Those Who Walk with Fire

Everyday People Discuss the Passion
That Fuels Their Extraordinary Lives

John R. Daubney

PublishAmerica
Baltimore

First printing

PublishAmerica has allowed this work to remain exactly as the author intended, verbatim, without editorial input.

Hardcover 978-1-4512-4858-6
Softcover 978-1-4512-4859-3
PUBLISHED BY PUBLISHAMERICA, LLLP
www.publishamerica.com
Baltimore

Printed in the United States of America

Dedication

Dedicated to the memory of my parents, John and Virginia Daubney, both of whom had dreams that were short-circuited by the disease of alcoholism. Mom's compassionate nature and her passion for music and the arts have been like a river that has never stopped flowing through my soul, bringing me great joy and freedom of expression. Sometime after Dad's death the beginnings of a western novel were found among his belongings. Despite his struggle with alcoholism, the memory of this "great unfinished novel" has remained with me as a symbol of the dreams and aspirations that lay within him. I thank you Dad for passing the seed of your desire on to me. Embracing and acting on my own passion took a long time but in so doing I have found a deep and everlasting tie between us. As well, the reality of the struggles he had to face in his upbringing and early life, have given me a greater appreciation for what he had to overcome and sacrifice in order to survive. I am deeply indebted to both of them and I miss them.

This book is also dedicated to all those brave souls who by finding and living their healthy passions bring a measure of healing, love, and positive change to our hurting world.

"God picks up the reed-flute world and blows.
Each note is a need coming through one of us, a passion, a long-
ing pain.
Remember the lips where the wind-breath originated, and let your
note be clear.
Don't try to end it. Be your note.
I'll show you how it's enough.
Go up on the roof at night in the city of the soul.
Let everyone climb on their roofs
And sing their notes!
Sing Loud!!"

The Essential Rumi by Jelalludin Rumi, mystical Sufi poet (1207-1273)
Coleman Barks (Translator)

"Life is no brief candle to me. It is a sort of splendid torch which
I have got hold of for the moment, and I want to make it burn as
brightly as possible before handing it on to future generations."
George Bernard Shaw

Table of Contents

All Interviews were conducted, transcribed,
and edited by John Daubney

Acknowledgements

A very special round of appreciation goes out to my copy editor, Tom O'Toole, for your skillful hand in editing my work, your humor which kept me loose, and for the patience you always extended. I also express my appreciation, to Anne O'Shaughnessy, whose Wild Soul Weekend in 2006 provided a safe and magical container in which my consciousness could open up to this dream which lay waiting deep inside of me.

My salute also to Andy Lavigne for his book photos and cover ideas.

A special thanks to my children: John, Michael, Sheila, and Anthony; my sister Linda and brothers, Bob, Paul, and especially Bill who showed me the way by his example; and *The March Winds Brotherhood:* Tim, Larry, Geoff, Bernie; Ted, Orrin, Dan, Johnny R., Marco, and Tommy Baseball. Whether you realize it or not, you've all played a part.

My gratitude goes out to my readers: Andy Lavigne, Diane Tuetschman, Tim Martin, Joe McTague, Ron Freedman, John Reith, Anthony Daubney, Shiela Daubney, Bill Laznovsky, Dave Spina, Dinkar Wagle, Gary Allocco, Geoff Little, and Larry Zimmerman.; and to my mentor Dr. Brad Biggs.

My thanks to Anne O'Shaughnessy, Phyllis Pulver, Grace Russell, Aaron Corman, and Dan Johnson for the time you spent sharing your passion and your stories with me. I learned so much from each of you.

I have profound gratitude also for the late, great author, Studs Terkel. The love and respect you provided the storytellers you interviewed in the many books you created, resonated deeply in me, and reminded me that every person has a significant story to tell, if someone is willing to truly listen.

Lastly, my deepest appreciation is for my life companion, Anne Valliere, whose unlimited patience, encouragement, and love has carried me over all the "humps and slumps" I have encountered during the 4 years and thousands of hours it has taken to complete my dream project. I am forever grateful to you.

Introduction

Filling the pages of this book are in-depth discussions with people from various walks of life who live their lives and follow their dreams passionately. They are not "hiding their light under a basket." While none would be classified world-famous personalities, these brave souls have all found a great depth of meaning and soulfulness in their everyday lives. In their passionate approach to life each of them has also positively affected the lives of others in some way. My hope for us all is that our own sleeping passions may be awakened by these discussions and that we may be tempted to take that first or even next step into the fires of desire that burn within our souls. To be conscious of and to apply this life-giving energy in our daily lives is the difference between existence for survival's sake and engaging each day as a daring adventure.

In April of 2009, 47-year-old Susan Boyle walked onstage before a panel of quite skeptical judges to audition for *Got Talent,* a British version of *American Idol.* Looking every inch "common," unprofessional, and without the appearances of a serious contestant, Susan opened her mouth to sing and within seconds astounded the judges and the studio audience with her musical talent and the passion of her delivery. Jaws dropped and tears flowed as her powerful singing voice shocked and dazzled everyone present as well the millions around the world who viewed her performance or would see her talent for themselves displayed repeatedly on the news or internet the following day. Ironically, the song she chose for her audition was *I Dreamed a Dream* from the play, *Les Miserables.* With her performance Susan was taking a huge step to fulfill her dream of becoming a professional singer, performing before a large audience. In being selected to move on to the next phase of this talent show she also touched that deep place in all of us that yearns to live out our fondest dreams and rise above our self-imposed limits.

I was deeply moved but not terribly surprised by her accomplishment. She was expressing a truth, a theory, I have long held, that most people hold some dream or yearning within— ignored, dormant or forgotten—just waiting to be ignited by their passion. That powerful enthusiasm, when stirred up, has the capacity to empower a person, change lives, and even shake the world in ways big and small. Our passion may not change governments or reshape cultures, or make banner headlines but it can alter the lives of others because it excites and ignites the deepest desires we all harbor. None of us are merely *common* unless we believe we are. In fact, passion is the fire that can make each of us extraordinary in our own way. For a few precious minutes Susan Boyle lit a candle so we could all get a glimpse of our God-given potential.

So often, when in the presence of passionate men and women, my soul has been stirred and energized with a sense of unlimited possibility for me. Such people, when in the flow of living life with love, compassion, and a purpose beyond self-centered gain, are fully engaged as human beings and in a position to influence others in a positive way. I truly believe that when enough people are similarly touched and energized, amazing things are possible for all of humanity! That is my ultimate purpose and hope for this book.

In this world, that at times can seem so dark, chaotic, love-deprived, and out of control, it is sometimes difficult to see bright spots where hope and the glow of love and peace can exist. It is my hypothesis, however, (based on personal experience and the shared experiences of others) that passion, at its best, operates out of a direct connection to the creative spirit within, and thus can elevate a person's consciousness in a highly spiritual way. A healthy passion is a positive energy brimming over with love and can be an antidote to the hopelessness that seems always to be waiting in the wings, ready to seize the opportunity to have its way with us. So, in today's world of powerful and often overwhelming forces, that can weigh heavily on my view of the world and my sense of well-being, the notion that I can bring a feeling of accomplishment, empowerment, and joy to my life, and to the lives of others, is a welcome one. A healthy passion offers that power.

"Passion burns down every branch of exhaustion
Passion is the supreme elixir and renews all things
Let divine passion triumph and rebirth you in your self."
—Rumi

Before I go further I must make a disclaimer regarding this book. It is not a scholarly or research-driven attempt to get at the theoretical underpinnings and the how-to of living the passionate life. I leave that to others. Rather, this book is a collection of individual stories, beliefs, and thoughts on living a life of healthy passion. I'm confident these interviews will reveal a number of qualities, skills, and principles that will surface repeatedly, providing some light on the "path," and a framework of sorts for those interested in discovering and energizing their own passionate quest. In the epilogue to this book I have listed a number of the ideas and opinions consistently identified by the interviewees as they described the essential elements that have guided and informed a healthy, passionate life for them. I trust that you will find and cherish the nuggets of wisdom and experience that speak to *you*.

Chapter 1

Author's Notes—The Journey
John Daubney

Let me explain a bit about how this book came into being, the process of interviewing, the various aspects of passion explored, and the part played by my own life's dreams and passion.

To begin with, I had no dream or ambition to write this or any book; no burning subject matter that yearned to be shared with the world; nor did I ever relish spending the time that creating a book would require. A couple of events took place, however, that pushed me quite unexpectedly in that direction. My brother Bill had recently engaged his longtime dream of writing a book, which he eventually published. Throughout that process, I was very excited for him and read his work as it progressed. He had been through some difficult times, had come out the other side, and was then engaged passionately in his writing. His excitement and sense of purpose was not lost on me; but while his success was a source of great happiness for me, it did not set off any sibling rivalry or light a fire under me to write. What did occur, however, was the stoking of my own creative spirit. Passion after all is contagious.

Around the same time a second momentous event took place. I was drawn to attend "A Wild Soul Retreat Weekend" in Vermont, led by Anne O'Shaughnessy, a very passionate and creative woman. Arriving early I made the acquaintance of another attendee, Gerry Cooper, a retired high school principal from Virginia. As we sat and chatted, he shared with me that he was in the process of writing a book on the history of the Jamestown settlement. His obvious enthusiasm for his project just glued me to my seat and created a profound stirring in me. I was experiencing an irresistible enthusiasm for something I love to do—help a person tell their story. I also felt an opening deep inside me that evoked my own creative potential. As I participated during the retreat that followed our conversation, I continually experienced a level of exhilaration, stimulation, and boldness I'd not formerly known as I listened to person after person speak passionately about what was important to them. When the retreat concluded, I was filled with excitement and gratitude for having been in the presence of so many passionate people and for being on the receiving end of their stories and deepest desires.

As I set out for home on that Sunday afternoon and drove south on Vermont Route 7, along Lake Champlain, the idea for writing this book suddenly exploded into my consciousness; I mean exploded! I became excited, energized, and so convicted that I could barely contain myself—I wanted to write it all down before it could be washed away by a flood of more mundane thoughts. I pulled off to the side of the highway and began rapidly writing and emptying my mind of all the thoughts that were now flooding in. Although I would not recommend this to anyone, the focus, structure, and method for the book you now hold in your hands were scribbled down on a notepad throughout my drive home. One inspired idea after another came to me and were recorded. It was an exhilarating process. I was as convinced of the need for me to undertake this project as I had ever been about anything in my life.

I was certain that I wanted to write a book which would provide a space where people could tell the stories of their passion, and readers would have the chance to be stirred, as I have been at times in my life. I was also aware that interviewing passionate people would be exciting. In my years of being a Union Representative, Employee Assistance Professional, professional counselor, and retreat leader I've had the pleasure and privilege of hearing and being inspired by the remarkable stories of thousands of people, at various stages of their lives. They've certainly shared their challenges and heartbreaks but I've always been amazed at the courage, wisdom, creativity, and the capacity for greatness that each person carries as well.

It is my personal axiom that anything of worth that I have achieved in my life has been inspired by the passionate people who have come before me. Without their example, passion, and vision, the scope of my life would be narrow indeed. I trust that, consciously or not, all who dedicate themselves to a mission with zeal and love shine their light for us all.

"In whatever you are called to, strive to be devoted to it in all aspects large and small. Fall short? Try again. Mastery is made in increments, not in leaps.
Be brave, be fierce, and be visionary.
Mend the parts of the world that are 'within your reach.'
To strive to live this way is the most dramatic gift you can ever give to the world."
Consider yourselves assigned."
—Clarissa Pinkola Estés, Ph.D., from An *Assignment for You from Dr. Estés.*

In Joseph Campbell's book, *The Hero's Journey*, he declares, "*An individual has to find what electrifies and enlivens his own heart and wakes him."* I am confident that the stories and passionate exploits of others can force a crack in the veneer of our ego defenses long enough for that "greater self" within each of us to become engaged. When that happens, we can become conscious of what awakens, electrifies, and ultimately will fulfill us. I know that has happened for me through events that took place in my early adulthood. I remember at the age of 22 reading a newspaper quote by the great spiritual sage, Jiddu Krishnamurti, (1895-1986) as I rode a bus to work on a Sunday night. I was "bummed out" that night because I was leaving my wife and newly born son at home to take an hour-and-a-half bus ride to my job, cleaning

14

and fueling busses for a local transit company. This was not how I wanted to live or to work. The realities of adulthood, fatherhood, and earning a living seemed so overwhelming to me. The quote I read was Krishnamurti's hypothesis that human beings use only a minute portion of their innate abilities and potential in their lifetimes. This idea caused such a jolt that hope was awakened in me. It was if someone shook me by the shoulders and screamed, 'Don't give up! You have the power to rise above all this!' This inspired thought also planted a seed within me. I would like to say it was onward and upward from that night, but the truth was that it would take many years for that seed to mature and bear fruit, owing to my immaturity and a highly addictive lifestyle. Later, as a 25-year-old Ford Motor Company assembly line worker in Green Island, New York, I read a book on the life of the great labor leader, Walter Ruether (September 1, 1907—May 9, 1970). I was fascinated and inspired by his passionate commitment to help working people around the world raise their standard of living through his involvement in the labor movement, particularly as president of the United Auto Worker's International Union, and his later involvement in the Civil Rights Movement of the 1960s and '70s. His dedication⁻ against great odds and powerful forces determined to destroy him⁻ to doing what he could to elevate the lives of all people, in and out of the Union, was his life's mission. For the very first time in my young life, something shifted within my being, energizing me to at least begin thinking about the plight of others. I even began to imagine that I could make a difference in this world of mine.

Inspired to learn more about labor and management relations, I was eventually elected a full-time union representative with the opportunity to serve my fellow union members. I don't know that any of this would have happened, however, without first being inspired by the fervor of Ruether and a local union leader by the name of Richard Cardinal. Richard taught me by his example how to create and follow a plan as I watched him strategize and execute his run for our local union presidency. His passion, focused action, and determination showed me that with hard work and the right attitude a person could succeed no matter what their circumstances were. Today, my "work" has changed, but this desire to give to the world by bringing people together in a way that gives them the chance to find their own power and truth has not been altered. My awareness of this desire has happily been my "true north" ever since. Whenever I discover that my ego is attempting to take over my efforts, I go back, sometimes reluctantly, to this greater purpose or higher intention for what I do. Most importantly I ask God or my higher power, if you will, to use me as a channel, as in the Prayer of St. Francis.

What began for me as an attempt to give meaning to my life in my 20s and 30s, became a high-powered drive in my 40s to deal with my addiction to alcohol which then naturally evolved into a desire to help others as I had been helped in my recovery. I must mention here that the zeal for recovery from addiction, as exhibited by a friend in the workplace, was a major factor for me in deciding to reach out for help—passion is contagious. Later I discovered my passion for creating situations where people could discover their own innate power, gifts, and beauty. Today those situations are primarily my workshops, retreats, and here on the pages of this book. My intention in creating this book has been to bring together readers and these wonderfully passionate storytellers in a common cause: to explore the role of this great energy that has the potential for bringing out the very best in all of us.

"Man is only truly great when he acts from his passions." Benjamin Disraeli, English Statesman and writer, 1804-1881.

What is Passion?

Webster's New World Dictionary, College Edition, defines passion as: "...*extreme, compelling emotion; intense emotional drive or excitement; specifically, a) great anger; rage; fury, b) enthusiasm or fondness, as for music, c) strong love or affection. d) Sexual drive or desire; lust. 6. The object of any strong desire or fondness.*

"For me passion is this upwelling of energy, drive, determination and enthusiasm that seems to just flow out of somewhere inside, and generates a willingness to follow an idea or a dream that I really want to achieve. When that happens it seems that the whole universe flows through me and a loud 'yes' resonates in my being..." Jennifer Hanson—long distance hiker

"I think of passion as a fuel that fires my furnace and life without that is just a dry, dull shell of a thing. Life with passion is vibrant and energetic. For a human being it's like the hydrogen in a star; without it I doubt we can ever be fulfilled or be a fully alive person. We can end up being a drone who does nothing more than keeps the economy moving. That's really sad and a waste of life to me." Steve Rock, Mycologist

Within each of us lays this often dormant, but always limitless energy just awaiting our summons. How it is used is up to each of us. As my friend, musician Phyllis Pulver who monthly leads Friends in Harmony, an ever-changing group of singers and musicians, at her home in Rexford, New York says, *"Passion, for me, is the feeling of desire that propels me to focus all my energies on something my mind and heart have wrapped themselves around."*

Passion has the capacity to empower the performance of great works of art, love, goodwill, or industry and be of great benefit, or it can be the powerful thrust that initiates obsession, fury, revenge, lust, compulsion, and ultimately, destructive and self-interested choices that can produce great pain for oneself and others. Passion is the power that propelled the art of DaVinci, the leadership of Lincoln, the compassion and poetry of Walt Whitman, and the vision of Martin Luther King. Passion, as well, is the force that launched the Spanish Inquisition, the American Civil War, the vindictiveness of the McCarthy era, countless assassinations, ethnic cleansing in Rwanda, and the horrific destruction of 9/11/2001.

Passion fueled by revenge, a thirst for dominance, power and control, and self-gain has accomplished little in the long run, but to set the table for eventual dissatisfaction, never-ending retaliation, and win-lose outcomes.

"Another aspect of passion for me is the emotional fuel of fire and excitement, which has the potential to be consuming as well as nurturing at the same time. There's an intensity and aliveness which goes beyond the commonplace of everyday existence."

Steve Carty Cordry, pastor

Because of its potential for negative outcomes, many feel ambivalent when even hearing the word, "passion." When asked how he would describe passion, author Chris Ringwald replied, *"Passion—although very honestly the word sometimes leaves me cold and drained of meaning when I hear it associated with violence and sex—is that, which I feel strongly about and see as important enough for me to undertake."*

I confess, for a big chunk of my life, I had a very wary approach to the concept of passion. Very angry, passionate people always caught my attention in a sometimes reverential, but always fearful way. In my personal life I had often attached anger and aggressiveness to my own passion and personal causes. There reached a point, however, in my late forties, where I became aware that passion used in a heated and antagonistic manner would ultimately result in frustration and dissatisfaction for me, even if I initially got my way. Most significantly, I often hurt others with this negative use of passion. Those painful memories are a powerful reminder of the potential for harm this great energy possesses. It would entail many years of fervor-gone-wrong before I could view passion as a life energy that if harnessed to compassion, proper intention, and a higher purpose, could enable me to achieve more than I ever thought possible. For that change of perspective I am eternally grateful.

I must admit that it seemed a daunting task when deciding how I would define *healthy passion*. In the epilogue to this book I will highlight some characteristics of healthy passion that have been identified by those I have interviewed. I will leave it to them to express their thoughts about the subject, except to say that I believe the end results of a healthy passion is typically joy, contentment, and a real sense of purpose. Now, for someone with a passionate nature or drive, those positive outcomes may not always be present, which is why I asked interviewees to consider how the elements of ego and obsession impact on their endeavors. As writer and lecturer, Cary Bayer says, "...*When I step out as a teacher, my higher-self is aware that I'm the instrument and the knowledge or wisdom comes from a higher source. The ego, however, tries to convince this higher-self that it's the source. That's why people go on ego trips and why we often see people fall from grace. It's something that I have to be conscious of every moment.*"

Passion, I believe, is essentially value-neutral neither good nor evil. As life energy, it exists in each person as a potent manifestation of spirit, awaiting the call of strong desire before springing into action. Thus it seems that ego, obsession, self-indulgence, reflection, integrity, compassion, and higher purpose can all have a profound impact on the way in which passion is used. It's been said the potential of a Mother Teresa *and* an Adolph Hitler exists within each of us. Our challenge is to choose the direction in which we will exert our passion and then to decide the forces that we will allow to motivate us.

I must add here there are those who by reason of culture, health factors, personal woundedness, or lifestyle choices may have lost touch with or perhaps never fully experienced the enthusiasm, exhilaration, and power of passion. Acquaintances of mine over the years have told me they wish they had my passion or confess to a total lack of passion in their everyday existence. To those people and to the millions like them, I hope the stories contained in this book can be an awakening, a spark, and a realization that regardless of our use, misuse, or disuse of this great drive, passion is built into each of us. To quote storyteller, Jackie Hawkins, "*Passion is something that I really don't believe you can control or create. It comes from within and has always been there. It can only be nurtured.*" Though the reasons for being out of touch with passion are many, for most people the flame of passion can be ignited and nurtured, and when lost, rekindled. When that happens our lives take on purpose, pleasure, and meaning. No longer is life just about survival and endurance. Our existence becomes a never-ending adventure and an opportunity to positively affect our world.

"Passions are about how you live your life. Goals are about what you choose to create in your life." Janet Bray Attwood and Chris Attwood, authors—*The Passion Test: the Effortless Path to Discovering Your Destiny*

Some of the contributors like Bob Lobue, author and producer of the play *Visions,* and documentary filmmaker, Amy Hart, saw their great passion as a spiritual mission to benefit others while others simply view passion as *how* they live their lives. Interviewees like clown, Carol Sue Hart, and hypnotist and showman, Sandesh Naik, have parlayed the joy of hobbies into passions that have brought benefit and joy to others. Hospice worker, Bonnie Kriss, spiritual teacher, Darci D'ercole, and artist and activist, John Frederick, initially focused their passion on self-discovery which consequently led them to use their passion in service to others. Self-Advocacy leader, Steve Holmes, landscape architect, Catherine Weaver, and professional interventionist, Jim Garrett are among several contributors who devote great passion to their careers.

Ann Waldorf, through her therapy practice, Mike Reilly in his business activity, and Francis Endryck as a body builder and trainer, all have an intense desire to help others as a result of their own healing and the hand-up they have received from others.

Both Paul Ehman's early love of writing and Jennifer Hanson's childhood fantasy of following the tracks and trails of Lewis and Clark were put on hold for many years. Both, however, reconnected to these desires later in life; the fervor they attached to those early dreams never died.

Pana Columbus engaged in a passionate and challenging 5-year journey around the world to find her mission in life: finally discovering through various personal trials, including being struck by lightning, that her life's mission was to create a ritual theatre group.

So the manner in which this powerful energy is discovered and utilized is unique to the individual. The purpose, as well, when mixed with compassion and self-care generally seems to flow naturally from self-interest into more altruistic purposes. This seems to also validate the principle of getting one's own house in order before being ready to help someone else. That was true for me before and during my many years as a helping professional. Time and again I have been challenged to face my own shortcomings so I could grow and heal, and then be of optimum help to others.

As a young adult, an unforgettable image of a loving passion that has never left me was contained in a human interest story I watched on a television news program sometime in the early 1970s. It featured an elderly, well-dressed African-American gentleman whose passion was to love people, by standing on a busy street corner in a major American city, and simply smile and wave to them as they passed by each morning in their cars. Whenever a lull in traffic occurred he would return to his metal folding chair and rest. When the next car approached he'd briskly rise and move to the curb and happily wave to the next motorist. I was captivated as I watched his smiles and hand waves returned from nearly every person he greeted, and then the joy he experienced as he extended himself to them. He did this day after day with such vigor and elation that I was amazed that such a person even existed. I couldn't imagine for the life of me ever taking such a risk (as it seemed to me) to be laughed at, ridiculed, or even attacked because this was a time of great tension between whites and African-Americans. Nevertheless none of these concerns deterred him. He freely expressed his love for people regardless of color or race. In doing so he gave me hope for mankind and for myself. I felt such admiration for him. When questioned by a television reporter as to why he did this day after day, in all kinds of weather, he responded that everyone needed to know they mattered to someone. He also told the reporter, that the simple act of greeting people made him happy and gave his life meaning. When motorists were interviewed, each felt that he or she was blessed by this man's daily greetings and in fact looked for him each day as they passed his corner. Many said they felt a loss when for some reason he didn't appear for a day or so. That memory remains in a freeze-frame. I can still see him, even today: this slightly built man in a formal suit, tie, and fedora, fearlessly sharing his love on an inner city street corner. He will always be an icon for the positive power of passion. Each recollection of him brings a smile to my face and a stirring in my heart that says, *there is love in this world after all. If this man has the courage to fearlessly express his love, maybe I can as well.*

As you read this book I invite you to remember those times when you were lit up, if only for a moment, by something you witnessed, experienced, or heard. Recall that event and how it felt. See what that memory has to say about what's important to you. It could be the seed for your great passion!

The Interview Process

"In those first thrilling days of wildly ruminating about this book, various people and potential conflicts came to mind as I considered who I would interview. Somewhat reluctantly I made a decision not to include close friends and family. I did not want to be in the position of choosing between them—most of whom are very passionate and interesting people—when it would come down to deciding who I would interview or which interviews I would ultimately include. That decision, though difficult, freed me to just be open to whomever life sent my way. A few people like Connie Messit, Steve Rock, and Catherine Weaver with whom I was well-acquainted, immediately came to mind. Others, such as Bob LoBue and Matt George came to my attention through newspaper and magazine articles. Howard Meyer, Mike Reilly, and Carole Sue Hart had attended some of my workshops and retreats. There were times I came upon people quite by accident, as in the case of Pana Columbus who I overheard, one dinner table away from me at a retreat, speaking about traveling through Europe and Egypt, in her twenties, on a five-year journey to find her life's mission. Later, I would run into writer, Chris Ringwald at a birthday party for my copy editor Tom O'Toole. Sandesh Naik, Bonnie Kriss, Debra Burger, and John Frederick all attended my church and Jim Fuller was my pastor. Others like Bill Thomas, Jim Garret, and Darci D'ercole were known to me through various civic organizations I took part in. Of primary importance for me was to stay open, listen with my heart, and notice when I would be drawn in by a particular person's words, actions, or enthusiasm. That was the litmus test for my interest.

My first step was to develop an overview of the project, which I then gave to each potential interviewee before they decided whether to participate. This overview enabled me to clearly define the purpose and scope of this book for myself, and it gave the interviewee a clear idea of my focus and intention. I was amazed that only five people out of 40 or so that I invited turned down the opportunity. That supported my belief that we all have a need to tell our story, to make our lives real, and to share it with someone who can hold that story with trusting and loving hands. I have tried my best to do that.

"Story is the song line of a person's life.
We need to sing it and we need someone to hear the singing.
Story told, story heard, story written, story read
create the web of life in words."
From the book *Storycatcher*. Copyright©2005 by Christina Baldwin. Reprinted with permission of New World Library, Novato, CA. www.newworldlibrary.com

Among the questions I asked those I interviewed to consider, prior to the interview were:

Describe the Great Passion that you will talk about?

When was the seed for this passion first planted within you?

What drives you to pursue this passion of yours?

What is the difference for you between obsession and a healthy passion?

How does your ego challenge you in your Great Passion?

What have you learned is required to live a passionate life?
What sacrifices have you made to follow your passion?
How have you benefitted from living a passionate life?
Explain how your spiritual beliefs impact this passion of yours.
How would you like others to benefit from this Passion of yours?
What would you say to those who say they have no passion in their life but would like to bring greater excitement and meaning into their life?

These questions had a two-fold purpose. One, I wished to keep the conversations confined to certain parameters rather than create a go-where-you-may conversation that could completely miss the aspects of passion I wanted to hear people talk about; and two, I wanted to *prime the pump* and help people reach deeper into their stories. I hoped the storytellers would also have an enriching experience as they walked back through their histories and processes. My years of working as a helping professional had allowed me to see the power and life-changing benefits that accrued whenever I could help people explore their lives in a deep way. As long-distant hiker, Jennifer Hanson told me after she came to tears, discussing her childhood talks with her father: *"It's been 10 years since he passed away, but I realize now how much I miss him. Until now, I haven't been aware of the importance of those conversations, which took place during a three-month period when I was 13."*

Although I was interested in hearing what it was that people were passionate about and their level of knowledge and expertise, I was drawn to the "story behind the story"—the deeper dimension of a passionate person's life and ambition. I think this wider focus holds greater wisdom than a simple discussion of how one does what one does. In his interview, Civil War buff Matt George discusses the values, compassion, and *better angels of our nature* as exhibited by heroes Abraham Lincoln and General Joshua Chamberlain, and the impact those ideas have had on his own desire to pass on something of value to the adults and children he speaks to in his living history presentations.

For many of the storytellers in this book the seeds for their passion were planted in the trauma of their young lives, or in some other painful event in their life. Storyteller, Paul Ehmann's love for writing, in part, grew out of the adolescent sexual abuse he suffered and later in his desire to tell his story and help other fellow victims of this terrible crime. As he puts it, "*...this bad thing—sexual abuse—happened to me, but redemption came from speaking my truth to those who would listen.*" Cape Cod Pastor, Steve Carty Cordry's painful childhood as an overweight, bullied, unpopular, and bookish kid motivated his fervent quest for personal transformation, and for helping others to overcome fear, self-doubt, and feelings of worthlessness. Jackie Hawkins, who grew up as an African-American child in the segregated South, was greatly influenced by her father, a Baptist minister and Civil Rights activist. As an adult, she became someone who nurtured a profound passion for loving and empowering people in a variety of ways.

In looking back at my own journey, one memory clearly portrays the principle that a gift is always present in the most trying times of our lives if we're only willing to look—

Standing, shivering in the doorway of a corner drug store on a bitterly cold evening, I waited for the bus which would take me home. I had just finished my part-time job selling newspapers at an outdoor stand. All around me people hustled and bustled buying prescriptions and last minute Christmas gifts. Although the sound of Deck the Halls filled the air and invited my anticipation for my favorite day of the year, a great sense of aloneness enveloped me as I viewed my solitary reflection in the store window.

I was 13 years old and I don't think I had ever experienced such a degree of alienation from the world about me. It seemed to me that I had very little in common with the rest of humanity. The world had, in fact, become a frightening place for me; more to be feared than explored and enjoyed. I was firmly convinced that I could really depend upon no one. My survival depended on strict adherence to self-reliance and pleasing others.

Today, I know my family members and I did the best we could with the cards we were dealt, but in those days I lacked the capacity for that understanding. In retrospect I can see clearly that the loneliness and ever-present apprehension that I lived with in those days would become the driving force for first healing myself and later for bringing people together in various ways for the purpose of connection and healing. This work continues, to this day, to bring healing and love to my life.

For many, a personal connection to some sense of God or a Higher Power, or universal love gave them a powerful resource for negotiating the rapids of living passionately, and an inner guide for discerning direction and for making important choices. As Albany, New York pastor, Jim Fuller states, "...*at the core of my passion for finding out who I am, and how God and I relate to each other, is the idea that as I trust my impulses, I become more willing to take the next risk, with the assurance that a benevolent intelligence is attempting to move me forward to my greater good.*"

I also was very curious to hear how passionate, purpose-driven people were able to be aware and then get themselves back on track once their egos had grabbed the upper hand in their lives. As I listened to these brave souls tell their stories, it became apparent that no one, in the throes of a passionate pursuit, is impervious to the challenges of ego and obsession, and it is indeed the *spiritual warrior* in each of us that must come to the fore and take over if we are to engage our drives in a healthy, centered, and satisfying way. Spiritual teacher Darci D'ercole believes an important characteristic of being a *spiritual warrior* is in knowing and being able to manage one's mind with all its wildly disparate thoughts, rather than having the mind manage the person. Ultimately most of our problems originate in our mind, in our perspective if you will, so I was very interested in inquiring how the contributors were able to manage their thoughts. The answers were varied and fascinating. Many also talked quite openly and powerfully about the role that spirituality played in providing guidance, and how it re-centered them whenever they would stray from their truth and higher purpose in whatever passionate activity they were engaged in.

Since I had been repeatedly inspired by the stories of those I've had the honor to work with as a helping professional, I had great faith in the value of the stories of *everyday* people. I did not feel any urgency to chase down larger-than-life public figures for interviews. This is not meant to be cynical, but rather, through experience, I've learned that most public figures are understandably more protective of their personal lives and revelations than the not-so-famous. Time and again I was humbled by the generosity, honesty, and vulnerability of the people who shared their stories with me. All are using their passion to engage in what they feel called to do. Without reservation, I believe those who engage life with a loving passion are the hope for the survival of our planet.

As I interviewed people and later during hundreds of hours of transcription, synthesizing, cutting, and editing of a half million words into a readable and interesting form I was inspired repeatedly by their passion and commitment to what they felt was their mission. While a task like this one can be tedious and seem daunting at times, my excitement for this process has never wavered and there wasn't more than a day or two over more than four years that I just couldn't wait to sit down at my computer, open up my document file marked Passion Interviews and begin that day's work. A case in point was the Francis Endryck interview. In transcribing our session a year later, I listened to him relate his 20 year-long evolution from a self-described 36-year-old "fat guy with poor self-esteem" into a man he could really like, and then into a trainer who could help others transform their lives. As I listened I became painfully aware of my own bodily neglect and a deep longing to treat my body with greater love and respect. That awareness subsequently motivated me to join Weight Watchers and a local gym in 2007. A voice deep inside me had said, *If Francis can do it so can I!* That began a monumental shift in how I now take care of my body till this day. Thank you Francis!

Another personal benefit of conducting these interviews was that I got to engage my curiosity for asking questions about what makes passionate people tick? The more of these interviews I conducted the more I discovered just what I had always hoped: That I am so much more like others than I ever could have imagined. I share many of their spiritual, emotional, and psychological struggles, and, like them have the innate potential to overcome, heal, and lead a fulfilling existence. What a gift!

An adequate expression of gratitude escapes me as I consider how honored I feel to have had the opportunity and the trust to receive these stories. I have done my best to transcribe and edit these conversations—with the invaluable assistance of my copy editor, Tom O'Toole—in a manner that is clear, thought-provoking, enjoyable, compelling, and inspirational without diluting or changing the essence of what each contributor had to say. Out of grammatical necessity and for brevity's sake, words, sentences, and sequence of events have sometimes been altered to create a more readable flow. My greatest fear was that I would fail to do justice to the interviews, so, if I have "missed the mark" at times, I hope you know my intention was always to honor the spirit and truth of what you had to say. In the end the best I can say, with all my heart, is thank you.

To the Reader

These stories, I trust, will contain the answers to many of the questions you've asked yourself and others about the subject of passion. Questions like: Why am I not passionate like others? How can I find what I'm passionate about? Can I be passionate without harming others? How do I prevent burnout? What sacrifices would I have to make to follow my passion? Is there a difference between passion and obsession? Where do rage and a healthy passion part ways? Where does spirituality come into the picture? What are the benefits of living life passionately? As you read this book, clarity about your passion might well reveal itself, and once awakened, that inner fire has the capacity to energize you to discover and accomplish your dreams, and to alter dramatically the course of your life.

As Peace Corps volunteer, Stephen Anderson conveyed to me *"...I don't want to be wishing at the end of my life: I want to do the absolute best with my life right now!"*

Howard Meyer, actor, writer, and director said, *"Before I discovered theatre I was pretty unhappy. Everything I have in my life today is all organized around this passion. I can't remember a day in the last seven years when I didn't wake up with enthusiasm and a kick in my step."*

Psychotherapist and musician Debra Burger stated, *"When I express my gift, I discover the amazing-ness in me and in all people. ...I'm not hiding my light under a bushel basket—I get to feel it, express it, and act on it... I'm able to see it in others too...it's not theoretical, I truly know it!*

As anyone who lives passionately will tell you, the rewards are numerous and make life an exhilarating daily adventure. For the reader, I hope that as you read this book you will engage your heart as well as your mind, and listen to that still, small voice within you, to hear what it has to say about *your* own potential and about what yearns to be expressed through *you*. May your love burn ever so brightly in all you do—the world waits.

Chapter 2
Action
Pana Columbus

"Here I stand six years after the lightning struck me and all I can say is this: Having had an initiation of fire in my system like I did, it became the difference for me between being a 'dreamy' or visionary person with lots of great ideas, or being a person of action. Having that much 'juice' running through my body, I could no longer just talk about heaven on earth: I had to do something to make it happen."

I first met Pana at a spiritual retreat I attended in the Pocono Mountains of Pennsylvania in the summer of 2005. Although I was attracted by her musicianship as she and her husband Scott provided a variety of great music to support our weekend journey, it was the passion she had for improvisational dance that caught my "inner eye." While engaged with three other women in an impromptu talent night performance it was apparent to me that Pana was in a zone of sorts and seemed to flow with grace and a connection to her soul. She had a sense of reverence for what she was doing. The next day over lunch, she shared with me bits of a fantastic, life-changing journey, which only a few years prior had taken her across many countries and locations in Europe, Africa, and the United States, but most importantly, into the truth of her own soul. Pana, her husband, Scott Eggert, and daughter Gaia live in Emmaus, Pennsylvania.

"My particular passion is Ritual Theatre. It's an art form that I discovered while I was traveling on a five year journey, after leaving the acting profession in New York City.

"My whole adult life up to that point had been spent acting in the theatre. Then my world began to fall apart after performing in three plays, back to back to back, that were all disasters. In one production, the guy playing opposite me disappeared the week before we opened, and it turned out he was in prison serving time because he'd hit a cop and had been too embarrassed to tell anyone. There was just one outrageous event after another until finally, after the third play I just decided to take a break.

"It seemed that something in my life was about to shift. I'd left my fiancé and moved to Inwood, New York, which just borders the Bronx. I had this little apartment there which was surrounded by woods that I would walk through as I tried to figure out who I would be if I was no longer an actress. I only knew at that time that travel would be part of it."

Why traveling?

"Well, after deciding to take a hiatus from acting, New York City lost its meaning for me. I wanted to get away. The next year seemed like a protracted death for me. I had been acting for 10 years, so all my identity and my friends had been part of the acting profession in New York. Simultaneously I began praying for the resources to present themselves so I could travel and discover the next step for me on my journey. One day I remembered that I had some stocks that my parents had purchased for me when I was very young, but never really paid attention to. I knew little about the stock market and the value of my stock. Each month I received a dividend check for a couple hundred dollars but thought little else about them. But now I thought, *Umm, I wonder what these are worth*? So my mom and I went off to see a broker. He looked up the stocks on his computer. Then he turned to us and said, "These are worth a lot of money right now!"

"We found their value to be over $40,000 and I immediately said, 'Great, sell them all!'

"Everyone tried to convince me not to sell them all; but I said, 'No.'

Part of my reasoning was that these were companies I was no longer interested in investing in. In going through this *death purge* of mine, I was re-examining everything in my life for its meaningfulness to me, as a person. These stocks were from a big, multinational corporation that I wasn't interested in supporting, so I decided to sell the stocks.

"I then reconnected with an old friend named Tata who I had attended acting school with. Together with her husband, who is a fabulous musician, and their daughter, we traveled to Greece and Hawaii. So began a process of an even deeper level of shedding things that no longer felt like me. One big thing, that I let go of, was fear, and another was a critical voice that I had carried around in my head my entire life. This voice judged myself and others; said that whatever I did was inappropriate or not good enough, and that the world was a scary place to live. As I was leaving various pieces of my old life behind, I also began to go through this total shift in consciousness which eventually laid the groundwork for an entirely different career path for me. This process was much more than simply deciding to switch from one career to another."

How would you describe your consciousness while engaged in your acting career?

"If you look at most dramatic literature and especially the plays created by Ibsen, O'Neil, Miller and my hero up to that time, Tennessee Williams, they were all filled with angst, and these magical, brilliant characters filled with deep longings that never get satisfied. There was: Blanche Dubois, in "'Streetcar,' who ends up in the 'loony bin.' My favorite lady character in "Orpheus Descending" is shot,—*such great tragedies*! The message is that anyone who has a wild, passionate, longing soul just doesn't work out in this society and usually ends up either hospitalized or dead. (Laughter) At that time I found these stories moving, important, and tragic because they were a reflection of the consciousness I lived in. I felt compelled to tell these stories as an actress.

"While living in Greece and the island of Maui, I also went through a shift where I found that I no longer had this desperate need to connect with others, as I'd had all my life. I now felt a fearless love and oneness with everything and everybody. I could now be with perfect strangers and there would be an almost instant connection wherever I went. There was no longer this terrible longing that I had previously felt."

Were you studying any spiritual philosophy during that time?

"The friends I was traveling with were very conscious people and had a great influence on me. I was born with natural parents, of course, but these people were *parents* for me in what I was to become. They weren't of any particular religion or spiritual path, but they were loving, spiritually conscious, and supportive people for me while I was wrestling with my demons, so to speak, in my head.

Even that relationship, however, fell away when I got a cottage of my own in Hawaii. I realized that I needed to do some of this journey by myself. I had reached a place where I knew I had to go beyond another person's words and guidance, and take a very personal inner journey. So, 'kicking & screaming,' that's what I decided to do. It was really a reprogramming of my mind. I had become very aware of how unconscious I was of my own thought process and how unhealthy my thinking and perceptions were. At the same time I recognized that I had the power to change or reframe those thoughts and perceptions in a positive direction. That became my greatest challenge!

"It was hell, and it was an amazing process at the same time. I can recall the day when I realized this process was over; I thought to myself, *Now I can begin living my life; now the real work can begin.* I had a deep awareness that everything up to that point was an exercise in clearing out the junk from my brain.

"I then began to travel on my own. Basically it became an exploration for me to discover what my future work would be. I knew that love and transformation would be a part of whatever my work would be, but I didn't know how that was going to happen. So I traveled on my own to various Hawaiian Islands, and then on to Egypt, a few European countries, and finally landed in the Southwestern United States. During my travels, ritual and ceremony really piqued my curiosity. I was fascinated by how people used art in various ceremonies, rituals, or prayers to generate a certain energy or transformative power. I loved it! I participated in as many of these rituals as I could, regardless of what the religion or tradition was."

What was there about the use of art in rituals and ceremony that drew you in?

"It wasn't art for entertainment; it was creative expression being channeled in a way that could really change things. There's power in that. One example for me took place when I was in Hawaii. There happened to be a lengthy drought, and the farmers were really suffering. It was the spring equinox, there was a full moon and some people that I had been regularly playing music with decided to create a ceremony to bring rain. Aroshn, one of the women in our group, started praying for rain in a beautiful, poetic way. She encouraged us to visualize the rain, the thunder, mist, and the clouds. At the end of it we were dancing and singing about the rain and just embodying this whole rain feeling. Four days later it began raining and it didn't stop for two weeks.

"When your prayers are answered, you can always ask, 'Was that a coincidence or did it happen because of the prayers?' You never really know. To me, it certainly felt like an answered prayer, and we were all very grateful. When this happened enough I came to understand the cause and effect of consciousness and attention, and could see there was really a powerful truth in what these people were doing.

"So I began to think, *Wow! Wouldn't it be great to do this as an art form?* I could do this consciously to create musical events that were kind of like a performance and kind of like a ceremony too, and we could do all this good in the world through these opportunities for transformation. I thought about it in terms of people using it as a vehicle for personal transformation.

"It would be years however before I was ready to attempt to use this process with anyone. I was living in Pennsylvania at the time, and had met a man by the name of Ben Iobst, who was a Massage Therapist. He had also recorded a best-selling meditation CD called *Seven Metals*. His music was created by playing giant singing bowls of various sizes. So we would get together, and I would sing and he'd play the bowls or drum. We enjoyed this so much that we agreed we had to do something with it. So at Little Pond Retreat Center in Nazareth—there's another of those biblical names—we presented our first event.

"I didn't really know anyone who'd be interested in this kind of event, so I visited the local health food stores and healing centers, picked up the business cards of the therapists and healers in our region, and created a mailing list of 150 people. We ended up with 77 people attending our first performance in the middle of an ice storm! It was truly amazing. I must add that the Little Pond Retreat Center was kind enough to let us do this free of charge because it was our first attempt at something like this.

"We told people exactly what we were going to do. There were no surprises. We said there would be an invocation to the universe and that we'd be praying 'for the manifestation of our most glorious and soul-stretching dreams.' It was a beautiful night and I was so excited. I thought, *Ahah!* I had figured out how to do this and now we had this 'thing' that we could present to an audience.

"With the money I'd made, I went back to Hawaii to tell my old friends that I'd created this wonderful art form. I told them, 'It's kind of like a ceremony and kind of like a performance. Let's do it!'

"I was then shocked to discover that they would have no part of it. They told me they do ceremony in service to others and not for money. I said, 'yeah but even priests get paid. If somehow we don't get paid for doing this spiritual work, then we'll always have to be doing it part-time and not be able to put all our energy into it.'

"They did not argue with me; they're very well grounded. So for three months I belabored my point of view over and over, and felt like I was hitting my head against the wall. Finally one morning, while pouting away in the bathtub,—and I must tell you this was the day of The Grand Alignment, where five different planets would line up,—it occurred to me that the way I had always done everything in my career was with storytelling. After all, I had been an actor and stories were my life. In a flash it came to me that if I created a story that incorporated ritual elements into it, I could then charge money, because it would be a performance. My friends would then have no problem with what I wanted to do. I leapt out of the bath tub, ran into my room, and wrote my first ritual play that afternoon. I didn't stop until I was done. It was called, "The Angel and the Shaman: A Metaphysical Love Story". I was so excited! I felt that I had invented a new art form.

"I called my friends and told them of my exciting idea. I also let them know I was thankful for their persistence, because it helped me to clarify this new 'thing of mine.' Once more they would have nothing to do with it. They thought it was contrived and they didn't like it. So I thought to myself, *well its time to leave Hawaii, something is not happening here.* I was disappointed. So I did leave, but I left having created this art form.

"So on to New Mexico where, in 2000, I met a deeply spiritual woman by the name of SoLea who became a very dear friend. While there I began researching Egyptian mysticism. I took a fascinating workshop with musician, researcher, author, and therapist, Tom Kenyon. Egyptian mysticism was now on my brain and I began writing my second ritual play, titled, *The Initiation*, the story of one woman's journey to enlightenment, through falling in love with a bright blue star. It eventually became a one-woman show that I performed. The production wove together ritual, ecstatic song, dance, and Egyptian mysticism into a beautiful story. My show with Ben at Little Pond had been the greatest night of my life, and now it was being replaced by this exciting new show.

"I bought a van, took the show on the road, and did a performance in Crestone, Colorado. My next performance was scheduled for Boulder, Colorado, but before that happened I was struck by lightning while hiking with some friends. It was all so crazy!

"I'll explain how I survived that later, but I must tell you that there was another related-story unfolding at the same time. As I was attempting to integrate my fascination with ritual and ceremony into performance, while in Hawaii, I started having incredible dreams. Some dreams came to me while I slept and some were sudden visions that occurred in altered states—usually accompanied by high fevers. In one, I had a husband who lived on another planet and I was told we were going to meet. The visions were so powerful and beautiful that I would

36

come out of them weeping! I knew that I couldn't just ignore them. I had to figure out what they meant.

"Then, through a series of events, I came to understand that the star in the vision was the Planet Sirius, which revolved around a star of the same name. This star is part of the Orion constellation as well as the brightest blue star in the sky. Recently it was found that the star has planets and they are called Sirius A and Sirius B. Scientists think that if they discover a form of extraterrestrial life it will probably first be discovered on Sirius, because of its closeness to our galaxy. In Hawaii, it's common to talk about people on other planets, so nobody, there, thought I was insane when I told them about my visions. Thank God this didn't happen in Pennsylvania. (Laughs)

"When I told my Hawaiian friends about my vision, one of them said, 'I'm going to take you to meet Neo, the astrologer. He will have something to tell you about this.' When I met him, he told me that whatever would happen for me with the Planet Sirius would happen in two years because that's when Saturn lines up with Sirius, and Saturn's the planet that governs *manifestation*.

"By the year 2000, I had grown tired of trying to figure everything out and decided to let it all go. But then one morning my friend SoLea came into my room, with tears streaming down her face. She said, 'I've been working *energetically* all night for you and I have some information!' I had no idea she was a mystic and could function in this way. I just thought she was this very cool lady. She said to me, 'The husband in your vision isn't a man. The husband represents the star, Sirius, and you will be receiving a transmission from the star. You must prepare yourself.' Now this was three months before I ended up being hit by lightning. So, exactly two years after Neo said whatever's going to happen between me and Sirius would happen in two years, and three months after SoLea said I would receive a transmission from the star, I get hit by lightning! Now in case I didn't connect the dots the name of the man standing next to me when I was hit by lightning was Asira Nova, which comes from the name of the star Sirius. I now understood on some deep level, that I was going to be involved in Ritual Theatre, and

I'd better *hold onto my pants* because things were going to happen. When I looked at the whole sequence of events that led me to this realization, I knew it was all connected and this was my right path.

"There was also a journey of physical healing to deal with. I had been zapped by this high voltage blast of electricity; I was knocked unconscious; and I had burn marks across my entire body. When I woke up in the hospital in Boulder, Colorado, the medical people told me that my survival was a total miracle. They said the heart is not designed to be able to handle that kind of voltage. They had a hard time believing I had survived. Beyond the physical healing, however, I had to integrate the energy of the lightning which was not easy."

Were you able to connect, right away, that being hit by lightning was part of this journey?

"I made the connection, but what I didn't know was *why* the whole thing happened. Why lightning? Why had I just gone on a two-year journey for that outcome? I understood at some level, from my earlier visions and intuitions that events would be happening for me that would prepare me for something greater, which in turn would be some kind of blessing and a mission of sorts. But I didn't know what shape that mission would take—I was in the dark! During my stay in the hospital I wasn't even sure if I would ever be able to walk again. After I did leave, I had a profound limp for years. In addition, my whole body was so sensitive to electricity, that for a long time it was hard for me to be in the same room with a refrigerator. I was afraid I was going to end up being some kind of freak. Thank God that over time, I fully recovered."

"Here I stand six years after the lightning struck me and all I can say is that having had an *initiation of fire* in my system like I did, it became the difference for me between being a 'dreamy' or visionary person with lots of great ideas, or being a person of action. Having that much 'juice' running through my body, I could no longer just talk about 'heaven on earth,' I had to do something to make it happen. That was the 'gift' of the lightning.

"I have continued to write new plays. One was called, 'The Water

Ceremony' which was performed at Muhlenberg College to a standing room only audience. I then met my husband to-be, musician, Scott Eggert. Together we incorporated Circle of Stones Ritual Theatre Ensemble, which is a beautiful, not-for-profit, professional company dedicated to using theatre to inspire positive community transformations. We have also produced some children's plays and then in April of this year, during Earth Week, we premiered our first big production, 'The New Earth,' at Zoellner Arts Center's Diamond Theatre at Lehigh University in Bethlehem, Pennsylvania. The play was written to ignite hearts and inspire action towards environmental sustainability within community and on our planet. It was a tremendous event! Now we're working on 'Gilgamesh', a new play for which we've just begun the research and development phase .This play will be an invocation and guiding spirit for a new arts center, for Emmaus, our hometown. The arts center will be the home of Circle of Stones Ritual Theatre Ensemble and dare I say a temple to peace and environmental sustainability. One aspect of the Arts Center will be multicultural programming aimed at getting at the roots of racism and the reasons why people go to war with each other. We hope to bring about understanding and appreciation of different cultures in the most exciting way possible, which for us is through the arts. Another major component will be a focus on programming geared to empowering the youth of our community to become all they can be."

You have a very clear vision of the future for your theatre group and this arts center!

"Yes I do, and it's happening! We currently have a committee of some really wonderful and powerful people in the community, including funders, who like us are very excited about the project. Our biggest challenge right now is finding the perfect site, one that will be large enough for what we want to accomplish."

What exactly is Ritual performance?

"Ritual performance is theatre that is consciously designed to invoke a positive transformation in the community. The context for the plays is usually myth. We are particularly drawn to ancient myth because it's a way to integrate spiritual principles without stepping on anyone's toes. When you're talking about Christianity, for instance, people whether they're Christian or not, have a very personal connection and interpretation of it; but if you're talking about Zeus, people don't have that same connection or charge—they don't feel like their personal God or religion is being attacked or even addressed. We also like to use archetypes in our plays and we're not much interested in psychological drama. Ritual Performance also integrates theatre with ritual, so there's a strong audience participation element. During 'The New Earth,' for example, there was a scene from the myth of Persephone and Demeter where Persephone, the daughter of Demeter, the Grain Goddess, is kidnapped by Hades, Lord of the Underworld, so she could help him destroy the fears that were preventing humankind from shifting to a new renewable energy source. We know that thousands upon thousands of people have died, and that our world is imperiled because of our dependence on foreign oil. We know all this and we're still not willing to switch to another form of energy use—why?

"The answers to that question lie in the four fears that we present in the play. They are: the cost of changing, taking the time to investigate it, ridicule, and the fear of change itself. Hades then called each of the fears out on the stage. They appeared as martial artists dressed in red and wearing painted monster faces. Hades and Persephone then battled the fears until the point where they turned to the audience and said, 'we need your help. To give us the energy to kill these fears, we ask that you clap in rhythm. The energy and the focus of your intention will enable us to kill off these fears.' The three musicians then played some fantastic, energetic African drum music, and the audience clapped and clapped (raises her voice very excitedly) in rhythm. I thought they would jump out of their seats. It was so exciting! In the end the fears were destroyed. That's an example of how we use Ritual Theatre to encourage the audience to use their energy and intention to create a positive transformation."

Later, people have said to me, 'I wanted to buy organic milk but my God, it's so expensive. After the play though, when I would feel the fear of that expense, I would think, *what is the expense of our military and of our cars, etc.?* I realized that, *no*, our real expense is our continued dependence on fossil fuels.'

"So they would remember that and say to themselves, *I'm going to buy that organic milk, or I'm going to walk to the store instead of driving.* That's the attitude we hope people will leave the play with.

"Ritual is not a dead event! It's very alive and not concerned with simply going through the motions of lighting a candle or making a gesture: When I participate in a ritual, my intention is to invoke a change: to make the planet, myself, or the community function better, and in the end, for the world to be a better place. It's a way for me of cultivating consciousness.

"So that's what we're doing and that's my passion!"

Did you have any of this particular passion or drive prior to Gaia coming into your world?

"Yeah. That day, eight years ago, when I had that great inner change in Hawaii, the focus stopped being about me and my career and personal happiness. It wasn't that I didn't want to feel happy and fulfilled, but from that day forth, my intention became, *how can I serve to make the world a better place?* I also knew that *how* I wanted to do this would be through the mediums of art, beauty, and most of all love. From that day onward there was never a question about what I wanted to do!"

How has the pursuit of this passion benefited you Pana?

"Well, I'll tell you, when I left the consciousness of being afraid, and I wasn't worried about my career and money anymore and best of all, doing something I love, my life took on a kind of playful, game—like quality. I mean there were years after I had left acting and I was wandering around the world, when I had no money—not a penny in my pocket! If the dream I have for the Arts Center never happens, I'll be OK with it. If the funding for 'Gilgamesh' doesn't come through, I'll be OK. I'm no longer governed by this ambitious, desperate, ego-driven desire I once had. Today I think, *wouldn't this be great, if enough people agree with me and we could make it happen?* That's what I mean when I say it's game-like. There's lightness to my passion now and most of the time there's no angst! *I sometimes think, in my dream of dreams what would be the most cool, fun filled thing to do? Oh! That would be fun. Let's do it!*

"The biggest challenges for me are in learning how to delegate, finding people who have the willingness and skills, and who I feel comfortable with, in representing our theater company, and in raising money for the projects we're engaged in. In the last year, others have begun to help with that, but during my pregnancy for Gaia I was working up to 14 hours a day, seven days a week on the computer, doing mailings, fund-raising, and answering the phone. There's only so much of that you can do in a sustained way and not have it affect your health. Our volunteers have been great and they're stepping up to the plate. We have a new president of the Board—she's great and she believes in the board being a working board, so we're moving in that direction."

How does your spirituality affect your work?
"There's no aspect of my work that isn't connected to my spirituality. Whether it's my choice of projects, seeking guidance, staying focused, or getting myself centered, every aspect of my work is immersed in spiritual principles, and guided by divine intelligence in some way. I attend a church here in Emmaus, but there are also six of us who meet monthly as a ritual community, and go out to a friend's farm, where we light a fire, pray, and set our intentions together. That's really wonderful. Scott and I used to do a lot of rituals together, but since Gaia came into our lives we're lucky sometimes if we can take five minutes to squeeze a prayer in. We maintain a little altar in our house and there are articles on it that remind me each time I walk by it, to stay focused on my intentions, and on what's important at this time in my life."

Where were you brought up Pana?
"I was born in Ohio in a town called South Euclid, my father died when I was eight, and mom moved us to Allentown to be closer to her family. Allentown was my home until I left to attend school at SUNY Purchase where they had an acting conservatory. Later, I moved to

Manhattan to attend the New Actor's Workshop, a two year program for actors.

"My background as a Greek-American really supported me in my early life before I started traveling. I loved all things Greek, which gave me a sense of identity. I even had the Greek national anthem taped to the front window in our home. When I began to travel around the world I realized that identifying myself as Greek—which I love to do—was too small an identity. The Universe would no longer allow me to derive my sense of self from something as small as one culture."

Where did your desire to act come from?

"I guess it really came out of my enjoyment of singing. I sang in choirs and various music groups when I was a youngster. In High School, I was playing Charity in the play 'Sweet Charity,' and I remember being backstage, excited and very nervous, and thinking, *I want to feel this alive my whole life!* That's when I decided I would act professionally. So my passion for theater began at that point, but would eventually shift, after my hiatus from acting and my time in Hawaii, into something which was less about how great an actress I was, and more into how I could make a difference in the world using my acting skills."

It's been quite a journey!

"It sure has! I've also been working on a novel that is the story of this journey I've been sharing with you. One way I was able to get around the world without money was by helping various people I would meet, who were in a state of crisis, much as I had been after I had left acting. They wanted to let something in their life go—like a job, a country, or a relationship—but were afraid. It just seemed that we would meet, and I would move in and help them with their process until they decided that they would or wouldn't make the change. So I helped them through their time of crisis and in the meantime I had a place to stay and food to eat. It was an odd arrangement that happened many times while I was traveling. In time, though, I grew weary of this way of living, and wanted a home of my own and my own money. That's when I decided I would write a book telling the story, sell it, and help many more people—God willing. I'd also break this cycle of telling my story and living in other people's homes, and would have gained some financial independence for myself."

What's the "juice" that keeps you going Pana?

"Well! One very inspiring part of my life that keeps me going is our beautiful daughter Gaia, who was born in June of this year. I would like her to grow up in a place where conscious creativity happens. I want her to be around more than just white people. I want her to be with great musicians, thinkers, and creative people from all over the world. I want there to be a beautiful, sacred place where she can see the windmills and the solar panels; and if anybody should say to her, 'Environmental sustainability is silly,' she could answer, 'that's not true, we're doing it; it's totally real, I can show you! Would you like to come see it?'

"I don't want to live in the realm of, 'wouldn't it be great if'…? I really want to give this *heaven on earth experience* to her. *Heaven on earth* for me is peace between the world's cultures, and all of us living in a sustainable way. So I'm in the process of creating that, not only because I think it would be a great thing for the community and the planet, but personally, because I know it would be great gift to her. Hopefully she'll like the arts. But who knows, maybe we'll be creating a *conscious* baseball diamond for her someday."

Pana Columbus may be contacted at **www.circleofstones.org** and at **www.facebook.com/pages/Circle-of-Stones-Ritual-Theatre-**

Chapter 3
Conduit
Perley Rousseau

"To be a conduit for positive musical energy in the world is truly my great passion. As insignificant as Sonny and I are in this great big world, I still feel that because we have been called to something, and are living out our calling, that eventually the musical energy we leave here, will have some kind of positive and healing affect on this planet."

Perley is a vivacious, warm, engaging, and deeply passionate woman who combines a love for singing and performing, with great artistry and a fervent desire to bring joy and healing through her music. Her ability to draw an audience into the *story* of a song creates an intimate connection between her and her listeners. Together with her husband of 24 years, pianist Sonny Daye, she brings her music to various venues throughout the United States as "Sonny and Perley." From time to time they also perform with their 20-year-old daughter, Desiree, who plays guitar and sings.

I interviewed Perley in her home in Cohoes, New York.

"I think I'm one of those people who live their lives in a passionate way, rather than being someone who has one particular passionate pursuit. Coming from a passionate Italian family, it seemed everything we did was done passionately whether it was cooking, eating, talking—look my hands are going already. (Laughing) We love passionately! We fight passionately! So yeah, I do everything passionately, and that's probably why I take high blood pressure medicine. (Laughing)

"One of my great passions is music. I just *have* to play music. There's no two ways about it. I'm sure I would find another creative outlet if I couldn't sing—maybe cooking or dance or painting or gardening—but for me, music is my *r'aison d'être* or *reason for being*. To be a *conduit* for positive musical energy in the world is truly my great passion. As insignificant as Sonny and I are in this great big world, I still feel that because we have been *called* to something, and are living out our calling, that eventually the musical energy we leave here, will have some kind of positive and healing affect on this planet.

"It's not like I think we're going to change the world or anything like that, but I think that whenever we can live out of our higher purpose or reason for being, it will have a positive effect on the world and on humanity in general. I really do believe that each one of us, going back to the beginning of time, has had a reason for being here that goes well beyond paying our bills and just living day to day.

"What gives me the most pleasure out of my passion for singing is seeing people healed. What I mean is, in that hour or so they're attending our concert, they've forgotten everything else: their pain; their worries, their emotional turmoil—whatever it might be, and they've received some level of spiritual healing. The reason I'm so convinced of this is because so many people have told me it's happened for them. So finally I thought *well OK, this is really happening; it's great!*

"So now, provided we remember, we pray just before we perform, that God will prepare our hearts so that essentially, we will get out of the way of the music—as an artist in this business you have to fight your ego all the time—and be open *conduits* for the Higher Power to come through us and flow to the people. We also pray for the hearts and souls of those in our audience as well, that they will be open to receive. This is key for us as performers and, also wonderful when I can apply it to everything in my life."

What's the benefit to you when you're able to be that open conduit for spirit?

"Oh my! We get so much. To state the obvious, we get to do what we love for a living. I'm constantly grateful that we actually make money doing what we love. I mean I've had other jobs and not that they were bad jobs, but they just weren't satisfying for me.

"For instance I was in sales for a long time. It was direct sales. I worked for that company for about eight years; traveled a lot, and ran some aspects of their advertising. I made a good living, but I knew there was something else that I was supposed to be doing with my life besides just going into my office each morning by ten o'clock. At times it was *torture* and I was unhappy. Often work into the *wee* hours, not leaving till 11 or 12 at night. It was crazy!

"One part of my work life that I *did* enjoy for a period of time, before music became my fulltime work, was working with emotionally disturbed and physically handicapped children. I really did love that and perhaps at some time in the future, I may return to that and use my musical ability. In those days I was starting out in the music business and only able to work with these children part time. That's one of the reasons that I'm now in training to be a volunteer for hospice. I want to use my music in that area.

"So I get a tremendous amount of satisfaction and joy when I see people smiling as they listen to our music. I'm also a vocal coach and I receive a lot of happiness from that. It's very rewarding when I coach someone who has some bad vocal habits, for instance, and in time I'm able to help them so that they're singing more on pitch or their expressing themselves more fully or their phrasing is better and they feel more confident. One of my students is a 17-year-old High School Senior. Her mom recently told me her daughter's confidence level has improved as her vocal habits have gotten better. That makes me very happy."

When did your love of music begin?
"It probably began when I was a little girl. I was born in Lawrence,

Massachusetts and I grew up mainly in Atkinson and Salem, New Hampshire. My mother and father had great taste in music, so I grew up being exposed to all the 'greats' like Ella Fitzgerald, Duke Ellington, Sarah Vaughn, and, of course, a nice dose of very sophisticated pop music like Barbara Streisand and Sergio Mendes and Brazil 66, which was the seed for the Brazilian music which I grew to love. It's funny that for a long time I didn't actually sing; instead, I sort of mimed the music with a hairbrush, pretending to be singing into a microphone. Then there were times that I'd make up words to sound Brazilian. At that age though, no one ever told me that I had a good singing voice. I didn't really become aware that I had an enjoyable voice to listen to, until I was in my twenties. At the time, I was working for the sales company in Milford, Connecticut. Every once in a while I'd visit this little piano bar there and *sit in* with the piano player when no one was around. One night after I'd sat in with him he said, 'You have a pretty good singing voice, a good feel for the music, and you seem to enjoy it. Why don't you take a voice lesson or two and see where it takes you?'

"I can't even remember his name, but he was the first one who urged me to study and get serious about music. So I took some lessons in Connecticut and then moved to Chicago with the company I was working for. I continued my studies and began *sitting in* more often in jazz venues. I resumed my music study again when I returned to Chicago, and continued, when my work led me back to the Berkshires of Massachusetts where I was born.

"I had my first paid singing gig there—I performed regularly with a pianist on the weekends. He worked for GE and when the plant he worked in closed, he moved to Schenectady. I followed him there and we booked some gigs. That's actually when I met Sonny, who was playing drums at the time.

"Within 4 or 5 years after that, I really got serious about music and studied classical technique for another four years with Sylvia Kutchukian, an international opera diva. Since then, I still take master classes at times, mostly with opera singers because I really believe in that foundation for my singing. I've also taken some jazz classes with *icons* like Sheila Jordan and Jay Clayton."

What is it about jazz that attracts you?

"Jazz just hits me right in the center of my being whenever I hear it. There are so many types of jazz these days—smooth jazz, bebop, fusion, and then there's a cabaret type of jazz which is relatively new, and combines styles. That's basically what we do. It's hard to define what I love about it. I know I love the freedom of jazz: the improvisational aspect of it; the chord structure; the harmonies; the challenge of the melodies—they're so interesting.

"Music is so subjective for me and because of that, it's very hard to dissect. I just like it! It's something that I'm naturally drawn to and in part it could be that I grew up listening to that kind of music. Even before I can remember, my parents were playing music—primarily jazz—in my house. I love all kinds of music. We often listen to classical, and lately I'm getting more into the *folksier alternative* stuff because of Desiree, my daughter. Annie DiFranco is someone I enjoy, and of course being 52, I have my whole teenage-through-early-twenties—time of my life caught up in the rock and roll movement of the sixties. I loved the Beatles and the Woodstock Generation of music stars like Jimi Hendrix, Janis Joplin, Led Zeppelin, and Jefferson Airplane. I mean I was really into that stuff and still love it today—in fact I've had it in my mind for the last four years to put together a concert that will focus on our generation's music, performed in our style, and with a jazz background to it. "

What drives you to pursue music performance so passionately?

"It's in knowing that I'm fulfilling my main purpose here on earth; 'my calling,' so to speak. Indeed there are other reasons for my being, and they may be just as important, if not more, but this calling is clear and obvious and confirmed by the fact that I love what I am doing! I periodically check in with God to make sure that I'm still meant to be in this business. I believe that a person can have more than one passion in a lifetime, and more than one purpose to fulfill. So, for me 'checking in' is integral in pursuing my passion. In addition to all that, as an artist, I passionately engage in creating music because I must…It's a way of life.

"Of course one of the more practical factors that drive us is that we have to pay the bills. So Sonny has got to get on that phone and make calls. He's an amazing person. I could not do what he does. He calls some people maybe 25 to 30 times, and often those people are rude to him or never call him back. I don't know how he does it. It's a real gift to be able to let all that negative stuff slide off your back. It's really sales, but he's not a high pressure person. So we don't go anywhere where we're not wanted and welcomed, and *that* is a wonderful aspect to what we do. A lot of times in this business you have to push to get your *foot in the door* and force it open, but I don't like to play in places where we have to do that. As a result we only perform in venues where we're really desired and they're excited about having us.

"That's another aspect of our character—we just ask the Lord to open doors and show us where he wants us to go."

How do you know if you're on the right road or not?
"It's that nebulous thing we call *peace of mind*. When you're on the right road evidence abounds. My belief is: *If you do what you were born to do, you'll be sustained.* Sonny and I have been sustained.

"We took a huge leap about 22 years ago. We left our part-time jobs behind so we could do what we love. We leapt into the music business full-time. Sonny had actually been working full time in a non music-related job, and he bought out a booking agency from a man he knew at the time, and that became our foundation. Because of the booking agency, we had established clients and many leads for our own music.

"That gave us some sure footing, but it was still a struggle at times. For quite a while, Sonny's mom would say, 'Why don't you get a job Mark?'(His real name)

"He'd say, 'I have a job mom' and she'd say, 'You do?' (Laughing)

"He'd say, 'Yes—I have the agency and I have music.'

"She finally stopped saying that when we bought our first new car. I guess that was a sign that we had made it.

"My parents, on the other hand, were supportive the whole time. I think that was because my dad was dabbling in show business at that time. He played piano and sang, danced, and did comedy. My dad, who was married to a lady who owned a dance studio, didn't actually learn to play piano until he was in his forties and divorced from my mom. Then he went full steam ahead with it. He would go to nursing homes and resorts, and put on shows. My mother, on the other hand, played accordion as far back as I can remember. I came from a very musical family."

Have you had heroes or mentors who've influenced your passion for music?

"Ella Fitzgerald was the first recorded voice I heard as a child and I think she became more of a mentor for me after I read about her life. She struggled to survive and often lived on the street as a child. Her original dream was to be a dancer. When Ella took part in a talent show at the Apollo theatre in Harlem, she did not go there with the intention of singing, but instead had gone with the aim of dancing. Now, there were also two sisters entered who were professional dancers, and when she saw them she lost her nerve; even though she billed herself as "The Best Little Dancer in Yonkers." When she finally stepped out on the stage she was terrified, and as Ella tells it, someone from the audience yelled, and I'm going to paraphrase here, *While you're out there kid, you might as well do something.* So she started to sing, and because she loved Connie Boswell, who was on the radio a lot in those days, she sang two Connie Boswell songs. She said the crowd at first heckled her something fierce, but by the time she finished, you could hear a pin drop.

"Carmen McCrae influenced me stylistically. My phrasing is a lot like hers and I love her delivery. She really tells a story when she performs a song. Carmen was overshadowed throughout her career by Ella and Sarah Vaughan. Ella was so perfect that her voice was like a musical instrument. "

You often perform before large, packed rooms, but I also know that you and Sonny play before very small crowds at times. How do you keep the disappointment of a small turnout from dampening your passion and enthusiasm when you perform?

"Thank goodness we have each other to remind us why we're there. No matter the size of the crowd it doesn't alter our purpose, which is *to get out of the way* and allow ourselves to be a conduit for the music, the lyrics, the healing, and whatever wants to come through us that night. That never changes. But very honestly, there are nights when I get *totally bummed out*—to borrow a phrase from the sixties—especially around here in the Albany area where *we're old hat*. Why pay to see us in a concert when they can wait and see us in a town library for free? So, yes, sometimes that bothers me a bit, but then I've talked to other performers and heard stories of *stars* that have played in Jazz clubs with six people in the audience. I attended a gig, a friend of mine put on just a few weeks ago, and there were just three people in the audience! There were more people on stage than there were in the audience; and this was for a fabulous pianist, bassist, and guitar player. That tells me it doesn't happen only to us.

"I think that's where the ego can get in the way. If I stay conscious on how small the crowd is, I'll never be in the moment, and totally focused on the music I'm singing. I think that's what can separate a passionate performance from a performance where someone just goes out and delivers the music. To truly present the truth of a song, I can't be thinking about anything but the lyric, melody, or music of that moment. I can tell if we're distracted. I can tell when Sonny's distracted and he can pick up on me being *out there*. I'll say to Sonny, 'Come back, come back darling—where are you?' That's a discipline that takes time to develop.

"It's also easier when you have an audience that is educated in the music you'll be presenting and familiar with what you're going to do. They're there because they love the genre of music and they're full of expectations. Recently we had a *fabulous* concert in New Jersey. There were 75 people packed into the room—some had to stand—you couldn't get another person in that door. One of the reasons these people came with expectations, was that the venue has an established reputation for presenting top quality music—not just jazz, but even more so, folk. We're their *token* jazz group. We do this gig once a year and the audience comes with this expectation of not only being entertained, but being *moved* and having an experience.

"That makes a difference, and it doesn't matter how large the crowd is, as long as that *vibe* is in the room and the reciprocity between us and the audience is happening. That's why I like to talk in between numbers. I'm sure you've been to concerts where the performers don't talk, and there's nothing wrong with that, but for me, I like to create community, and that's what I'm doing in those moments. If we're having one of those nights where we aren't connecting with an audience for some reason I can sometimes get really grouchy (Laughing), so I'll work hard at changing the vibe in the room. I might prod them by being a little outrageous or by making them laugh so they'll loosen up, relax, and feel a bond with us and with the music. It's not always easy though.

"In our recent newsletter, I took a quote from a Catholic priest, Father Francis Gargani, who we've been involved with musically, and as a friend for a long time. Francis is a passionate and fascinating person in his own right. He often presented entertainment at his beautiful retreat center, Mount St. Alphonsus, in Esopus, New York. He's the first person who got us into this form of performing that's called cabaret, where you discuss the music you're playing, and connect with the audience. The quote that I used this month is: '*What Sonny and Perley offer is love, pure and simple...they weave a tapestry of affection among their listeners, such that a real sense of community and beauty results.*'

"Those words really personify what we strive to do, in an articulate and succinct way."

Has personal woundedness had a part in creating or energizing this passion of yours?

"For an artist there's always that old adage that you have to *suffer* before you can truly create a worthwhile work of art or beauty. (Laughing) I laugh, but I think there's a lot of truth to that idea. A person gains more compassion, as well as passion, for humanity when he or she has suffered. That's definitely played a part in my music and in my ability to relate to music.

"Forgiveness also keeps coming up in my mind. I've found that my woundedness, and as well, my wounding of other people⁻ intentional or not⁻ has manifested forgiveness in my music as well. One of the first Brazilian songs that we rewrote into English was *One Must Forgive* or *E Preciso Perdoar* in Portuguese, and that song came about during a very painful time of my life when I was facing things within myself that I didn't even know were there. It was a four-year period of intense counseling where emotional pain I'd been carrying, was being validated for the first time in my life. So I went through the whole gamut of emotions, and months and months of just crying almost everyday as I worked my way through the process of grief, which resulted finally in forgiveness. It wasn't pretty, yet this beautiful song came out of that journey, and I can't tell you how many people have been touched by it. I get e-mails all the time telling me how this song has affected listeners."

What is the difference for you between obsession and a healthy passion?

"I find that the line between obsession and a healthy passion are so blurred at times that it's often difficult to tell the difference between the two. You should ask Sonny about that."(Laughing)

-Sonny enters the room

Sonny: 'I think when you get into obsession you're thinking too much of yourself and not enough about other people."

"That's beautifully put honey"

Perley said that you are able to pull each other up when one of you seem to be drifting away.

Sonny—"Yes, we try to do that. We seem to know what the markers are."(Laughing)

"Yeah, our little antennas go up and go, 'beep, beep, beep."

Sonny: "It's an art to know how to do that when you're up on stage in the middle of a performance. Sometimes it's just an instant reaction in listening to her singing—I'll quiet down, put more space in my playing, and she'll listen more. Sometimes if I become

aware that I'm *out there,* I'll just get livelier. But then there are times while performing that your brain just doesn't work as well as you want it to."

"I was telling John that I'll sometimes simply lean over towards you and say, 'come back Sonny…come back.'

Sonny—"I certainly know what she means when she does that. Sometimes though it may just be an idle thought that pops into my head, and if I follow it I'm *gone.* I don't wanna follow any thoughts, unless it has something to do with the arrangement of the piece I'm playing at the time.

Sonny—"You also don't want to focus on the expressions on people's faces because they often don't represent what you perceive them to be anyway. Some people are very happy yet they look miserable. The other effect of focusing on what you think people are feeling is that you can destroy the music and your performance. I try to keep my focus on the music. When I do that I find that, in most cases the music, when it's played well, will draw people in. That's not to say that there aren't some people that you just can't draw in no matter what you do."

"That's why I don't wear my contacts anymore on stage. That way, the audience is a beautiful blur of color, and that's the way I like it. (Laughing) If I concentrate on people's faces, it can drive me crazy."

Sonny—"Sometimes you have to draw them (the audience) into the situation, so they realize they're present in the moment and not just a distant observer."

-Sonny leaves the conversation-

"I make a point at every concert we perform now to tell them, '*If it wasn't for the reciprocity we're experiencing in this moment, no matter how perfectly we might be playing, it would all be for nothing if there wasn't this energy moving back and forth between us.*

"At a concert we gave this past weekend, the audience was just unbelievable! Every person in that room was smiling. It's not always that way—some people just listen very seriously or others may wrinkle up their faces. When I sing I like to close my eyes, but I have to force myself to open my eyes to connect with the audience once in a while. What I'll do then is try and find someone who's smiling and always go back to the person who has that kind of energy. Thank God for those folks."

What sacrifices have you had to make Perley, to follow this passion of yours?

"I've had to sacrifice my dream of being the richest person in the world. (Laughing) Seriously, I didn't want to be the richest person in the world, but I did want to have more money than we have now. I wanted to have the freedom to travel more and to have a larger house because I love to entertain people in my home. I wanted a better car—I drove a nice little sports car when I was in sales. So I did sacrifice some material things but the tradeoff for me has been absolutely great.

"Sometimes, when we're traveling to perform, we might say to each other, 'How can we be traveling like this and having such a great time, when most people would consider us poor?'

"Sadly, in our country, the middle class is disappearing, but we do just about everything we want to do. It's truly amazing to me. That may be because we don't need as much as we once did—we're content with what we have. I really believe that if you do what you were *called* to do, you will be sustained."

What would you say to those who say they have no passion in their lives?

"Somewhere in our concerts I will say to the audience, 'If you don't like what you're doing you can stop doing it, and find what it is that you were meant to do. Besides bringing you great joy and happiness, when you do what you love, you will most likely benefit others.'

"I say that, because I believe it, but more than that, I want everyone to be as joyous in what they do, as I am in what I do. I can't tell you how many people come up to me and tell me how miserable they are because each day they have to get up, go to work, and perform work they hate. I feel so bad for them. I hear them say, '*Oh thank God it's Friday.*' I say, 'It's Friday, yea! I can't wait to sing.! I can't wait to get there.' I mean

I didn't always feel that way. Sometimes, we'll get a gig where I say to Sonny,

'O-h-h-h-h, I don't want to go to this gig,' but those days are far and few between, thank God."

How are you able to perform at a high level when you may be experiencing difficult events in your life?

"It's not easy sometimes. There have been times where I've been crying just before going on out on stage. Right now my dad is very ill and that's a real source of concern for me these days. Sometimes I dedicate our performance to the person I'm holding in my heart, and allow all the energy from that performance to go to the healing of that situation. Other times, and I'll be quite honest with you, I say, 'God, you have to do this performance for me; I don't have one ounce of love in me right now.' I've prayed that prayer many times. Thank God that I have Sonny—he'll pray with me or squeeze my hand or give me some little expression of love or support. There are other times when I'm not feeling great, and I'll be up on stage and see someone in the audience wave to me and I'll think, *Oh my God, I haven't seen that person in so long, I'll do this next song for her*, and then I'm able to refocus myself on why I'm there. It's important, as Sonny said earlier, to get the focus off myself—get me out of the way—and then the love can come through. As soon as you get your *self* out of the way, the love comes through…always…Don't you notice that about life?"

Perley may be contacted at ***www.sonnyandperley.com***,

Chapter 4
Breaking Free
Jennifer Hanson

"The next day I set out without water and eventually came to a mountain pass near the border of Idaho and Wyoming through which Lewis and Clark had traveled and where there was reported to be a spring. After searching for a while, I found water and cooked the dinner I'd not been able to have the night before. I then wrote a letter to my friend, and slowly became aware my feelings were changing from despair to confidence. I can do this, I thought, I can really do this!

Jennifer is a computer consultant and full-time mom, living in Latham, New York with her son Noah, daughter, Eliana, and her life partner Denise. Her passion for hiking, and a desire to always find out what's *around the bend,* led her to hike the Continental Divide from Mexico to the Canadian Border. In the process she broke free of old limits and fears which had limited her development as a person. When first meeting Jennifer, one is struck by her 'dancing eyes' and high level of energy, which are fueled by her curiosity, openness, and excitement about life.

"My passion for being in the wild has always been with me. As a young child I would sit in the back seat of my parent's car, and as we were driving, I'd look out the window and imagine myself running, walking, or horseback riding through the fields and forest that were passing by. I could feel myself moving through the land, and going on and on and never wanting to stop! I loved that experience. During grade school I was an avid reader and would read stories about the pioneers who crossed the country on the old wagon trails. I would often wonder if I was born a hundred years too late. I'd seen many pictures of the Great Plains and the Rocky Mountains and so wanted to walk through those places and experience the beauty of it all.

"Walking is exhilarating and peaceful for me, and I always felt very comfortable in the woods. I joined the Girl Scouts when I was very young and attended Girl Scout camp four years in a row. The fifth year our troop planned a two-week backpacking trip. That had me very excited. But my father, being a Colonel in the Army at the time, got orders to transfer, so we ended up moving from Fort Benning, Georgia to Indiana and my backpacking trip was cancelled.

"I recall fondly the conversations my dad and I would have about camping and backpacking at that time. We were a large family¯I am the sixth oldest of 10 children¯so the times of having my father's individual attention are memorable to me. I can recall a few times when we were alone and he would share some simple tips, and he'd talk passionately about hiking and camping. (Tearing up) I could tell how important it was too him because he was taking time from watching the news or whatever else he would do in the evening to relax. Those conversations so excited me.

"It's been 10 years since he passed away, but I realize now how much I miss him. Until now, I haven't been aware of the importance of those conversations, which took place during a three-month period when I was 13. Dad was not easy to connect with, and when I was nine, he went to Viet Nam for the first of two tours. He saw a lot of heavy combat, so when he came home, he drank a lot, was frequently angry, and wasn't the same person he'd been. During high school I don't remember any special times with him. At 17 I left home for college and never returned. So, that time we did have together was very special to me.

"Much later, when I was a cadet at West Point, I learned a lot about hiking, orienteering, land navigation, and terrain analysis¯all the things you need to be a successful backpacker. For a number of years after graduation, I did all the hiking and camping I could, but never really did any backpacking because I didn't have the proper equipment nor was I very well versed in what I would need. Slowly, however, I began accumulating the equipment and, in 1989, I went backpacking for the first time.

"I met Greg, my ex-husband, when I was backpacking. Over time, he and I did a lot of backpacking and hiking together, and we slowly increased our mileage. In 1994, with our confidence building, we tackled the 100 Mile Wilderness Trail in Maine, which took us 12 days to complete. When we started that hike, we really didn't know what we were doing; yet that's the way you have to begin—where you're at. You have to be willing to make a fool of yourself and just kind of learn as you go.

"On that trip we gained a lot of experience, and best of all we were hiking in the company of quite a few thru-hikers, since this trail was also the last 100 miles of the Appalachian Trail. I found it fascinating to read the trail registers in the shelters each night because these thru-hikers who were finishing, were recording what they had learned and how the Appalachian Trail had impacted them. Reading these entries inspired Greg and I, and got us thinking about doing a long distant hike of our own. It would be a few years before it happened but the seed got planted here.

"In 1989, when I lived just off the Appalachian Trail in Sheffield, Massachusetts, I met two women thru-hikers on a day I was out hiking alone. I was flabbergasted when they told me they were hiking the entire trail! That can take four to six months. They were probably in their 40s, weren't athletic-looking, and even a bit overweight, but they were very excited about this trek of theirs, and told me that if I liked to hike I really had to do it too. It seemed impossible to me, but it was the first time I started to believe that maybe I could do it too."

"Greg and I were married in 1995, and that same year I suffered a miscarriage, which was a big disappointment because I truly wanted to have a child. In the aftermath of that loss, and with help from a therapist,

Greg and I realized that if there were things we wanted to accomplish, we'd better do them *before* we had kids. At the time I was 35 years old. I thought, *I'm running out of time if I want to hike the Appalachian Trail and then have kids too. We just couldn't afford to sit around and think about it anymore.*

"In February of 1996, we decided we'd hike the Continental Divide Trail, so we set about planning and getting organized. Then in June of 1996 I was fired from the retreat center, where I'd been an administrator and teacher, because I'd been butting heads with the owner. That was truly a blessing, because it took care of the problem of, *how do I get enough time off to do a thru-hike?* For 22 years, beginning at the age of 14, I'd been working non-stop, so I'd never actually taken a break, nor had I even conceived of one. During that ensuing year I worked part-time as a downhill ski instructor, worked at a home for severely disabled children, but mostly planned and organized for our adventure.

"When you mention passion, I remember how excited we were despite the enormity of what we were undertaking. I was also afraid to tell anyone because I was afraid they'd say it was silly and crazy, and besides *ordinary people don't do these things.* When I first told my parents, I imagined that my dad would think I was running away from my problems, trying to escape, or taking some kind of 'geographical cure.' At the same time, I felt very passionate and determined to do this hike. Somewhere in me there was a voice that would keep saying, *But I just want to hike.* (Tearing up) I guess I feel a little sad that I had to work so hard back then to justify following my dream.

"In my family we had 10 children. Because my father was in Viet Nam for a long stretch of time and my mother raised us alone, we had a lot of structure and rules. So, I internalized rules from my family, from society, and from being a cadet at West Point and later as an Army officer. In undertaking my passion for backpacking, however, I was able to make major breakthroughs out of how rule-bound my life had been. My passion combined with a growing spirituality would allow me to risk doing something very much out of the norm.

"I was hesitant to tell my father because he can be strongly opinionated. I don't believe I told him until I'd heard that he'd been diagnosed with stage-four lung cancer in early 1996 and had only a short time to live.

"The cancer actually was a *gift* for my dad in the sense that it caused him to engage in psychotherapy, which led to a spiritual transformation for him. During this period, I decided to tell him about the hike, and to my surprise, he was immediately supportive. (Tearing up)…He'd always been so driven…he had a rough childhood. His father died when he was only a year old, and by the time he was eight or nine he was helping to support the family. As a result, he always had the attitude that *nothing comes easy; nothing comes free,* and he just worked, worked, worked all the time, and expected the same from others. While dealing with his cancer, however, he came to see that life was too short not to do what you dream of. Dad was at the end of his life, but he truly wanted me to enjoy my life. He was very interested in our plans; he gave us $300, and told us he didn't want us worrying about anything *frivolous* like money when we were out on the trail. This was a huge shift for him and for me as well—knowing he was behind what I was undertaking.

"I also needed help in preparing for the hike. People at the Continental Divide Trail Society were very helpful. We also contacted rangers at the different sites we'd be hiking. Ten years ago when we did this, there was very little marked trail. People just did the best they could to find their way. *Backpacker Magazine* said that only two to four people completed the trail each year, so there was little well-documented experience for hikers to draw from.

"I could see from a map of the United States where the Continental Divide is, but how to get from one point to the next on the hike was very unclear. This would be a trek of 2,500 miles through five states, and without trail maps there would be no way of knowing what type of terrain we'd be facing.

"For example, we had only a US Forest Service map to help us find our way through a 300 mile stretch of Montana. I knew I'd have to call the rangers to get more information about what we'd be facing. At the same time, I had a huge fear they would be indignant that we were going to hike through their forest, and then be forced to go out and rescue us. Once again my fear was proven wrong; the forest rangers were wonderful. They advised us of what maps to use as well as the best locations for camping and finding water. I was truly being *taken care of* while breaking through deeper and deeper levels of my fear. My passion was also energizing me because I wanted so much to hike and see every inch of this land that Lewis and Clark had traveled through!

"So the organizing and planning for this trip required a great deal of work. In thinking about this interview I perused a lot of the resource material I'd accumulated for the book I wrote about this hike. I had five pages of food items that I was comparison-pricing in the various super markets, department stores, and even on-line. We went into such detail because we knew conditions could get really serious on the trail. We were scared that we'd run out of food, water, money or supplies and we'd be in deep trouble—maybe even die!

"There were many logistics to figure out as well. At the time I didn't have a job, but Greg would need a six-month leave from his work. We had to give up our apartment and find storage for our possessions. There were questions about our health care and even about where our mail would be sent. This was a major upheaval in our normal day-to-day existence. Fortunately, Greg was great at taking care of a lot of those paperwork kinds of things. There was so much to think of!

"We also had the fear that maybe we'd become miserable once we got out there on the trail. There's a big difference between imagining doing something new and then actually doing it. We had many little fears. Did the maps we'd acquired—some as much as 50 years old—accurately portray the land we'd be walking through? Did the windmills used for pumping water to the surface of the arid landscape of New Mexico still exist? Would we be able to attain water from them? Theoretically, we knew our plan could work, but we were still unsure whether we would be up to the challenges that we'd be sure to face.

"Early on in our planning, I sensed Greg was really conflicted between wanting to do the hike, and supporting my desire to have a child. After the miscarriage, he was very sensitive to how upset I'd been about losing the baby; and also to the fact that I was 35 and my *biological clock was ticking.* Eventually, after a late night discussion one evening, I asked him, 'In your heart of hearts what do you truly want to do?'

"After pushing and pushing him, he finally said, 'Jen, I've always wanted to take on something big in my life. I really want to do this hike.'

"I said, 'Okay, we'll do it.'

"That discussion took place on day 31 of my menstrual cycle and I'd been pretty darn sure I'd was pregnant. I went to bed, woke up around one o'clock in the morning, which is very unusual for me, went to the bathroom, and discovered I was menstruating. It was as if I'd had another miscarriage because we had decided on doing the hike instead of having a baby. I was okay with that because I'd prayed and reflected on our conversation, and I knew both Greg and I wanted to do this hike. I thought: *As much as I want to have children, let's go do it!*

"We left New York on March 27, 1997, made some stops to see family along the way, and finally arrived at our jumping off point, Columbus, New Mexico, on the Mexican border, on April 1st, the traditional starting date for people hiking a trail south to north.

"The Continental Divide trail is difficult to finish in one season because 60 percent of it is at high altitude and is under snow for all but three months of the year. Consequently, you head north, finish New Mexico, and then run into snow in Colorado. At the north end, you encounter more snow and ice in Glacier National Park in Montana, and in Wyoming's Wind River Range. We made a decision to chop the trek into five legs in order to do it all in one season. Hiking all the lower elevations first and scrambling through the mountains at the end, which would be the warmest time of the year, was what we settled on.

"Still wondering if this would all work out, but with great excitement, we set out from Columbus. For me, this was the realization of that childhood longing to just go and go and go, and see everything on the way. This passion had been burning in me for a long time, and, now I was doing it!

"We left the highway for the first time and headed into what looked like desert to us. There were no trees, no telephone lines, and very few planes flying overhead. After hiking for awhile, we saw the first of the windmills and headed toward it hoping to get some water for the freeze-dried meals we planned to have for supper. I also spied a cow in the same area and became immediately scared. Now it was one lone cow (Laughing), probably a mile away, but I had no experience at being with cows, especially in a field with no fences. We did find water at the windmill that day, and we found some the next day after some frantic searching.

"On the Continental Divide we encountered a lot of cows, but I continually became less fearful until, by the end of the hike—after Greg had left the hike and I was on my own—I walked through a field of about 30 fully grown bulls, with no fences between us, got to the other side of them, and went on my way without an incident. I was scared but I prayed and sang the Prayer of Protection as I walked.

"We reached Deming, New Mexico three days later. This was the first short leg of our hike, and we had learned a lot. We were sunburned, I had blisters on my hands from the hiking poles, and my feet were sore and swollen from carrying too much weight in my pack. We decided there were supplies we could do without and mailed those things home. Although novices, we were learning as we went.

"It was tough. Our bodies were trying to adjust, so we tried to be gentle with ourselves. We had preplanned a one night stopover in Reserve, New Mexico, but Greg had such horrendous blisters by the time we reached there that we decided to stay an extra night. It messed up our schedule but we stayed for an extra day so we could sleep more, watch a movie, eat some popcorn and just relax."

It sounds like it was a real lesson in letting go?

"It was!

"An even bigger 'letting go' took place when we reached Grants, New Mexico. Throughout the three previous days of hiking, it had been snowing and the clay underneath the snow was very slippery and clinging to our boots in big, heavy clumps. Our equipment was soaked and we were soaked; I was developing shin splints; and we were both feeling miserable. As we slid and limped along the trail, with 11 miles still left to go, Greg turned to me and said he wanted to hitch hike. Well, I wanted to keep going, so we agreed we would hitch-hike, and then return the next day and hike the 11 miles.

"After reaching Grants, and finding a place to stay, we rested for the night. In the morning, however, we found that our bags were still soaked. In addition we were both limping from our blisters. So Greg suggested that we take a day off.

"I can't tell you how hard that was for me. It was a true *letting go*. Part of my agreeing to it was to satisfy Greg's wish, but I was aware that another part of that decision was due to some healthy self-reflection on my part, and an intense and honest conversation between the two of us. I remember him saying, 'You know Jen—I really wanted to come out here, hike from one end of the country to the other, and accomplish something that would really be a tough challenge: but I never said I was going to do *every single little mile*! Just because we lose this one little stretch doesn't mean we didn't come out here and do a really great job. Let's be kind to ourselves.'

"Despite my fear this was the beginning of the end, there was something in what he was saying that resonated in me very deeply. In the end I agreed to take the day off.

"By the time we got close to the northern border of New Mexico, we were getting into mountainous terrain with more snow, and then, further on in the Pedro National Forest, we got to see our first actual trail sign for the Continental Divide.

"After finishing up in New Mexico we visited family in Denver, Colorado and then drove north to the Northern border of the Great Divide Basin in central Wyoming. Along the way we cached water every five miles so we'd have plenty of water stashed along the trail when we hiked south. Later, when hiking through the Red Desert in the southern part of Wyoming that would be the only water we'd see for three days. There was absolutely no water or spring for at least 75 miles! We never could have done it without the water we stashed.

"When we finally reached Wamsutter, Wyoming, which was the end of our trek through the Red Desert, my feet were killing me. We had wanted to be done with the desert so badly that we hiked 31 miles that last day—most of it over hard rocks. I had to stop every half hour just to rub my feet. I used meditations some friends had taught me along with Ibuprofen to manage the pain. I was in so much pain that I couldn't even cry! The meditations really helped because it brought energy and awareness into the balls of my feet. But as a result of focusing my attention there, the pain really flared up, and I experienced greater pain than I'd ever felt in my life. There were even times when the pain brought me to my knees! By staying with the pain, however, and breathing into it, it eventually eased enough to where I was able to continue hiking.

"In Wamsutter, we met the sheriff who told us there was absolutely no water between there and Muddy Creek, where we were headed. I didn't believe him. I knew there were cattle down there, and if there were cattle and ranches, there would be water. The sheriff meanwhile kept insisting we'd find no water. To myself I said, *Screw you! I've planned for a year and a half, and up to this point I've hiked 850 miles, so whether you help me or not I'm going!* I was willing to hike without water being available for two days, if I had to. So we hiked down there and although finding water was a struggle, we found a big pond that was about three inches deep and was totally silted. We filtered the water through a bandanna and our filter, which kept clogging up, and ended up with a pretty gritty soup that night. (Laughing) We did find enough water and we managed.

"On top of Bridger Peak in the Sierra Madre Mountains of southern Wyoming, Greg struggled for the first time, instead of me. It was snow-packed and we'd been snowshoeing for about six hours when we reached the peak. A storm was heading our way and the wind was picking up, so we knew we really needed to get off the ridge and down to lower ground. Greg, at this point, was slowing down and beginning to lag behind, which surprised me. I said, 'Greg, what's going on?'

'I don't know, I've hit a wall,' he said.

"He was totally out of energy. He'd broken trail with his snowshoes all the way up the mountain, so his energy reserves were just gone. I gave him some food and snacks, and even transferred some of his equipment to my pack to make his load lighter, but it was very tense and I was scared because the storm was coming in fast. We'd done a lot of hiking together and I'd never seen him in this condition. Greg is six feet tall and weighs close to 200 pounds, so he was always the strong one. Now, he needed my help to get off the mountain. So I broke trail and when we finally reached the end of the ridge we cooked up some meals, which restored our energy. On the way down we were even leaping from snow pile to snow pile all the way down the mountain, just having a lot of fun.

"This was truly a significant experience for me. I was able to find my old strength and confidence again. That's not easy to do when you're a woman and married to a guy who's a match for you. Now, however, I was taking charge: using the map and GPS, figuring out what we're going to do, and assuming the role of leader. It was empowering! It was fun. I felt really good about myself. I really appreciate my leadership skills today.

"Eventually, Greg, who had a chronic foot condition, would leave the trail because of a foot injury and I would hike the rest of the way by myself. Up until our ascent of Bridger Peak, however, the condition didn't bother him. Then we started using snowshoes which have a steel plate right under the balls of the feet; and in the three weeks it took us to reach central Colorado and leave the snow, Greg was in great pain and had greatly exacerbated his condition."

Deciding to continue on when Greg could no longer keep going must have been a real conflict for you.

"The decision really wasn't, because we arrived at it gradually. We knew his foot was getting worse; we'd talked about our options if he couldn't go on, and by the time we'd hiked down through Montana and half of Colorado, we knew we just had to get out of the mountains. His worsening condition had slowed him down, it was endangering both of our hikes, and injuring his foot even more. Because we were slowing down it also meant that we would be encountering difficult snow problems later on.

"I remember the scene: I was hiking between two big trees and I heard Greg say, 'You're going to go on without me if I have to quit, aren't you?'

"I said, 'I'd really like to Greg.'

"I'd never considered quitting. Even today I have trouble understanding people doing that. It was only going to be another two months to complete the hike so I never considered dropping out for his injury.

"I've got to backtrack here for a moment. There was a point right after we'd finished the desert and the Sierra Madre Mountains, where we left the trail and returned home. My dad had taken a turn for the worse. He was very close to the end because the cancer had spread to his brain. Dad continued to hang on and after three weeks we knew we had to get back to the trail because time was closing in on us. If we didn't get back soon, weather conditions would make it hazardous and impossible to finish. So I told my mom we had to get back. She said, (tearing up) 'Go ahead; he wouldn't want you to jeopardize the hike by sitting around while he was in the hospital.' She knew that's the way dad would want it.

"So we took an all-night bus ride out to Butte, Montana and rejoined the trail. After just a short distance, though, I called home and my sister said the doctor had advised her to get us to come home. We flew home and that night stayed with my dad in the hospital, which was a good thing because he passed away that very night.

"Following the funeral we returned to Montana, but three weeks later Greg decided to leave the trail. Now I was really on my own. With the loss of dad and Greg, I'd lost two of the biggest supports in my life.

"My decision to continue alone for the last 900 miles also raised some new fears: namely Grizzly bears, men, and the additional pack weight I'd have to carry by hiking alone. I also was aware there would be situations like river crossings and injuries, where it's definitely safer to have two people. There was also no cell phone coverage at that time, so I would really be out there on my own.

"So here I am, facing some of the highest mountains on the trail, which we had saved for last. This was the Bitterroot Mountain range and my father had worked up there for the forest rangers one summer when he was 18. I remember him telling me how much he loved that time. He had also hiked in those mountains, and all of these memories were helping me to feel very close to him. In a sense, I now had my dad with me.

"At the same time I experienced a new bond with mom because we'd both lost our husbands and were now on our own. I'd call her whenever possible, and since we were both grieving and very vulnerable, our talks became very emotional, which bonded us in a whole new way. In fact, when I finished the hike, my mom who had not taken a trip by herself in 46 years of marriage to my dad drove out to meet me.

"On that first day without Greg, I was very scared. I walked the first couple of miles on the highway without hitchhiking—I just couldn't do it. Then I said, 'Goddamit! I've got to do this! I'm wasting time and I've got to get out there.' So I stuck my thumb out and a young guy in his 20's, probably on his way to work, picked me up and gave me a ride. We didn't talk the whole way, but he didn't look like a rapist (Laughing) and everything was fine.

"Once I reached my destination, I received permission from a cattle rancher to walk through his property and climb up through the foothills to get back on the trail. As I walked a dirt road through the property, I encountered a wide stream meandering through a big field ahead of me. At the water's edge I saw that what I had thought were cows were, in fact, young bulls. I was scared! They were totally ignoring me as they grazed, so I thought, *Okay, I can handle this. I've already handled a lot on my own.* I pumped myself up and I was so excited that as I passed them I raised my arms and yelled, 'boo!' as loud as I could…(Laughing)…and you know what? They charged me…the whole herd charged me! I was frozen in terror and frantically trying to figure out what to do. The bulls, however, lost interest before they

70

reached me and just kind of wandered back to where they had been. I never did that again. (Laughing) I think that was the universe's way of telling me I had a little more to learn.

"For the first four or five days of being on my own, I did what I had to do, but was still not confident that I was up to the physical and emotional challenges that awaited me. It's very challenging when you're facing the prospect of climbing up rock slides in the rain, not sure where you're going in areas where there are no trails, or you're being attacked by armies of mosquitoes who are oblivious to bug sprays.

"One day I hiked down off a ridge to find some water and when I came back, there were so many mosquitoes that I didn't even bother with dinner. I just protected myself inside my bivy sack. The next day would be my 38th birthday, but the position I found myself in, definitely did not feel like a life-highlight for me.

The next day I set out without water and eventually came to a mountain pass near the border of Idaho and Wyoming through which Lewis and Clark had traveled and where there was reported to be a spring. After searching for a while, I found water and cooked the dinner I'd not been able to have the night before. I then wrote a letter to my friend, and slowly became aware that my feelings were changing from despair to confidence. *I can do this*, I thought, *I can really do this!*

"Within a few days I was on a *high.* I was enjoying marvelous sights and beautiful sunrises and sunsets. Everything had changed for me and I found myself in a real groove and just loving it all. These were probably the best days of my life up to that point in time. I was euphoric—singing at the top of my voice as I walked.

"During this time, I also used the 'Prayer of Protection' when I got scared. A major part of the forest in Yellowstone Park had burned nine years before, but on windy days many of those burnt, tall pines would still fall. On one of the days I hiked through there, an 80 ft. pine dropped only 12 feet from me. That really scared me, so thereafter I used the prayer so my fear wouldn't overwhelm me.

"By the time I finished the hike, I'd become aware of my strength and truly liked who I was. Shortly after I got back, Greg asked for a divorce. It wasn't that we had fought while we out there, as much as I had profoundly changed in so many ways. Primary among them was that as I regained my personal strength, I felt like a lesbian again. I had identified as a lesbian for 10 years prior to meeting Greg. When I met Greg, it was during a time when I'd been encouraging myself to be straight, in part because I wanted to have a family. Now I could see clearly that it wasn't working for me or for him. He could feel it and, in fact, didn't even recognize me when he met me at the completion of the hike. It had been two months since we'd seen each other. I was feeling my power and I liked it! I did not want to give that up, in fact I didn't want to go back home; I didn't want it to end. For a couple of years after I finished, I continued to relieve it in my mind and could still recall where I'd camped each night.

"The hike was so transforming for me that I decided to write a book about it. My hope was that my story would inspire others on their journeys. Stories about people setting out on great, long journeys have always fascinated me, so I wanted to do the same thing. Writing, itself, is also something I love to do. I didn't know what I was doing, but I sat down at the computer the day after I got home and began putting down my memories of the journey. Putting this book together from my journals and from letters we'd sent to friends, has been a 10-year project. I now have a contract with Rainbow Books, and they hope to have the book out sometime in 2008. I've been calling the book *Alone on the Divide* but an official title has yet to be decided on."

How would you describe a healthy passion?

"For me *passion* is an upwelling of energy, drive, determination, and enthusiasm that seems to just flow out of somewhere inside. It generates a willingness to follow an idea or a dream that I really want to achieve. When that happens it seems that the whole universe flows through me and a loud 'yes' resonates in my being, and the people and things that I need begin to appear.

"Obsession enters the picture when I introduce fear into the process. At one point on my hike, I was totally exhausted after hiking 57 miles in two days through mountainous terrain, in an attempt to reach a small town, 90 miles away, where I had booked a room. My goal for each day was 30 miles and here I was 3 miles short of my daily goal. I really wanted to camp because I was exhausted and the spot was beautiful. What a conflict! I remember I was getting water from a stream and just so pissed that I had fallen short of my goal, when I suddenly recalled something Greg had once said to me when I was pushing myself mercilessly. He said, 'Jennifer, look me in the eye and listen to what I'm saying. I want you to be gentle with yourself.' In the end I did stop and I was gentle with myself that night. For a time, obsession had taken over, but since that day I've remembered that conversation with Greg, and not gotten myself into that same degree of drivenness. "

How have your spiritual beliefs impacted this passion of yours?
"Well, as time on the trail passed, I was distinctly aware that I was praying more. Sometimes I was simply saying *Help me,* and other times it was a prayer of thanks which I said a lot! Each day, with maybe the exception of the days it rained, there was such beauty out there—the water, the mountains, the sunsets—and I felt so close to Spirit.

"On the other hand, you're also vulnerable out there and continually at the whim of forces you cannot control. Here at home I assume that I can control certain aspects of my daily life if I exert enough effort, but out there my efforts were simply fruitless at times. I couldn't make the sun come out or get the temperature to warm up or make the trail easier. As time on the trail passed, that reality sunk ever deeper into me.

Synchronicities that occurred, however, like: suddenly finding the trail when I was lost or seeing wildlife or discovering water when I badly needed it, happened frequently as time passed and produced a sense of being taken care of and being part of the flow of the natural world. That's a beautiful thing, and my gratitude just overflows from it. I have a level of faith today that I didn't have before my journey."

Where did the trail end for you?
"Since we had already hiked portions of the trail from the Mexican border north, and southward from Glacier National Park, I'd be ending at Chama, New Mexico, which is just south of the Colorado state line. I finished just two days before a huge snowstorm completely blocked the pass and would have made it impossible for me to get through. I was

very fortunate. So we started on April 1, and I finished on October the 6th, and in the process I hiked a total of 2,400 miles.

"Years later I flew out to Colorado for a week of solo backpacking in the Rocky Mountains. In the course of my hiking, I really got in over my head: too many miles; out of shape; not acclimated to the altitude; and daily lightning storms. The last day I was aware *I'd had it* and I had to get down out of the mountains. I knew roughly where my truck was parked down in the valley, so I decided I'd just bushwhack straight down off the ridge and get to it. I had idea what I'd encounter as I made my way down.

"I scrambled down a couple of rockslides that were a little dicey, and then I begin finding myself in these very steep chutes where water was gushing through. The temperatures were 40-45 degrees and rainy; I was wearing tennis shoes because my boots had gotten too heavy; and I realized that no one knew where I was. I was very aware that I was making some bad decisions.

"At the end of one of these very steep chutes that hung out over a cliff, with a raging river of water flowing under it, my feet slipped out from beneath me and I was hanging on by holding fast to a tree branch. At this point my shoulders felt they would pull out my sockets because I was carrying so much weight, and my feet were dangling over the edge. I was frightened and near panic! I eventually righted myself, and, to stop my slide into outright panic, I spoke out loud saying, *'OK Jen, you're going to take 10 steps and no more; just 10 steps!'* So I'd take a step and count *one*, then *two*, right up to ten. Then I'd stop and say aloud, *'Thank you God for ten safe steps!'* I kept doing that for probably an hour-and-a-half until I eventually got myself out of there. Those prayers kept me going and it was the first time I'd actually spoke out loud to myself.

"The woods demand respect, so I learned a lot from that trip. I'm grateful for the many challenges I have encountered on my hikes. They have allowed me the opportunities to deepen my spiritual beliefs and break free of old limits."

Jennifer Hanson may be contacted at jennifer.hanson@earthlink.net

Chapter 5
The Circle
Anne Waldorf-Hoff

"I've learned that the pinnacle of being human is in truly being myself. Humanity is diverse, yet it's the same in its desires. I am no different from anybody else. The realization that I am human is a beautiful thing because it means I have my place in the world. I have my own God-given gifts and my dreams; and I can love and honor the gifts and dreams of others. I don't have to be something that I'm not— I'm free to be me. I mean a duck, after all, doesn't try to be a hippopotamus."

Anne is a nurse, educator, and psychotherapist, and as she describes herself t in semi-retirement, 'more of a coach these days.' She and her husband, Bill, her childhood sweetheart, divide their time between homes in Schroon Lake, New York and Hilton Head, South Carolina. Anne has had a private therapy practice in Rensselaer, New York for the past 28 years. Her passion for helping people find love and self-worth is matched only by the love she has for her family, which includes two grown sons, 3 stepchildren, and 11 grandchildren. I had the great pleasure of working with Anne as a peer for 14 years.

"One passion I would like to talk about is using the gifts that God has given me in order to help people discover more about themselves, and in that process to find serenity, love, and self-actualization. That's what I needed when I started on this path, and that's what my passion and purpose have given back to me. It's kind of a *circle of life* if you will. I always thought if I could help just one person I would have done something worthwhile. As I've learned who I am and how I fit into this world, in the company of other brave souls, I've then been able to give something back. That's my *'circle'* and that's my passion.

"This is how I live my life today, and it makes me want to cry *(tearing up)* because *I haven't always had* it. Talking about this is striking a lot of emotion for me. I'm surprised. My tears are caused more by gratitude than by sadness; because I have a life today I never could have dreamed of when I was a kid. Living this passion of mine has worked—even with my family. I was always afraid that what I was passionate about would not have any positive effect or impact on my children and their families—but it absolutely has. Because of the passion I have for this process, and for how I've lived it, I think my children have a greater capacity for loving, and for discovering and living their own passions. I'm extremely proud of both of my sons.

"So, this passion I have for helping others seems to flow out like ripples in a pond."

When did the roots of this passion for helping others first take hold?

"Well let me go back to the beginning. That reminds me that I've just turned 66 and *I'm not happy about it.* (Laughing) I was born and brought up in Albany, New York; the second child of two. My brother was closest to my mother; my father was alcoholic and distant, so I grew up in a family where I was virtually on my own emotionally. The impact on me was that it created a belief that I had little value—I was the 'underdog.' I would often use that term to describe myself as a young person.

"I felt alone and different—not really connected to anyone. I would pick up and care for little animals (weeping)…birds…I do to this day. I had lots of material things and was secure in a lot of ways—I had a roof over my head and my mother showed her interest in me by getting me dance lessons—but I still didn't feel a *part of*. At age 11, on my own, I took a bus from West Albany to Albany Medical Center, which was a long distance in those days, and signed up to become a 'candy striper' volunteer, and helped care for kids in the pediatrics ward three days a week after school.

"So how and where I grew up had a huge influence on my passion for helping others. What it did was give me a great sense of value and compassion for others—especially for little kids. I always remember this one *little guy* I would care for who was 3 years old and had a severe case of Eczema. He was always strapped down because he would scratch himself to the point of bleeding. The nurses and aides were so busy that they just didn't have time to spend with him. So I looked forward to the time I'd spend with him. He'd say to me, 'Meat and gatatoes, meat and gatatoes! You get me meat and gatatoes?' I fed him food, along with love and reassurance when I was with him; and then we'd sing a little. Those times with him gave me great joy and a sense I was giving him something that he wasn't getting and badly needed. There was also a little gal who was born with her stomach outside of her body. She spent over a year in that hospital recovering from surgery for this condition. Her name was Laurie and her dad was in the service in Korea at the time. Her mom *wasn't in the picture*, so it was usually her grandmother who would visit her. Her special-duty nurse and I became very close to Laurie, and knowing that she would be put up for adoption, we plotted to get my godparents, who were childless, to come and visit Laurie and see if they might adopt her. Laurie was essentially *an orphan* so I could identify with her in a lot of ways.

"Laurie died before my godparents could figure out whether or not they wanted to adopt her. The diagnosis was basically that she had died of a *broken heart* because nobody wanted her. They had taken her private duty nurse away; I had started high school, and had less time to devote to volunteering, so she was essentially alone.

"That profound first-hand experience of what could happen to someone who isn't loved or cared for, became a part of the passion I would follow.

"I haven't thought about these events in a long time, so I really feel it.

"As I got a little older I tried to distance myself from all the pain these children were experiencing because it mirrored the pain of aloneness I felt in my own family. In high school I was a good student, worked to become one of the crowd, and in the end became very popular. I was a cheerleader and got involved in music, dance, gymnastics, and theatre; all an attempt to become something I really wasn't, thinking it would make me feel better about myself. It worked for awhile as my popularity increased and I had boyfriends. I remember appearing on and even directing a little, on 'Teenage Barn,' a local television program for aspiring performers. I was very busy and really had a wonderful time.

"My mother, however, wanted me to be a teacher. This began an ongoing conflict between us from the time I was a sophomore in high school. I wasn't interested in teaching. I wanted to be a nurse and that left her pretty unhappy. Ironically, when I did finally begin nursing I gravitated toward childbirth, and the bonding between mothers and babies. I actually got a master's degree in Obstetrics. I did the clinical work for my degree at Metropolitan Hospital in Harlem, in New York City.

"Working at that hospital and learning my nursing skills just didn't seem like enough to me, so I *moonlighted* at Flower Fifth Avenue Hospital as a nurse's aide. One of the aides came down with breast cancer while I was there, and asked me if I would provide some home care for her. I did until she died. I'd help her on the weekends when I didn't have school and I felt truly privileged that she wanted *me* to help her. She was a big part of my life during that time.

"At the same time, when I did my psychiatric affiliation at Pilgrim State Hospital, I connected with a patient there by the name of Michael. I was not *in love* with him, but I did have a lot of love *for* this man. He was born in Spanish Harlem, became a 'raging' alcoholic, and was involved in the 1957 gang wars in mid-town Manhattan. He was a man who was out of control in so many ways. Eventually Michael was convicted of a crime and sent to Pilgrim State where I first met him.

"I took some great risks to help Michael, but I learned so much from my experiences with him. When he was released from Pilgrim State, he was given 50 dollars and a rat-infested room in the Bronx. He and I were both afraid that if he moved in too soon, he would become depressed and relapse back to his addiction. Not sure what to do, we walked the streets for four days and nights, until finally, on that Saturday, we found a clubhouse for recovering alcoholics on 47th St., where they gave us some food and we were able to rest. That evening we also attended an AA meeting which was my first experience with Alcoholics Anonymous. That meeting relieved a lot of the pressure I'd put on myself to help Michael. He was this beautiful human being struggling to stay sober, and here I was, trying to help him, knowing absolutely nothing about the disease of alcoholism except that I had experienced it with my own father. We stayed at the clubhouse through the night, and the next day we got to talk to some members of AA. Michael was then able to make some connections for himself. I returned to the Nurse's residence and went back to work. For the next three weeks, I accompanied him to AA meetings every evening, and literally received a crash course in alcoholism as a disease. Unknown to me, these events were the seeds of my desire to work with people with addictions. At the same time, I became aware that my own family was peppered with addictions of all kinds—primarily alcoholism.

"I became very attached to Michael. Meanwhile my parents were saying, 'You've got to come home; we haven't seen you in six months!'

"So I went home for a visit and unbeknownst to me, Michael followed me by a couple of hours. He wanted to see where I lived and meet my family. I was terrified to have Michael meet my family because I was afraid of what their reaction would be to him and to me. If you can picture this: Michael was dark-skinned, had no front teeth; was parts: Polynesian, Puerto Rican, and African-American. He arrives at my house, rings the doorbell, and when my mother opens the door, he greets her with, 'Where's Anne?' (Laughing) Needless to say both my mother and I were a *little* stunned!

"The irony of it all was that Michael and I ultimately went our separate ways, realizing that we were two very different people and could never consummate any kind of healthy relationship because we came from two very different worlds. Much later, when I was married and had a family, I invited him to come for a visit. He accepted, visited, and had dinner with us. He was 39 at the time and shared with us that he was married and had a lovely wife; but wanted no children because he didn't know how many children he'd left behind or abandoned during his days of addiction. Michael had never relapsed once he got sober and had in fact created a thriving antique-dealing business. About 10 years ago, I received a letter from him in which he told me he'd been diagnosed with blockages to his heart and didn't know how long he had to live because of the severity of his condition. He didn't give a return address so I was never able to write him back, and consequently lost touch with him.

"I think Michael and I both had an important influence on each other, and on the directions our future lives would take. A gift from that relationship was the realization that I had a talent for being able to verbalize thoughts and ideas, and offer encouragement in ways that were helpful to another person. That was when this gift of mine first started to bud. Michael contends that he never wanted to get sober, but his attitude changed during the time that we were together talking, walking, and attending AA meetings. He had a tremendous impact on me, and on my ultimate career of working in the addiction field.

"When I earned my first master's degree in family obstetrics, I developed a clinic, at Samaritan Hospital in Troy, New York, for women who preferred natural childbirth but couldn't afford the services of a physician. During this time, I was traveling back and forth to night classes at Russell Sage College with a woman by the name of Suzanne, who was experiencing marital problems at the time. For almost two semesters she would share her problems with me, ask me questions, and sometimes invite my opinions. One day she said, 'You should work in the counseling field and get paid for doing this.'

"I was stunned by her suggestion because I couldn't recognize that talent at the time. I still saw myself caring for people as a nurse, and besides, that was my job. What Suzanne was proposing to me was something very different. Her idea was a gift to me, and I'd say she was *the person* who most encouraged me to get the training I would need to become a therapist or counselor.

"After attaining my masters in nursing, I went back and got a second master's in psychiatry. For my elective clinical work, I chose an alcoholism center. There I worked with people who were alcoholic, angry, defensive, and usually in trouble of some kind. In the process I discovered I could really care about someone even though they were resistant and different from my background.

"I also learned a great deal from my clients. Unknown to me, I had come out of my family with an addiction to anger. Sometimes in my therapy groups I'd get angry when I wanted someone to hear me or when I was confronting someone. This was before I seriously began attending 12-step programs for myself. Previously I'd attended meetings more to help my clients than to help myself. I just wasn't cognizant of my own needs at that time. Several times during the first few years I did group work, my clients, many of whom had more self-worth than I had, would challenge me and tell me how angry I was. That's the point where I began to conceptualize anger as an addiction, and see that it was a consequence of the family system I grew up in. I didn't become an alcoholic, but I had this anger, and it was addictive. Anger did the same thing for me that alcohol did for my family members: It made me feel *bigger and better*, and less vulnerable. My clients gave me a great gift when they challenged me and my attitudes.

"About the same time, fellow professionals, including a young counselor I was supervising, were telling me my anger was formidable and off-putting. That was the last thing I wanted to be putting out to people. This revelation was a real eye-opener and it set me on a very different path. This was my incentive to start my own twelve-step work and my own healing in an effort to bring out this passion I had inside me. I wanted the *Ann that was outside* to be the same as the *Ann that was inside*. I knew I was a kind and compassionate person on the inside, but what would come out of me at times would be arrogant, righteous, and angry. This awakening in me was also the beginning of my theorizing and conceptualizing anger as an addiction as well as a growing awareness that addiction wasn't just about ingesting chemicals.

"Motivated by the work of people like Sharon Wegscheider Cruise and Claudia Black, who were real pioneers in exploring and writing on Alcoholism as a Family Illness, we began treating people from addicted families at a nonprofit, free-standing treatment center in the middle of the inner city, in Troy, New York. I was asked to speak at the first Governor's Conference on Children of Alcoholics, along with a woman named Justine Caldes, who I was working with at the time, and who was a great help to me. That conference was an awesome experience for me because I also attended a workshop given by Dr. Janet Woititz, author of *Adult Children of Alcoholics*, the very first book on the subject of Adult Children of Alcoholics. I believe I cried through the entire workshop because she was identifying *my story*. It was wonderful! I wasn't bad or crazy after all!

"Janet Woititz had this list of characteristics and symptoms of children of an alcoholic that I could identify with—every one—right on down the line. This self-identification was a spiritual experience for me. It was like; *I'm free now, to be me*! The experience was a true milestone in accepting myself. Helping others effectively would not have been possible had I not first learned about myself in the ways I've pointed out. It's been a true circle for me."

Could you spend some time talking about how you learned about family systems and how they operate in an addictive family?

"Well, that's a subject I love. When I was at Sage College in 1978-79, earning my degree in psychiatry, Family Systems Theory really began to *click* within the psychiatric treatment field. After graduating from Sage, I decided to do postgraduate work with Phil Guerin and Tom Fogarty, who were writers and theorists of Family Systems, based on the work of Dr. Murray Bowen.

"I loved it. Tom Fogarty had developed the concept of 'Triangling in Families,' which defined explained the process that caused children to replicate dynamics in a family as they progressed through life. I could identify with these dynamics. Personally, it was another way for me to understand my own history. In using this process with my clients, they could now understand that what had happened to them, how they became who they were, as well as directions they could follow, which could produce a significant difference in their lives."

Living life with passion can sometimes become a challenge when a person becomes ego-driven. How can you tell when your passion becomes unhealthy?

"To me, the difference is in my spirituality. My ego gets in the way of my passion and purpose when I'm out to prove something or to impress someone. On the other hand, when my motivation is my love for them and for what I'm doing, I'm really present, grounded, and enthusiastic in being of service, whether it's in simply listening; providing what's needed at a certain time, or in offering options to someone's pressing problem. There is such a difference in the quality of that experience, as opposed to what happens when I'm in my addiction to anger and trying to force my will in a situation. When that happens, my interactions become difficult, and my behavior is controlling, abrasive, and confrontive in an uncaring way. It's vital for me to focus on my highest purpose—that of love—whenever I attempt to be of service to someone."

What part does your spirituality play in this work you love to do?

"I've always seen myself as a spiritual person, going back to my childhood. Even as a little girl, I felt spiritual picking up that robin or in helping that little boy at Albany Medical Center. I knew there was a God and I prayed as a kid, but I didn't always trust him, nor did I always have the faith that if I needed him he would be there. Often times, when I really needed him and he wasn't there, I would wonder about the quality of my spirituality.

"When I started working in the field of alcoholism and began imparting my thoughts, ideas and feelings; and teaching those I was working with, I often sensed that *something greater* was working through me. I mean there were times I would have an intuition or say something, and I would have *no clue* where it came from! Obviously I then began to pay more attention to these moments. Even to this day I'm astounded when I'm in a situation with a client or someone who may really be hurting, and there are words that I think or say or do that I *don't plan*. Nothing is contrived in that moment and it just comes.

"I believe in God and I use the terms God and *universe* interchangeably. It seems the more I learned and accepted about me, the more open I was to messages from the *universe*, to the needs of others, and to my own needs. In the last 15 years, I've had so many remarkable *coincidences* that I don't actually believe in *coincidences* anymore. I know there's a master plan, but I don't think it's about God coming down and changing the tires on my car when they go flat. I believe there is a flow and movement in the universe—part of God's design—that works through people. I believe it's God's love for people, just moving through them and I think it's miraculous! I can't fully explain it and I don't want to, I just love it.

"Some of the other spiritual directions, like how I came to marry my *childhood sweetheart* and all of the things that happened that gave me confirmation that we should be together are not always as clear. I'll tell you about one event that stands out for me among the confirmations I received regarding Bill and me. I'd always wanted to be in a relationship with someone who'd be honest and candid with me about their likes and dislikes, or how they might disagree with me. I knew that would help me to grow. A lot of times when you're in the helping professions, you're *alone at the top* unless you seek therapy or you're in a group yourself. So, to have someone who is intimately close to you, be candid, loving, and honest is just huge! The first time that I spoke with Bill on the telephone, I said something about him having 'potential.' He took exception to the remark, and very gently but convincingly, confronted me about how he felt about it. I can't even begin to tell you what a spiritual moment that was, and how his honesty connected me to him in a very deep way. That type of intimacy has been a profound quality of our relationship ever since. His honesty was one of those affirmations from the *universe* that said I was on the right track in choosing Bill."

In your experience, what have you seen is necessary to stay on a healthy, passionate path?

"I would say that staying in touch with myself in a loving and disciplined way is very important because I've noticed it's not terribly difficult for me to revert back to my old ways. That also pertains to how I relate to my loved ones. To not revert back to the *mother* that my sons know, means that I have to be disciplined and heartfelt and loving toward them but at the same time, accepting of them. It requires me to remain close to my spirituality and take that *next sane and sober step"*

So being consciously aware of your thoughts, behavior, and feelings is key?

"I have to be. As someone addicted to anger, I have to be aware at all times of the possibility of becoming reactively angry—especially with those closest to me. That's where I'm most vulnerable; they mean the most to me, and they would be the people who'd *get it first*! I'm not perfect at this; I work hard at *owning my stuff* and unconditionally loving and accepting the people that I live with or are close to me."

Where are you with your career these days?

"My work with people these days is less what you would call therapy, and more in the area of coaching. I think I've actually mellowed over the years, (laughing) so the work I do now is gentler. Now I'm primarily working with people who *know how to work*. I give feedback to my clients, but I don't work as hard as I once did.

"I think I'm slowly distancing my self from this work, but at the same time, I'm not ready to quit because I love helping people to learn more about themselves and their choices—in a sense, empowering them to live the lives they desire."

What has your work with others taught you about what it is to be human?

"The first image I have is of my mother. *I'm 15 years old and I'm drying dishes, and she says, 'You should marry a doctor so you won't have to ever worry about anything.'*

"I would feel revolted when she'd say that and I'd get so angry at her! What I've since learned is that the pinnacle of being human is in truly being myself. Humanity is diverse, yet it's universal in its desires. I am no different from anybody else. The realization that I am human is a beautiful thing because it means I have my place in the world. I have my God-given gifts and my dreams, and I can love and honor the gifts and dreams of others. I don't have to be something that I'm not—I'm free to be me! I mean *a duck doesn't try to be a hippopotamus.* I just want to be human and live the life *I want.* That's a great privilege. Again, here's the circle—what I want for myself is what I teach to others.

"Despite this journey of mine having been a struggle and very difficult at times, it's also been very rewarding. In the last 10 years of my life, I can now say that I've come to know something about serenity. For many years I'd say the Serenity Prayer, but I didn't really grasp the meaning of serenity. Today, I may not know everything about it, but I have a peace inside of me that I haven't had all my life."

"After I'd gotten my undergraduate degree in nursing, my husband, Rob and I moved to Wyoming and he entered law school in Laramie. He subsequently dropped out and bought a house-moving business in Denver, Colorado. Almost immediately he was involved in litigation with the former owners, so we had little income and I went to work part-time. I wasn't going to go out and sacrifice the well-being of my children with babysitters, so it was a real struggle financially. At times, the only thing I had in my cupboard to feed my children was Campbell's pork and beans. It was a nightmare! It was not long after, that I left him, came back to New York, and filed for bankruptcy. My relationship with him was really difficult. I was an anger addict and I wasn't nice. I was fearful and angry much of the time.

"One day while nursing my baby in the living room of our home, the front door suddenly opened and in walked three IRS agents. They told me they had come to take our construction equipment as payment for unpaid fees, income taxes, and road taxes. I was terrified and mortified to have them just walk into my home like that. I've often thought that if I could survive those kinds of challenges, I could survive anything. I think that's a huge part of my spirituality. I discovered a degree of strength in myself that I never thought I had. Looking back, in 25 of the 29 years we were together, there was always some type of litigation going on in my life and I wasn't the one causing it. I was, however, deeply affected by it all.

"As tough as that era of my life was, our two sons were born while we lived in Denver; and I was invited to become part of Dr. Robert Bradley's natural childhood practice in Denver. While working part-time there, I met and had the pleasure of working with two beautiful women who were happy, positive, and passionate about helping women give birth. Those years of my life were extremely difficult, yet here I was happy and inspired by my work. I really believe the challenges of our lives can make us stronger—they did for me.

"When it comes to inspiring others to live passionately, I realize that talk is cheap and what I say may not hold a whole lot of water but I'll say it anyway. (Laughing) Many of my clients have told me that one of the things that has meant the most to them in working with me is that they know I *walk the walk*—I've done a lot of healing myself. In some ways, I guess I've become a guide through the modeling of my own living.

"That's the most powerful thing I do, but I think if I were to say anything to people I would say, *learn more about yourself.* When I learned how I was blocking my own happiness, and was able to take my addictions out of the way, that new freedom allowed me to become more of who I really am. I no longer had to latch on to another's *coattails* to be fulfilled. The bottom line is that anyone who wants to discover their gifts and find their passion or mission in life has to first learn who they really are, and then come to believe in and accept themselves as individuals with the power to determine the course of their life.

"Being an individual gives you the gifts of emotion, authenticity, courage, strength, and spirituality to bring into your daily life. When we get to know and accept ourselves, there exists a level of joy and serenity that's unattainable almost any other way. That's when I know without a doubt that *I'm OK just the way I am;* and in that knowledge there's a peace beyond all understanding."

Anne may be contacted at **hoffann2003@yahoo.com**

Chapter 6
Courage
Howard Meyer

"When I was a kid I had athletic courage—I was a real warrior on the ball field. Facing my demons as an adult, however, demanded a much deeper level of courage. I was challenged to become a warrior on a whole different plane. In pursuing my dreams I've had to cultivate faith and a belief that good things can happen, rather than focusing on the bad things that might occur. That seems to fuel my courage."

Howard Meyer, 44, is a high-energy, friendly, and enthusiastic man who has a deep passion for truth-telling. He is a writer, actor, teacher, and artistic director of Axial Theatre. Our interview took place in his acting studio which is located in Pleasantville, New York, a short distance north of New York City. The studio is a beehive of activity and positive vibes, as actors, staff, and workmen come and go throughout our interview time.

"I would say that my passion, today, is different from when I walked into my first acting class at 23. I didn't have a dream to be an actor. I was just a confused kid who didn't know what he wanted to do with his life. I had been working in the business world, knew it wasn't for me, and was searching for my *dharma*—the Hindu word for life purpose. When I was first exposed to that term it hit me like a ton of bricks. I was convinced that being a 9 to 5 guy and looking for fun after hours would not work for me. So began a quest to find that purpose.

"Acting was suggested to me by a number of people over a few years. Later I would see those suggestions as my first big *leading (a Quaker term pertaining to inner guidance or direction).*

"I walked into my first acting class without any expectations and just thinking, *OK, I'm checking this out as one of a variety of things I'm exploring.* What happened within a couple of weeks, was that something inside me started to stir. At the time, I wasn't sure what that stirring was, but it was the first instance of me being in a place where authenticity and honesty were held at a premium. That's what grabbed me and kept me coming back.

"Exploring acting wasn't about feeling that I had this wonderful gift for imagination. In truth, my imagination at that time was pretty shut down. My whole environment in my formative years was much too frightening for that to be encouraged. My dad had a mental disease, so any time he would move into his wild ideas or fantasies, it would look like craziness. So, for me, it was dangerous to imagine. I did not want to be seen as crazy like him. Thankfully, my long-dormant imagination finally got permission to come through, in my acting. Today, I have what I feel is a pretty good access to my imagination.

"It wasn't the imagination, however, that first hooked me—it was truth telling. The door that first flung itself open for me, in the practice of this craft, was my emotional door which had long been shut down. For the first time I had a safe environment in which I could honestly express all my pent-up emotions. That kept me going back, long before I knew I wanted to be an actor or theater artist. Acting is about bringing your empathy and deep understanding to the character you're portraying. In that way, the character portrayal provides the actor a pathway into understanding him/herself better. When there's a role that I feel really connected to, I think, *Wow, this is a story that I've got to be inside of!*

"In wrestling with the question that you pose, ⁻ *What is my great passion?* ⁻ I realize for me, that it is truth-telling and authenticity. The vehicle for this passion has been the theatre, whether it's through the plays that come through me, or in acting, directing, or teaching. Gratefully, the communal work of Axial Theatre combines all the things I'm most passionate about.

"As a central form, however, playwriting is really where it is for me right now. I just love inventing stories that emerge from our deeply held places. I think that's what good playwriting is about. If there's something that's held deeply inside, there's a better chance of a good play emerging, rather than, *Oh, I think it would be fun to write a play about such and such.* The great writers that I've known have said 'Write what you know, because that's where you're *juice* is.'

"I feel very lucky because my passion for truth-telling and expressing this *juice* has shaped how I live my theatre life. There are people out there who are happy to be 'hired guns' and go where the work opportunities and the money are; but I need an ongoing place, a *home*, where the spiritual and the emotional and the creative all come together. It's necessary to make money, but fortunately I have been able to follow my particular path and the money has found me."

I'm wondering how this approach to your work affects the rest of your life.

"I live holistically, so this work has affected the rest of my life, and, in fact, has given me life. Without this passion, I don't know what or where I'd be today. Before I discovered theatre I was pretty unhappy. Everything I have in my life today is all organized around this passion. I can't remember a day in the last seven years when I didn't wake up with enthusiasm and a kick in my step.

"The one area of my life that has probably taken second place to this passion is my relationships with significant others. I've been fortunate to have had deep and wonderful relationships with women, but this passion has always come first. It's probably why I'm not married yet. I say, yet, because maybe I will be one day. I love being in a committed relationship, but there are conventional demands that

I don't do so well with. I compare it to the calling to the religious life, which carries with it a purpose that precludes any desire for a traditional family life. I'm not someone who wants to divest myself of earthly things and devote myself exclusively to the spiritual realm, but I know that my passion for theatre and truth-telling is the central organizing principle of my life, and I have no interest in placing conventions before that.

"Occasionally I have thoughts like, *Oh God, should I get married? I'll think, I love this woman and she really wants this and…it's not necessarily what I want. Maybe I do…maybe I don't…but maybe I should.* The word, *'should,'* has become a flag for me, so I have made a concerted commitment to an *anti-should* way of life.

"Direction for my life presents itself, to the extent to which I can really listen to: my inner self, to whatever leadings I'm getting from God, a bumper sticker, a song on the radio, or to others who are carrying messages I need to hear. I have a friend who talks about putting on her 'listening ears.' Over the years I've gotten better and better at knowing when a leading is coming from a higher place and when it's not."

"I've been meditating for about 25 years and attending Quaker meetings for ten years. The Quakers have taught me that you never rise at the first impulse. If that thought or feeling persists, however, you will start gaining confidence that it's probably something you're being called to say. I then take that leading out into my life and act upon it.

" *EXAMPLE*…I think the decision to move into playwriting was assisted in large part by this process. Man, was there confusion and fear about leaving a directing career where things were happening—I even had an agent! Who was I to think that I could drop all of that and make a transition into a form where I was a beginner? But my desire to write just kept coming back to me in all sorts of ways. Finally the need to begin that process became inevitable for me…a spiritual imperative.

"An aspect of identifying a true leading is asking: *What quality does this leading have? Does it feel peaceful? Is it going to lead to some good in the world? Is it going to hurt anyone?* To me, ego-driven or obsessive impulses always have a quality of suffering or fear about

JOHN R. DAUBNEY

them, and are usually about *me—me—me*...What can I get for myself and screw everybody else! Another aspect of the 'shadow side' of leadings is that fears exists, like, *Oh my God; if I don't get this or do this, I'll go broke or I'll lose this person,* etc. Most of my decisions driven by this kind of impulsiveness have not been that healthy for me.

"A big fear of mine when I was young, was, that if I didn't act now I'd be done! So this new way is an entirely different idea that says that if something is truly coming from God, it will keep calling me, and there is no 'missing the boat.'

"I think there's a widely held belief that you have to know what to do, (snapping his fingers) and you gotta know now! Hurry up! You gotta seize the moment. *The window of opportunity*! I think it's all conventional nonsense. (Laughing) It's taken me a long time to learn this. There are times when you have to act and acting is important—it's just knowing when. It reminds me of the idea of the Serenity Prayer: *To know the difference between having the courage to act and the wisdom not to act.*

When I'm not sure, I'll say, *Okay, I think this is a leading,* and then try it and I'll eventually know if it is or isn't."

Where did you grow up Howard? What was your childhood like?

"I was born in New York City in 1962, and raised in the borough of Queens. I grew up with my mother, father and my younger brother Andrew. I lived in an apartment building and, since my school was close by, I walked to school every day. My world was basically the apartment, my walk to school, the walk home, and later the run to the park to get into whatever game was being played. That was my world for a very long time. Occasionally, as I got older, I'd hop on the train or the bus, and I'd go over to a movie theatre in another part of town. That was considered 'stepping out,'—a huge adventure in those days. My friends and their families were all in that neighborhood.

"Since my dad had mental illness, which really colored the world-view of my childhood, my early family life was unique in many ways. Daily, we had to deal with this man who was not well. As a result, everybody learned to adapt and adjust to that reality. I used whatever

94

innate survival skills I possessed, just to exist. That's pretty difficult stuff to negotiate for a nine or ten-year old. I had to grow up a lot faster than other kids.

"Dad was able to hold a job and provide for us, so it wasn't like we were starving or destitute. In fact, during those years we had a summer rental in Vermont that provided less stress, a lot of happiness, and even pockets of joy for everybody. He was a very attentive father, very athletic. So sports became very important for me as a way to connect with him. Dad and I were big Mets fans, and since we lived only 20 minutes from Shea Stadium, we attended a lot of games. I was seven years old in 1969 when the Mets won the World Series, the Jets won the Super Bowl, and the Knicks won the NBA championship. It was a magic year for me and my dad and for New York City.

"As an athlete, my primary sport, and the one I most excelled in was baseball. I played Little League, but at the point I could have become more competitive, the problems at home really exploded, which dealt a real blow to my confidence level, self-esteem, and effectiveness. In the past I'd want the ball hit to me, but after the family problems exploded, I began thinking, *Please don't hit it to me!* When that happens it's time to put down the glove and get off the field because that's no way to play.

"My artistic path began as a musician, playing piano and the standup bass violin in school. I never really excelled, but playing those instruments awakened the artistic side of me. When I got to junior high school, I had to choose between mechanical drafting and orchestra. This was an easy choice. I'd had a growth spurt during the summer, so on the first day I entered the orchestra room, the teacher looked at me and said, 'Meyer, go get a stand-up bass.' Music became an interesting adventure! Back in those days, the ball field and the music room were sanctuaries for me."

Who encouraged you in the direction of the arts?

"My mother was a school teacher, highly intelligent, and cultured in her own right. It was important to her that her son was well-rounded, so those values were encouraged, and even though there wasn't a tremendously enthusiastic reception to my theatrical involvement later on, the cultural influences of my early life and for what was to follow were significant.

"Playing and learning piano required a high degree of discipline, and it really was the only area of my life where I submitted myself to that kind of discipline. With both the piano and the bass, I was not better than the people I played with, so it required that I apply myself in order to keep up. This application of daily practice ultimately carried over, years later, into my daily practice of writing plays. I'm grateful that I have the discipline today, to follow through on my passion, so it becomes more than just a nice dream or a fantasy. I've found that discipline actualizes fantasies.

"I was a rabid Mets fan during the Dwight Gooden-Darryl Strawberry years, so I went to games early and watched batting practice. I particularly remember Wally Backman, the Mets scrappy little second baseman. His talent was probably not equal to that of Darryl Strawberry, but Wally worked his ass off, and you could see how that impacted his intensity and level of play. That was very instructive for me even before I became an artist. I observed that one could have great natural gifts and a real passion for something, but unless you work it and hone it, it may not amount to much."

It's very evident that you're a high-energy person; has that always been the case?

"When I'm in sync with myself, I'm happy, and this is how I am. In the times of my life when I wasn't in touch with my energy source, I wasn't happy. But I think that's all about being in sync with my life purpose."

In times of disappointment what keeps you going?

"If there's something that has kept me going, it's my vision of how I think theatre should be conducted. When it's right, theatre can have a powerful effect on all who participate—and that includes the audience. Like I said earlier, theatre brings together the spiritual, emotional, and artistic aspects of a person. When I first walked into the acting room, as a young lad, it was a definite spiritual experience even though I didn't have the words to describe it that way. It was a place where spiritual ideals were being fostered.

"As I grew up in my rather bizarre household, I pursued things that I thought my parents wanted me to do, always doing my best to preserve peace in the home, and constantly looking for praise. There wasn't a lot of space during those years for me to investigate who I was or what I wanted to be in the world. I did what I *thought I should do.* Initially I wanted to be a doctor. In addition to my family's encouragement of that choice, I think the fact that my dad was ill and I so wanted to cure him, contributed to that desire. I didn't question it; it was too frightening. Our house was fraught with hyper-vigilance and caution, always anticipating when the other shoe was going to drop. So, I went off to college and lasted as a pre-med student for one semester. It's hard to consider competing for medical schools with a C in Organic Chemistry. Later, I was accepted into Colombia's five-year medical program. This time it was Physics that did me in. I didn't even make it two weeks. Clearly this path was not going to work for me.

"After that, I was at a total loss, and terrified! All my life I'd thought this was what I was going to be. Now what? I had no clue…Without even knowing it, I was having my first spiritual experience. The complete despair I was experiencing in this period of *not-knowing* was cracking me wide open. I was willing to try anything…and that's when I was lead into my first acting class. Gradually I began to think, *Wow man, I don't know where this is going to take me, but theatre is what I'm supposed to be doing. This makes me feel good! This is what's stoking my fire.*

"I must tell you that as exciting as this realization was, it was equally terrifying, because it was such a radical choice for where I came from. At a lunch, just five or six years ago—after my theatrical career had begun to hit its stride—my mother asked with total sincerity, 'Where did this all come from?' It was inconceivable to her that I would have chosen this path, and it was a valid question because it wasn't something I had any interest in as a child. At the same time, I would think, Oh *my God, I've discovered acting and theatre, but I have no role models! How am I going to do this?*

"In some ways I'd found my religion—I was lit! It was similar to a person wandering around in the wilderness for 20 years and suddenly stumbling onto his *Mecca*. It became a life-giving path for me. That's why my relationship to theatre has always been so profound.

"As a result, it took me a good 10 years to reconcile how I could make money at it without compromising my values. In other words, *How do I integrate my soul and my career path?* As I was being challenged to maintain a high level of integrity about my choices, I wound up turning down many opportunities. That was very scary.

"For a long time it seemed that the acting and directing possibilities that were coming into my life each contained a lesson of some kind for me. For instance, 10 years ago as my father was lying in a hospital during his last days, I was hired to direct a play called *Hello and Goodbye*, by Athol Fugard, a South African playwright. The play took place in the aftermath of the death of a father, and focused on the impact that death had on the son. A month before I began the directing job, my father passed away. It was impossible not to see that entire job as a huge gift from *beyond.*. My theatre projects always feel like uncanny meditations on whatever life issues I am being asked to consider. In some sense, that has been my guide in my decisions to accept or turn down a job. The dilemma of acceptance of work is not as much an issue today, since for the past eight years I have had my own theatre and devoted my life to creating new work.

"That is not to say there weren't a lot of *herking and jerking and lurching* as I've gone along. Prior to the establishment of Axial Theatre, there were many successes and failures and frustrations as I attempted to integrate my value-based needs with the demands of the New York theater marketplace. Sometimes I'd think, *I'll just try and do some commercials.* So I would audition, end up feeling terrible, and I wouldn't get the job. Even when I was getting introduced to the right people in seemingly 'big break' moments, it wouldn't work out. Finally after the continual lurching back and forth, and my grandiose ego getting shattered enough, I was able to let go and accept what I needed to do to pursue this career of mine.

"At the same time, I became increasingly interested and involved with theatre projects that had more of a community-based vision of the world, and of creativity. I found, over time, that I was building relationships with actors, writers, and collaborators who had the same confusions and desires as I did. They encouraged me in my vision to form some kind of collective theater group. That's not an easy thing to create in this day and age. The economic pressures on actors are extraordinary, so to have a permanent company of actors, with my limited financial resources, would require flexibility, ingenuity, and vision. Did I have that vision? I didn't know. But I had to try.

"Even before I knew what my life path was going to be, I had mentors and guides helping to shape my future journey. As the great German philosopher, Goethe (1749-1832) wrote, and I will probably badly paraphrase it: *When you move in the direction of your dreams there are forces that gather around you that defy your wildest dreams and expectations. It doesn't happen, however, until you take that first step.* I have lived that idea, and the experiences have been awe-inspiring. One such guidance occurred in meeting and developing a friendship with Merrill Brockaway, a TV/film producer, who directed and produced a PBS series called 'Dance in America' back in the 80s and 90s. He was a man who was fiercely protective of the integrity of theatre and art. He also told me of a man by the name of Athol Fugard, who would become my next mentor. Today, Fugard is considered to be one of the world's great playwrights. His personal story was inspirational, and a role model for living life with integrity. As a white South African writer he took risks and challenges during apartheid that most people wouldn't be capable of taking. He was working with mixed-race and black actors in black townships when it was illegal. He could easily have been arrested or killed. Fugard needed to tell his stories for his country and for himself, and those stories became world renown. It's legitimate to say, he was one of the voices that brought apartheid to the world's attention. I don't believe, however, that when he set out he had this grandiose idea that he would be an international spokesman against apartheid. His ultimate journey emerged out of his passion to write plays and tell stories about his world.

"To go back a bit, in 1990 I had become a partner in a venture called

Total Theater Lab in New York City. This was my first foray into having a place where I could do the work I envisioned. There, I cut my teeth in acting, teaching, and directing.

"The Lab was where I met Athol Fugard and his wife Sheila, also a writer, when their daughter, Lisa, auditioned for one of our shows. We ended up casting Lisa for a part, and later, she and I developed a long-term, romantic relationship. I pretty much spent the next 10 years as part of this family, where living the artistic life was a way of being. In a way, I was being *re-parented* artistically. They embraced me and clearly validated that I had what it takes and that I could achieve my desires in theatre if I chose to. I don't blame my parents for not recognizing that; it's just who they were. This time with the Fugard family was my initiation into a world I'd always wanted to be part of, and a passage into a new life and a chance, which I embraced, to claim my birthright.

"Axial Theatre was created in 1998 out of my vision to begin a company of professional actors with a mission to generate new works. The name, in part, derives from the time period, 500 BCE to 0 BCE, a time of great spiritual outpouring, known as the Axial Age by mythologists and spiritual historians. The first year we failed for a variety of reasons. I think the early incarnation of Axial was too ambitious. Being a young playwright, I simply bit off more than I could chew. This apparent failure dropped me into a state of depression. So, I was at a juncture of trying to decide what I would do next. *Do I try again or do I abandon theatre altogether?*

"What I really wanted to do was try again, but I had been thinking, *Here I am up in Westchester County and who's going to care?* I had lunch with Athol during this phase and I told him I was creating new works but not quite sure that I could pull it off. He said, 'How do you think I felt in Port Elizabeth in South Africa?'

That remark left an indelible mark on me. I thought, *Here I am in Westchester, just one hour out of New York City, the theatrical Mecca of the world, while this man lived and worked courageously at the very southern tip of South Africa during apartheid.* It became very clear to me that it wasn't about where I did the work or who would see it or how famous I'd become; it was about having something to say and bringing my passion to it. I had to tell my stories! If those stories had meaning, people would find us…and of course that's what's happened. I decided I was going to try again."

What is required to live a passionate life?

"Well, listening is very important, but I think an equally significant requirement is learning to deal with fear. I've had to go up against tremendous fear because not only am I going up against conventional wisdom about how one conducts one's life—*get a job, get married, have kids,*—but I've also been up against the conventional standards of my own family, where there were no artists, poets, actors, or writers. As a result, if I was to follow this path I'd chosen, it became essential for me to learn to manage my fears and then act in spite of them."

How did you learn to do that?

"Oh God! There were countless hours of therapy, retreats, and time spent in recovery groups doing a hell of a lot of emotional and spiritual work. Then throw in the people who came into my life that I've already mentioned. I know that without those experiences I wouldn't have been equipped to follow my passion because I didn't have the tools that would be essential in facing my fears.

"When I was a kid I had athletic courage—I was a real warrior on the ball field. Facing my demons as an adult, however, demanded a much deeper level of courage. I was challenged to become a warrior on a whole different plane. In pursuing my dreams I've had to cultivate faith and a belief that good things can happen, rather than focusing on the bad things that might occur. That seems to fuel my courage.

"When I first saw a therapist, I told her I had no faith except the faith that things would not go well. She told me I had to create a *faith file* in my *filing cabinet* and start making contributions to it. It was a powerful metaphor for me and it's proved to be entirely true. I still have fears but they don't dictate my decisions about my life or about the business anymore."

"I have faith in our ability to grow and expand. Early on, I don't think everyone entirely bought into my vision, so I had to hold that vision until people came around. Today there is a tremendous amount of collective energy fueling the health and growth of Axial. I feel happy and fortunate to work in this space. Prior to moving here a year and a half ago, we'd been renting classroom and performance spaces in a variety of Westchester County locales. Having *a key and a lease* is a big deal!

"This is what I do full-time, and though it can be challenging, it's no longer difficult. Axial theatre functions as a nonprofit organization with a board of directors. Not only do we generate revenue through our acting classes and ticket sales, but we also receive some very generous donations and grant money as well. We've proven to ourselves that we possess the ability to co-create a success."

.

How would you like audiences and those who are part of your company to benefit from this work?

"My path is creating truth-based, authentic theatre experiences for myself, my collaborators, and the audience. For my theater company, I've submitted to a vision of a place where people could be nurtured, learn, and work together to create theatre that has emotional meaning, substance, and authenticity.

Theatre, unlike film, is a shared experience. Film is in the *can*; it's already been done, while theatre is in the present tense. The performers and audience are going through something together. As a member of the audience, it's always been thrilling for me to be present to a piece of theatre that has heft and substance, and where the performers are truly putting themselves *on the line*. Those are truly memorable moments. I remember flying all the way to London to see a production of an old Fugard play called *The Island*. The play took place in a detention prison on Robin Island, the same place where Nelson Mandela had been imprisoned many years before. So I got on a plane with a dear friend and spent all that money to go see a play! All I can say is that it was worth every penny. The direction, those actors, those words…priceless! I will never in all my days forget that experience.

"My hope for our audiences is that they will be touched by our work. With the lights down, and the actors bravely carrying all of that for us, it becomes a deeply collective experience; we watch the characters go through things and we can identify. Theatre holds the possibility that we can see something about ourselves that maybe we've forgotten or perhaps we are too scared to confront on our own. That is always what we are aiming for."

It's interesting that these very regions of self that you and your actors are able to enter were the same areas that you described earlier as much too scary for you to be in touch with as a kid.

"Exactly! It's what I craved even before I knew I was craving it. When I finally was able to experience it, I knew it was what I needed and wanted all along. "

What would you like your legacy to be Howard?

"Legacy? Wow…that's a big word. I hope people will think of me as someone who was unrelenting is his pursuit of truth, creativity, and integrity. I hope too, that the plays, the productions, all the classes, and the effects they have had on people will *ripple out* and made a positive difference in the world. In addition, I would like to see the plays that have come through me stand the test of time and continue to touch people long after I leave this life."

Howard may be contacted at **www.linkedin.com/howardmeyer** or at **hmaxial@aol.com**

Chapter 7
Commitment
Francis Endryck

"During this time I was being transformed from an overweight, out of shape, low-esteem fat guy into someone I really began to like! I didn't quite understand it at the time, but my commitment to the training and my physical changes enabled me to have a spiritual and emotional transformation as well."

Francis, a personal trainer, body builder, and triathlon participant, resides in Rensselaer, New York with his wife Tammy. His passion for training both himself, and those who come to him wishing to physically transform themselves, has literally saved his life and brought him a sense of purpose and pleasure beyond his "wildest dreams."

"My passion for the last 20 years revolves around my love for personal training, bodybuilding, and triathlon training. I began my quest into this at the age of 36. A close friend of mine had died of cancer, and I was concerned about my own health, so I went to my physician for a cancer checkup. Well, there is no such thing as a cancer checkup, but he told me that I was more likely to die from heart disease since I weighed 290 pounds which for me was 50-70 pounds overweight! My cholesterol was at 300 or 400 and my triglycerides were 300 or so. He said I needed to deal with my weight and my heart issues—that was my problem. My bad state of health had resulted from a combination of overeating and passivity with exercise.

"So I left my doctor's office, went home, and began to think about what I could do to help myself. I never could play sports because I had a lot of fear and little self—esteem. My dad and I didn't have a great relationship during my youth, and he was my main role model. I remember playing little league and just shaking in my boots as pitchers threw fastballs at me, at what seemed like 90 miles an hours. I tried football, but that was another disaster for me. I never seemed to succeed in anything, nor had I been encouraged to really act on what I wanted to do in sports, so I didn't have a good taste in my mouth for them.

"In high school I'd played some soccer and I was fairly good at it, mostly owing to my coach Jim Hotaling who mentored me, genuinely liked me, and was very kind. That had a positive influence on me. So I played soccer, a little baseball, and participated in a few other sports in High School because I felt pressure to be a 'jock.' With the exception of soccer, I'm not sure I enjoyed any of it but I played anyway. My journey into athletics was marked by a lot of activity but little real determination, enjoyment, or success because I took part for all the wrong reasons. I always wanted to gain someone's approval—often my father's. I just didn't feel I measured up as a young man.

"When I attended Nichols College in Massachusetts, I went out for the swim team and quit after three or four practices. I could barely swim the length of the pool while the others could swim literally thousands of yards without stopping. I also dropped out of soccer in college because I was just too lazy for all the drills and running. I just didn't have the necessary drive or passion!

"I'd also never had a good body image. I was a fat kid growing up and then overweight most of my adult life. When it came to doing things athletic, I also experienced a lot of humiliation and negative messages from coaches that left me with little motivation to improve myself. I remember one time I had a hole in my shorts and ended up with a rash on my thigh. In front of the whole gym class, the coach told me I was too fat and that's why I had the rash. I was eight years old! So as you can see, participation in sports had become a very negative experience. I later got married, had children, and over the years gained a lot of weight. As I mentioned previously, my friend's death when I was 36 motivated me to see Dr. Daggett, my physician, who told me that although I was not going to die tomorrow, my heart was not in great shape due to my current lifestyle, and that I had better begin to make some changes.

"I went home that day and started reading about lifting weights. I'd never tried that, nor had I failed at it, so I thought, *well here's a fresh avenue that I can investigate*. To begin, I borrowed a solar-flex machine which is not much more than a bunch of rubber bands, but because I really wanted to do this, I read the manual that came with it and started to work out.

"Dr. Daggett had ignited something in me! Amazingly, two years ago, he and I competed against each other in a triathlon and I beat him. After the competition I wanted to thank him and give him a hug, but he disappeared. I'm not sure he knows how much he helped me.

"So I worked with this solar-flex machine. After a couple of months, I saw that I had lost some weight, my body was looking better, and I could see that I was on the right track. The machine however, limited what I could accomplish, so I went to a fitness store to buy more equipment. I wanted to buy a big, fancy esoteric piece of equipment, but the store manager, Dan Pruitt, strongly recommended that instead of the equipment I consider hiring a trainer and have the trainer show me how to use free weights. He told me that working with free weights is an old and proven method, and the quickest way to transform my body into how I wanted it to look. I didn't like what he had to say, so I left and totally dismissed what he'd told me. Nevertheless Dan had me thinking and within a couple of weeks, I went back to the store and asked him, 'OK, who's the guy?' He then introduced me to Rene Huntley, a young man, who'd won a number of bodybuilding competitions. Rene had spent his formative years in jail, but following his release had met Dan who trained him to be a body builder. I agreed to work with Rene. We became friends and I paid him a weekly fee of $40—which I thought was outrageous at the time—to train me. In order to afford it, I took on construction work, evenings and weekends, in addition to my day job. I believed strongly that it was a worthwhile investment in my health and self-esteem.

"Initially I was thinking I would work with him for four weeks, take the knowledge I'd gained, and do it on my own. What happened during those four weeks, however, was that I was falling in love with lifting. In just a month's time, my body was beginning to change and, besides, I liked Rene. He taught me to love weights and he taught me what he knew, and did it in a very kind and gentle way, which was vital for me.

"After three months, the gym we were using went bankrupt and closed. I then decided I wanted to get in this business myself, so I suggested to Rene that we rent some space together where he would train me for free while he'd continue to train others, and I in turn would teach him how to run a business. He agreed, so we rented a little place on Lark St. in Albany, bought some free weights and two exercise machines, and Rene started training people and also training me three or four times a week. We carried on in this manner for about three years and then I began to take part in body building shows.

"During this time I was being transformed from an overweight, out of shape, low-esteem fat guy, into someone I really began to like. I didn't quite understand it at the time but my commitment to the training and my physical changes enabled me to have a spiritual and emotional transformation as well. As I mentioned earlier, I had never really liked myself, been content or happy, but body—building, at least for the hour I was engaged in it, allowed me to transcend this merry-go-round of life that I'd been on. My weekly routine was such that I would go to my day job at the Health Department .each day and then do construction jobs at night or on Sunday. When I wasn't doing that I was teaching a Drinking Driver program. My life was pretty much work, work, work! It had always been that way with me.

"Eventually I wanted to go further, and learn more about bodybuilding than Rene was able to teach me, so we parted ways. Throughout this time I'd gotten to know some professional bodybuilders and from them I began to understand that bodybuilding was a science. I'm an accountant by trade and have a business degree, having graduated Magna Cum Laude from Nichols College and later attained a master's degree in Public Administration from Russell Sage College in Albany, New York. I didn't have the physiology or kinesiology courses that are called for in this kind of work, but I was determined that I was going to learn how to do it.

"I began by getting certified as a Personal Trainer. Next I bought a book called, "The Iron Man System of Training." In it the author, described a concept called *periodization*, developed by a Czechoslovakian man, Tudor O. Bomba, author of "Periodization Training for Sports." Bomba's idea is if you work a muscle out, you must then rest and relax it so it can recuperate. If you reach a certain level of intensity in working out and remained at that level, you will eventually get weaker, which I had been experiencing in my workouts. Bomba suggests that you work the muscles for a month in a certain regimen and then you back off. Then you would once again go forward, much like a pyramid where you would move up a step, rest, move up a step, and then rest. He wrote the science of that system over a year period and called it *metho-cycle*. What it gave me was the key in how to be a trainer!

"All of a sudden I had a lot of information about being a trainer but I wasn't quite sure what to do with it. The *Iron Man* book laid out what you do for the first four weeks to six weeks, fat-burning, training for various events etc. It gave me the structure I needed and I then proceeded to do some research into Bomba's resources. I found that the East Germans were pretty good and I studied some of their books. I also went to Canada and took some courses with Charles Poliquin, a body building expert, whose books I'd also read. After a couple of weekend training programs in Montreal with Charles, I was not only looking good because I knew how to train, but I now understood *why* I was doing what I was doing. He had given me the *keys to the kingdom* of body building and body transformation.

"I was charged up. My business also geometrically increased because of my confidence in myself. In the past someone's negativity could easily steer me off my course: but now nothing could back me off from where I was going! I knew I could contribute something positive to the Universe and best of all; I wasn't doing it because I had to satisfy someone else's wishes; I was now dancing to my own tune!

"One of the main reasons I became good at this work and have continued to improve is that I have continually pursued additional education to learn all I can. When a person comes to me and says, 'can you help me train for a Triathlon?' or 'can you help me do some bodybuilding so I can look better?' almost immediately a light in me gets switched on, and I begin scanning his or her body for structural imbalances and physical limitations. I think about how I can help them. My *'master's degree'* in training came from a man named Mel Siff who wrote the book, "Supertraining," which most sports coaches and trainers have read. Tammy and I traveled to Denver and spent four days at Mel's house and in the gym where he trains members of the Denver Broncos. I have read Mel's book, which is about 1500 pages, and although I didn't understand a lot of it, it probably added about 40 layers of knowledge to what I knew about bodybuilding and training at that time.

"At this time, I had a computer person working for me, so I agreed to train him in exchange for him creating some computer programs for me around my system of training. Now I have a nice system and don't have to manually figure any of this out. Tomorrow morning for instance, I will be doing a body assessment for a client, and within two hours, I will have gone over her entire body, and know how strong she is in eight different muscle groups. That data, when entered into the computer, will produce a detailed workout for her, covering the next four weeks. When I test her at the end of the next month, she may have improved 30 percent, and the look I will most likely see in her eyes, will be the look you see coming from a kid on Christmas morning as he looks under the Christmas tree and sees every toy he ever dreamed of owning. When I give them the chart and they can see they've lost two pounds of fat, gained three pounds of muscle, and the strength in their arms and legs has increased considerably I see a radiance in them that's beautiful.

Many of the people who come to me have been struggling with weight and self-image for years. They may have tried running, jogging, Pilates, swimming, or yoga, and up to then nothing had worked for them. Being part of their transformation is truly a natural high for me. Alcohol or drugs could never touch that. It has become my life."

When you describe your experience while training a person, it seems that you're doing something which truly expresses who you are.

"That's true, and—I never really knew that I needed to express myself in this way. I sometimes (and this may sound egotistical) feel like Leonardo Da Vinci. He had his paint and I'm fortunate enough to have a person's body to work with. If they will follow directions around training, food, rest, and lessening stress I can help them to transform themselves beyond their wildest dreams!

"I usually work for about an hour with a client. When they come in they may be thinking about a conflict they had earlier with their spouse or some other issue in their lives, but within fifteen minutes of beginning their training routine something changes in them. You can definitely see the endorphin-rush happening and simultaneously dopamine is flooding their body. I will also push them beyond their capacity when I can see that look in their eyes and know that 'magic' is happening for them. I may put an extra 20 to 30 pounds on the bar and they'll lift it 12 times. When that happens the person may say, 'I've never done that before. Thank you.'

"Wow! What a feeling that is for me. At the same time I know this person had that capability within them all along.

"What I provide is a window for them to see what's possible and where they can go. Whenever they say, 'I need you,' that's a real ego booster, but I tell them, 'You're doing this, not me. Somehow you've reached inside yourself and became more than you thought possible.' So there's a self-confidence in them that builds, and then spills over into all areas of their lives."

So this work they do becomes life-changing!

"Yes, and that's the whole point! I began this work myself with the shallow goal of looking good. Little did I know how it would benefit my whole life? For example, last week I got some difficult news. I learned that my heart is defective. Because of heavy drinking early in my life, I have a condition that affects the right atrium and left ventricle of my heart. Consequently the blood pumps through at a lower ratio than it should. What all that means is, if I didn't undertake this lifestyle change when I did, I'd probably be dead right now! There are no accidents; I'm here because of this passion of mine. Not only has it been life-giving but it's been life-sustaining for me.

"With the help of drugs my doctor has prescribed, I'll be able to actually repair the damage I did earlier in my life. Now, I have to say, my ego has been humbled here because I've always been proud of my ability to heal myself naturally. But I've thrown in the towel and I'll start blood pressure medication next week. I was in a funk for a couple of weeks, but I don't want to look at this as a negative. In fact, I'm looking for the silver lining. I'm even thinking that I may actually be able to run faster and improve my triathlon scores as my heart heals. It's very ironic that as I'm dealing with this health challenge, I'm in the best shape I've ever been in. It seems that every year I say, 'It can't get any better than this' and then it does!'"

Does spirituality play a part in your passion?

"That's a difficult question. It's tough for me to define spirituality, but one thing I do know is that personal training is the one thing in my life that I know I'm really good at. I think that's how God expresses himself in Francis Endryck. I intuitively know how to work with a person when I see that person in action. I don't want to say this out loud because I'm afraid something will happen, but in 20 years of training people, no one has yet gotten hurt. I learned that as a trainer your most important mission is injury prevention. Don't do any harm! I've had people who had quadruple-bypass surgery train with me and they've been all right. One man, 55 years old and unable to do much of anything, told me he'd always wanted to ice skate. Within six months of beginning training him, he was ice skating. So I see my ability to train and help people, as a gift. When I'm in touch with that I'm in sync with God's purpose for my life. That's the spiritual connection for me.

"On July 22nd of 2007, I will be 55 years old and on the 25th, I'll be retiring from my job with New York State. I'm hoping that I'll be able to re-create this model for what I do, when I move to Beverly Hills, Florida, where my wife and I have purchased a home. I feel very grateful that we're able to make this move, and frankly I'm just blown away by the direction my life has taken. I never thought this could happen for me. It just about brings tears to my eyes.

"In the area we'll be living, there's a firehouse a short distance away. On one of our recent visits, I offered to train the firemen there for free and they accepted. I've learned that doing some gratis work is a terrific way of using the *attraction, not promotion*' principle of marketing."

Where did your desire to help others come from?

"In my career at the Health Department, I had an opportunity to be an Employee Assistance Representative for a few years. In doing that work, which is assisting employees who are having personal problems affecting their work and personal life, I learned that when I'm able to connect and be of assistance to another person on an emotional and practical level, I'm all the richer for the experience. In a way it's a selfish motive because I feel better when I can join with someone in a way that's helpful to them. As well it seemed, that as I was able to help people heal the broken places in them, the brokenness in me was healing as well.

"The trainings that I attended were very illuminating in the sense that I got to learn a lot about me. I had a real listening deficiency, so through the classes I attended, I became a much better communicator. Consequently I became better able to assess people when they walked into my office and not let *my* 'stuff' get in the way. I walked away from those years in that job, realizing how important it is to help another person, and how much I benefit from doing so."

Do you have any heroes Francis?

"I get glimpses of spiritual heroes in quotes from Plato or Mother Teresa, and from other sources, but I don't think I ever said to myself at 16, *I want to be like Mickey Mantle* or at 37 thinking *I want to be like three—time Mr. Olympia, Frank Zane*! I try to stay open to little pearls of wisdom that might come from someone such as the man who picks up my trash. My job I think is to be aware that the information I need is coming at me, and I have to be present to catch it. I've missed a lot of wisdom in my life.

"I become more aware and present in my daily life by living in the now. Each morning I read a meditation, get myself centered and eat right. If I go on a food binge and get *drunk* on ice cream, I have trouble even getting up the next morning, and might have stomach problems, or even pass out from a sugar rush. That's very self-destructive behavior, but thankfully, as long as I'm careful it doesn't happen a lot.

Body building became a part of my life 10 years after I'd stopped drinking alcohol; in part because I discovered that I'd replaced my addiction to alcohol with an addiction to food. So I have to eat every three hours and in a balanced way with the proper amounts of protein, carbohydrates, and fats. This is a bottom line for me. If I take good care of the physical side of me, it positively affects my spiritual and mental health as well. I also require at least 7 hours of sleep every night.

"I think what helps me to be spiritually centered is the knowledge that God is there all the time, expressing himself to me if I will just listen. I can even experience God when I get to play and spend time with my grandsons Hunter and Tanner. My daughter and her husband are struggling with addiction problems right now and it just rips my heart out knowing that. The only way I know to handle that is by going to God; the same God that watched over me during the periods of my own insane behavior with alcohol and drugs.

"So, my daily process keeps me focused. I think that when you don't have a structure to your life, 'life' will get in there and make it difficult to handle what comes at you each day. Part of my daily structure is my job with New York State. It's not the favorite part of my life, but right now it gives me structure, and from noon to one o'clock each day I exercise as well. I also attend a few self-help meetings each week, follow an exercise protocol, and have a rough plan for each day.

"How I stay passionate without becoming obsessive is mainly by allowing myself to do what I'm reasonably able to do each day. If plan A isn't workable, I may do plan B or C. I'm not anal or *afraid I'll die* if I don't get to do a certain thing. There's no *have-to's* in my life any more. I see compulsiveness in some of the people I train who come from addictive backgrounds—if they can't work out on a certain day, they panic! There's no freedom in that. Earlier on, I think, I used exercise as a way of controlling my life and myself. Now it just flows. My personal bodybuilding regimen feels more like a loose-fitting garment these days. I work out when I know its right for me instead of having to do it every day. I notice that when I'm not fanatical about my working out, that same attitude spills over to my clients.

"I also work with runners. Just recently I was working with a 16 year-old runner who'd been breaking down. I learned proper running technique from Dr. Romanoff, a Russian living in Miami, Florida, whose writings I'd discovered in some of my research. I worked for him and now I'm a POSE running coach. It wasn't a very profitable venture, but it did teach me to run properly. I had been breaking down in my running and needed to find a different style.

"In this country, we're taught to run heel to toe and what that does, it sets up a shearing force on the heel, that will then affect the ankle, and when the leg straightens, the knee gets hit, and then the hip gets hit with this jarring force. Romanoff studied ballet and animals and in his doctoral work in Russia, came up with this concept for running which was much like the way a cat or a 2 year-old child runs on the balls of his foot with a bent knee. What he conceptualized is that it is possible to capture gravity and use it in the movement of the feet and legs, thereby diminishing running injuries. It's a simple concept but not easy to learn. This is what I teach to runners who come to me. In my own life I was a lousy runner.

"In Triathlons, I also couldn't swim well, so I took a weekend course with Terry Laughlin, called Total Immersion, and then added some follow-up work with one of his trainers. In the last Triathlon I competed in, I think I was 20th out of 300, out of the water. That's pretty amazing considering that five years ago while visiting my daughter Liza in Germany, I couldn't even swim a lap. I turned to Liza at one point and said, 'Liza, this Triathlon thing might be more than I can chew.' (Laughing)

"I now have a deep conviction that says that I can do anything if I really want to do it! It's a belief and a drive that motivates me to read, check out websites, and seek out people who have the experience and expertise to counsel me on what it is I desire to do or accomplish. I take what I've learned in the gym and apply it to anything new that I'm attempting to learn. I focus, I try, and if I can't accomplish it in my first approach from angle A, I'll go to angle B and so on. I try to remember there are 360 degrees in a circle, all pointing in to that center where my goal is. So that means I have 360 different degrees or angles to pursue in accomplishing my goal. Knock me down and I get up again. I don't quit! Maybe Harold Macy, who created Macy's department store, is my hero. He failed hundreds of times in his various ventures before he became successful. I guess you could say I no longer take my failures personal. I'm more apt to take it as a message from God that I'm going about something in the wrong way; and there's a smarter way of doing it.

"My grandfather, Frank Endryck, who I greatly admired, told me that 'necessity is the mother of invention' and I've taken that to heart. On one hand he thought he was just an ignorant, uneducated, blue collar guy who tended bar in his family's grill, but in reality, he was able to build a house, install plumbing, run electricity, and put a roof on without anyone showing him how to do it! He's another role model and a hero of mine, for sure.

"What I hope people take from what I teach them, is a way to come to grips with themselves, and to love what they see when they look in the mirror each day. My vehicle for helping them to achieve that is in my gift for training and teaching of body transformation through exercise and practicing a healthy lifestyle. You know, a person whose a hundred pounds overweight is hiding the best part of themselves beneath that weight, and their true radiance is trapped and hidden from both themselves and from the rest of the world. I'm currently working with a woman who came to me about 6 weeks ago—very quiet and subdued. I just recently saw pictures of her at a wedding where she just radiated life and peace. People learn that it's possible for them to make their wildest dream come true if they're willing to believe it and commit themselves to the goal!"

Postscript—June, 2008 Francis is training people, in Beverly Hills, Florida where he and Tammy now live following his retirement and their subsequent relocation from New York State.

Francis Endryck may be contacted at: fendryck@tampabay.rr.com

Chapter 8
Creating Beauty
Catherine Weaver

"I would love to create spaces that would enable people to have the sort of profoundly inspiring outdoor experiences I've been privileged to have in my lifetime."

Vivacious, passionate, and convicted about her love for her life's work aptly describes Catherine Weaver. At present she is a self-employed landscape architect, living on the outskirts of Providence, Rhode Island. She has a deep love and reverence for nature, and a burning desire to create outdoor spaces where people can connect with each other and with the natural world, and, where the planet can be honored. Her passion for landscape architecture blossomed at the end of a long and rather unexpected journey through various paths to find work which truly fit the person she is. I interviewed Catherine on a park bench on a balmy June afternoon next to the Providence River, in Providence, Rhode Island.

"In early elementary school my daughter, Meghan, had a teacher whom I greatly admired. She was one of those extraordinary people that not only enjoyed her work, but, also was seamlessly one with it. It was a joy to be in her presence when she was working, and I knew she had something I wanted. It was a passion for what she did. She was in her right livelihood; not only was she doing her job but she was using her gifts to perform work that she was meant to do. It was obvious there was something very different about her. I remember looking at her and thinking, *that's what I want—I want to find that for myself.*"

What were you doing at that time?

"That was about 20 years ago. I was involved in raising my daughter—I don't think my son was born yet—and I had a college degree in anthropology, which I loved, but quite honestly, I had studied anthropology because that subject was the one thing that made school tolerable for me. It held my interest enough so that I could get through college, get that *piece of paper,* and say 'I've been there and I've done that.' I also knew that I didn't want a career in academia. So I ended up becoming a career waitress. (Laughing) My degree in anthropology did however hold some value for me because I love people, and I love to see how they work and what makes them tick. There's also nothing more fascinating to me than exploring the ways in which people interact with their physical world. I just didn't want to ruin my love for anthropology by making a career of teaching it. Because I have this very artistic side of my personality, I was also aware that anthropology alone wasn't going to fulfill me. I'm a very *hands-on kind of person* which wouldn't work with teaching anthropology.

"So I floundered for awhile. I waitressed and I also got heavily involved in photography. While engaged in a work-study program, I worked for a woman, Jane Brawley, who was a very talented photographer and became a mentor to me. She convinced me that I was gifted. I was always very creative, but hated art class because it just terrified me. Somehow Jane convinced me that I had the talent for photography, and that when I left school I should go to New York and pursue it. Photography, however, wasn't *it* either, so I continued to waitress. There were, however, two more big pieces of my life that ensued from my first college experience. One was meeting my husband and second was giving birth to my daughter."

How did your love for the outdoors come about?

"My long-time connection to nature came from both sides of my family. My father, Tom Weaver, was a research economist and worked in academia, so his *"Prozac"* was gardening. It kept him sane. My mother, Peggy Maxwell, came from South Georgia, where she grew up on her family's farm and lived very close to the fruits of the earth.

"When I was growing up, the outdoors was where I sought solace when I was troubled or upset. Wherever we lived, one of my first tasks was to find my *special place*. It was more important to me than the house or my room, or even finding new friends. I needed to know where I could go whenever the going at home would get rough."

Do you remember your first special place?

"I do—it was in India when I was five years old. There was a huge fig tree outside my bedroom window with these giant fruit bats that can be the size of large birds. They would come and feed there at dusk when the fruit would ripen. Anyway, at the base of that tree I had a nook that was just right for me.

"Before that, when I was 3 or 4, I had a spot in my yard. I can't remember what the spot or the yard looked like, but I can recall how the place itself felt. It was like the comfort of a mother's arms or a father's lap, only in a bigger way. This was an awareness of safety, warmth, and a deep love, and I just wanted to stay there.

"I guess I was subliminally aware at a very early age that nature was an important source of good feelings for me. Some part of me knew even in this early time in my life, that a big part of my life's work would have to encompass being connected to the natural world in some way. That has been a constant ever since for me, and I've noticed that in other people in the various cultures I've lived in.

"I lived in India from the age of five to seven with my brother, my mom, and my dad, who happened to be a graduate student at Cornell University at the time. This was the early 1960s. Dad was an irrigation specialist studying rice production, so in order to complete his PhD research; he packed up his little family and hauled them off to the rural interior of India. While there, we lived in an old British bungalow next to a mission hospital in the tiny village of Tilda. My father helped the farmers in that area figure out how to improve their rice yields. Tilda is now famous for its rice, and the agricultural station there continues to help farmers solve agricultural issues.

"Living in a foreign culture is a very profound experience for a child, because a child doesn't intellectualize the experience, he or she just lives it without any preconceived notions or expectations, as an adult might do. As a result I just embraced it and was totally immersed in the Indian culture which became part of who I am.

"About 40 years later, I had the opportunity to return to India with my daughter, Meghan, who had just graduated from high school and had experienced a very tough adolescence. As a result, she'd really struggled at times and barely graduated from high school. After graduating she decided that she wasn't ready for college but wanted to do something worthwhile with her time. So she worked and saved some money, and then joined a program that offered cultural exchange, through community service in other countries. Growing up, she heard me tell of my childhood in India, so that's where she chose to go. Consequently, at the tender age of 19, I put her on a plane bound for India.

"She spent three months there, performing community service in the slums of New Delhi while she worked with the destitute and dying at Mother Teresa's Mission. It changed who she was!

"When she completed that program, I flew over and the two of us traveled around India for a couple of weeks. We were able to locate the village I lived in as a child, which made me very happy. I wasn't confident we'd be able to find it. We found the house, with the tree I loved, still very much alive, and I was able reconnect with the woman who'd taken care of me as a child. She was still living there in the village, so we spent time with her and her family. It was an *amazing* experience. I could now see the place of my childhood with an adult perspective.

"I think that trip definitely affirmed my commitment to take the work of landscape architecture, which I was doing at that time, and deepen it. In rural India I learned of the 'magic' that happens when people have a really strong connection to their outdoor environment. They harvest their sustenance from it, they worship in it,—they just live very closely connected to it. While it certainly has its problems, I experienced a beauty associated with the more primitive and natural life that disappears when you enter the world of concrete and cities. The beauty is about the relationship between people and the land, and how that informs them in their ceremony, religion, work, and everyday life. That fascinated me. It also reaffirmed in me what I had felt as a child while living in that culture; more than I'd ever experienced living here in the states.

"As well, I wanted to figure out why that connection to nature was so magical for me, and how I could bring more of that into my work, creating physical outdoor spaces that respond to people, and that people in turn respond to. So I knew that I now had this amazing opportunity to create and enhance a beautiful connection between people and the land."

How would you describe the work of a landscape architect?

"Wow! How do I explain what I do? I didn't know that landscape architecture was a profession until I was 33 and pregnant with my son, Evan.

"I have an aunt, Elizabeth Heimbach, whom I've been very close to since birth, and who has always maintained a garden. Whenever our family would come back to the states for a visit, we would make it a point to spend some time with her, and she, being a very passionate gardener, taught me quite a bit during those visits.

"Over time, her home became a sanctuary for me. Her garden was a place I could visit when I needed to recharge my batteries. One day, when I was quite pregnant and unsure about my vocational direction— mind you I was still waitressing—she invited me to her house. I went, figuring this was probably my last foray out into the world before giving birth to my son.

"Prior to my visit she said, 'I'm glad you're visiting this weekend because there's someone coming to the house I really want you to meet. He's a landscape architect.'

"The man she wanted me to meet was David Campbell, a well-known landscape architect, who owned a firm in Washington, DC. He was coming to do a home design for her and my uncle on their new home. So I walked through the property with him and my aunt, and listened to their conversation. It was really one of those corny moments that you read about when all the bells and whistles go off and the bulb lights up over your head. But there it was; I thought, *That's it, that's what I want to do*!

"I realized as he was conversing with my aunt that his work combined many elements I'd previously identified as passionate pieces of myself. That included interacting with people to understand how they related to their physical environment and what made them 'tick' within that setting. It definitely addressed the artistic side of me because that involved a very creative process. Another element is that landscape architecture, whether you're doing something that is a residential design where you're very closely aligned with *a* client, or public design, which calls for involvement with a whole community, or habitat restoration where you're more directly involved with a natural landscape, has an aesthetic sensibility to it. I believe that nothing God created is ugly, so this work is really an opportunity to participate in the creation of beauty. What could be better than that? It also involves working with plants, which I love. As well, there are the visual and graphic arts, which are important mediums for communicating your design concepts in ways that can be easily read and understood by your client. So I was excited, and absolutely knew I wanted to do this work.

"When Evan was 2 years old, I took an Introductory to Landscape Architecture class at the University of Rhode Island. I wanted to find out more about the profession and decide whether I wanted to move forward with it as a career. It turned out that I had such a knack for it that the professor pulled me aside after finishing the class, and told me I should enroll in the program. Then I thought, *I really have to do this now*? I mean I was terrified! But I went ahead and applied to the program. By this time my son was three and my daughter seven, so after being accepted, I set out in pursuit of my second degree.

"The program at URI was very good, but it was a demanding program, and because of having two young children and a husband who was not highly functional due to his personal issues, I had to go slow. It was a long and sometimes grueling six-year haul before I finished my degree work. I was so enamored of the coursework, however, that it gave me the necessary energy to get through it all. Since then I never looked back!"

So you achieved this at the same time your personal life was going through some difficult challenges?

"Yes, it was challenging! I think I knew, out of some deeper wisdom within me, that my marriage was not going to get better and would probably get worse. I could very well end up in a situation where I was the sole financial support for myself and my children. That possibility motivated me to keep going, because I definitely did not want to be stuck in waitressing in to support my family.

"The process of my schooling was amazing because everything now came so easy to me. At times I seemed to be remembering what I had intuitively known at one time. It's hard to describe the sensations of that process.

"Some very astonishing things happened while I was in school. For a period of about two years, I had dreams that were very out of the ordinary. I had the good sense to write them down at the time, so I could see there was a connection between those dreams and the skill of conceptualizing an idea—seeing and even feeling it in my mind's eye, and then bringing it into a physical form. I had been developing those skills at the time. In the dreams I would be in some breathtakingly, otherworldly, drop-you-to—your-knees beautiful place that I never could have imagined in my waking life. I would wake up, completely blown away that my brain could tap into that kind of information; and then I'd attempt to get the details down on paper. Over time, I saw the connection between those dreams, and my learning about how to take something from my mind's eye, write it down so it could be understood, and then create it.

"I navigate through the world on my intuition—it seems I have little choice in that because that's the way I operate. As a result, when I design a project a lot of what I come up with is very intuitive. Other designers use a more functional or logical orientation to figure out the nuts and bolts of making an idea work. I'm more intuitive when it comes to assessing and choosing from among the infinite number of ways in which something can be created. I love that part of the process and I often think, *What can be better than this?*

"When I'm able to combine a client's ideas for a project with mine, it's like mixing the ingredients of a stew together. There's also much negotiating back and forth between myself and the client over ideas. It's a very collaborative process between the client, me, natural forces, and maybe even supernatural forces. A lot goes into the *stew*.

"To this day, I'm in awe when the form of my design goes through construction and I come to the site for the first time and get to see the spaces beginning to take shape. Later, when it's finished and the plants go in, I get to see the final result, much as I had imagined it in my mind's eye. There it is…what a sense of awe and wonder! That's why I do this work." (Laughing)

How do you discern when the time is right to follow your intuition and when it's not?

"The truth is I don't always know. There have been occasions where I did not trust my intuition when I should have, and at the end of the day I'd think, *You knew that was wrong and you didn't stick to your guns — you let them talk you out of it. Now you have to live with it! (Laughing)* In this business you usually have to suck it up, and live with your decisions or what you agree to. The older and more experienced I get, however, the stronger I become in my ability to stand by my intuition. That's important to me. I've also learned there's more than one way to do something and my intuition can sometimes be influenced by my ego. There have been times when, even though my intuition was right on the money, no matter what I did, I couldn't bring my client to my way of thinking. When that happens, I have to trust there is some greater process going on, which, for some reason isn't readily apparent to me at the time. When that happens, I change direction and see what I can do to make their idea work. Those occasions can be very challenging.

"Honestly, I hope that some of my work survives after I'm gone, not so much so I will be appreciated, as much as I'd love the beauty I create to be appreciated and enjoyed by people.

"My aunt, Betty Heimbach, whom I mentioned earlier, took me to

Italy when I was younger, so that I might have the chance to see some of the great gardens of that country.

"I had just finished college and had begun my first job, working for a very well-known firm, staffed with many talented people. Of course I didn't believe at the time that *I* had any business being there—I didn't believe I measured up to them—but there I was anyway! This firm did private work for extremely wealthy clients. It was difficult for me seeing people spend so much money on things that I just didn't see as very important, and that actually went against some of my personal values. My mindset was to help the world through doing public work, which was what we primarily focused on during my schooling. I imagined myself doing work like habitat restoration, and designing public parks and gardens at homeless shelters. I actually tried **not** to get this job, and, in fact, tried to sabotage my getting it *every which way to Sunday,* but the job eventually got me.

"I later came to recognize this work, essentially estate gardening, would eventually make me better at aspects of the work that I wasn't very good at. In the private sector, an architect designs the home, but once you step outside the threshold of the front door, you're entering the domain of the landscape architect. So the entire exterior of the property, which could include: lawns, trees, driveways, tennis courts, pools, driveways, and walls are within the realm of the landscape architect.

"Although I struggled with my job for a while, I realized that I could actually make a living doing it, and that was a major factor for me to consider. In the end I decided to stick it out and learn everything I could.

"When I was traveling in Italy with my aunt, and visiting these gardens that had been created six or seven centuries ago, I was aware that *beauty lifts the spirit.* As I walked in those gardens I could sense the layer upon layer of not only design, but also people's responses to that design. I became acutely aware of how these amazing places had *gifted* people throughout the centuries. I thought, *Wow, maybe there is some real value in this kind of work for me!*

"While I was walking in a garden outside of Florence, a voice from somewhere whispered in my ear, saying *Beauty lifts the spirit.* I just knew those words were right, because I'd always considered beauty to be sacred. No matter how you define beauty within your culture or your personal understanding, it's love, and it's an energy that makes our existence here on earth worthwhile. After that, I gave myself the message that it was okay to be doing the private work I was doing.

"In residential work, you're much more intimately involved with your client. There are many people in this profession who don't like that because it's usually a long association with the client, and it requires that you have good relationship skills. For me, the time I spent waitressing, which I never could have foreseen, served me extremely well in that aspect of my work. I remember one day, while attempting to resolve an issue with a difficult client, becoming aware that, *This is just like a crazy Saturday night in a restaurant, when a drunken customer wants to kill me because I don't have his food yet, and I have to work it out right there on the spot to keep everybody happy!"*

So, many of the pieces of your past seemed not to be disconnected at all, when you look at the work you do today?

"Right, they're not disconnected at all! The past was not a waste and no piece was insignificant; the pieces have all worked together to get me where I am today."

I remember visiting the famous *summer cottages* of the extraordinarily rich families of the 'Gilded Age,' here in Newport, and initially being repulsed at the thought that much of their wealth came from the cheap labor of poorly paid immigrants, women, and children who worked long hours in the mills and on the railroads during the 19th century. At the same time, however, I was captivated and awed by the beauty in the buildings, the grounds, and the artwork that some of that wealth created. Today that beauty inspires millions who visit there. It reminded me of the patrons of the great artists of the Middle Ages who used part of their fortunes in the service of creating great beauty.

"Yes, and visiting the Taj Mahal in India reinforced that for me. There are no words to adequately describe the beauty and majesty of that place. There's no question that when man is at his best, beauty is divinely inspired.

"In doing this work for wealthy clients, I also create work for very talented craftspeople who are then able to practice their art and skills. That's very satisfying to me. Not only am I able to provide opportunity for them, but I get to work with these truly amazing people.

"Every day I feel that it's an honor to perform this work, and to meet the people I do, and to learn and experience what I have. I'm very grateful."

How do you work with a client who may be very opposed to your vision and ideas for a project?

"It can be very difficult. At present I have one such client who challenges me weekly. Each project has its own life and lessons for me—no two are the same. They're like children in the sense that each project is unique. With this recent challenge, I've decided that the project and our conflict are about something else for me. The test for me is to look beyond the persona or veneer of another human being, learn not to judge them, and then look for the deeper lesson for me. I would like to think I am prejudice-free and I don't judge anyone, (Laughing) but I must admit there are a *few* things that I allow to push my buttons. So this project presents me with an opportunity to see beyond the individual and really let go of my ego. I've reconciled myself to the fact that this project is about my struggle with my ego more than it is about the finished product."

"Among my heroes or mentors, my mother and father both stand out.

"My father taught me 'the sky's the limit,' and anything is possible. He never took no for an answer. The Coastal Institute at the University of Rhode Island, a collaborative of scientists and technology dedicated to advancing knowledge and developing solutions to environmental problems in coastal ecosystems was his brainchild. He was a resource economist and head of the Department of Resource Economics at URI for many years. He worked tirelessly to see his vision come to fruition before his untimely death in 1996. The Coastal Institute building on the main campus was dedicated to him and the Weaver Auditorium bears his name. When he wanted to get something done, there was no such thing as *It can't be done,* which at times could make him a real pain in the ass! It seemed that people generally loved or hated him—there was no in-between. I certainly butted heads with him more than once. By his life and his work he taught me that anything could be accomplished.

"My mom, on the other hand, taught me that no matter how strange or nonsensical a recurring thought or desire might be, it was worthwhile to listen to it, because the process of following it could take you somewhere. She taught me to *trust the process,* so to speak. Without her encouragement I think I also might have given up because there were so many times I stumbled and wanted to quit. She would always encourage me to get up and take that next step. I feel very fortunate to have had her behind me.

"I think of myself as being a deeply spiritual person, and that spirituality informs everything I do in my life. I definitely feel that my passion for this work at least puts me in the *ballpark* of carrying out what God put me on this earth for. In that way, there's definitely Divine inspiration for me in my current profession. It's a satisfying and humbling feeling to be fortunate enough to be using the talents I've been given, in a way that feels right to me. When I get to a time in my life where I don't have quite the financial burden that I presently have, I would like to take this work to a deeper level.

"For example I would love to be able to design outdoor churches or spaces, created to support people in worship or ceremony. The birth of that idea came about from a design I created while I was in school. It's a little scary to even talk about it, but I would love to create spaces that would enable people to have the sort of uplifting outdoor experiences I've been privileged to have in my lifetime.

"One of those occurred for me when my children were young and we were living in a rural area where a dirt road ran behind our house and out past a farm. One day while we were walking that road, my dogs took off on me. I followed them through a wooded area until I suddenly found myself in an old-growth field full of cedars, blueberry bushes, and native grasses—a place that at once seemed so familiar and 'at home' to me. It seemed as if I'd been there before. I felt almost like Alice in Wonderland as I came through a thicket of bushes and stepped out into this field. I seemed to be in another state of existence during my time there. It was magical!

"Sadly, I had to watch as this very special place was turned into a housing development years later. I can't adequately describe the depth of pain that caused me. It was as if I had lost a loved one! I remember thinking, *What kind of freak am I? What's the matter with me?* It wasn't an intellectual loss like, *Oh, they're building another housing development!* It was a pain that I was aware of in a much deeper part of me.

"It causes me great pain to see what we're doing to the planet. At the same time, I realize that people can only care for and protect that which they love and feel an emotional connection to. If they don't have that connection, what do they protect? In my work, I attempt to help people feel more closely connected to the outdoor places that support their lives. I try to help them fall in love with the natural world. I want them to feel the same sense of awe and reverence that I feel outdoors.

"You know, I have some clients that love and really care for their properties, and then I have others that are not that bonded to their land. Those people may be more interested in keeping up with their neighbors, yet even they can be affected by what I do. For them, my work could provide the beginning of a deeper appreciation and a tie to their land."

How would you describe the greater purpose in what you do?

"That's really easy. It's to create beauty.

"To me, there's no excuse for ugliness. With everything I do, I ask myself, *Is it beautiful?* I'm not saying that it's necessarily the right way to look at the design process or what I do, but for me I get such a deep sense of fulfillment and love from engaging beauty. If I'm not getting that from my work, there's no point in what I do. Although I don't always succeed, I strive to create beauty in every aspect of my work."

What has you're journey, thus far, taught you about what it is to be human?

"Well, first of all, I consider myself to be very lucky. My life hasn't always been easy. I've had my share of struggles and I'll probably have more, but I feel so fortunate and blessed to have something that I love to do and feel so passionate about. To be able to experience that kind of fulfillment, despite my struggles, is just amazing to me! It's right up there with having a child."

"When I think of people who go through life without any passion in their day-to-day existence, my heart just breaks for them, because I've certainly *flat-lined,* myself, in different periods of my life. My best friend, in fact, has a daughter who's 17, and will sometimes call me in tears and ask, 'What do I say to this child? She doesn't have an interest in anything!'

"I've been asked this question by many people and my answer always seems to be, 'Well, sometimes you've just got to jump in and try something, even if it's wrong. You've just have to start somewhere with something. You take your *best shot* at the time.' If you have an idea with some zest to it, set-aside as little as five minutes out of your day, and discover a little more about it. Check it out.

"I think people become frightened because they think, *What if I take the wrong step,* or, *this might not be right for me.* There is no wrong step! It's just about starting somewhere and if you're paying attention, that first step, even if it's not exactly the right one for you, will take you to the next step, which is a giant step closer to the right place for you. You just keep chipping away till you find the thing that really fits for you."

Catherine may be contacted at **cnw@tupelogardenworks.com**

Chapter 9
Effort
Mike Reilly

"When I was a kid I remember feeling very excited when I read that the average person uses only 15 percent of their mental capacity. I thought 'If I can squeeze a little bit more out of myself, even though I may not have the same level of skill as some others, I can still reach the level others have risen to.' Improving myself has always been important for me."

Mike is the President and CEO of Energy Insurance Brokers in East Greenbush, New York., He resides with his wife Terri and their children Ashley, Jim, and Kate on the outskirts of Albany, New York. Mike has a passion for playing basketball that is not unlike the way he lives the rest of his life. When first meeting Mike, one is aware that his initial shyness quickly yields to a sparkling smile and a focused and dynamic energy. Despite growing up in poverty, Mike has become a successful businessman and a role model for the American ideal that whatever one's circumstance, a person can realize his or her dreams if they are willing to believe in their dreams and work hard. Mike has also made a commitment to do whatever he can to give those who've grown up in similar circumstances a hand up, much as he was during a difficult childhood.

"Although basketball is my passion, it didn't become a major part of my life until I was in the ninth grade. Baseball, my best sport at the time, and football were my favorites until the time when basketball came into my life. Willie Mays had been my hero. I often dreamed about being him and playing in the major leagues. When the Mets would be playing the San Francisco Giants out on the West Coast, I would sneak my transistor radio into my bed so I could listen. I might only be able to stay awake until the third inning, but those were very exciting times for me.

"I grew up in a housing project in Schenectady, New York with my mom and my sister Kathy, who was four years older than me. My dad had left early in my life. Kathy, I think, struggled a lot more with the divorce and with life than I did. At a certain level I decided that I wanted to survive, and to accomplish that, it was necessary for me to find something that I could do well. Consequently, in everything I did I looked to find an advantage for myself. Whether it was in math or reading, I tried to squeeze the most I could out of what abilities I had, because I saw *that* as the one way I could hope to rise above the environment I grew up in. Eventually I would come to love sports and see that as my path.

"Though I never played basketball on my high school teams, in junior high I began to see that others were much better than me because I lacked the experience they had. So I realized that I had to learn how to compete with others who were better than me if I wanted to be successful. That became my challenge and in fact still is today.

"Sports became a mental game for me. I would figure out how to make an opponent uncomfortable and then force him into mistakes. Later on, when basketball became my favorite sport, that mental aspect, along with doing what I could to make my teammates better, led me to see that consistency in those areas would generally produce favorable results over time.

"Winning is a lot of fun, but I can honestly say that my *life or death* approach to winning in sports has lessened a bit as I've matured and gotten healthier. (Laughing) About 12 years ago, I brought my son Jimmy with me, to play basketball with some of the guys I regularly play with. Late in the game our team was losing by a lot, but we came from behind to win. I'd played real well—my ego was pretty inflated and *my peacock feathers were right out there*—but in the locker room my son, with complete honesty, said, 'Dad, you don't have to be a *ball-hog*. We don't have to win all the time.' I was totally deflated by what he said, but that lesson still sits with me as an important one. I will always love to compete because passion is part of that. There's a passion that goes into figuring out how to win when you're not shooting the ball very well; there's always something else you can come up with to be competitive. At the same time, not everything I'm competing in, or challenged by is a matter of life or death. That's a big change for me.

"Going back to the beginning, I played on the junior high school team, and I remember a real sense of achievement, when in the second half of the season I was chosen to be a starter over players who had more ability than me. I was probably the smallest power forward in our league, but becoming a starter, I think, had more to do with my determination than my ability. Twenty years later, I happened to bump into one of my teammates from that team and the first thing he talked about was how competitive I'd been and how I pulled everyone together. He said that although I wasn't the biggest kid on the team, I was the one who made sure that we were all *on the same page*.

"Through basketball I learned to become a leader, in the sense that I worked at making everyone around me better. That skill goes well beyond sports; it has been very helpful in my workplace. I've learned how to challenge people to fulfill more of their potential, while also learning that different people must be challenged differently. I believe in the adage that the *sum of the parts can be much greater than the individual parts added together.* I also love the challenge from sports where you sometimes end up on the worst team but still do your best to compete. I've always got a healthy *high* from that. I love in some way, to make everybody better, so that when we compete against a team, organization or company that may be superior in some way to us; we can not only compete, but in most cases win. I think it's an idealistic notion of mine that allows me to do that."

Where does that notion come from?

"I believe it's what I wanted as a kid. In my family, I would have liked my mom to be more present. I would have liked my sister to somehow feel more a part of the family so that she didn't have to leave at 16; but I didn't have the power to make those things happen.

"When people can play together, take care of each other and trust each other, a team can be like a healthy family. One of the biggest challenges for any sports team is learning to trust one another. People and teammates who learn to trust each other and work together, will have more successful outcomes than more talented individuals or teams who are motivated primarily by selfish needs. I think that holds true for all of life. Talent, I believe, ranks behind desire, teamwork, and knowledge when it comes to success.

"Home life for me went like this: my mother went to work in the morning; she went to another part-time job in the evening; and I pretty much fended for myself. My sister, being four-and-a-half years older than me, just wasn't around much. There was no physical abuse in our home but there was also nobody there. I made my own breakfast, and when I was in elementary school, I'd come home at lunchtime, make my lunch, and more often than not I'd cook my own dinner. That was why sports teams and coaches filled my need for family during those years. My friends' homes, where I spent more time than I did at my own, actually became my primary places to go. Without my friends and sports teams, it would have been a very lonely existence. That's one of the things I love about team sports.

"Years ago my basketball team was playing in a playoff game and we were getting beat. Absolutely nothing we did that day seemed to work. At one point in the game, my friend Eddie and I couldn't figure out what to do. The score was close, but we weren't going to win the way we were playing. So I went down court, deliberately pushed a player on the other team, and accused him of playing dirty. Then one of his teammates came over and I began screaming at him, at which point the referee got into the argument, and soon everybody was yelling at each other. What people didn't know was that I was acting out a temper tantrum. When my friend Eddie asked me what was going on I told him, 'Nothing, but I have to do something to disrupt the way the game is going.'

"In the end, we came back and won the game by six points. That's the survivor in me. That's how *Michael* learned to survive. When I look back at that desperate act, I know exactly what that was about. It was about, *I've done everything I can to barely keep us in the game, but there's got to be something else in my bag of tricks to help us win.* When someone is passionate about something, they'll look deeply within to figure a way to be successful. Today, I probably would not do what I just described, but I still would look for ways to make me and those about me perform better.

"At forty years of age, I learned to shoot left-handed, as a way of improving myself. Then, a few years later I blew my knee out,—which slowed me down a bit—so I learned to improve my outside shooting. I constantly have to adjust so that I can continue to participate. My wife would like me to stop playing, but she knows the passion I have for basketball.

"When I do end my playing, it will be a huge loss for me,—a death of sorts—but I will still greatly enjoy watching high school, college, and professional games, and keeping track of how various teams are playing. I've prepared myself a little for the day I quit playing, but I'm not looking down that road right now."

It sounds like basketball for you is much more than the final score, or who wins and who loses.

"Through basketball, I've learned a lot about myself and about other people. People who are selfish, only interested in personal statistics, or easily intimidated, or not hard workers on the court, will usually be the same in their everyday life. As an example, I'm a so-so shooter until the end of the game when I become, as my friend Eddie says, a very good shooter. I like the pressure, where someone else may not handle it as well. It's really about how you view things. I see the end of the game as an opportunity to win rather than to lose. I view life as filled with abundance; so I want to take that last shot. That's one of the ways basketball skills are transferable to the rest of life and I've always been interested in these corollaries."

Can you say more about this belief of yours that the world is filled with abundance?

"In business, I believe there's an infinite amount of money and business opportunities available. People, on the other hand, who have a finite view of life think, *If Mike Reilly does well in business, he's taking something away from me.*. Fear-based people often have this finite belief that there's only so much out there. The reality is: there's more than we can ever use.

"I get excited when I see others do well. It inspires me. I don't worry about people who are in the same business as me. Professional people will often say to me, 'Mike, you have a nice business—you're doing well.' The reality is that in the scheme of things, I have *a couple of grains of sand,* and that's more than enough to take care of me."

Where does that view come from? It's a rather uncommon way of thinking in today's business world.

"I think just from looking around. Some of it came from reading and some from traveling. The more I look at the world, the more I realize how insignificant I am. It is possible for me to make a difference in some significant ways and that's important, but the world itself is bigger than I ever imagined.

"As a kid I was always looking for ways to get more out of me, so I could expand myself and increase my chances of success. I remember feeling very excited, when as a kid I read that the average person uses only 15 percent of his or her mental capacity. I thought to myself: *If I can squeeze a little bit more out of myself, even though I may not have the same level of skill as some others, I can still reach the level others have risen to.* Improving myself has always been important to me. In my recovery from alcohol addiction, I learned that the only person who has ever limited me in my life has been me. Once I came to grips with that reality, I realized that anything I want to accomplish is possible. Again it goes back to the idea of effort and consequences—if I put in enough effort I stand a good chance of getting a positive outcome, while if I put little or no effort into what I'm doing, I'll most likely get little in return.

"As a youngster I was always trying to broaden my horizons. I bought books on speed-reading and quickly improved my reading capacity. I can also remember being outside the house, and doing exercises to improve my peripheral vision. My belief was that *the more I could see the more I could have.* I also had a speech impediment and was acutely pigeon-toed. I would walk into a room like I had tripped. By working at them, I eventually was able to improve both of those challenges.

"I believe that the obstacles I face and am able to overcome, make me stronger. When I first tried out for little league baseball at ten, I was *devastated* when I wasn't picked for even the minor leagues—and I knew I was a good player! That was when my mother told me, 'you earn what you really want in life.' So, I played all that summer. The next year I tried out again and was the #1 draft choice in the league! I can still remember the pain I felt at not being chosen and then the redemption I experienced at being successful the following year. Losing is something I don't like, but I believe that out of losing comes a personal obligation for me to work harder. I don't ever want to fail for lack of effort whether on or off the basketball court.

"I believe that's true in all of life. I remember something a counselor, who was facilitating a therapy group, once told me. I think I was being a little cocky. He said, 'No matter how well you're doing in your recovery, there's always more to learn.' At the time, his words really *pissed me off*, but he was right. I think that metaphor holds true for life, and, for basketball.

"This morning I played and we lost. It was a very difficult game and as always—humbling to be on the side that loses. The first thing I did after congratulating the other team on how well they'd played was to question myself: *What did I do right? What did I do wrong? How could I have helped my teammates to play better?* I think introspection is so important to success in life—that's how I learn. That's one of the elements of basketball I love. There's always the *next game or there's tomorrow*, when I can redeem myself

"Self-evaluation is a real key to life. It's me, not others, who has to change and adapt to the environment, my realities, and to people around me. I'm only five-foot-eight, so I often guard players who are as much as a foot taller than me. I have to figure out how to use my abilities and strengths to negate their strengths. As long as I want to continue to play competitively, the reality is that I will need to broaden myself and my skills, and the same holds true for life. I've also learned to stay out of the *extremes.* In the past, I would allow losing to destroy me; but today I'm able to see it as just a part of life. I give *it my all* when I'm playing, and when it's over I'm able to let it go.

"Today I'm more comfortable with myself and who I am. I don't *always* have to win. The fear that I wasn't good enough always lurked behind my overly intense drive to come out on top in almost everything I undertook. Today competition is fun for me and it can be intense but it might also include more kidding around. It's no longer a matter of life or death. I usually like the guys I'm playing against, and besides, if I do lose today I can play again tomorrow. On the other hand, although I no longer have to prove I'm *good enough,* I have to admit that it's still a *kick* to go out on the court and compete against young kids.

"Basketball has also allowed me to make friends and continue my passion for this game in almost any city I've traveled to, as long as I have the courage to go where the competitive games are. When I lived in California and Atlanta, I played in many all-black neighborhoods and made many good friends there. These days I also have a home in Florida. When I'm down there, I play on Monday, Wednesday, and Friday mornings. The basketball court has always been a place where I can meet people, make friends, and compete. I love that about this game."

Who are the people in your life who've been major influences?

"As I mentioned earlier Willie Mays inspired me when I was growing up because of how effortlessly but passionately he played. I could see he loved what he was doing and would do whatever it took to win.

"In terms of mentors, I've frequently been blessed to have people in my life people who've pushed me in the right direction. Theone Bob was my fourth grade gym teacher. To keep me out of trouble and because we didn't have the money, she would put me on scholarship for the Summer Sports School at Linton High School. I would take three classes: baseball which I loved; basketball which I was just learning at the time; and modern dance, in which I was the only male. In the baseball and basketball classes I learned more about competing and the finer points of the games, while dance improved my speed and flexibility. Because of Theone I had these great opportunities that probably kept me from going down roads that could have led me into trouble.

"My mom always stressed that if I was going to pursue something, that I do the very best I was capable of. Of course there's good and bad in that advice; so I had to learn to pick out what I really wanted to do. She taught me a lot about the importance of self-evaluation. She also taught me, though I didn't grasp it at the time, that if I made a mistake and learned from it, then mistakes are okay. But if I make a mistake and don't learn from it, I'm a fool! Like a lot of things she taught me, there were parts that were helpful and parts that weren't?" (Laughing)

What is your greatest challenge today in living a balanced and fulfilling life?

"I can still go from *zero to 60* really fast when I feel threatened or I even begin to think someone might be trying to take advantage of me or is playing me for a sucker. The hairs on the back of my neck stand up straight, but at the same time, I've come *light years* from where I use to be with that. I use to take things more personally than I do today, and the volume of those *voices* has probably dropped from a 10 to a 3 or 4. But, yeah, that sense of heightened alertness is still there, and it's probably my biggest challenge.

"Today, however, I can use that heightened-alert response of mine in a constructive way. Like John McEnroe used to do, when I think I've been treated unjustly, I'll use that anger to spike some adrenaline energy in myself. I'll then experience some *fire in my belly,* and use it to raise my level of play. I know this challenge will be a lifelong one, but I've gotten much better at using my anger to motivate me in a positive way. I want to continue to lower the volume of that *voice* that comes from my childhood."

Would you describe your *day-job* Mike?

"My *day-job* (laughing) is being the President of Energy Insurance Brokers. We're a specialty insurance company that sells insurance primarily in the energy, trucking, and environmental areas of business. Other specialty areas are companies like K-B toys which is a national account. Most insurance agencies are very salesman-oriented, while we are mainly referral-oriented. That means that when we are doing our job right, people want to do business with us. We do minimal advertising, mostly through charitable organizations. Many other brokers refer new business to us because they're not equipped to deal with an individual's request and because we're considered experts in what we do. Our company was created in 1989, five years after I'd started in the field as an independent operator.

"How our company does business is much how I play basketball—it's the same deal! We spend time developing relationships with the insurance companies based on honesty and trust. We see the clients and the insurance companies as our teammates, which enables us to create a bond of trust that makes such a big difference in our relationships and to our success. They know we have their best interests at heart. In this way, we're truly bringing the parties together in a way that insures a better outcome for both, rather than '*screwing*' the insurance company when it's in the best interest of the client or '*screwing*' the client when it's in the best interest of the insurance company.

It's a very different business model from the one most companies in our business use. As a result, we have a positive national reputation that says: *We can get done what others usually can't.*

"I got a kick out of you telling me earlier how you experienced a *buzz* when you walked into the office this morning. A lot of people feel that when they come here, as opposed to many business places,—especially in this field—where you experience tension and an eerie silence when you walk in. That tells me that people working there are afraid to make a mistake. They're afraid to 'take that last shot,' to borrow a sports term. In this office, I tell the people who work for me, 'If you don't make a mistake that means you're not working hard enough, you're not competing. The important thing is to learn from the mistakes you make and move on.'

"Some of my staff, if they have come from violent backgrounds, may get scared by my passion or the *fire in my belly* until they really get to know me. I've had to find out what those people's reference points are and let them know that I'm not a threat to them. For the most part, we have long-term employees who understand my approach and have learned to enjoy healthy competition. And like my teammates in basketball I often create challenges for them so they can become better at what they do.

"Most companies generate business plans based on dollar amounts, while the basis for every type of business plan we have is based on the process of *how* we conduct business. If we work as a team, the outcomes we want will be there. This *process* however is not always easy to quantify. Five or six years ago for instance, I had a client come to me who was a potential three million dollar account. An opportunity like this one doesn't happen every day, but because we work our *process* that opportunity came. We don't make financial forecasts, but instead we: plan on talking to so many clients in a year; focus on how we respond and how we provide services to our clients; and continue to conduct business and work with the insurance companies as teammates. This is our process and when we do it well, we have fun and good things happen for us."

It seems that you view your business as a game.

"Absolutely! I have the same passion for my business as I do for basketball. It's fun, and a long as its fun, I'll keep doing it. Many people have told me that to be successful; they believe they have to find a job or career that pays a lot of money. To that notion, I say, 'No, find something that you love doing.'

"I love what I do for a living. When I take apart a policy and look for coverage deficiencies; ways that I can do things better; and how I can make this account better, I'm no different than a master craftsman building a cabinet. My craft, our craft, just happens to be putting insurance policies together, and that's how we look at ourselves here."

How do you see your passions for basketball and for your business making a difference in your little corner of the world?

"Well, there are a couple of things. First, it allows me to grow and experience joy in my life, and it allows the people I work with, the same, while helping them to make more money than they might in other places. I'm at a point in my life where I really don't have to work again unless I want to, but I continue to work because I love it and because it allows me to give back in various ways. That includes contributing financially to a first of its kind Transitional Living Program—named after my mom—at the Addiction Care Center of Albany, NY. There's also a meditation garden named after Terri's parents at the same place. We also do a lot with the Cancer Society. I give back to various AAU basketball programs for kids as well as to an Urban YMCA that provides a place, as it did for me, where kids can enjoy themselves on Friday and Saturday nights as an alternative to hanging out on the streets. Most of what I do in this area I prefer to do anonymously. I feel very grateful that I have the ability to contribute and be part of helping others.

"I truly believe that I have an obligation at a certain level to give back. I can only have so many pairs of sneakers and TVs. My wants and needs are not great. I use to have guilt about how much money I earned, but I don't today. I use it in very positive ways.

"A couple of years ago I attended a Black and Latino Achievement Award Dinner at which Bill Russell, the basketball legend, spoke. During his talk he said that it was very important to give something back when you do well in life. As a caveat to that, he said it's important to consider how you give back. In other words, giving as an equal, rather than in a condescending manner which says *I'm better than you.* That made a deep impression on me because when I was a kid, I often felt upset when I sensed people giving to me in condescending ways. I know that memory is a piece of why I like to remain anonymous in my giving.

"The most interesting part of that evening came when a speaker began introducing who would be given the Person of the Year award. I realized they were talking about me, and as I'm prone to be at times, I turned to Terri and being *ever so gracious* said, 'Did you ____ know anything about this?' (Laughing)

"With a big smile on her face she said, 'Yes.' She knew that if I was aware that I was being honored I might not have showed up that night. So I have a passion to give back, not to gain recognition, but rather to help people receive some of the opportunities I've had along the way.

"I play this *game* of business and it gives me, my family, and my children a plentiful bounty. We truly have whatever we need. The excess, I give back. I did a rather convoluted business deal a while back involving my company, with proceeds from that deal being used to fund a charitable foundation named for my children. If all goes well, the foundation become self-sustaining from the interest, in a few years. I know each of my kids will have their own careers, but if they can work together at this project, it would please me and help them in many ways. They'll get to work together, and learn about the importance and benefits of giving back. So again, the ability to give back has probably been the biggest gift for me, of my *playing at life."*

Do you see your spirituality as an integral part of this passion of yours?

"My spirituality is my passion; my self-evaluation; my sitting with myself, and coming to grips with who and what I am, and how I want to better myself in what I do. My belief is that all of this emanates from my Higher Power, and comes through me. People sometimes ask me to describe my Higher Power and it's difficult, but I know that this *ride* I've been on couldn't have happened without a greater power to help me.

"I wouldn't say my *ride* has been *storybook,* but some of the things I've been able to accomplish and what has happened to me have been well beyond my own power. It almost sounds Calvinistic, but some of the wonderful situations I've found myself in, could only have happened by some higher power putting me there. I'm not egotistical to think, *rah, rah, rah for me—look what I did*! I believe I've been *allowed* to participate and that my contribution is that I've showed up.

" John Wooden, the legendary basketball coach at UCLA, said the first thing he taught his new players each year was how to properly lace up and put on their sneakers so they wouldn't get blisters. His comment, and I drive my kids crazy with this, is: "Failing to plan is planning for failure." Showing up and having a plan has always been important to me."

How do you experience passion?

"It's that *fire in my belly,* at times positive and at times negative, but always a sense of excitement, that says *I want to do this thing*. There are days I may be tired, but I get up and head down to the gym to play ball. I want to be with the guys. I want to participate. When I'm passionate about something, there are no excuses for me, to not show up.

"I've told my children that if they have a passion for something I'll help them in any way I can as long as they *show up*. My daughter Katie has a passion for glass-blowing and she does whatever she has to do in order to *show up* three days a week to practice her art.

"Some passions, like my business, can be vocations and some, like basketball, can be avocations. My daughter and I recently had a conversation about this subject and I told her that I would loved to have been a pro basketball player but that didn't happen for me—*God was mean, he didn't make me six-four or six-six.* (Laughing) On the other hand, I *love* selling insurance and as a result I'm able to be a negotiator, an accountant, and a lawyer. Focusing on these various aspects of business makes me happy."

As I tell my children, 'participate in life—keep searching and try various things until you find the thing that moves you—then grab hold of it. I believe that unless people are willing to *participate*, they're alive but *dead*. At this time in my life, my greatest wish is for my son and daughter to discover what they're passionate about and grab hold of it."

Mike may be contacted at mreilly@energyins.net.

Chapter 10
Enthusiasm
Sandesh Naik

"Living passionately is not about success or about accomplishments. It's about the journey. When you are passionate, even the smallest things become enjoyable because you are living in the moment with awareness and enthusiasm. I think that unless you're living passionately you're missing the force of life."

Sandesh Naik, 53, lives in Albany, New York. He brings great enthusiasm, curiosity, and drive to all he does. As Dr. Bengali, he regales audiences at a wide variety of venues around the country with his high-energy showmanship, humor, and ability to playfully manipulate and hypnotize groups of willing volunteers at his performances. For the past few years, he's also been developing his "chops" as a stand-up comic. To say he brings passion to all he does would not be an overstatement.

"I really appreciate this opportunity to talk about my passion. My personal objectives and goals have changed over the years, but my effervescence and drive has never changed. Whatever I do, I do it passionately. It's the way I travel from point A to Point B in my life!

"I came to this country from India at the age of 29. I had been selected for a National Health Post-Doctoral Fellowship to conduct research on the link between AIDS infection and Tuberculosis. When I got here, I felt intellectually inferior because of the expectations I had for myself, and for what I believed the expectations of the scientific community in the United States were. After a time, I realized I had what it took to be successful here, but I had to adjust to the politics of the workplace and the scientific establishment as well as facing my own constant drive to earn more and more money.

"The first time I realized that I had this ability to really connect with an audience, was when I had the chance to present a workshop on Mentalism at SOS (Singles Outreach Support) in Albany, New York. This is an organization for people who are going through breakups, divorces, or just single people who are looking to socialize and make the best out of their lives. I took this challenge on, even though they don't pay much, because I was excited about the opportunity, and they didn't really care whether I was successful or not.

"So when I finished the workshop the comment from the attendees was that they loved my passion even more than what I did or said. That was the first time I realized, *O My God! Passion is so infectious. If you can be a passionate person you can literally charge up a group of people. So many people are missing this and craving it in their lives.* Unless I had heard these comments from the audience though, I never would have known it. I had never thought about it because I'm just naturally passionate about everything I do and like.

"Now that comes to the question of what passion is. For me it's a drive that says *I'm willing to care about something; I believe something; I appreciate something; I want to make a difference with something; I want to create something; It's how I go*! That's how passion comes into the picture for me. On the other hand I can do exactly the same workshop in a dispassionate way, and there would be no *charge* for me or for them.

"Living passionately is not about success or about accomplishments. It's about the journey. When you are passionate, even the smallest things become enjoyable because you are living in the moment, with awareness and enthusiasm. I think that unless you're living passionately you're missing the force of life.

"One key ingredient to living this way is love, and I think passion without love will not last. I believe you must have a level of appreciation or love for what you do. I mean when I perform, I don't even think about how much I'm being paid. Sometimes I make ridiculously low amounts in comparison to what my other performances pay me. I give one hundred percent all the time irrespective of money. It's a joyful expression of my creativity.

. "I went through a lot of difficulties to get my doctoral degree, but I faced them with enthusiasm. When I was finishing I had three examiners who disagreed on the quality of my work. Two felt my work was fine and the other one didn't think so. I was able to convince the two to drop the examiner who was against me. They did and I received my doctorate. You have choices: you can quit or you can fight it out. I think that when you live passionately you feel energized; you feel empowered."

Where does this passion come from?

"I think it might be inherited. My father's side has a lot of passion. My mother's side is more intellectual. I was fortunate to have a perfect blend of both of them. I can be very analytical, but also have a hands-on, practical side where I just go *at* things. Sometimes I think it's better to fail and learn from your effort, rather than contemplating and never actually trying anything. I also think it's equally stupid to keep repeating some—thing that just doesn't work. I think that's where the intellect comes in.

Gandhi said that his definition of a hero was someone who makes mistakes but doesn't repeat them.

"I come from the middle-class, and the middle-class in India is very interesting. On one side you've got all the glory of great wealth and abundance, and on the other side, you have the lower class with horrendous poverty, dependency and *lack*—very drastic differences. It's like walking a tightrope! So there's a fear that if you don't work hard you'll be nothing. You have no option, you have to work hard and do your best all the time."

So that's become part of your motivation to work hard at what you do?

"Yes, because I was born into this cultural level where there was so much push and pull to survive. Owing to this tension, I surrounded myself with people who were enthusiastic and would encourage me. Now, there were some family members who were very discouraging. They will tell you how you will fail; how it can't be done and how you will go wrong. I try today, to avoid those people. There is really no future if you just sit around and see the negative side of things."

Was there anyone who encouraged you when you were younger?

"Some of my uncles on my father's side of the family were encouraging to me. If I came into the house and I was crying, my father would say, 'Why are you crying?' So I'd say that someone beat me up and then my mother would want to protect me. My uncle though, would come to me and say, 'I'll teach you some techniques, so that you can beat that guy.' That kind of pushed me past my limits, so that I acted, rather than reacted by sitting and crying. I had to learn to rise above so that I did not fall into poverty. This drive I was being taught helped me to have a sense that I could become prosperous, empowered and free.

'I believe encouraging yourself internally is also very important. There's an internal dialogue going on inside of every human being. We have to be very vigilant about what that *tape* is saying. If that *tape* is talking about past failures, opportunities that were lost, and mistakes you made, then you're creating a pattern that will set you up for failure. I would rather say, 'Ah, screw it' and just do it—take the chance that I might fail or I might be successful. If I lock my mind onto those memories of when I have succeeded, and give myself a positive affirmation, then I have 'my car in the right gear.' Sometimes even if I lose at something and I've given it a good fight, I feel empowered and contented irrespective of the consequences, because I gave it my all.

"I've also realized there's a lot of junk in life and sometimes I've got to turn a deaf ear to it all. Recently I and some good friends bought a book to study that had been given great reviews by authors, Larry Dossey, Depak Chopra and Bernie Siegel. They were all saying it was a wonderful book. In the end, we all agreed that it was not even a *good* book. I was very upset, so I sat down and wrote a letter which I was going to send to each of the reviewers. I was very angry. We had bought the book based on these reviews, and I felt we had been taken. My friend Paul saw what I was doing and told me that nobody would read my letter, and that I was only wasting my time and effort. He told me to move on. There was a lot of wisdom in what he was saying. I used to have the tendency to have to fight every battle, which I realized was a waste of my time and energy. Now I choose what battles I am going to put my energy and passion into."

Who are your heroes?

"Well I don't have big heroes like Gandhi or Martin Luther King: They're too high for me. There are elements of Krishnamurti's personality I like, and some elements I don't. There are no perfect people. I think you can get into trouble if you start worshipping people. I pick heroes from my daily life. I realize that no one person has everything, so I pick some elements from each person. One of the best elements I've learned from you is that you appreciate everyone, and I think that when we can appreciate our life and other people we can be happy, and the people we appreciate are touched. I have a couple of agents who work for me and they are so effervescent—no matter what happens, they always put me in a good mood. They are so good to me. Many times I've been depressed or upset and they will cheer me up; help me get up on the stage and remind me of my skill and potential. I'm very thankful for them. It's easy to put someone down, but it's another thing to cheer them up and to lead them to their highest self. My friend Paul Bernard is one of those people. He's a very good and gentle man. He sees the best in people and he just ignores the rest. That's the way I want to be. It's a quality I admire. These are my heroes and role models. They show me what I'm capable of.

"When I was in medical school, we had an annual student get-together. I was interested in hypnosis at the time, and some of my friends and fellow students came to me and said 'Why don't you put on a show?' Now I was using hypnosis with a few people one-on-one, but

I didn't think I could do a show in front of an audience. They said, 'Well you're guaranteed four or five people. Give it a try.' I did, and I ended up with about 40 people up on the stage with me. So I got confidence through the encouragement and support of my friends.

"Then I started watching other hypnotists and I learned from the mistakes I saw them making. For instance, one of the worst mistakes people make when public speaking is moving around when they speak. People can not pay attention to you if you are walking around when you're talking."

Does Ego ever pose a problem for you with what you do?

"Because I came from a very competitive world, when I started out I was very ego-driven and wanted colleges to hire me over others. But I don't do that anymore. If a school asks me about another person who does my kind of show I will praise the other performer, and might ask the representative of that school if they would give me a shot some time in the future. It works out well that way. Sometimes the other performers send business my way and sometimes I send business their way. I don't have any need to be cut-throat. The world is full of opportunity.

"When college students at my shows ask me about how I was able to learn the skills I have, I tell them that its an acquired science and they could learn it if they decided to put their minds to it. That makes me happy. I don't try and tell them that I have any great power that they lack. At one time I had an assistant, to whom I had taught these magic and hypnotism skills to, and now she's very successful. In fact some people like her more than me (laughs)."

Have any of your relationships been effected by you following this passion of yours?

"Oh yes! In my family, in India, I'm like a 'fancy car.' Recently I worked in Washington D.C. and my mother was telling her friends and family members over here to go see my show. She'll tell them I'm performing in Baltimore or Boston or wherever. Many of them then come to my performances—they enjoy it and so do I. They feel as If they belong.

"Now sometimes my passion for what I do can be healthy and then begin to overlap into obsession. That can negatively affect my relationships. Obsession in my work and in my life can lead me to depression, anger, and compulsion where my mind can be totally consumed with my work. Healthy passion however is a choice and it empowers and gives me a sense of freedom and peace. In obsession my creativity gets blocked, my relationships with others are affected, my skills suffer and my thoughts get into patterns that repeat and repeat. My life then becomes one-dimensional, and that's not healthy for me. So I have to be careful and stay balanced in my life."

Are there any sacrifices that you've had to make to follow this path of yours?

"Well, when I left my job with New York State, I earned just $5000 the first year and I lived in a one-room apartment. I was just barely able to pay my bills. It was a very difficult time for me.

"I had a license in lab medicine, so I was eventually able to pick up a job in a hospital on the weekends, and work on creating my dream during the week. Fortunately within four or five years everything worked out for me and today I can just do my performances."

I imagine your greatest leap must have been in leaving your original profession in this country. What was that like?

"That was the biggest leap. It was very difficult. I had come into this country with a lot of passion around doing research and helping to find a cure for Aids. In my position in state government I was put in charge of people who I absolutely was unable to move into action. They had permanent jobs and had no worries. When I started there, money and power were not my primary goals. My purpose was being able to put out meaningful publications and presentations. I took a lot of risks. Eventually I was made the director of 150 laboratories all over New York, and it became too much for me. Handling all the politics and personnel was very stressful and I began to reconsider my career.

"During this time, there happened to be a conference at Roaring Brook Ranch near Lake George, New York. My boss suggested that I do a performance of my (hypnotism) show, which I had been developing. I had done this in public in India, but at that point I had not yet performed in the U.S. So I did a show and the attendees at the conference loved it. The management of Roaring Brook also saw the show, liked it, and asked me to perform it for some of their events, which I did. My new career just took off from there.

"Compared to the work I had been doing, this is so much better. I love it!! It's fun! I still have my Lab Medicine License, and from time to time I get calls and offers to go back to that kind of work. I say, 'no thank you.' I could make a lot of money in my old profession, but I ask myself how much money do I really need, and how important is to my life? It's just not worth it to me.

"I have so many good friends today and they are such a blessing to me. They stimulate me and support me in what I do. The people at the Unity Church of Albany Coffee House and open mike shows have given me the chance to try out new things that I could never try when I'm performing under contract. My God, I could stand there and drop my pants and they'd all applaud!' (Laughter)!

Will you talk a little about your hypnosis show?

"Well, first of all I tell people what hypnosis is and isn't, and how one way or another we all get programmed in this society. I tell them that if we can learn to reprogram our minds then we can avoid all the junk that comes into it. My performance helps them to experience how they are programmed by outside influences and how they can learn to program themselves in a healthy way.

"I think a great fear of most people is the fear of public speaking and I'm just the opposite. When I get up on the stage with a microphone in my hand I can't stop myself. Sometimes my agent will say, 'My God where do you get this stuff from?' Sometimes I pull out new things and I'm not sure where they come from. I try to give one hundred percent all the time, and I feel 'expanded' when I do.

"I also feel an obligation to help the crowd enjoy what I'm doing. When I see a large crowd I feel very happy, and I do my best to make the people happy. That's why I'm out there.

"I used to be very intellectual, actually giving lectures about what I do. At Babson University, a couple of students came up to me after the show and asked me why I was giving them a lecture, when I was a performer. They said that they had lots of professors and had heard numerous lectures, but that's not why they had come to see me. They had hired me for entertainment. So I stopped doing *lecturing,* and from that time, my obligation is being a performer. During a show, I talk only a little bit about what I do.

"When I am doing my hypnotism I bring my enthusiasm and passion to the audience as opposed to some hypnotists who are apathetic. I make a big deal out of everything that the participants on the stage talk about. I also talk loudly. That way their attention stays focused on what we're doing. I also never turn my back to the audience and I stand tall. I have to be totally present in the moment. I can't plan every show. Every show is new. I don't know what will happen. I don't know how my audience at each performance will react to me and what I do. My shows are like a meditation for me—I'm present in the moment and doing my best with the cards that are in my hand—a heightened awareness experience! That's what it is for me."

What is your purpose in performing this work?

"I think its God's gift to me. I would do this free of charge! It's a joyful expression of who I am. To make people laugh is a very difficult thing. Seinfeld says that it takes him six months to write 10 minutes of comedy—Seinfeld! I have noticed that comedy is a very complex deal. It falls flat many times. I've fallen flat many times. But when it flies, no amount of money can give you that kind of joy. I feel empowered at every performance I do, even though I feel tired at times. It's absolutely a gift for me and a great blessing. I was not trained for this. It's my hobby. Imagine that! There's no business like show business—amazing!

"I no longer expect to change the world. But I think that if I can make somebody's life a little easier by giving them a good laugh, that's a lot. That make's me happy. Someone I hypnotized in a Quit Smoking Seminar has been smoke-free for over 20 years now, and her gratitude for that, gives me great joy. Doing this work and seeing some people become empowered is very satisfying.

"I don't focus on why I do it most of the time. Sharing what talents I have is what I want to do. If they enjoy it that's fine: If they don't, that's ok too."

"When I am living passionately—with compassion—I'm living completely in the moment. I don't want to harm anyone. I feel content and filled up with great enthusiasm for life."

Sandesh may be contacted at spnaik@yahoo.com or through his website at www.bengalihypnosis.com

Chapter 11
Faith
Norma Seaward

"When I'm scared, but operating at my best, I can approach a goal or a project by imagining myself crossing a creek, with new stones rising up out of the water to meet me as I take each cautious step toward my goal and my safety on the other side."

Norma's passion for life and for greater spiritual meaning has carried her through the difficulties of painful life experiences, and her ongoing search to find personal worth and peace. A former teacher, Norma is also passionate about her creative endeavors, which include writing, music performance, and art. Our interview took place in a beautiful old farmhouse, nestled in the hills of West Glenville, New York. Norma has an adult daughter, Mehera, who is 24.

You've described your passion as a journey to tap into a deep connection to the Source or God. What impact does that connection have on your life?

"It makes all the difference. When I'm tuned in to God, in any way I'm able to experience a sense of well-being in all areas of my life. Everything's okay and I'm conscious that I have resources to help me.

I then become naturally inspired to creatively engage in projects where my efforts can contribute to the well-being of others."

'**When was the seed for this passion first planted within you**?

"Where teaching is concerned, I remember that I had an opportunity to tutor a fellow student in geometry, while in high school. She was very grateful for my help, believing it had enabled her to pass her regents exam. That really *lit me up!* I was able to make a difference in her life! The notion that I could actually help someone was also counter to my long-held belief that I was unimportant. As time went by, I became aware this student and I had connected in a real way, and that her success was in part, the natural outcome of that connection. This meant there was something inside me that had value. It felt wonderful. I've found that anything I can do to help someone else get close to their sense of value, helps me get closer too. Each opportunity to serve another is a gift that enables me to experience joy."

"A thread of wanting to be connected to God has run through my entire lifetime. As a little girl I viewed God as this benevolent guy on a throne, up in the clouds. I recall how my grandmother would take us to the local Catholic Church for Sunday mass and I would put my pennies in the collection basket. I had no idea what was going on, but I loved being in that church. When it was time to make my First Communion, I was very excited. Unfortunately Grandma passed away before that day came, and that was the end of my churchgoing, *and* my dreams of making my First Communion, since my parents were nonreligious people. It was very disappointing for me.

"While I was attending junior high school, my dad went through a personal spiritual transformation. As part of his searching, he explored many of the world's religions and spiritual practices, and began to practice various forms of meditation. As a result, his library contained books on St. John of the Cross, St. Thomas Aquinas, and even stories about the lives of the great Indian holy men. He and I would often take long walks and discuss spiritual matters. Looking back, I believe that had a big influence on me.

"Out of my desire for a personal connection to God, I'd often ride my bicycle to another town to attend a weekly church service. The pastor touched me deeply. He had a wide-open heart and didn't limit his sermons to the scriptures.

"When I was nine, we moved up to Rockland County, and everything changed for me. I felt a great sorrow around the loss of my old friendships, and for the next 11 years it seemed I was a square peg in a round hole—I just never seemed to fit in anywhere. One bright light in the darkness of that time, however, was finding that I loved being in the woods. Spending time with my cat and being out in nature was my solace. Our property butted up against the woods where a utility company had their pumping station, so I had quite a few acres of woods to enjoy. I loved climbing trees, watching the birds, and the peace and security that I felt there.

"Somewhere around the age of 13 I began to become very depressed. I was later told that it was largely hormonal. Puberty had hit and my stress level was high, especially at school, where it seemed I was being bullied all the time. I frequently felt suicidal, wanted to run away from home, and generally felt miserable most of the time. My mom would joke that, 'Norma's always been a yo-yo.' The school was aware of my depression and attempted to alert her, but mom's answer always seemed to be 'She's just going through a stage.' I have a buoyant personality, so, when I went to school, I forced myself to be cheerful, and my friends never saw my tears. My motto was: *Never let them see they're getting to you.* Despite all these difficulties, I always had the idea that God was the answer. So I kept going to church and by the time I'd finished my first year of college, I'd read just about everything in my Dad's library.

"I was launched into adulthood with very few life-skills. I never saw my parents hug or grieve, which I'm sure they did, but it was done behind closed doors. My mother was very insecure. She never let me do anything to gain domestic experience around the house. For instance, she would not let me touch her washing machine. Consequently I never learned how to operate it. When I got married and had to do laundry, I ruined a lot of clothes before I learned to separate the dark and white clothes. Mom had grown up with an abusive, bible-thumping father, and passed her insecurities and walking-on-eggshells strategy for getting along with my dad onto me. So, I learned to not 'rock the boat' and kept a very low profile.

"We also had very little money which meant we seldom bought new things. Spending money on myself or being a little frivolous is still a real challenge for me. We pretty much lived hand-to-mouth with nothing left over to buy things like music or a piece of nice clothing. Consequently, I grew up with the belief that I didn't deserve having nice things.

"I don't know if I'll ever completely shake those messages, but in the last four or five years I've come a long way in not letting those messages determine how I think and how I live my life.

"During college I discovered the mystic, Meher Baba, through my then boyfriend Ken, who became my first husband. For the next 10 years I read and absorbed all Baba's writings. I'll admit that I had a hard time with some of his ideas, such as *Don't worry—be happy.* That was real hard to grasp because I'd worried all my life. What I did learn from him, however, was that God isn't *out there* somewhere; He's as close to us as our own breath.

"But in those days I was emotionally numb. I'd married Ken, but our relationship did not work out and I was pretty much on my own as far as parenting went. We eventually divorced and I then went to work in a job corps program in Oneonta, New York. I taught employability skills to disadvantaged and at-risk youth from the inner cities. What I taught them encompassed respect, courtesy, well-being, tolerance for others, open-mindedness, and awareness. I made it a point to know all of the students who entered that school, whether they were in my class or not. I'd like to think I touched each of them in some way. My light really shone in that school and I loved those students. This was my work for the next 15 years.

"During this time I also suffered from long bouts of depression, sometimes taking a couple of years off before I was ready to resume work again. Despite my ability to teach competently, the work was very demanding for me, and coupled with being a single parent, I broke down emotionally and physically from time to time.

"So much of my life it seems, has been lived *on the edge.* In the past, I've been in and out of depression, even suicidal at times. These last few years, though, have truly been the best of times for me.

"In 1995 I began to read author and teacher, Carolyn Myss, and she had a major impact on me. She discovered, on her own spiritual journey, that she could offer her spiritual gifts to the world *and* also have the kind of life she wanted *and* not have to live in a monastery to accomplish that. She gave me hope that changing my beliefs could change my life for the better.

"I also attended my very first Meher Baba conference in September of 1982. At a workshop that weekend, a man talked about this inner *voice* that would talk to him and give him direction. Now here I was, still thinking that God's *up in the sky*, while this guy has God, or whatever spirit, speaking *to him!* That really lit me up! I remembered that as a kid I use to get this little tug or feeling inside that would motivate me to look in just the right place for something my mom had lost. That was one of the first experiences of this thing, *greater than me*, interacting with me in a way that I was conscious of. In nature—I can't explain how—I just knew in my bones that only a divine force could create a beautiful mountain or a tree. I had no clue as to how it all worked, but I wanted to understand it and get closer to this power. I have spent most of the years since, listening for that *voice*, and doing my best to follow its direction."

When did the idea of an inner God, or a greater power, first begin to emerge?

"The first memory that comes to mind took place while I was in junior high school. I was writing in my journal one night, trying to come to grips with the question every kid faces at some point: *What am I going to be when I grow up?* At that point, a deep awareness emerged that said *my life would be a journey of seeking an outer existence that would be in harmony with my inner truth.* (Tearing up)

"I've come to see that my challenge is to love myself enough to risk being who I really am. That meant that I would have to overcome a lifetime of decision-making based on expediency. In many ways I'd been a *wallflower* in my own life—afraid to step out. I'm 45 years old, and as I look back, my whole life has been a quest to truly be me!

"Now that's quite a contrast with this loud Italian, with the waving hands and big voice that I can be a good bit of the time. I mean I sang in the choir as a kid and you don't do that if you've got a *little* voice! So I go back and forth between quashing myself in order to fit in with people and then letting it all hang out until the *volume gets shut off again.* Nevertheless this enthusiasm or passion that I have is still there.

"Going back to the man who heard the *voice,* I recall that I asked him how he was able to hear it. He said, 'by listening and loving it.' So I then considered myself on a mission because I'm pretty headstrong and I don't listen very well. An incident that illustrates this mission occurred when my daughter was about two years-old. We went to a deli one day and I ordered a sandwich. When I received it, I was aware that I'd been undercharged by ten cents. The *voice* said, '*Norma, if you rip this lady off for ten cents, karma dictates that you'll be ripped off, yourself, at some point. Do you want that kind of Karma over ten cents?*' I responded *no* to myself and let the clerk know she had undercharged me. She looked at me like *I had two heads* but she adjusted the price. So I proceeded to the check-out and as I paid for my sandwich, my gaze shifted to my feet and there next to my right foot sat a shiny dime. I got it!

"Although I haven't always listened because of my fear, I've increasingly learned to pay attention to this *still, small voice* within me, especially where it concerns major decisions in my life. I'm encouraged because I trust that guidance, which I believe is God, more than ever, and I see that I'm okay when I do. I don't have to run out and get a psychic's *take* on my situation whenever I'm fearful.

"I've also experienced being in touch with this *source* or God, if you will, when I've been in the creative mode through my art, cooking, making clothes, decorating, gardening, and performing music. Once, I was coloring Easter eggs as a thunder and lightning storm approached.

Now, I had a life-long terror of storms like this; but in the midst of lightning flashing and thunder booming, I totally engaged with my artwork, and I was able to experience peace. From that time on, I've never been afraid of lightning and thunder. When I'm connected to this creative source I'm connected to God and all is well."

Norma takes me into another room to show me her latest piece of art: a wall hanging of various layers of fabric depicting a natural waterfall.

"I make art quilts, and use fabrics as my paints. This particular scene was inspired by a cliff-face I saw with this beautiful waterfall cascading over it. So I started with these strips of fabric to simulate the face of the cliff, the strata of the rock, and the cascading of the water. I've created about 20 pieces so far: some I've given away and some are hanging in art galleries in the area. I'm hoping to progress with this work and just see where it goes. I'm also aware that I have an old tendency to jump from one interest to another. I can begin a venture with great enthusiasm, but abruptly drop it or begin avoiding my project. Suddenly I notice it's been a week since I've worked on my piece. If I'm going to get deeper into my artwork where I'm truly creating art at a high level, I'll need to go deeper into myself, which means working on my *stuff*. To the extent that I'm afraid to be in touch with myself in a deep way, my art will be limited. My challenge is to trust that I'll be able to handle whatever comes. When I'm scared, but operating at my best, I can approach a project or a goal by imagining myself crossing a creek with new stones rising up out of the water to meet me as I take each cautious step toward the other side. A major challenge for me when I lack peace and serenity in my life, is remembering that I'm not separate from God unless I choose to be.

"The first time I experienced that I could create peace, without a spiritual teacher, was in 1998 when I began studying the Course in Miracles. I remember a prayer I read that I'll paraphrase: *In the stillness of my mind I sit knowing that you will not fail to answer me…*(chokes up) An incredible calmness opened up in me, as a result, and I had my first conscious connection to what I call the Source. Since then, I've been pursuing this serenity and discovering the roadblocks I throw up to prevent it.

"Today I'm very aware that all good comes from God. When I have a need I turn to Him. God is now tangible and something I can lean on and go to for guidance. That's a new step for me. I previously feared that what God wanted for me would not make me happy, so it's taken me a very long time to unlearn that idea.

"I've also become aware that my thoughts have power. Loving thoughts can strengthen me, while holding on to fearful thoughts can weaken me. Having just a few loving thoughts can overcome the fears I might encounter during a day. Back in the early 90s I was going through a very difficult time, actually feeling suicidal at times. One day on my drive home from work, feeling hopeless and defeated, I surrendered and said, '*Okay God, I'm letting go of trying to be happy. If I can help at least one other person in my lifetime, maybe I won't have been a complete washout.*' Suddenly I had a profound sense of joy. I realized that redirecting my thoughts toward bringing joy to others had the power to change my feelings and my outlook. That outlook has brought much more peace and happiness to me."

How does your ego challenge you on this journey you've chosen?

"When I accomplish something good, my ego wants to say 'Look at what I did! I'm great after all.' But the truth is, anything that I can point to and say, 'Wow that was really something;' if I'm being honest I have to admit it came *through me* not *from me*. I'm not really the one who pulls it off. If I don't acknowledge that, the bliss I feel will quickly fade away.

"I believe we all have the ability to be in touch with this deeper connection. Until we earnestly seek it, however, we spend a lot of time pursuing things like money and careers which don't really have the ability to give us what we want. When we decide to look inward, the connection to that power is right there, inside of us—waiting for our call."

What have you learned is required to live a passionate life?

"First, a great deal of courage! Living my truth and truly being myself is scary at times. I never quite know how people are going to react to me. Because it can become somewhat lonely when being *yourself*, it is important to find companions who also have the courage to be their unique selves. At the same time, it seems that when I am truly myself, other like-minded people will join me on this path. Paradoxically, it's taken me years to learn that when I am with my *true-self*, I am never really alone.

"There is a big difference for me between doing what I *have* to do every day just to pay my bills and gain some measure of success, and, feeling fully alive and passionate because I'm doing what I *love to do*. I believe we know that difference as young children, but it gets trained out of us. Little kids are so *lit* in kindergarten, and then by third-grade they only go to school because they have to. I am just like those children. I haven't always been able to know what I want because I'd never been allowed to really ask. Now I am claiming that right, and, as scary as that can be I am giving myself permission to find out who I really am, and what I really want. I'm allowing my passion and my inspiration to guide me."

How would you like the world to benefit from your journey?

"First of all I believe that all of our minds, the world over, are linked together. So the more that I can heal myself, the more love and non-exploitive cooperation I'm capable of bringing into the world. The world will benefit by my being a more peaceful, healing, and loving person. .

"To those who have the desire to for a more passionate life, I would say to not be afraid to feel the desire for something more. If you keep asking to find a way to lead a more passionate life, or a more fulfilling life, things will start to shift. You will meet people who will have a small piece of it, or a book will come to your hands. As you let yourself feel the desire for a greater life, the path will unfold before you.

"Pursuing what I love and appreciating each day makes my life worth living and is well worth the upheaval of any transition that I might be required to go through. Do I have to jump off a cliff to live this way? No.

All I need is a willingness to keep taking small steps in that new direction."

Norma may be contacted at **normaseaward@gmail.com**

Chapter 12
Gratitude
Bob LoBue

"After most Visions shows the audience jumps out of their seats cheering, applauding and thanking us. The Visions troupe, however, who have suffered great losses and pain in their own lives, always wants to thank the audience, because in serving them, they know they are serving the ONE who is carrying them all."

Robert LoBue or Bob L. as he is known to many of his close friends is the Author/Director/Producer of "Visions," a play depicting the story of drug and alcohol addiction from an insider's perspective. Over the past 19 years and despite having no previous experience as a writer, his play, performed mainly by volunteer actors,—recovering addicts and many who have lived in the orbit of those addicted—has offered hope to thousands of people in the Northeast who have lived with the destructive affects of addiction. Bob, a retired auto worker, lives in Ridgefield Park, New Jersey and is the father of Robert, 33 and Michelle 22.

"My great passion is to carry the message of recovery from drug and alcohol addiction through the medium of theatre. I'm particularly interested in getting this message of hope to those in the early stages of recovery. I'm soon to be 57 years old and this is definitely one of the finer things I've done in my life. My theatre program called *"Visions,"* depicts the journey from the despair of addiction to the light of recovery, using volunteer performers who now number over 400 members. The play has reached thousands of people: predominately in treatment centers, shelters, and prisons, but many in churches and community centers as well.

"Our acting company is strictly voluntary. As individuals we've declined media coverage just to keep our egos out the way. It's been my experience that if you put a microphone in an alcoholic or addict's hand, they're apt to forget and become *monsters* (laughing).

"Beginning in 1991, I've trained people from treatment centers, prisons, and homeless and battered women shelters to put on this production. It's been a healing process for all of them. Although most of our troupe was never on stage prior to this opportunity, they go where few actors would ever dare to go to put this play on: into prisons, treatment centers and hospitals, battered women shelters, and youth houses. Out of our own pockets we've accumulated about $10,000 worth of equipment. When we come into a location, we bring in staging and a very professional lighting and sound system—our equipment makes it look like we're putting on a rock concert! My techs have become very good at what they do. My lighting director is a one-legged amputee who believe it or not climbs up and down the ladder to adjust the lights. Many of my crew members had been caught in the talons of drug and alcohol addiction but other members have been afflicted with conditions such as HIV and mental illness. This is the Visions Troupe; a bunch of "rogue gypsies" that have been given an opportunity to carry a message of hope to the world.

"It's been a long, slow process for us to get recognized and invited to perform our play as much as we would like. The most effective publicity we've received has been one treatment center saying to another, 'you've got to see this play—they're able to emotionally move audiences of hard-core addicts.' If I took some of the media coverage that was offered, recognition probably would have been faster. On the other hand, if I had, I think my ego might have gotten in the way, and that would have hindered our mission. Most of the media was interested in sensationalizing our actor's lives—what drugs they did, what trouble they'd found themselves in, etc., while we have been mainly interested in providing a message of hope. At the same time we have had some wonderful coverage from sympathetic press and radio people who have respected the anonymity of the members of our troupe and audience, and focused their stories on the play. It took years before we were able to show our play to a thousand people, but as of today, over 30,000 people in six states have seen the play.

"For the last couple of years I've concentrated my energies on bringing the play to people who've been incarcerated for drug-related crimes. I feel so grateful to have had that opportunity. At New Jersey's Kintock Prison, we trained a group of inmates over three week's time, to perform Visions. It wasn't easy but the day came, I brought in one of my techs and our equipment, and we performed the play twice. One of the inmates, the man who played Tony the Pimp, one of the play's main characters, came up to me after the play and said, 'I will never forget you man.'"

Why do you think he said that?

"Well, these are talented people and like most recovering addicts and alcoholics, they have very intense feelings. They know what it is to experience isolation, shame, emotional *bottoms,* despair, or the joy of simply hugging a child, which so many of us take for granted. I find that actors who are not addicts have to dig much deeper for these feelings and some don't even have a clue about the experiences they're being asked to perform. I think this is also a dream come true for some of our actors—possibly fulfilling some deep aspirations to be on stage—to shine, to express themselves. Even more important, however, is the chance to give something back after having *taken* for so long. I think these people are very special. That's why this man said, 'thank you.' He shined, and many people complimented him that night. He was in the spotlight and it wasn't because he'd robbed someone! (Laughing) It was because he was reaching out.

"Most members joined our troupe after their release from prison or rehabilitation. There have been a few who didn't stay clean and a few have died over the years; but the majority of us have remained clean and sober. I don't attribute that solely to the play, but I do believe it's helped us. There's something about carrying the message of healing and recovery that makes a person feel whole again. I'm absolutely sure of that!

In 2006 after 15 years of traveling with the play into treatment centers, shelters, and prisons, and usually performing without a real stage, I took the play into an off-Broadway theatre, the Hudson Guild Theatre in the heart of New York City, for two—week runs in April and November. We had a real stage; theatre seats; real curtains; and dressing rooms—the whole bit. I formed a troupe with professional actors complimented by some of my Visions troupe's non-professional regulars. Among those attending were people from HIV groups, some 65 rehab and treatment centers, young mothers in need, as well as various adult and adolescent recovery groups. After each performance the actors would go out and connect with the people in the audience. It was an incredible experience!

"Most of the performances were sellouts, but roughly half of the tickets were given free of charge to treatment centers and shelters. I thank God that despite only charging $10 a ticket, we broke even financially. That was our goal from the beginning."

"Between the two runs we used over forty actors. One woman who was wheelchair-bound told us she wanted to act in *Visions*, and we said *absolutely*! She hopped up the steps, wheeled herself around the stage, and acted magnificently.

"Following these two runs, we performed the play in many different venues in upstate New York and New Jersey. In 2006 we did shows in 25 different venues; a real challenge because we have very little funding to offset our expenses.

"Except for the off-Broadway shows, we have never charged

anyone to attend a *Visions* performance. All we ask from our hosts is a pot of coffee and, if they can afford it, we might ask for gas or mileage expense for the truck. Whenever we can secure a site that will accommodate people, we notify treatment centers in that area, and their clients are bussed in to see a night of free recovery theatre. In Paramus, New Jersey, where we are right now, I rented a church hall and over 500 people came to see the play.

"After most *Visions* shows, the audience jumps out of their seats cheering, applauding and thanking us. Our troupe however, who have gone through great losses and pain in their own lives, always want to thank the audience, because in serving them, we know we are serving the ONE who has saved us.

"Throughout the 19 years of performing this play, and my 21 years of recovery there has been something profound I've continually experienced, but until now, just couldn't describe adequately. I believe God is very present during the play. We didn't know it in the beginning ourselves; all we knew was that it was our mission to perform this play. There's a scene in the play where a person hits a bottom in their addiction, and there's a lot of yelling and anger. Then suddenly the person's head is down, they've hit this ultimate bottom. You just know they're crying out silently for help. I call that moment the Great Silence. Then they have an awakening that's depicted through the use of music and lighting, and in silence they reach out and look into this magnificent light as they experience a spiritual awakening.

"After getting clean and sober, there were times when I would say, 'I can't get another guy sober' or 'I can't help her, I've got other commitments.' It seemed like too much to handle. I don't look at it that way any more. I believe that if I do the best I can, and say, *God, do whatever you will. I turn it over; I have no control,* God can work through me to help others as He worked through others to help me when I first came into recovery. Those days were my first tastes of what I call divine love, and that's where my passion for *Visions* comes from."

Where did your interest in theatre come from?

"When I was newly clean and sober, and working on the assembly line in a Ford Motor Company plant, I enrolled in a company-sponsored Dale Carnegie Course for public speaking. During one of the classes I got up, and, with everyone looking at me, told my personal story. Do you have any idea how long I sat down at the end of the bar waiting for somebody to ask me something? (Laughing) Nobody ever asked me anything! So after I spoke, they gave me a pen as a reward—it was a big deal and I was pretty darn good. I thought, *wow…I like this. I'm not hiding anymore!*

"After that, I realized I had a desire to be in theatre. I wanted to take an acting class, but a wise friend told me that I should wait awhile because I was newly sober. My wife was in early recovery herself, and my kids had suffered—one was very angry and one was still a baby. So I took his advice, waited a year-and-a-half and then joined a theatre group, took some acting lessons, and even landed a small part in a play. It was a murder mystery and at the end of the play, where the female lead gets killed, I carried her off the stage on my back while wearing a black hood. My part lasted about 5 seconds. I'd invited all my friends to come and see the play and later asked them how I was. They all said 'You were great!' (Laughing) I was so proud.

"Then I became interested in writing a play. So here I was working on the assembly line, mindlessly putting my boxes into the chutes as I did all day, every day, and trying to come up with an idea. Eventually I began to write about what it was like to be in the middle of addiction— from my own and from my family members' points of view. After writing a few pages, however, I became discouraged. I thought *I can't do this. I'm a failure at this just like I've failed at everything else in my life.* At that moment I got on my knees in the little metal cage I worked in, and said, 'God help me,' just as I had earlier done in my recovery. Once more something transforming happened to me. I became inspired again, and was able to finish the short script I'd been working on in a matter of days.

"At that time, I had no idea whatsoever about how to go about writing a play, but I'd made what I considered a rough draft and took it to my theatre group for their consideration. They said it was too harsh, too real, and not their cup of tea. Next I brought it to my theatre class at school and they basically said to forget about it. So I went home, despondent, and locked myself in my room. I questioned God. I said, 'God, this play is inspired. Why doesn't anyone like it?' Just then a friend came to the house, knocked on my door, and yelled, 'Bob, come on out of that room!' (Laughing) He wouldn't let me feel sorry for myself.

"What finally happened was that the play found its way into the hands of one of my recovering buddies, who passed it on to a twelve-step convention committee who loved it and suggested I perform it at their next convention, four months down the road. I thought *Wow, this is terrific! But I don't know any actors and I don't know how to direct or produce a play.*

"So I started by renting rehearsal space and then choosing friends of mine, from among the recovering people I knew, to audition for the roles. I remember saying, 'You'd be great for this part'...and 'You'd be perfect to play William the alcoholic bum'...and in this way I formed a nucleus of 20 actors.

"By September of 1991 we were ready to go. I remember that we were two days away from the convention and *Visions* needed to be tested. So the night before its first performance, I took the play to Integrity House, a long—term drug treatment facility, in Secaucus, New Jersey. We did two performances that night (the play was only 25 minutes long at that point) and when we finished, this huge man in the audience was just weeping like a baby. He hugged me and told me the play reminded him of all the wrongs he'd done to his son. Many in the audience hugged us, and several people were in tears. I could only say, 'Oh my God!' I was stunned. When we finally performed at the convention the next day, the reaction was similar.

"In the 19 years since, *Visions* has evolved to an hour-and-fifteen minutes in length and is comprised of a collage of raw and wrenching scenes that depict the journey from active addiction to recovery. Over the years, the actors themselves have suggested and added some vignettes from their own lives:

We watch Jim steal money from his wife's purse so he can buy drugs.

We are introduced to Monique, a young hooker who is HIV positive from intravenous drug use. There is Joan, a victim of domestic violence, and her young son Bobby, who turns to drugs to escape the reality of his home life. And there are others, each of them piercingly portraying some aspect of addiction. To many in the audience, these actors are mirrors, while to others they are omens.

"*Visions* is a cautionary tale, but it is also a tale of hope. In the first scene we hear a voice singing "*I shall be released,*" and we are given a ray of hope that these characters will move into the light of recovery. That hope is realized as individually, they move into that light, and finally all come together at a twelve-step meeting.

"Everyone in addiction and recovery has their own unique story, but what's clear in the play is that they all share the common emotions of anger, loneliness, sadness, and denial. The emotions are what the audience connects to, and most of the time my intuition—a gift that I'm truly blessed to have—enables me to choose the right people for the roles. They really *know* their character and that particular scene in a very deep and personal way.

"One of my personal ego challenges is thinking that I'm been putting this play on for 19 years yet I've only reached 30,000 people. I think *why haven't I reached more people?* When that happens I have to go back to my original intention which is: *If I and my cast do the best we can, in an unselfish way, God can use us!* I believe that He's using not only me but all 20 members of our troupe as a channel or as some sort of prism through which He creates an intervention with our audiences.

"I don't know if I would get the healing that happens between the audience and the cast using only professional actors. The deepest desire for actors from the *Visions* troupe is to be part of the healing for those who attend the play. I think the primary agenda for the professional actors is about being recognized for how good their performance happens to be although they have told me the play was a wonderful experience for them. Each night when the play ended, the members of the cast who were in recovery, would go out to mingle with the audience. The professional actors, however, were timid about doing that until I encouraged them to give it a try. Once they did begin to mingle they found they liked it, and thereafter were out there after each performance. No one in the audience ever asked these hired actors or the volunteer actors if they were addicts or not—they just hugged them in gratitude for the performance they gave.

"Recently I became aware how our audiences, many from shelters and prisons, are giving me the opportunity to serve the God in them. That's unbelievable! It's taking me a while to get used to that thought. It's a very Eastern way of thinking.

"I've been inspired over the years by the teachings of Meher Baba, an Eastern spiritual master, who has followers all over the world. His philosophy and writings have helped me tremendously with the *Visions* play and in my relationships with my volunteers. Meher Baba stayed in silence for 44 years, had no attachment to money, lived with humility, and wrote only of love. I'm continuously fascinated by his writings and do my best to follow his teachings in my life. I grew up in an Italian Catholic family. My dad was a barber, I had two brothers, and we had pretty good family ties. But, in my 20s, as I was seeking spiritual answers, I became involved in studying some Eastern faiths. Today I believe there is only one God, and all religions are sources of the truth.

"In 1993, we were invited along with others from various fields to the Governor's mansion in New Jersey where we were awarded the State of New Jersey's Volunteer award for the Arts and Humanities.

"The play has received accreditation, for professional training, from the Addiction Professional Certification Board of New Jersey as well as from five other states. In 2001, our troupe received the Presidential Points of Light award from President Bush. Then in September of 2002, I took the play to Washington D.C. where it was performed at the Rayburn Room of the House of Representatives in an effort to secure more funding for alcohol and drug prevention and treatment. I'm not sure what kind of a difference we made, if any, but I'm proud that 22 of us made it there and performed the play. We'd gone from staging *Visions* in shelters and prisons to now performing at the Rayburn Office Building. You have to remember this occurred shortly after the 9/11 terrorist attack in New York and Washington; so when we told security that we had prop guns for use in the play, they searched our truck and took the guns away. We were forced to improvise by using our fingers. (Laughing) I think we did make some impact. People in the fields of policy, health, and addiction treatment now knew we existed, and maybe had a better understanding of the journey of recovery.

"In 2003, after 31 years, I retired from Ford Motor Co. in order to put more time into pursuing this passion. Following that, I was invited down to the West Virginia University Medical School in Morgantown to train a group of medical professionals and social workers to perform the play. The counselors who were present received graduate credits in Behavioral medicine and counseling. Later that year I was invited by the Catholic Archdiocese of Lansing, Michigan to train 20 of their parish representatives to perform *Visions.* Subsequently, they went on to perform the play for their congregants. At the end I was truly amazed and grateful to be in this position."

"In 2004 we gained tax-exempt status, which led to some small contributions to our troupe. Previously, I hadn't wanted to accept any big donations because I didn't want to have to use tax lawyers and everything that goes with that. Any income we do get goes to outreach, equipment, truck maintenance, and gas. In 19 years, *Visions* has never made any money and I would guess that I've probably spent $60,000 to $75,000 of my own money. But hey, everybody has some kind of hobby; for some people it's guns or fishing—for me it's *Visions*! (Laughing)

"After five years of sobriety, my wife resumed drinking and in time we divorced. That was very difficult for the children. They split their time between the two of us. I later hooked up with my very first girlfriend from 25 years earlier, and in due course we were married and settled in Teaneck, New Jersey. Things however began to go wrong for us and eventually we divorced. So I'm single again and living with my daughter in Ridgefield Park, New Jersey.

"Earlier you were saying how passion can turn into an obsession and I think at times during my marriage that happened with my involvement with *Visions*. It can be pretty intoxicating when people are telling you that your work is moving them and making a difference in their lives. I went overboard at times, but there were other issues between my ex-wife and I which I'd rather not talk about here.

"All in all John, life is not bad. Some days I don't get up until 10:00 o'clock! (Laughing) I have my daughter living with me and I have great friends. Sometimes I'm not all that well in the head. (Laughing) In fact I went to a retreat one day and the facilitator gave me a coin and announced me as *Bob Lobotomy* instead of Bob L.(Laughing) Some of my friends then started referring to me as *Lobotomy Bob*. How're you gonna get rid of that nickname?

"I wish I could say that as a result of me being clean and sober, everyone around me is better. Sadly, that's not the case. I've had to deal with addiction and its effects in my family and in others close to me. Sometimes I wonder why this *addiction thing* isn't over and done with. I don't have an answer; it's just the way it is I guess."

What has your journey with Visions taught you about Bob?

"I've learned that I have the gift of insight into people, and in the process, I've been able to see the real worth of human beings. I've also learned that I might be a decent guy: I'm not a bum like I once thought I was. I've discovered that I have feelings for myself and for others. When Bill Wilson (one of the co-founders of A.A.) visited Carl Jung (1875-1961), the great Swiss psychiatrist and thinker, Jung told him that he believed the alcoholic's thirst, in reality, was a spiritual thirst that had got lost on the way 'home.' To me, this means that the alcoholic and the addict are highly spiritual souls who got lost in alcohol and drugs and then pursued those things with a passion. I think addiction is as much a spiritual illness as it is anything. The founders of AA knew that if they were able to remove the booze from their lives, the desire to search for meaning would still be there—questions like: *Who am I? Where am I going?* So the Twelve Steps, a way to help alcoholics get on the right path, came out of that spiritual thirst.

"In 1976, in the midst of my addiction, I went off on an alcoholic bender when the girl who I was planning to marry traveled to India and wrote me, telling me that she had found true happiness in the teachings of a spiritual teacher She was basically saying goodbye to me. When I heard this, I went out and bought myself a 750 Bonneville Triumph Motorcycle, and one night, despondent and angry, I went barhopping and became very drunk. Around 4:00a.m., after being thrown out of a couple of bars for causing trouble, I got on my bike, and just *opened it up.* I hit 80 mph as I sped through the city streets. I was so mad at God! As I roared through the city I lost myself and imagined that I was a knight on a charger, challenging God himself to just wipe me out.

"The last conscious thing I remembered was seeing a light. It turned out to be the head light of an oncoming car. My next memory was coming to, as people were trying to wake me up. The bike was 100 yards down the street and I had somehow ended up underneath a parked van. All I knew at that point was that I was *so* tired, and just wanted to sleep. People at the scene however were telling me not to sleep—they were afraid I'd die if I did. When I arrived at the hospital, the doctors had already put metal plates in my arm and told my parents that I *might not make it.* I had head, leg, and arm injuries, as well as internal bleeding. I did survive, but it was close to a year-and-a-half before I was able to return to work.

During that time I drank alcohol like there was no tomorrow—like each drink was my last. On the Thanksgiving Day prior to my entering treatment I was arrested for Domestic Violence. My wife had called the police because I was drunk and attempting to break down the front door in my own house. I was insane! Following my arrest I was jailed. At one point the inmates tried to shove my head into a toilet bowl because I was banging on the bars and screaming that I was going to kill everybody. The guards broke it up, thank God. Later that day, in desperation, I got down on my knees and prayed to God for help. Almost immediately, I experienced a wonderful sense of peace, which I had not felt in a very long time. That event is actually one of the vignettes in the *Visions* play.

"In spite of the tragedy of what happened that day, it was a blessing for me because God gave me what I couldn't give myself—the chance to see the truth about myself and my situation. Before that, I felt certain that I would die the way I was living. That time in jail was my spiritual *bottom* and the beginning of my sobriety.

"During the years, when I was acting out my jail scene—I no longer play the role—and I'd be on my knees, I could feel it! I could feel God's presence and I could hear the audience reacting to what I was going through. Some nights it's like a church revival meeting. The audience will be relating personally to the vignettes and urging our actors on. I also recognize God's presence by the audience letters we get and in the way people hug us after the show. I feel so blessed."

How do you stay on track with your Mission and not get overwhelmed or sidetracked?

"For one thing, I'm calmer today in promoting Visions. There was a time when, not only was I spending a lot of my own money on the show, but I was spending 40 to 50 hours a week of my personal time promoting and performing *Visions*. It was do…do…do! I was going all the time. Today I feel more connected to the spiritual source that guides me with *Visions.* That's very exciting to me. I also have to look at the reality of my ideas. When I think, *I'm going to take Visions all around the world;* I have to ask myself how reasonable that thought really is. *Where am I going to get the money to take 20 people on a tour of Canada? With the effort I'll expend, is it worth it?* I guess I'm maturing. (Laughing)

"Balance is the key for me—especially in dealing with this part of my life that feels so wonderful. I have a nice girlfriend, and spending quality time with her is important for me, as is the time I spend with my friends in recovery—talking, sharing, and supporting one another. I've also learned that I need time away from the play. I love to work in my garden, read good books, spend some time fishing and even take time to work out. I need time alone these days. My garden is small but I have a table and chair set up in the middle and I'll sit there and feed the birds who visit me. I need that time to be present. I've always felt that *Visions* has been a gift to me so one of the ways I stay grounded has been through my involvement in the addiction recovery program that I continue to attend and that has saved my life.

"I also don't consider myself cured. Staying teachable and humble, taking life one day at a time, and being around the people who inspire me and give me hope, help me to stay in alignment with the message of recovery that I bring to others through *Visions*. I mean how could I *pick up* again and still bring this play to people? I'd be living a lie!"

What does the future hold for you Bob?

'Well, I've had a long-time dream of making a film. If it happens, it happens; if not it'll be OK. In October 2008, I travelled to Topeka, Kansas and trained a group of volunteers in to do outreach with the play. Now the *Visions* play will echo in the heart of America.

"When this is all over, I'll go fish! I often say to God, 'How come it's not over? When it's over, let me know and I'll be done.' (Laughing)

"Every once in a while in my very human mind I get to thinking, 'I could be on Oprah and we'll be seen by millions.' On other days, I can imagine God saying, *Oh Bob, could you give me a hand? I'm kind of busy this week.* "(Laughing*)*

"Seriously, I've received so many benefits beyond the wonderful citations and awards and praise we've received. I've made many, many new friends but best of all, I know it's not over."

POSTSCRIPT—In 2009 Karl Bardosh, award winning director, producer, and writer of short films and documentaries began work on a documentary film of the Visions play and its outreach. It is scheduled to be finished in the spring of 2010.

Robert LoBue—contact and info at www.visionsrecoveryplay.org or at rlobue@peoplepc.com

Chapter 13
Loving Freely
Jackie Hawkins

"Recently, I had an opportunity to publicly perform a song, based on a poem I'd written, and even though I was nervous and a bit apprehensive, once I got up there and really did it I thought, Oh, my goodness…what a high! It was another way for me of channeling love, and feeding this passion of mine, and it was a demonstration of God working through me. It's been my experience that, spiritual passion is God working through me in a way that just sends me to another place."

When Jackie enters a room her, graceful presence, dancing eyes, and uninhibited friendliness and laughter can literally wake up any gathering of people. Her passion for expressing love is evident in her warm smile, her deeply held beliefs about spirituality, and in her caring thoughts and actions for others. Jackie, mother of an adult son, Demond, lives in Schenectady, New York, and is currently employed as a Deputy Comptroller in the Human Resources Department of the New York State Comptroller's Office. She sat for this interview at Unity Church in Albany, New York, where she is a member of the Board of Trustees.

"Thus far God has blessed me with having 57 years on this planet. My birthdate is December 20, 1949, so whenever this book comes out the readers can do the math to figure out how old I am. (Laughing) I'm the third of four children—the second girl, and I have two brothers as well. I was born in Troup, a small town in east Texas, not far from the Louisiana state line, an area of oil and cotton fields; and during my adolescence, much segregation and discrimination.

"The modern-day Civil Rights movement—in its prime during the 50s and 60s—and Brown v Board of Education in 1954, were very important events in those years. In Longview, Texas where I mainly grew up until I was 16, the schools were segregated. Not until the Civil Rights Act of 1964 was there any real opportunity for me and other black children in Texas to experience an integrated educational environment.

"My father was a Baptist minister during my youth, and prior to his call to ministry had been a High School teacher and principal. My mom was a music teacher. As you might imagine, that really did inform my way of being and thinking as a young black girl growing up in the 1950s.

"In my junior year of high school, my father was called to be the minister of a church in Lansing, Michigan, so off we went to Lansing, Michigan. Initially we lived in East Lansing where I was thrust into an all-white world. That was a huge shock to me. It took me a while to be able to handle that. Outwardly it probably appeared that I was handling it very well but, internally I was experiencing stomach problems and emotional turmoil. I was 16 years old, and aside from the race issue, I was adjusting to a new school, attempting to make new friends, and making the shift from the South to the North. It was difficult for me most of the time.

"My father, in his commitment to being a religious and community leader, as well as a civil rights activist, instilled in me a passion for helping others, doing the right thing, and for making my voice heard— though softly, because my father was a very humble and kind man. He was also very passionate and had strong convictions for what he believed to be right. He was convinced God had put him on this earth to help others find their way. So looking at my father as a role model and seeing him as the kind of person that I wanted to grow up to be, I formed and nurtured a profound passion for caring about people, loving them, and not being shy about showing that I cared.

"I guess you could say I've always been a 'people person,' someone who believed that I was put on this earth for a purpose. Early on in my life I didn't always know what that purpose was, but as I've grown into adulthood and have been involved in just a whole host of community activities, I've come to realize that my mission is to do my part to advance human development—especially by helping young people, and in particular young women of color, find their way by *going within* to discover who they are. I do that by sharing with them how I've *gone within* to find what my core being or essence is, and what a difference that has made in my life.

"For me, that happened when I began attending Unity Church about a decade ago. I immediately felt as if I'd come home. It spoke to my very being. It spoke to my core—it said, *YES*, God *is* love and truly loves everyone without regard for gender, race, and ethnicity. I learned that God is not a vengeful or punishing God; He loves all of us and we're all part of this great human mosaic. I now believe each of us is here to love one another and to insure that we protect everything that is good. In fact I believe everything God has created is good. When people do negative things or things they wouldn't ordinarily do, I believe they've become disconnected from their true identity; that is, to their *Christ* within or spiritual self, if you will. I admit that it did take me awhile to disengage from the Baptist Church, but when I found Unity I truly found my spiritual home.

"Getting back to my passion, it includes caring about how people learn, and helping them to realize who they really are so that they have the chance to develop their full potential.

"When I was a young girl growing up in Longview, Texas, in addition to my parents and family, I was fortunate enough to have a number of people in the community who cared deeply about me. One, who demonstrated just how much she cared about me and the other girls, was my 4-H leader, Jeanetta Probasco. I will always remember her as a tender and kind person who expressed her love for us without any reservation. Our energy was high—we were, after all, 8-to10-year-old girls—but she knew how to redirect that energy. When we'd make mistakes she also knew how to correct us in the most loving of ways. This woman did not have children, but she and her husband, a very kind man, opened their house up to us. Mrs. Probasco took the time to teach us life skills like sewing, cooking, caring about each other, how to redirect our anger, and how to work together as a team. How she related and worked with us left a very deep impression on me, and I loved her *so much*. At the same time she was teaching me these life skills, she was also showing me how to be a human being in a way I think all of us are meant to be. That is, she taught us to love unconditionally regardless of a person's *station* in life, what has happened to them, or what their socioeconomic status is. My father and mother then reinforced these principles at home, and in the way they lived *their* lives.

"Mrs. Probasco also showed me that an adult could *give back* to the community by loving its children. When I became an adult, I then had the opportunity to do the same thing. My first two years of college were spent at Spelman College, a women's college with a predominately African-American student body in Atlanta Georgia. To show you how much of an influence Mrs. Probasco had on me, I majored in Home Economics and my first professional job was as a Cooperative Extension agent for a home economics program. So *I* then taught 4-H leaders, who in turn would teach skills to 4-H'ers in *their* programs, and the cycle would go on. Later on Mrs. Probasco found out that I had become a home economics program leader, which made her proud and I believe helped her to understand what an effect she had on me.

"As a 4-H leader, I lived and breathed my work and, even though I would become one of the first African-American 4-H leaders in Schenectady County, I was able to impart my passion for working with youth to the broader community. I was also able to create a presence in the African-American community and provide an opportunity for African-American youth in Schenectady's inner city to have exposure to 4-H. For those who participated, 4-H gave them a sense of possibility and potential for their lives that they may have never considered before.

"Through 4-H, I was able to start an outreach to the African-American youth community and have an impact, because programs of this sort had never been attempted before. With the aid of a grant that had been given to Cooperative Extension I was able to partner with Hamilton Hill Arts Center to start an inner-city photography program. Young participants were given disposable cameras with which they took pictures and then entered their work in a photography show. I felt happy and proud to have had the chance to help them, and see what a positive experience it had been in their lives. Within a couple of years we were able to build a dark room at the center. Later on, I was chosen to be on the board of directors of the arts center, which enabled me to continue my work there and again be able to share my passion for the arts and for youth development in a way that I never would have thought possible.

"Quite frankly you can trace it all the way back to when I was a 4-H'er myself, and someone took the time to guide me in developing my potential."

What was the experience at Cooperative Extension like for you?

"It was absolutely thrilling. I have to tell you that it did not feel like work. At the time my husband would get angry at me, complaining that I was always working. What I was doing however did not feel like work to me because I was doing something that was very much a part of who I was, and at the same time, was having a positive effect on others. I knew it was meaningful.

"Jeanetta Probasco had taught me life skills as a young girl, but my father instilled in me, my sister, and brothers, by his example and words, that we had an obligation to give back to the community. Therefore I knew that part of my purpose in life was to give back. I was fortunate later on, to discover my passion for working with youth, not only with 4-H and the Hamilton Hill Arts Center, but through my sorority, Delta Sigma Theta, which I joined in 1996. I found that one of the committees I wanted to be involved with was the youth committee that reached out to young people in the community.

"I knew I wanted to work with young girls, 6 to11, because at that age, they're very impressionable, which gives you a chance to have a big impact on their lives. These girls, primarily from African-American families, come from all walks of life—some have very little, while some are middle class. As a result, some of the girls need a lot of attention, while others don't need as much. Regardless I found it was really important that the principles and ideas I exposed the girls to, were introduced in such a way that all of them had an opportunity to *get it*. These were values that really counted and would be significant to their development as young women.

"We call our program *The Delta Pearls* and we meet one Saturday a month, from 9:30a.m. to 4:00p.m., and typically get together at the State Museum, the Albany Academy for Girls, or some other supportive environment.

"I'm in charge of some of the programs, so I can decide which programs we'll use during our meetings. We have reading programs where we choose books for the girls to read, talent shows where we set the criteria for the types of music and dance that they might use, Women's History programs in March, outings to African American Family Day at RPI in February, and fashion shows that the girls will prepare themselves for, typically in the spring. Our organization also invites women in to speak to the girls on a variety of topics. We've had the mothers of some of the girls, as well as women from the sorority and the community, speaking about their careers as professional African-American women, so that the girls can see what these women have overcome in order to succeed in the professions they work in, and understand the many options they have for their own lives.

"We believe they also need to have a sense of their cultural history, so that's why we stress the importance of reading. When they first come into the meeting each month, we'll spend time reading from pre-selected and age-appropriate books.

"We also provide classes, for example, on designing their own sweatshirts, which provides for creative self-expression and a sense of ownership. Several of them are musically inclined, and others have amazing talents as poets and speakers, while some may have to be coaxed a little. We'll often partner those who are more confident in these ways with girls who might be less developed in self-expression or in reading.

"So we're teaching them teamwork and the importance of helping others—that it's not all about *me*. So there's a leadership component in what we offer them.

"Of course we also have fun activities as well. We took them to the Great Escape amusement park during the summer, and just a couple of weeks ago we traveled to New York City to see the Broadway show, "Beauty and the Beast," preceded by a visit to the Forest Gump Restaurant. Later we did a little shopping. Again it was fun, enlightening, and a cultural experience, all very important components in shaping the life of a young girl.

"Passion, I think, can be negative, but mine is positive. I would describe my passion as a positive, innate drive. Passion is something that I really don't believe you can control or create. It comes from within and has always been there. It can only be nurtured. A person can discover their passion whenever they become aware of a *spark* or a feeling of excitement coming from something they encounter or become involved with.

"Anyone who claims to be passion-less has just not connected to their passion. The *Christ within,* or the spirit, is always there but a person is not always connected to it. All of us are forever seeking, whether we articulate it or not, experiences that are pleasurable, feel good, and will give us a real sense of life. What we're really seeking, in my view, is the Christ or God, or your love if you will, and when we're able to join with that energy and stay with it, it will continue to grow and expand."

What is the biggest obstacle you've found to staying focused on your passion and your life purpose?

"Probably all the things that society dictates that I *should* be: *Since you have your education you should be doing___; Since you're an African-American female and you're educated you should be* *doing___; You should be earning $___ a year; etc…*It's those outer expectations that can be very seductive for me.

"When I'm "out there" and disengaged spiritually, which happens from time to time, I can tell I'm *off* by the sheer exhaustion I feel. Something will usually give me a sign—physical, emotional, or mental—that tells me I'm not right.

"What will then anchor me are prayer and my connection with God. My exposure to organized religion through my father gave me a strong spiritual foundation growing up, even though I no longer believe a lot of what I was taught at that time. (Laughing) I was positively influenced by growing up in the caring and loving environment of the church. Every Wednesday, Friday, Saturday, and Sunday I was in church, and the summers meant Vacation Bible School, and the regional and state congresses. All those church activities gave me a real feeling of being loved. I can always go back to that; I can always feel that; and those very positive teachings that I received in the church continually gave me a sense of comfort and grounding. As time has passed, however, I've built on that earlier spiritual foundation. Once I discovered Unity Church I knew I'd found my spiritual home or wellspring, because it gave me the spiritual sustenance through meditation, the teachings, courses, and spiritual principles that keep me going in a way that nothing else has ever done.

"One of my passions is teaching. The work I do with the *Delta Pearls* at our monthly meetings is a type of teaching. Although I don't teach formally, with the exception of a little teaching I did at the university, I've found that teaching is a way of giving back or passing it on. I love, for example, to be a platform assistant at church on Sunday. I will think about what I want to say and the prayer I will use. Then I'll write it out. I love helping people to center themselves so they can receive the message that will follow. Doing that feels so good! That preparation centers me and that gets my blood flowing and my heart pumping—it gives me a true high!

My day job is Deputy Comptroller for Human Resources and Administration at the New York State Comptroller's Office. People there see my passion in my work—*it leaks out*. All of the people issues and concerns are my responsibility, as is all of Human Resources and Administration. Colleagues of mine as well as employees often come to me for counsel. It's nothing I advertise, but because I express my love freely and naturally, I become a magnet for people who need to talk with someone. Again, it's another way of expressing my passion. Often I haven't been aware that I was expressing what God has generously given me—my love for humanity—until someone has publicly called me their conscience, or their therapist, or their counsel."

It seems like that could be a lot to handle.

"If I were to think about it, it would, but I don't. I just let God take care of it. My volunteer work with the girls brings me as much or more joy as my day job. As an example: one of the most wonderful things that happened to me was when a grandmother of one of the Delta Pearls said 'Nzinga always talks about Miss Jackie, and says she's her favorite.'

"When I heard that I was so touched and surprised because I never thought I was having that kind of effect on the girls.

"Recently I had an opportunity to publicly perform a song based on a poem I'd written, and even though I was nervous and a bit apprehensive, once I got up there and really did it I thought, *Oh, my goodness…what a high!* It was just another way for me of channeling love, and feeding this passion of mine. It was also a demonstration of God working through me. It's been my experience that, spiritual passion is God working through me in a way that just sends me to another place."

Jackie Hawkins can be contacted at jhawkin1@nycap.rr.com

Chapter 14
Giving the Best of Me
Ruth Alsop

"I believe it's important for human beings to continue to develop and evolve. We weren't made to stagnate or stand still. I don't want to go out of this world saying 'I was a blob, I stayed a blob, and I'm leaving a blob!' I want to hear at least one person say, 'Ruthie helped me, she gave me some joy.'

There may be *snow on the roof,* but in the sparkling eyes and heart of Ruth Alsop there exists an ageless and joyful child who dances and plays her way through life, always looking forward to her next adventure. Ruth lives in a 200-year-old Victorian home in a pastoral setting on the outskirts of Saratoga Springs, New York where we met for this interview. She also maintains an apartment in New York City, where she is a cellist for the New York City Ballet Orchestra during the spring and summer. Through her performing, teaching, and her volunteer work, Ruth gets to express her zest for life, and brings joy to many people. Ruth is the proud mother of Marin Alsop, the conductor for the Baltimore Symphony Orchestra.

"I guess you could say that I feel passionate and excited about my whole life. I've had rough times, but so has everyone else, and we all find a way to get through them. I'm going through a divorce now, and it's painful because I feel very hurt by someone I've really loved, and in fact still do. One of the most difficult aspects of this divorce from Lamar is that I performed so often with him. At times I felt sorry for him, because I always performed as a *professional*, and not as his wife. I would say, 'that's out of tune' and he would take it as his wife criticizing him. I think our musical partnership was more difficult on him than it was on me.

"I've been a cellist for close to 70 years now. I'm the fourth of five Irish-American children. My father was an immigrant. He was largely unschooled, but he *adored* music, so I became the one he chose to learn the cello. The family story is that when I was an infant I would scream each time he listened to the old radio show, *I Love a Mystery*, until he would eventually shut it off. The theme song was a Sibelius piece (*Jean Sibelius, 1865-1957, Finnish composer),* and it's ironic that I now love that piece of music and often play it in my work.

"So he bought me a little cello when I was six. I was already taking piano lessons at the time in school and that's really what I *loved* and wanted to be, a pianist. But he brought this half-size cello home, and he found me a teacher for, I think, 50 cents a lesson. I remember she had to carry the cello for me because I was so little. My mother didn't have another 50 cents for piano lessons so I had to give that up. My siblings were also playing instruments, but not very well. I would still teach myself piano and could play rings around them, and in fact I learned to play all the instruments they were playing better than they could, so I was learning that I had talent.

"We lived in Melrose, a small town outside of Boston, Massachusetts. At the time there were very few young people my age playing instruments seriously, but I just kept with it. Throughout my high school years during which World War II was going on, I would travel to Boston and play in orchestras with a lot of older musicians. Boston was only nine miles away, but I think it took roughly an hour-and-a-half to get there. I was a little kid traveling alone, at night, on subways and busses to get to Boston, but I was fine. Nobody paid me much attention one way or the other.

"At that point, I wasn't sure that playing the cello was what I really wanted to do—the piano always stayed in the back of my mind. But I did know it was music I wanted…I always knew!"

How did you know that?

"Oh! In my dreams I'd be singing. I'd be moving. I'd be dancing. I mean music was in me and I couldn't get away from it.

"Along the way a lot of kooky things happened. One time, I heard they needed someone to play the glockenspiel in the town's public high school band. I was attending the Catholic school in town at the time, but I volunteered and they let me play it, without having had any lessons on the instrument. The love for music and the ability to play was just always there.

"When I graduated from high school, I won a scholarship to the New England Conservatory of Music in Boston, but instead decided to attend Manhattanville College in New York City. Although I was aware of my talent, I knew I wasn't as good as I should be, because I didn't have the schooling I needed, nor did I practice all that much. I had a good time growing up. I wasn't home practicing every day. My father, who was so musical, was away in the Army, so he wasn't around to push me musically. He was the second-in-command at Fort Devens, an Army base at the time, and was able to arrange for famous musicians like Jascha Heifetz, the world famous violinist, to come and play concerts at the Officers Club there. I wasn't invited since I was attending school, but Dad would always tell me how wonderful the performers were.

"I got more serious in college and was able to earn a music degree from Manhattanville. Following graduation, and a few years of study with a private teacher, I got to study under a really famous teacher by the name of Luigi Silva. I then went on, with Luigi's urging, to the Julliard School of Music to work on my master's degree. I didn't finish because I got a call to audition for Arthur Judson, the biggest manager of classical concerts in the country, and the head of Columbia artists.

"I won the audition for this important job, but I didn't really know what I was doing! I went out on *the trail* and played solos as well as being part of a Chamber Music Trio. We toured for about three years and because of my schedule, I had to withdraw from Juilliard, since they didn't allow for such lengthy absences. I saw my touring as a benefit for them in the sense that they'd be getting favorable publicity. Unfortunately, they didn't see it the same way. (Laughing)

"During the time I was touring, I learned so much about performing. I was initially very nervous, but I learned to get over that the 'hard way,' which was to just get up there and perform until the fear began to lessen. We toured all of the United States and Canada. It was a wonderful experience. We were young American musicians and our shows *sold*. I was 21 and I didn't realize how prestigious our performances were. This man had said, 'Sign this contract,' and I said 'sure.'—What did I know? Later on I would learn more about the business end of things.

"During this period I had a boyfriend, Lamar, who was a violinist, and later became my husband. He was from Salt Lake City, Utah. He was studying music in New York. Between tours he and I got hired at Radio City Music Hall as part of their orchestra, which only employed three women at the time. The organization was very chauvinistic in those days, so we women would seclude ourselves in a little room and not bother the men. Lamar and I eventually married and worked together a lot in New York. I continued with the trio until I left after giving birth to my daughter, Marin. I continued to play in the orchestra at Radio City, which did four shows a day, seven days a week. I was a substitute though, so I could come and go. Some days I would ride home on somebody's motorcycle—through Central Park between shows, and take care of the baby. It was really crazy at times.

"I also started teaching at this time, and really enjoyed teaching someone how to be musical and 'do what they heard.' It's very difficult to transfer what you hear into what you do.

"Lamar and I bought a house in Westchester. The local church needed an organist, and, without really knowing what I was doing, I filled that role. When Marin was three I started her on piano—she had no choice. She would ask her playmates, 'What does your mother or father play?' (Laughing) She thought everyone played music. She eventually graduated to the violin when she was six or seven. There was always music in our house. When we had company we played chamber music. So Marin was constantly surrounded by music. I guess I wanted her to experience what I didn't have as a child. My mother was absolutely tone-deaf, and dad was away in the Army for a big part of my childhood. So I enrolled Marin at Julliard School of Music when she was eight. I would drive her in at 7:00 a.m. every Saturday morning and come home and teach, and then go back and pick her up when she was finished. At that time, I also started subbing as a cellist with the New York City Ballet Orchestra and I also did a lot of playing and performing in-between subbing for Broadway shows. 'Golden Boy' with Sammy Davis Jr. was one show that sticks out in my mind from that time period. As you can tell it was a very busy time.

"Once my daughter went to school full time, I returned to studying with coaches and anybody else I could learn from. I wanted to be better, to play up to my potential."

Why was that important to you?

"Well, I think that's the essence of any success, if you know you're capable of doing better. There will always be people around you who are more skilled than you, but if you're really observant and open, you can learn from them. You can grow. You can reach another level, and this process of learning goes on and on if you want it to. For example, I received an *education* last night by attending a concert by Yo-Yo Ma, the world-famous cellist. I learned so much about what I can do with my thumb. He broke a lot of *rules* about how to place your thumb, yet the music was absolutely gorgeous. So this morning I was practicing something I learned last night. Learning never has to stop."

"I feel it's important for people to know there's so much they can do to grow and to put fun in their lives. Believe it or not I started tap dancing when I was in my 60s! Oh yeah…I was in recitals with six or seven gray-haired ladies, all of us acting like kooky people. Who cares? We had a great time. I had last done it when I was five years old. I still remembered many of the steps. It came right back. The only problem was that the teachers kept getting arthritis in their knees. (Laughing) As long as you like tap dancing though, you should do it. It helps your rhythm…you can do 3s again…it's a little complicated but so much fun.

"I could be a good painter, as well, but I'm not going to do it for many reasons; one of which is that painting water color is very time consuming and I don't have that much time to give to it. I want to play the cello and play it well. I just can not do everything I'm drawn to. One of the main reasons is that it's very important to sleep and eat properly, and that takes time.

"I remember that I once met a woman who was taking piano lessons, and I immediately thought, *why am I not doing that*? I always loved playing piano. So here I was in my 40s, and I got myself a piano teacher and began practicing six to eight hours a day, which was much more than I ever practiced cello. I loved it and I was good, but then I came down with tendonitis and realized that I just could not play two instruments. I had to make a choice, so I chose to stay with the cello. I don't play piano at all anymore because I could injure my hands."

It sounds like staying focused is crucial to your success?

"Focus is the most important thing. The most difficult part of my passion for music is in the actual public performance. It's a lot harder than anyone would know. You can't lose your focus for one second! You can't do it! Believe me, things can go wrong—your bridge can break; you drop your bow, or the sheet music might fly away in the wind. Everything that can go wrong has happened to me in my years of performing. Sometimes I think I would *die* if such and such a thing happened; but in the end, you just learn to laugh at things when they occur. The only way a person can really learn that however is through experience.

"Performance is hard because the energy level and the pressure are much higher than when you are simply sitting and practicing. You've got to give your best in those moments. That's also when you learn that the way you practice and the manner in which you work when alone will insure that you always do your best or pretty close to it.

"I practice every day. It's an athletic thing—the muscles and coordination that are crucial to your playing will get sloppy without practice. As a performer, I can not afford to have that happen.

"I played in a quartet for forty-some years with Lamar, but he no longer plays, so I recently formed a trio with two other *mature* women—not as old as me. (Laughing) and now I feel free to start over again. These are women I played with for years, in orchestras, but never as part of a chamber group. They're in their 60s; one lady is from Japan and tiny, while the violist is about six-feet-two; we're a *motley-looking crew*! (Laughing)

"I wanted to keep growing so I said to the violist, 'I want to save my life…do you want to save yours?'

"When I said that, I was referring to my talent and my mind, which is my life to me. We were all on tour with the New York City Ballet at the time. I told them I wanted to form a group. I wanted to save my sanity! I want to be more! The violist in our trio is *wild* now; she's practicing two to three hours each morning. She recently told me, 'Ruth, you've changed my life!' She's so happy and so grateful. We're just having a wonderful time. This fall we'll be performing two concerts up here, in Saratoga at the Museum of Dance. I really want these concerts to be fun for us and for the audience. The last time we performed, we played what I would describe to a non musician as an 'ugly-sounding contemporary piece of music.' What I did first however was prepare the audience, and give them examples of some of the *weird sounds* they would be experiencing in the piece. What happened was that the audience really listened for these sounds during the performance; in fact, they were fascinated, and said they wanted to hear it again. So for all of us, audience and players, it's a learning process and it should be enjoyable. I think it's pretty neat to get smarter throughout life.

"I also believe I'm a good teacher but I'm not doing it anymore—I need more time for other parts of my life. For instance, I love to volunteer; I've survived cancer twice, and I *give back* by helping out in a hospice program. I want to give back to people who need help and by giving a little of my time and effort I can make a big difference in people's lives. When I first got involved with hospice, I thought, *I can not be with people who are dying. Let me work in the office or something like that.* Over time though, I've found the work to be so rewarding and I love it. I mean I know these people will die and they know it too, but if I can offer a joke, read a little something or reminisce with them, they have some happy moments and I can feel good about myself. I mean what's life all about anyway? None of us really know all the answers, but we can do the best we're capable of, and give what we can to each other with love.

"For me, my love of music gives me the chance to give the best of who I am! I really…really…really…love to play! It's such a privilege. I don't compose—that's not a talent I have. But I get to play the music that great composer's wrote. Take someone like Mozart—the music simply poured out of him. It was such a God-given gift. He didn't have to work hard at it, but he did have to remember the music that he *heard* in his head and write it down very quickly. Beethoven on the other hand, slaved over each note. His talent wasn't any less than Mozart's, it was just different.

In all of this, I have the most wonderful daughter in the world. She's just become the first woman to break through into the *major leagues* of conducting. She's the new conductor of the Baltimore Symphony as well as the Bournemouth Symphony in England. When she has days off, which is not too often, she conducts big orchestras all over the world. She *put her violin back in the case* and found her true gift."

You're beaming.

"Well, I'm so proud of her. It wasn't easy for her in many ways growing up. I was always *running away* at night or dragging her along with me. Her daddy worked very hard; he was always playing somewhere. In some ways she received a different kind of attention than other kids get. Although I wanted her to be normal and play with all the other kids, I also wanted her to practice her instrument. It wasn't until Marin was in her late 20s that I found out she wanted to be a conductor. She started at the top by forming her own orchestra and then she just 'took off.' She won the McArthur Award for being the first woman to conduct a major symphony orchestra and with the money given her; she created a foundation for aspiring women conductors. She's done a lot for women who want to pursue their dream to conduct, because not only is she doing it, but she's had to overcome a fair amount of prejudice and other obstacles to reach her dream. That's the kind of daughter I have and that's why my face lights up.

What is your present work schedule like with the orchestra?

"Well, I play for the New York City Ballet which is based in Lincoln Center in New York City. We only play full-time six months out of the year because dancing is so hard on the dancers' bodies that they need rest. It's very hard work. We'll rehearse in the morning for three hours if we have even one performance or we'll do two performances on other days, all of which requires a great amount of focus over a long period of time."

What motivates you to continue this work, Ruth?

"I want to play! I also don't want to get lazy, which is easy to do and can result in playing badly. My muscles need the regular work that practice provides. I love playing with the Trio and I want to continue that as well. It's great to be able to do what I love to do."

I would think you inspire many people with your dedication and love of your art.

"I hope so. Actually we inspire ourselves. I get so excited about playing and performing. When we perform we play for the audience. When I practice, that's for me. I'm preparing myself, so that I'm ready to go. I always want to do my best or close to it. I don't want to let myself or the audience down.

"About a week ago, our trio played as part of the 38 year-old Mohawk Trail Series in Charlton, Massachusetts. I felt honored to do that. A woman who was one of the founders came up to me, following our performance and said, "It finally happened!""

"I said, 'What finally happened?'

"She replied, 'You three were smiling at each other, and you have no ides what a great feeling that gave us in the audience.'

"Well, I always smile when I play music, with the exception of an infrequent frown if I miss something. I don't really smile consciously; its just part of me that comes through. I'd really like people to be able to enjoy the music the way I do, even though they will not hear it or experience the music in the same way that I do.

"In the late 1960s, Lamar and I, together with one of our best friends, decided to give a debut concert, as a trio, at Alice Tully Hall in Lincoln Center shortly after it opened. We had been playing concerts for a while, but we felt it was time for us to perform in a major concert hall. I just recall how frightening that was for me. I mean *suicide looked so good!* I was a nervous wreck. I worked so hard—four to five hours a day for the year leading up to the concert. I couldn't sleep. I drove them *nuts* just listening to me. You pay a lot of money to give a concert in New York City. Somebody doesn't come and hire you; you pay thousands of dollars to hire the hall, pay for publicity, etc. So I just kept thinking, *I can't let them down.* In the end, the performance was beautiful and it taught me a good lesson. From that day on, my greatest wish when I perform is that the audience can experience something beautiful, exciting, passionate even ugly and be touched in some way by that connection. That's why I love performing so much, and feel so lucky to have the chance to do that. That's also why I don't want to give it up, even though I know the day's coming when I will.

"God gave me a talent and I think it's my responsibility to share it with the world. I'm always grateful when I perform, especially when it goes well; so I talk to Him, but I probably talk to St. Anthony more than I talk to anybody. (Laughing) All I ask for before a performance is to find me a way to get whatever I need, whether it is calmness, energy, or even physical strength. It takes a lot of physical strength to do what I do and I'm often in kind of a tailspin for a day or two following a performance. It's something I've gotten used to. Then I'll begin working on the next piece I want to learn and excitement takes over once again. I may never perform that new piece I'm learning, but I give it my all."

Do you see your music somehow making a difference in the world?

"Oh yeah! It's not that I see *me* making a difference as much as I know that the music has the potential to make a difference in people's lives. After all, most people who listen to good music, or at least have respect for it, know that music is good for their body, soul, and spirit. It's good for all mankind. It's similar to how great writing or great poetry has the power to elevate us out of the *mundane*, and sometimes carry us to emotional or spiritual heights we don't normally experience in our everyday lives.

"I believe it's important for us to continue to develop and climb as human beings. We weren't made to stagnate in our development or evolvement. I don't want to go out of this world *saying I was a blob, I stayed a blob, and I'm leaving a blob!* I want hear at least one person say, 'Ruthie helped me she gave me joy.'

"That's all I want. That would be enough of a difference to make!

"One of my hospice patients was an African-American woman who lived in a trailer court and was dying of cancer. She was wonderful to be with. I used to climb in bed with her and we would watch movies and eat Chicken McNuggets. I remember telling her, 'You know I don't do much for you. I don't even rub your feet.'

"She said, 'Are you kidding me? You make me laugh; that's more than anybody else does.' I'll never forget that. It's really important to bring a little light and laughter into people's lives when you can. It's sure helped me to survive.

"There was a time where I drank alcohol quite a bit, thinking it would help me to survive life's difficulties. I would often say that my problem was that I had married the wrong man. I didn't realize at the time that I had inherited the family gene for alcoholism. I've since come to see— it's been a long time since I've had a drink—that I don't need alcohol as a crutch to get myself through life's difficulties.

"Lately, when I look in the mirror I see wrinkles. I guess I could get them fixed if I wanted to spend the money. But you know, inside I feel 20, and I just keep praying to Saint Anthony to give me the energy to live long and healthy. I have a friend Joanna who is really fabulous. She gets me into such *trouble!* We've gone tubing down the Battenkill Creek a few times. We have a club now: we're a *bunch of old ladies,* eight or nine of us who do all sorts of fun things like that. I never knew getting old could be such fun. Life just seems to get better all the time. I'm over 75 and most days I don't believe it. I divide my days into sections so I can accomplish what I want. I'm very selfish with my time. I'm a potter which I've been working at for 20 years, and I also like to weave. Those activities help me to relax and think clearly. I also like to read often in the bathtub. Marin recently asked me if I'm going to take up basket-weaving next. (Laughing)

"I also want to say that teaching, which I did for 30 years, has been a great help to me. It's been a wonderful way to give away what I have inside me. When I teach I really feel as if I'm passing on what I know. One day, an old student of mine called me and said, 'Mrs. A., I think of you every day. I'm teaching my sons what you taught me.' He asked if it would be OK to call every five or ten years to let me know how he and his sons were doing.

"I said, 'You couldn't have said a nicer thing to me.' It brings tears to my eyes just thinking about it. I'm so grateful to that young man.

"Another time I happened to be perusing some cello music at a music store and realized there was a young woman looking over my shoulder. I asked her if she was a cellist, and she answered 'No, I'm a conductor.'

"I said, 'Oh, my daughter is one also.'

"What's her name?' the young girl asked.

"I said, 'Marin Alsop.'

"She replied, 'Oh my God, she's my teacher! You know there's something wrong with your daughter. I come from Mexico and I'm here in New York and it's hard at times, so your daughter will not let me pay her. She told me that I have to do this for the next woman who wants to become a conductor.'

"What a wonderful surprise for me to hear this from this young woman.

"I'm so fortunate. I mean we are blessed if we can have even one of those things said to us. I think that passing on what you love to others is one of the most important things you can do in life."

Ruth Alsop may be reached at **ruthalsop@earthlink.net**

Chapter 15
Helping Others
Bill Thomas

"I've since found the key to happiness. It's not about money, by any means. It's about being of service to and caring about others. I look at things differently today. I want to be a good person. I want to respect people, help out where I can, and be comfortable with what I see when I look in the mirror. I remember times when I'd get up in the morning, look at that image looking back at me, and think, 'Who the hell is that in there?" (Laughing)

*Editor's note—Bill's name is fictitious. He wishes his true identity to remain anonymous because of his membership in Alcoholics Anonymous and his wish to honor its tradition of anonymity. All other names have been changed as well.

Bill has a passion to help people who are less fortunate than himself. The seeds for his drive to support others in various ways were planted in the pain of childhood, as well as in his near death experiences, heart transplant, and ongoing recovery from heart disease and alcoholism. The caring that Bill received from friends and strangers alike during his healing left a strong desire to lend a hand to those in need of help.

"My passion is helping people who are in need and don't have the ability to do things that I can do. I very seldom talk about this but it's very important to me. When I read a newspaper story about some child who has cancer, for instance, I may send $50, $100,$200 or whatever I can afford, to help. Most times I don't even let on to my wife that I'm doing it. I don't usually talk about this because I don't want anyone slapping me on the back and saying what a good guy I am. I just want to do it because it feels good inside me. I don't want my ego to get in the way. I'm better off than they are and I simply give what I can afford.

"Sometimes my wife will see a cancelled check and she'll just say something like, 'You helped out didn't you?' (Laughs) I'll just say, 'Yeah,' and leave it like that. I guess that's part of why she married me.

"When friends get into a difficult financial spot, I'll help to bail them out the best I can. I get *stuck* sometimes but that's OK. I never give more than I'm able to, so I don't depend on anything getting paid back to me.

"I could probably contribute in other ways, but it's tough for me because I have to work. My medicines are very expensive. The cost came to roughly $52,000 last year. It's not all out-of-pocket, but each of the 14 prescriptions I take each day has co-pay, sometimes as much as $50, which I have to come up with. The medicines that my wife and I take probably cost us around $700 in co-pays each month. If I didn't have to work I'd be doing some kind of volunteer work.

"I'm 59 years old, and I've looked out for other people since my high school years. As the youngest of four children—two sisters and a brother—I had to fight for everything I got. I was always the kid being picked on, so I compensated by striving to be the best at everything I did. When I got to high School I became a 'jock' and excelled in football, basketball, and baseball. In my senior year, I was awarded a college scholarship for basketball.

"During my high school years, I always seemed to be attracted to the people who were disabled or in need, emotionally. There were times I'd even be defending the smart kids, who others considered the *brains* or the *nerds*, because they were frequently picked on. They became my friends because they knew no one would pick on them if I was around. I wouldn't stand for anybody being bullied, and all the kids at school knew that about me.

"I guess I've been doing that most of my life,. When I went on to college, I studied Special Education. During my final year, however, I quit college and went into business. I still kick myself in the butt for that decision. It's one of those choices you sometimes make in life that you're sorry for later."

You talked earlier about being picked on by an older brother, so I'm wondering if that's part of the reason you relate so strongly to the person whose down and needs help?

"Yes, that's true. My brother was a year older but a lot bigger than me when I was growing up. Until high school, when I had a growth spurt, I was very small. By the time I was a senior I was actually bigger than him; so things changed. One day he picked on me and I beat the living hell out of him (laughing). Today, he's one of my best friends.

"I was a tough kid back then. I had to be. We moved into a new school district when I was a high school freshman. I went out for the freshman football team, but after one week they moved me up to varsity. I'll never forget: we had a kid who was the fullback on our team. He weighed about 175 pounds and was one of those guys who had his hair slicked back into a D.A. (*duck's ass*), rode a motorcycle, and wore a black leather jacket. During pre-season practice for the varsity football team he continually gave me a hard time. About a week before our first game, we were leaving the field and he spit in my face. I kicked the hell out of him right there. He was considered to be the toughest kid in school, so nobody ever said 'boo' to me after that. They realized I was nobody to mess with. (Laughs)

"If anyone picked on any of the other kids at school, I'd always jump in and tell the attackers to back off. That's one thing I've never liked. I drive a school bus, now, and I still tell the kids not to pick on each other.

"Back in 2002, I was really sick and ended up having a heart transplant. I experienced a lot of pain, aggravation, and worry. I prayed a lot.

"Right after the operation I got very involved with a very special young man by the name of Jack. He has Cerebral Palsy and had been in a wheel chair his entire life. He recently graduated from college where he was a member of the varsity baseball team as the team manager. Jack considers himself a jock. I hung on to Jack because of his positive attitude. Many people who've had lifetime problems like that get very negative; but not Jack. He's one of the most positive people I've ever known. He's *up* all the time and though I know he's often in pain, I seldom hear him talk about it. I feel so good just being around him. I'm in touch with Jack every day, and have been since I first met him six years ago when he was in high school.

"My stepson played on the varsity baseball team, and Jack being a big baseball fan, attended all the games, as did I. That's where I got to know him. After my heart transplant, I began driving a van for handicap and wheelchair-bound people. Jack happened to be one of my very first clients. At that time, I brought him to school at a local community college each morning, got to know him very well, and we became close friends. Since then I take him on weekend trips, out to dinner, and to ball games. We just spend a lot of time together. It's worked out great for both of us."

How has your relationship with Jack benefited you?

"Well, it's given me an entirely different outlook on life. For a few years I went through a very difficult time, but when I see what Jack has been through, I'm so thankful for everything I have. He inspires me! He's an amazing young man. Through him I've also been able to reach out and give to others.

"There are a couple of other kids I've met through driving the ambulette who have handicaps. One of them was a junior at a local college and he was just the opposite of Jack—mad at the world and just so negative about life. He'd been in a terrible car accident in his childhood, has been wheelchair-bound ever since, and he'd let this experience negatively affect his entire life. It took me a long time, but eventually I was able to get him to laugh and help him to feel a little better about himself. But he and Jack—whose entire left side is paralyzed—are so different in their outlook. Jack sees the up side to everything. When he accompanies me to the corner in his wheelchair he says, 'Let's walk to the corner' or 'Lets run the bases.' It's just the way he sees things."

How was he able to become the manager of the college baseball team?

"Well, first of all, he's a huge baseball fan; so in his last two years of college, he would keep the scorebooks, shag fly balls, and be out on the field with the team (in his wheelchair). He was also studying for a degree in sports management. The team and the fans loved him. The basketball team had a special spot for him in the front row and wouldn't go out on the floor to play until each member had *hi-fived* Jack first. The girl's volleyball team, which was nationally ranked, would hand him the team ball before they went out to play each game. He's very special. He has inspired many of the athletes at the school. "

When you talk about giving, it seems that you're giving comes from your heart and not out of some kind of guilt.

"Well again I think, *I'm a lot better off than they are. Let me help them out.* I think that idea came out of my own illness and recovery. I received an unbelievable amount of help.

"I was 34 when I had my first heart attack. I'd traveled out to the Grand Canyon with a group of 12 friends for a 10-day rafting trip on the Colorado River. The first night there, I wasn't feeling that great when I went to bed. Nevertheless, I awoke at four-thirty in the morning, got myself a cup of coffee, and then proceeded to wake everyone for our trek down into the Canyon at five. Then, just as I left my room I had a heart attack and collapsed on the floor. Fortunately, for me, at the point I dropped, I was only about 50 to 75 feet away from the Ranger station, where the medics and paramedics were stationed. They got to me really fast. I was dead when they arrived, and despite their belief that I wasn't going to make it, they were able to bring me back to life. I was then taken to the hospital in Flagstaff, Arizona, about 90 miles away. When I awoke two-and-a-half days later, the only memory I had of the heart attack, was of the paramedics working on me, as I—out cold at the time—was looking down on them as they were attempting to save my life."

So you were having an out-of-body experience?

"Yes! On about the third or fourth day of my hospitalization the paramedics came to visit me. They told how they never thought I'd survive. When the two paramedics who worked on me came into my room, I knew them by name without them having to identify themselves. They said, 'You never met us, you were unconscious the whole time. How could you possibly know who we are?'

"I told them that although I was unconscious, I was able to watch them put a needle into me to get my heart going. They were amazed!

"That event changed the way I felt about things. I was positive and grateful at first, but as time passed, I became very negative. In the next three years, I had three more heart attacks, and I became sicker and sicker. In 1989, doctors did an experimental operation on me at St. Francis Hospital in New York City. The surgeon, Dr. Joseph Levine, later told me how happy he was that the operation had been a success. He told me that *I now I had three more years to live*! I was shocked and disappointed. I thought this operation would permanently fix the problem.

"Following the operation, I returned home and just gave up. Prior to this I was not a drinker; but I now started drinking and pretty much stayed drunk on a daily basis for the next five years. During that time I lost my business, my family—anything of importance, I lost.

"I was fortunate that I woke up one morning and said, 'I can't do this anymore.' So I began attending Alcoholics Anonymous meetings, got some professional help, and things slowly began to get better for me. It took a long time because I was in a lot of emotional pain and scared to death of dying.

"After a couple of years in recovery from alcoholism, I began to realize that I didn't have to deal with life alone anymore. I guess I was a person who was very self-reliant. Before I went to AA, I seldom asked anyone for help. Being in control was how I lived my life. Slowly, however, I began to give up that idea and reach out to others for help.

I also began to give help where I could. The main thing I got from friends in recovery was moral support. That was so important to me. I remember there was a guy named Bob who I'd call even before I'd call an ambulance. He lived a half-mile from me, so he'd reach my house before the ambulance would. There were so many people who'd take me to the doctor or to the hospital when I needed to go."

You told me earlier about your trip to New York City a few years back, to wait for a heart, for your transplant operation. As you told it, you were in real dire straits. Can you talk some about that?

"In June of 2002, I'd gone down to New York City to be evaluated, and as a result was told that I most likely would die in a few weeks if they weren't able to find a new heart for me. So I was put on a transplant list and set up in a hotel close to the hospital. That way I could get to the hospital quickly when a heart became available for me. I *lucked out* because I had a rare blood type and within 13 days they had a heart for me. On July 23rd I had my transplant. The normal wait for a heart is ten-and-a-half months. It was a miracle! I was the only one on the list, in the Northeast United States, for that blood type.

"There were two other people in that program that I became close friends with, and they both died waiting. They lived in the same hotel that I did.. Many people die while waiting for their transplant. If I'd been type O, that probably would have happened to me. I believe there was something like 15,000 people on the list for type O hearts at the time.

"While I was waiting I did all I could do to stay positive and free of fear. I attended morning mass each day at St. Cecilia's church, in Englewood, New Jersey. Knowing my situation, the parish sent somebody to the hotel to pick me up for 8 o'clock mass. The people down there were wonderful to me. I met one fellow who ran a restaurant nearby and he'd send someone to pick me up whenever I asked. There were even people from a local AA group who'd pick me up and bring me to a meeting if I wanted it. It was a tremendous experience.

"When the call finally came that a heart was available and ready for me, it was at 11:00 p.m. They said I should get there as soon as possible. I was very excited but at the same time I felt calm. I picked up the phone and called everybody back home to tell them, and then went down to the hotel's main desk to tell them I'd need a taxi to get over to the hospital. The man who drove the hotel shuttle had just ended his shift and happened to be standing close enough to overhear our conversation. At that point he told me that I that wasn't paying $50 for a taxi—he'd take me there himself.

"I even got married at the hotel! Sally and I were engaged the day after the transplant and then married 18 days later on August the 10th. I was still convalescing at that point. All the people who attended the ceremony were either waiting for their transplant or were recuperating transplant patients. We all wore Hawaiian shirts and I wore shorts, because that's all I'd brought with me. The people at the Radisson hotel where we were staying even gave us a room, for free, for the wedding. A minister who happened to be a friend of a Radisson staff person performed the ceremony inexpensively. We had a great time.

"As I mentioned earlier, a sad part of this story is that Stewart, who with his wife Jackie, helped to set up the wedding for us, died about two months later, still waiting for his opportunity to have a heart and lung transplant. I had called the week before he died and made plans to have dinner with him when I came down for some tests in the early part of the following week. He died in his sleep two nights later.

"Before I went down to New York for the transplant, I was aware that I had many, many people looking out for me and wanting to help. One day while I was an inpatient at Albany Medical Center, I was really in rough shape. My heart had stopped for the fifth time that day and they'd called a code blue on me. I later learned that they were about to stop treatment and pronounce me dead. During all this I was having a very peaceful out-of-body experience: watching the doctors and nurses work on me as I was calmly floating away. But a Pakistani intern who kept hitting me with the paddles and bringing me back, said 'No, I want to give it one more try!' He did and that last jolt brought me back. When I woke up about five hours later, my chest was raw from the many times he'd shocked me. He would not give up on me. I guess I'm like a cat; *I've got nine lives!* (Laughing)

"That was just the start of the miracle, though. Very seldom does a person ever get to know who the heart donor is, so the only information I got after my transplant was that the donor of my heart was a 20-year-old boy. The people in charge said I could write a letter thanking the family, but it had to be anonymous from my end. So I first sent my letter to the hospital, who proof-read it, and then mailed it on to the family. The family subsequently replied with a letter of their own, to which I responded with a second letter. This time I included some pictures of me before, and then two weeks after, the transplant. In their proofreading of my second letter, the hospital lost the pictures, so that when the family responded to me they said they were upset about not seeing the pictures. They then asked if they could contact me directly. At that point the hospital said we could sign off on all the protective measures if we chose to, which we did. We then began writing to each other directly, phone calls between us followed and eventually Ted, the father, came to visit me in September of 2003.

"During our conversations he described his late son, Steve, and I came to find out that we had many things in common. We'd participated in the same sports in High School, and both of us had attended college on sports scholarships. At the time of his death he was majoring in Special Education and had begun working with an autistic boy. As I discovered these amazing coincidences, I started laughing, and I told Ted that I had played all the same sports in school, had gone to college on a basketball scholarship, had started a local Special Olympics program for autistic children, and Special Education had been my major as well!"

Have you ever thought that you might somehow be carrying on the work Steve had begun?

"No! I've read and heard about many transplant patients whose activities, tastes, likes, and dislikes had changed after their operations. I really didn't experience anything like that although I've noticed that my love for reading has left me since the operation. At one time I would read three novels a week, but now I hardly read at all. Amazingly, Ted told me that Steve didn't like to read; he was always busy.

"Each year I travel down to Maryland where the family lives and I participate in a walk-a-thon in Steve's honor. I feel that's the least I can do to express my gratitude. His dad works at a school for handicapped and disabled children and through the walk-a-thon, has raised roughly $25,000 a year to help these people."

Would you talk some about your recovery once you got back home?

"Well, when I got back here I just thought about how lucky I was— I could work again, I could breathe normally, I could do most anything—even run a little if I wanted to. In fact, each year I'm required to undergo a very thorough physical exam in order to drive a school bus, and I pass that with flying colors. I was also supported by the prayers and words of a lot of friends back here. Many people reminded me to keep my attitude positive. Then I thought of Jack, the young man I talked about earlier, who had such a positive outlook despite his disabilities. He became a great inspiration and role model for me."

What would you say to those who say they have no passion in their lives?

"I would tell them to look inside themselves. That's what happened to me. In the end, I looked inside myself and realized that I needed help and wasn't alone anymore. I reached out and got help, and then I was able to give help to others.

"I had started out in life wanting to help others, but then it slipped away. For awhile all I cared about was me...me...me! When I left college after my junior year, it was because I wanted to make money. I accomplished that, but in the end I lost it all. In those days, I would assess my self-worth and the quality of my life by how much money I had in the bank, and by how big my house was.

"I've since found the key to happiness. It's not about money by any means. It's about being of service to and caring about others. I look at things differently today. I want to be a good person. I want to respect people, help out where I can, and be comfortable with what I see when

I look in the mirror. I remember times when I'd get up in the morning, look at that image looking back at me, and think, *Who the hell is that in there?*(laughing)

"My spirituality is something that I've had to just let happen naturally. It's a hard thing to explain to a newcomer in AA. I tell them that it's inside them, and to give it time to come out. 'I've got to find a God in my life!' they say. I tell them, 'No, let it come from within you. It's in there. Let it happen.' I find that it occurs in a different way for each person.

"I'll tell you, the first time I'd felt any peace in a long, long time, was right after I'd gotten my first apartment and was living alone. This was before I had my transplant and just after I'd had a defibulator implanted in me to keep my heart going. Up to this time I had a great fear of dying. After waking up one morning, I jumped in the shower to get ready to attend an AA meeting, when suddenly my heart stopped. The defibulator went off and the only way I can describe how that feels is to imagine someone hitting you across the chest with a baseball bat. That's how much it hurts. By the time I was able to reach the phone to call 911, the defibulator had gone off three more times. A very peaceful feeling came over me after the third time. I suddenly knew that everything would be OK: I could stop worrying. That morning the fear of dying left me and has not come back.

"It was then that I knew there was some power within me—holding onto me. I was no longer alone. Everything changed for me that day and I began to look at life in a very different way."

"As I look back at all the good things that happened before, during, and after my heart transplant, I can see that my spiritual beliefs were strengthened. I was able more than ever to see the goodness in everyone, and able to experience my higher power in every part of my life. That's why today, when I see an opportunity to be of help to someone, I just can't pass it up. It's an opportunity for me to give something back for all I've been given."

Chapter 16
Immersion
Bob Moore

"Once I immerse myself in a subject I feel passionate about, another door will usually open, and some other direction will evolve for me; it always happens...I also open to the possibility of magical things happening in my life."

My interview with Bob took place at his lovely home in a peaceful, residential neighborhood in Albany, New York. Bob divides his time between Albany and Rockville Centre, on Long Island, where he shares a home with his life partner, Tina. Bob's vision of making *all* of his life an art and a passion is beautifully revealed in the art work, photographs, music, and the sense of serenity that envelopes his home. Although an admittedly shy man who likes to remain in the background, Bob has overcome his internal struggles to the degree that he is able to put himself front and center in order to pass on his love and passion for learning, art, music, history, culture, and self realization to the students he has encountered in over 30 years of teaching.

"It's difficult for me to choose just one activity that I have passion for, because I feel passionate about many things. I often think of a Robert Louis Stevenson story titled *Providence and the Guitar*, which I first read while a student at Siena College in Loudonville, New York.

Stevenson talked about his passion for life, and how art is not simply a *watercolor painting*; 'Art is life to be lived.' I always think of that story and attempt to live my life *as an art,* infusing sensitivity and feeling into every activity I'm involved in.

"I'm now 57 and I was a middle school teacher for 30 years before retiring. One thing that got me through and helped to make me a good teacher during those years was my sense of humor—I was continually challenged by my 12-14 year-old students. Another aspect of my teaching style was that I brought my-*self* to the classroom. I believe that's one of the main reasons I became a good teacher. The kids knew for example that I loved music and read books. I believe they appreciated knowing who I was beyond just being their teacher. That doesn't mean that I revealed my personal problems to them, but I did let them in on what I loved and felt passionate about in life. I shared my love for learning with them."

How did you come to teaching?

"My first bit of teaching came as a Boy Scout leader. At 14 I instructed 11 year-olds in how to pack a knapsack and what to bring on a winter camping trip. Later, at 17, I became a water safety instructor and lifeguard, and began teaching little kids how to swim. I sensed there was a bond that developed between us and they were able to trust me. I remember standing in the pool in very cold water at 8:30 in the morning, thinking *they must feel safe with me*, as one by one, they'd jump into the water.

"Soon after entering college as a business major, thinking marketing would be my career, I realized that I was in the wrong place—my head and heart were just not into business. Having gotten a love of history from my dad I began to believe that becoming a history teacher would be the best path for me. My love for history goes back to being a kid, when on our vacations in upstate New York, we'd stop the car at each historical marker we'd see, and dad would tell us a story related to that marker. I don't know how true the stories were, (Laughing) but they captured my interest and stirred my imagination. So, in my freshman year at college, I transferred to the Arts Division and I ended up graduating with a degree in history.

"In 1975, after 3 years teaching in a Catholic school, I was hired by the Averill Park, New York, public school system and worked at Algonquin Middle School for the next 27 years as a seventh grade Social Studies teacher. I loved it, especially, because studying Iroquois culture and Native American history, which held a real fascination for me, was part of our curriculum. We also covered American history, a little bit of New York state government, geography, and of course current events. My curriculum constantly changed as I'd become inspired by things I'd read, in the newspapers, that related to what I'd be teaching. I liked to tie history and current events together for the students, so it was fun for me.

"Over the years I've been asked me if I didn't become bored, teaching the same subject for 27 years. I didn't because I was always developing new programs and lessons. Once such program which would take place during the two weeks prior to spring break each year involved a study of the future. I would have the kids make videotapes of each of their fellow students expressing their vision of what the future would look like. From these videos they would create *Future News* broadcasts.

"My life has always been influenced by what I was teaching. Because I was ever on the lookout for new and interesting subject matter for my students, it led me to do a lot of reading, traveling, and other activities related to what I was teaching or wanted to teach. I created a vacation project within which, groups of five students would plan an imaginary vacation,—including expenses, accommodations, and historic sites visited—using the New York State vacation guide. The group would later do oral presentations about their vacations, using microphones and a sound system, so they could gain some familiarity with making a public presentation. It was always fun for me and I think for the kids too.

"I wanted to give them as many experiences as possible within the structure of teaching Social Studies. I loved to have them discuss and debate current events. Sometimes I'd arrange their chairs in a circle, choose a topic, and have each of them share their opinion and feelings, and then listen while others responded to what they had to say. Kids are so surprised when adults let them speak their minds.

"Since I've retired, I've taken my excitement and love of learning, and together with a few other people, created a program called Renewal for Teachers which is now 11 years old.. It's given in a two or three-day retreat format where I afford people the opportunity to reflect on who they are as teachers. It's a great way for teachers to get away together, share with each other about their teaching and personal lives, do some experiential learning, and have some time for reflection. Another labor of love I still do, once a month, is to work with some of the students at Averill Park School to create an orientation video for incoming fifth grade students. The kids write the script and *star* in it.

"I have an idea about what I call *connectivity*. For example: In one of our workshops on a Renewal weekend we gave the teachers certain exercises to facilitate the experience of leadership. The secondary theme in this exercise was collaboration, and I used the Beatles as examples of creative collaborators. Now that was part of sharing me, because I grew up with the Beatles, who literally changed my world. It's a place where art and psychology connected for me. One year, I immersed myself in pulling together as much information as possible about the Beatles for the retreat theme of Collective Collaboration and Leadership. After the retreats were over for the summer, an amazing thing happened. Tina and I were vacationing for a week on Long Island, and while driving back from Montauk, the traffic slowed down and came to a standstill. While waiting for traffic to move, I noticed a jogger running right next to my jeep. To my amazement, it was Paul McCartney, and at the time I'd been reading a biography about him. There's an example of that spiritual connectivity I've been talking about..

"A while back I became interested in comparative studies of various religions, and found that Hinduism has a belief called *Darshan*, where the deity actually reveals himself to people through various disguises. It may sound far out but I remember hearing people say that *thoughts in mind produce in kind.* Looking back, it seems that seeing Paul McCartney after reading about him, and using the Beatles in our workshop was more than simply a coincidence for me.

"Once I immerse myself in a subject I feel passionate about, another door will usually open, and some other direction will evolve for me; it always happens. Years back, after much counseling and doing a lot of work on myself, I started seeing that once I open myself to the world and to my truth, I also open to the possibility of magical things happening in my life. It seems that the world becomes a different place. I remember the first time I went to a self-help meeting. I heard all these people talking, and I thought**,** *Maybe this is what I need to feel better about speaking in public.* Now I admit that's a very superficial reason for attending a self—help meeting, but being a shy person, I was able to find my voice through participation in those meetings. It ultimately enabled me to share my truth and, for the first time, let people know who I was. I'd come out of a shame-based family system, so I struggled a lot with my self-esteem and with expressing myself. I still do at times, but I've found that I can work through those challenges and be successful in life.

"Another connection happened for me when I saw the Joseph Campbell-Bill Moyers interview series, *The Power of Myth* on PBS a few years back. Like me, Campbell had a big interest in Native American culture and mythology. When I was a kid I was fascinated by Indians and always rooted for the Indians in movies and stories. (Laughing) So, a few years later, I attended a Native American workshop in Northampton, Massachusetts and I heard this white, Jewish man from New York City relate his experiences with Native culture. It really turned me on! I then began attending workshops on the Seneca reservation in Western New York, with a Seneca elder by the name of Twyla Nitsch. I essentially immersed myself in a different culture from my own, and gained a much greater understanding of native peoples as a result.

"To get to the first workshop I attended, I drove all the way to Buffalo from Albany, arriving at 8:00 p.m. I paid my fee, and asked for a copy of the program from the woman who registered me. She was very polite but (Laughing) said there was *no* program. She said, 'We ring the bell and you come down. You're on Indian time now!' I then asked, 'Well don't we get a list of who will be attending and presenting, and what their degrees are?' Again the answer was, *no*! Very little structure and the absence of degreed teachers were foreign and a total shift in consciousness for me. Here I was, a teacher who taught my young students about the Native American culture, and now *I* was being called upon to be the student and change *my* way of thinking. This work and *Black Elk Speaks*, a book written by Dr. John Nyhart, in which he describes his experiences with Black Elk, a Native American spiritual teacher, made a connection to something very deep and spiritual inside me. "

What has teaching taught you about yourself?

"It's taught me that I will always be a learner. It still brings tears to my eyes when I recall the exercise of courage, and the lessons I learned from some of my students. When I first worked at the middle school I was in charge of setting up the audio-visual equipment whenever a sound system was called for. Being a teacher you'd think it would be easy for me to speak in front of others. Because of the background I came from, however, that was not the case. I recall a day when I was setting up the equipment on stage in an empty auditorium and just very aware of a deep fear inside me. I'd always been interested in movie and film making—had even helped students to produce their own videos— but I'd been forever reluctant to put myself in front of the camera, instead choosing to be behind the scenes as producer. At the same time, I also had a deep desire to be in front of the camera. I mean who doesn't want to be a star sometimes? I simply lacked the courage and the skill to do it. Well, I had a student who had been in an auto accident and was left with some facial disfigurement which has since been corrected with surgery. Despite her appearance, she just loved being in front of the camera. She was a living testament to how courage could overcome difficulties and accomplish great things while I had always held back because of the dread of being less than perfect. She stirred me so much that I did eventually get in front of the camera. Later, I even had some success on local access television.

"Inspired by "Saturday Night Live," which I saw in person, I created a local variety show called the "Bob Moore Show." Although quite nervous, I was able to get some folks around me that I could trust and work with. Their support encouraged me to take some risks. The *Albany Times-Union* reviewed the show and although the reviewer was very nice and kind in her review, she thought the comedy was rather sophomoric. Nevertheless the show was a great learning experience for me.

"After many years of creating programs for my students I was invited by the New York State Education Department to develop and produce an interactive satellite teleconference that would allow people around the state to watch and learn how I make videos with kids. They could also call in and ask me questions. Besides feeling excited and a little shocked by the offer, I was scared. At the same time, I remembered my students who'd inspired *me*, and I knew that I couldn't ask them to do something I wouldn't do myself. In exploring my fear, I realized I was most afraid of not being able to provide the right answers to callers' questions. I actually had to give myself permission to say *I don't know the answer*. That permission eventually brought me peace and the confidence that I could do the project.

"This creative video work then became a *"gospel"* I just had to spread. I saw how the students were turned on by it and how it empowered them to learn in a new way. I also started giving classes on video-making for a Teacher's Center where I met many people who suggested I give my classes in other venues. Through contacts that continually appeared, I presented week—long classes for children and adults at the beautiful Chautauqua Institute in Western New York for many years, and also taught a week-long, credit course at the University of Connecticut for the Gifted and Talented Children Program. While teaching at Connecticut. I met a man who advised me that much could be learned by studying Eastern thought and spirituality. So I purchased a copy of the *Tao Te Ching* by Lao Tsu as well as books written by the great Zen teacher, Professor Shunryu Suzuki which was a logical progression from my introduction to eastern thought through the Beatles right up to my now sober lifestyle which began when I stopped drinking in 1986. It seems that each time a door would open for me, I'd step through it, see what it had to offer, and then eventually another door would open."

What is it about teaching that really *lights you up*?

"I think it really has to do with the opportunity to change a life by giving someone an interest in something new. I love to share thoughts and ideas that excite me, knowing that someone's life might be enhanced by it. For example, I loved to have my seventh grade students evaluate my teaching. These were very simple evaluations, but what the kids revealed was very touching and informative for me. For example: As much as the kids might complain about the particular type of music I might play while we were working on projects, one kid in his evaluation said, 'I play trombone in the band, and in our class I heard a piece of music that I love.' You're normally not going to hear this type of feedback in the classroom. I've been blessed to get letters from students that tell me I've touched their lives in some way.

"One day I saw a young woman, who'd been one of my seventh grade kids and was now a senior in high school, singing at an event I attended. She was someone I always liked and had been a really good kid. It was great to see her and I had it in my mind as I left the concert that I should write her a letter of praise and support. But a day or two later I received a letter from *her*, thanking *me* for inspiring her years before.

"My mother was a very sensitive person when I was growing up. I remember there were times I'd come home and I'd hear her listening to George Gershwin and she would be in tears! I'd think, *Oh! Oh! She must be into the cooking sherry again.* I don't think I understood the depth of feeling she had for melody. She was a singer but because of her worry and fears she never really reached her potential. As a kid I believe I internalized the message that *because mom couldn't do it I couldn't either.* I think that belief held me back a lot. Nevertheless mom did pass on to me a great sensitivity for art and music.

"In 1986, which I think might have been the 50th anniversary of George Gershwin's death; the record company released a lot of his material and I started really listening to his music—especially the melody and sentimentality which it evokes. I found his music could bring me to tears much as it had my mom. He'd died when he was 38, and here I was; newly sober, with a fresh lease on life at the same age. This created a strong bond for me with him and with my mother.

"From my Dad I also gained an appreciation for music, but he would annoy the hell out of me when he'd be singing 'Adeste Fidelis' around the house at Christmastime. He was usually *drinking* at the time. He also taught me a lot about craftsmanship and doing things right.

"Despite their shortcoming, I owe my parents a lot. In healing my relationship with them, I've been able to let go of my anger and appreciate their contributions to my life and to my growth. I grew to love and respect them on an entirely different level, and even began to tell them I loved them, which was not easy for me after all I'd been through with them. The relationship between us changed for the better and that's brought me much happiness and peace.

"When I was a student I was fortunate to have great music and art teachers. As a student, I visited the Metropolitan Museum of art in New York with the school art club on one-day bus trips and came away greatly moved and influenced by what I saw. As a Social Studies teacher, I tried to incorporate fine music and art into whatever we were studying, so my students could have the same opportunity."

I'm thinking that art museums and great musical works are not subjects that turn most junior high school students on?

"That's right. I was listening to Dave Brubeck when I was 12 years old because, thank God, I'd had made a connection years before with Dr. Zieger, my music teacher, during the seventh and eighth grades. He helped me to appreciate a wide variety of music. The other kids were listening to the Beatles, which I did too, but because of Dr. Zieger and my parents I was being exposed to many other forms of music. Another big inspiration happened in sixth grade when I took part in a class trip to see "The Sound of Music" on Broadway in New York City. Being tuned onto music the way I was when I was a kid, I became very excited when the orchestra began to play the overture. I remember thinking, *whoa, this is great!*

"Art to me is a language and it speaks to me. I think artistic expression comes from that very deep place inside us. I view artists as shamans that create their art through a connection to spirit. For some people numbers are a language, but for me its Jackson Pollack or George Gershwin.

"Because of my parents support, I became the kind of kid who would always keep trying. If I was afraid to do something, I'd study the activity and ask myself, why *am I scared to do this?* A friend of mine says I'm solution-oriented and I think that's true. If I can understand a problem, I can solve it and act on it despite any fear I might have. When I first walked into a therapy group and heard slogans like '*One Day at a Time*' or '*Feel the fear and do it anyway,*' I judged them as being very simplistic. Over time, however, I was able to incorporate these different positive ideas into my life, and I came to realize how personally powerful a change in perspective can be."

You seem to have a persistent thirst for knowledge?

"That's true. I have a love for learning, picking up new ideas, and developing fresh ways of looking at things. When I'm doing that I feel alive and I experience a sense of awe.

"For anyone who doesn't feel passion in their life, I would say, *just open your eyes and look around!* That may sound flippant, but I truly mean it. When I was a teaching, my students were not allowed to use the word boring. In my own life there's so much I want to learn and experience that I can't ever recall a boring day.

"When a person feels no passion, the problem could also lie in the unexplored self. He or she may need to dig a little deeper into their personal history and investigate how they came to be who they are. They may need to look around, take a closer look at where he or she came from, and who they are. What are their values? What's important to them?

"Just recently I found my father's discharge papers from the U.S. Army in 1945. It listed his home address—the house he grew up in. Finding this house is my newest project. I might add that I discovered that my father gave interviews to local seventh grade students about his WWII experiences. That touched me.

"In this country I think we lack a true sense of history. Forget about politics and just look at how we learned nothing from the Viet Nam War. We're repeating it all in Iraq. I'm horrified that so many people are dying, so each day I begin my morning by reading the death notices of our soldiers. I read their whole names, age, rank, and where they're from…(Tears up). That's my way of honoring them. I also contribute to Fisher House, which helps support the families of wounded soldiers. Although I've never served in the military, I try to support the soldiers in various ways. I love this country and I consider myself patriotic, but what I see makes me frustrated and angry! I get too emotional. I wouldn't make a very good debater."

How does your spirituality inform your life?

"That's such a difficult question. I was raised Catholic, but my parents were infrequent churchgoers. Nevertheless, I'd ride my bike to church every Sunday morning for the children's mass at 10:45— something drew me there. I've always felt some kind of connection to spirit, whatever that spirit is. As a college student, I became increasingly angry about religion. Some things just didn't seem right or make any sense to me. My parents' struggle with the issue of birth control also left me with a bad taste for the church. I was also married and divorced, so I carried a lot of guilt about that. As a result my churchgoing was pretty much relegated to attending recovery group meetings in church basements after I'd quit drinking. At some point I attended a service at a Methodist church, where the folks were kind, loving, and inviting to me. I cried while singing the hymns that week. I realized that I had to look around and find something that fit for where I was spiritually, at that time in my life. Over time, through reading and exploring various cultures and ideas, my spirituality has been strengthened and I've become very interested in Shamanism, Buddhism, and Hinduism, and even explored in a deeper way just who Christ was. A message that I get from all these spiritual sources is that everything and everybody is sacred and should be treated that way.

"For me, this house is *my temple*; a holy place. I feel comfortable and safe being here. That is very different from the fear I experienced growing up. Tina and I have worked very hard to make her house on Long Island a place of beauty and serenity, for us and for all who enter there. You can sense it as soon as you walk in the door.

"I briefly touched on a few heroes of mine when I was a kid and I'd like to say a little more about Teddy Roosevelt. I had asthma when I was a kid which left me rather sickly. In 4th grade our class visited Sagamore Hill, Roosevelt's home, and I learned that like me, he'd been very sick growing up but had overcome it and went on to accomplish great things in his life. That had a strong impact on me and I believe played a part in my overcoming many obstacles in my own life as I grew up. With President Kennedy I loved the whole idea of the *New Frontier*. I was turned on by his belief that each of us should do something for our country and for the world. Those few years were a very optimistic time and they still have a profound impact on me. Not that they didn't have their drawbacks and problems, but like millions of other young people, the Beatles and Kennedy made me want to give of myself to somehow create a better world, and fulfill the promise of a brighter future. As angry and pessimistic as I can be some times about certain things, I believe I have a deep-seated hope for a better world, and that hope goes back to those times and those people."

What gets you back *on the path* when you become aware that spiritually and emotionally you're off-kilter?

"I have to remember to *'sit loosely in the saddle of life.'* When you try to ride a horse and you stiffen up, you bounce around a lot. When you relax, however, you have a much easier ride. That's a real challenge, but as long as I stay vigilant about that tendency, I get a little better all the time. Being in touch with my emotions and then being vulnerable enough to admit my fear or anger without lashing out at someone also helps me to feel connected again. I have some symptoms of Post-Traumatic Stress Disorder from growing up the way I did, so I've had to learn to react in new ways to these old feelings. It's given me a new appreciation for what the Iraq vets have to encounter when coming back from the horrors of war and trying to lead a normal life back home.

"I also want to mention my sister Kathy, who lives on Long Island with her husband Bob and sons Jimmy and Robbie. She also grew up in the crazy world of our family life, so she and I have really stuck together and we have a great love for each other."

What kind of legacy would you like to leave behind Bob?

I think there was a consciousness among my generation that we were going to make the world a better place; so I'd like to think that maybe I've helped move the world in that direction, if even in a small way. I have no children of my own but I think of my students as my children and hope I've helped them in a positive way. I would really like to know in my heart that I made a difference through my teaching. Tina has three sons, and I believe that I'm someone who can help them at a formative time in their lives; the same with my sister Kathy's two boys. I want to do all I can to help them become happy and loving people. That would make me happy."

Bob may be contacted at bob-moore@netzero.net

Chapter 17
Higher Purpose
Chris Ringwald

"In the midst of that daily effort, a writer may ask: "Why am I here in front in front of this typewriter, alone in this mountain cottage or cold-water flat? What does God want of me and what role does faith play in my life and work? Is there a higher purpose to my writing—and did I keep that in mind for just one minute today?"
Excerpted from Faith in Words by Christopher A. Ringwald

Christopher Ringwald, a journalist, author, and educator, lives in Albany, New York with his wife Amy and three children. He has written for *The Washington Post, Newsday, Commonweal,* and *The Wall Street Journal.* Chris is a visiting scholar at the Sage Colleges and a journalism lecturer at the University at Albany. He speaks on religion, spirituality, and behavioral health to audiences around the country. His passion for writing has led him to author the books: *Faith in Words, The Soul of Recovery: Uncovering the Spiritual Dimension in the Treatment of Addictions,* and *"A Day Apart: How Jews, Christians, and Muslims Find Faith, Freedom, and Joy on the Sabbath."*

"I've always had a deep interest in the lives and circumstances of people with problems. In a larger, personal way I've wanted to know and do the will of God. When it comes to writing, I'm fascinated by how people find God and how God finds people. I think *The Soul of Recovery* is about people, through many different avenues, getting their lives back by developing some kind of spiritual or religious life. That subject attracts me because it's a great instance of where religion and spirituality have produced concrete results. A lot of times religion or spirituality is a more ethereal topic. People often believe things, but are unsure what difference it really makes. But with addicts or alcoholics, who turn toward some sort of spiritual life, their beliefs can create concrete results. They had to do it, in a way that works for them, or they could suffer and die! For them, their faith is a life or death issue."

How did the fascination for writing come about, Chris?

'Well, I got into journalism when I was in my thirties because I had always liked that kind of work—reporting and writing. Prior to journalism, I had worked as a carpenter for a long time in my own construction business after graduating from college. I also worked for a human rights group on Capitol Hill in Washington D.C.; lobbying to reduce foreign aid to various military dictatorships, primarily in South America. It's easy to forget that some things have actually gotten better—20 years ago, more than half the South American countries had a dictator for a leader. I enjoyed that work a great deal because I was involved in issues that mattered—basic human rights. I had been an intern in a congressional office and I then worked for this human rights group on a one-year grant. Subsequently, I had to decide if I would get more into this area of work or get out.

"Writing would continuously come up for me whenever I'd get to thinking about what sort of work I wanted to do. I thought that even as human rights go, groups can issue reports, but what really has an impact is the initial reporting on the subject in newspapers and magazines. While editorializing, and the later stages of educating and lobbying can have some effect, it's the earlier steps of investigation and reporting—for example, who's being oppressed, how are they being oppressed, and then getting that word out—that most interested me.

"I thought a lot about that kind of writing, but then ended up volunteering in Peru for a year, teaching carpentry in a small village in the Andes Mountains. It was a great experience and while there I did a good deal of writing, which led me to the belief that this was what I wanted to do. I went down there with a backpack full of clothes and a suitcase full of books. All the books you would never read unless you were marooned on a desert island—Dante's, "The Divine Comedy" and things like that—and by and large I did read most of them!(laughs) It was clear to me by the end of that year that I wanted to get into journalism

"When I came back to the states, I worked in construction for another year, and then entered Columbia's journalism school, because I didn't want to start out on the very ground level of newspapers. I knew that was the traditional career track—start at the bottom and work your way up. I didn't start at the top but I did learn a lot and it was a great experience. My first newspaper job was at the *Watertown Daily Times*, and I lived in Massena, New York.

"In 1989, I moved here to Albany and went to work at the *Albany Times-Union,* where one of my first assignments was a series on the Iroquois Indians. That was great. In fact it spoiled me because it was an ideal assignment for me. I was able to spend months traveling around the state to different reservations and really digging deeply into the subject. When I was working on that story, I began to see how beliefs shape culture, and how culture and beliefs then shape a person's daily life. This dynamic really drew my interest.

As the years passed, I covered business, labor, small towns, and demographics. That's when it became so clear to me that people's beliefs do shape their lives. We're not just economic actors. I remember when I was writing in business, the supposition was, that *people are economic agents and they'll act in their own financial best interest.* I found that to be false! People have higher goals or aspirations or even lower goals, and they're motivated by beliefs, morals and values.

"So it was a natural for the *Soul of Recovery* to be in that vein, and my most recent book on the Sabbath, "A Day Apart" is even more explicitly religious in that sense."

Where did the title, "A Day Apart" come from?

"I don't know for sure. I have since heard the term mentioned in a

1961 Supreme Court decision but I wouldn't say I took it from there because I had the title before I had read that decision. It seems that people, in a shallow way, often think of the Sabbath as a day apart. In writing the book, however, I came to view it not so much as a day apart, as it is a day of entering into a greater reality. I think that is an almost mystical truth about any holy day; especially in Judaism and to some extent in the Christian Sunday and in the Muslim Day of Prayer which is Friday."

Can you talk a little about your book, *Faith in Words*?

"Sure. It was published in 1997, and profiled 10 different writers—poets, journalists, editors—and explores the relationship between their religious beliefs and their work."

" 'In the midst of that daily effort, a writer may ask: "Why am I here in front in front of this typewriter, alone in this mountain cottage or cold-water flat? What does God want of me and what role does faith play in my life and work? Is there a higher purpose to my writing—and did I keep that in mind for just one minute today?' "

(Excerpted from Faith in Words, Christopher Ringwald)

Why does this subject of how beliefs shape individuals and society interest you?

"It fascinates me and I think it drives life. It drives humanity. We're all endowed with free will and some degree of intellect. It suits my talent and skills to write about the subject and it's a subject that matters to me. A lot of issues like politics for instance, will come and go, and I'm glad there are people who write about them, but they just don't grab me. I was looking for something that had a little more meat and depth.

"Even politics is driven by people's beliefs. What one politician says about another politician's views is going to come or go, but ultimately people are going to vote for someone because their campaign literature or their speeches address some deeply held beliefs that the voter holds. I think beliefs are the key to life. People believe certain things because they serve a purpose, not just for the heck of it. Addicts and alcoholics, for example, come to believe in a higher power and the importance of turning their will and their life over to that higher power, not because it's written on a piece of paper somewhere, but because it makes a difference in their life."

Please describe the evolution of your own spiritual understanding of a God or Higher Power?

"Well, in a general sense I grew up Roman Catholic, and I had periods of rebellion against it, but never felt the need to leave the church. My path just evolved over time. I had periods when I didn't think about God too much or didn't sense his presence, but even in the worst periods of my life I maintained some connection to the church by going to Mass once a week. That routine probably saved me in some periods and was one of the reasons why I became interested in writing the book about the Sabbath. Just being in church each Sunday reminded me of God, and helped keep some focus on a higher purpose to my life and work. It also helped me to keep the concerns of the other six days of the week—like, *does the world know how important I am?*—in a healthier context. (Laughter) It worked for me and made a concrete difference in my life. It still does today and probably more so then when I was younger."

How did your relationship to the church and to your God become part of how you lived your life?

"I think it always was. I believe we're made in the image and likeness of God. God's put his stamp on us. We come from God and I believe we go back to God. So I think it behooves me to get to know God better and what He has in mind for me. One thing I like about Catholicism is that it has always joined faith with reason; it's not solely an intellectual proposition for me. I can't really articulate all the reasons why. I just know some of it is very deep-seated in me.

"A lot of life is finding out who God wants us to be and not so much figuring who *we want us to be*, although I do think that our deepest desires correspond to the Divine plan for us. I think this is where passion comes into the picture, because when we discover that passion, in our deepest desires, I believe we discover what God wants us to be. I might wish a certain article or book I've written, would make a bigger splash, but *Soul of Recovery*, and my other books were satisfying to me because this is what I was moved to write about at the time. If I trust the instincts of the market I'll be lost. I wouldn't want to write a book and sell a million copies just to appeal to a bigger market."

Is that where the ego comes into the picture?

"Yeah. In *Faith in Words*, I wrote that you don't need a big or inflated ego, but you do need a strong one. I think writers sometime spend a long time building up their egos to be strong, because they're faced with so much rejection and other problems. So when they do become successful they can become egomaniacs! You hear stories of famous writers who were just unbearable; although most writers that I've met are pretty nice once you talk to them and get to know them a little. Writers often struggle for so long; and it can be such a lonely existence"

How do you keep a balance between being that "solitary, struggling writer" and being well-centered and connected to others?

"I don't know that I always do keep a balance but I try. My friend Tom O'Toole called me up one night after I'd written an op-ed piece about the harm done by psychiatric medications, and he said, 'I thought you might be interested in what I have to say about your piece'…and I cut him off saying, 'What makes you think I'm interested in what you have to say.' (Laughing) I was joking but sometimes I have that impulse. I think, *write your own column! Write your own book! I don't really care what you got to say.* Now that's slightly egotistical and defensive I know, but it's funny that when you do write about a subject, some people are very interested in telling you what they think about it. So *no,* I don't always keep a balance.

"How do I keep a balance? I have a small circle of journalists whom I talk to a lot. I'm sure that I sometimes wear them out. I'm very social, so almost every day I call up a couple of journalists, I know, just to chew the fat. And I do like to work on projects that involve other people. Both the Sabbath book and *Soul of Recovery* involved a lot of reporting which was fun.

"I also remember that while writing the *Soul of Recovery* I thought that I might crack up! I mean there was just so much material and it was my first big book. There was a point where I felt a little *loopy*. I recall that when I got around to writing the first chapter, I'd collected so much material; I'd traveled to twelve states, visited 20 different treatment programs, and interviewed close to 200 people. I was writing the first chapter last, so I had arranged all the materials for that chapter on this— very same—long conference table. It wasn't just a stack of paper; this entire table was covered with piles of papers and books, some of them very dog-eared. There came a night during that period where I was laying in bed and had a vision of the table tilting up, and an avalanche of all these materials burying me. That's really how I felt at one point. So, as you might imagine, talking to others is very important for me.

"Getting my work out there and getting stories *about* the work into newspapers along the way is great fun. It gives me another chance to talk to people about my work. With both books, I had asked other people to read them, and, later discuss with me what they had read. Sometimes when writing, it's just pure research in the library, which I love; the less I do on the internet the better. I love wandering the stacks of a library.

"It would also be nice to teach more on a subject I'm writing about, since I build up such an amount of expertise. I would really enjoy sharing that information in ways other than in the book."

As I read *The Soul of Recovery*, it was overwhelming when I'd considered all the people you had interviewed, the places you'd been, and the books that you had researched, in writing the book. How long did the entire project take?

"It took between four and five years. I was on a fellowship for a year, which got me started. That's when I did most of my traveling. There was a period of time where I was working on it just a few hours a week and then there was a six-month block of time where I did the bulk of the writing. I was also working on it and freelancing while I was finishing the project. I was back and forth between full—and part-time writing since I also had to support my family. The Sage Colleges was a great support to me. They gave me a place to write, as well as the use of computers and their library."

Who are the people who've inspired you along the way?
"A lot of people have inspired me and many I probably can't think of at this moment.

"My parents were very supportive of me. I grew up in New York City and that was the *stage upon which my parents walked*, so to speak. They loved the city and the mix of people down there. My mother was a fourth—or fifth-generation Irish-American; her family had come over in the mid-1800s, and my father was a first generation German-American. They were both devout Catholics and they made that the center of their life.

"It's unfair to the nuns and other female teachers I had a long the way, but there was a male teacher who sticks out, by the name of John Schipa. One of the things he imparted in me was that I didn't have to be a 'goody two-shoes' in order to be a moral person. He really embodied a healthy virility for me. He never personalized anything, he was a good teacher, had a good spirit, and was very alive and alert.

"Joe Touhey, a high school math teacher and debating coach is another person who embodied a deep moral sense, without talking about it a lot. From him, I saw that the pursuit of truth and logic in a logical way could be a moral activity. That's just come to me as I'm looking back.

"Thomas Shelley, a diocesan priest, who had a PhD and taught high school history, was a true gift for me. He was a real scholar; He would translate history from German or French books that he owned, without ever intending to show off. That opened my eyes to the joy of scholarship and to thoroughly getting to know a subject."

"I later attended Georgetown, and there my eyes were opened to the depth, both intellectual and spiritual of Catholicism. My faith was deepened and my study showed me there was a lot for both my spirit and mind to engage in within Catholicism. Among the many fine teachers there was Carroll Quigley, a great example of someone who really followed his instinct and his interests. He had a very eccentric take on history *but it was his and he made it his.* When President Clinton talked about his experiences as a student at Georgetown, I believe Quigley was the only professor he really mentioned. From Joan Holmer, an English professor, I learned that close attention, study, and intellectual effort could produce real joy and insight. Her enthusiasm in teaching Shakespeare was inspiring and contagious.

"When I went to Columbia for graduate school I had this *old-line,* eccentric professor, by the name of Melvin Mencher. It seemed that half the administration and students hated him, but he had a profound influence on many outstanding journalists, some of who became Pulitzer Prize winners. He wasn't interested in writing a story about people in a surface way—it had to illuminate some larger truth. I remember that he said, 'Don't be a stenographer for unfortunates,' which may sound very harsh and almost cruel. He was telling us that many people have sad stories and it would be nice to fix them all by writing about them, but focus instead on writing the bigger story. In that way you can help to resolve the larger issue and not just their immediate problem."

What is passion to you Chris?

"Well, for me I think it's about finding the thing I want to do and experiencing joy and purposefulness in the process. Passion—although very honestly the word sometimes leaves me cold and drained of meaning when I hear it associated with violence and sex—is that which I feel strongly about, and see as important enough for me to undertake. I try to balance that against what I think God's will and direction is for me.

"I went to Iraq for a couple of weeks in 1999 and reported on what life was like for the average Iraqi under the sanctions. Through a friend I had heard of a Christian pacifist group that was going there to distribute medical supplies, as a way of protesting the embargo on trade with Iraq. That trip was wonderful because it was an opportunity to report on a story that was not being told in this country. At that time, Iraq had been under these sanctions for nine years or so, and the country was a wreck as a result. It seemed to me, that at the time, Saddam Hussein was really not a threat; although I had not done any exhaustive investigation of the Iraqi military. When I came back there wasn't much interest in the story, although I eventually did pieces on it for the Albany Times-Union, and for various Catholic publications. Thank God for the Catholic press! The topics/issues that deserve coverage are often not very popular, but in this instance I felt this story really needed to be told.

"I'm very grateful for my life. It's been rewarding for me, but it's taken a lot of sacrifice on the part of my family—financially and otherwise. I mean it's been a long haul. When I left the newspaper almost 10 years ago, it was to take a one-year leave of absence to write my first book. By the end of that year my book was only half-written and I just couldn't see myself going back to full-time reporting again. I really wanted to finish that book. For me, this decision was a big leap off a very high cliff. At that point, we had kids and my wife was only working part-time. God bless her. She ended up working full-time for a year or two while I finished my book. Sometimes I still regret her having to do that. I remember when I first mentioned the possibility of my going to Iraq, she immediately replied, 'You have to go!' A good friend of ours told me that I must really want to be poor, because I had to beg, borrow, and steal in order to go. It just seemed to be the right thing for me to do. I'm so grateful to Amy for her support.

"Now she didn't say the same thing when I wanted to go to Uganda last year. (Laughs)

"Originally, I had been considering going to Sudan with some of the same people who'd got me involved in Iraq. Sudan, although a terrible situation itself, was getting a load of attention while what was happening in Uganda was not. A real possibility also existed, that we might be arrested and held by the authorities in Sudan for an indeterminate amount of time if we went there. For that, and for other reasons, I decided on Uganda, which had an awful humanitarian crisis that was going largely unnoticed. So I set about getting some writing assignments, raised some money, and off I went.

"For 20 years there's been an insurrection in northern Uganda by a small gang called the Lord's Resistance Army, led by a man by the name of Joseph Coney. They've been kidnapping children, making them into fighters, and mutilating people. Their specialties are cutting off limbs, lip, and noses. They believe in the biblical injunction of *an eye for an eye*. These kids are captured when they're little and are often made to kill their parents right away. Then they're continually terrorized and told that if they ever go back to their villages the Ugandan army will kill them. So they grow up to become these little soldiers. It was crazy and awful, but the great story I saw was that in the middle of this chaos and horror, there was and is a tremendous energy that's going into peacemaking and community building. It's needed because the people in the Lord's Resistance Army are in the same tribe as the people they are killing. Again I thought it was an important story that needed to be covered, so I went."

It seems that you really march to your own drummer.

"I try—life is short. Sometimes I think it would be nice to have greater financial security and a nice pension plan. It's tough working in Albany. Because it's the state capital, many of my friends, neighbors, and the people I play tennis with, are state workers who are looking at a retirement with a great deal of financial security and inflation protection. This can kick off some anxiety in me, but on the other hand, I have a great wife who has supported me and, besides, *we haven't died yet*.

"A lot of times we think we can have all the 'good things' in our present life if only we'd had a slightly different circumstance. Some days I'll catch myself second-guessing my book-writing decisions or my educational level. I'll sometimes think, *Oh! I should've gotten a PhD, been out of college, and then written this book. It would have been so much easier.* The truth is that if I did get a PhD, I'd most likely be writing things that were much more specialized but would not be work I enjoy doing today."

This idea harkens back to what you said earlier about finding out what God's plan or path is for you.

"Yes! A good example is that I recently began work on a new book that will look at the spiritual lives of people with mental illness. I want it to be focused exclusively on the people, unlike *Soul of Recovery* which contained a great deal of research. The book will be built on in-depth interviews with about 12 people talking about their spiritual beliefs, practices, and experiences.

"The project is going a little faster than I expected. I sent out a couple of queries that got sent around the country to various groups. So far I've heard from 120-plus people with virtually all of them saying, 'I'd love to tell my story!' I asked for one graduate assistant, and five volunteered. At the same time, I'm still finishing up the detail work of my most recent book *A Day Apart*. So I got to thinking I never should have started this new book and I should just drop it. Then, one afternoon, I called one of these people to say that I was going to postpone the interview—maybe forever. Well, as we started talking, he began sharing parts of his story, which became so fascinating to me that I got caught up in it. The same day, somebody else who was interested in being interviewed for the book called me. I was only going to take his name and number, intending to get back to him later, but then I decided to ask him a question and it wasn't until 45 minutes later that we finished. It was amazing!

"Yesterday I interviewed a fascinating woman, who is very articulate and sophisticated in many ways, and has a severe Bi-Polar disorder. She grew up Jewish, went to college and graduate school, and then started having psychiatric problems, which caused her to lose memory of long pieces of her life. She's now doing pretty well. Two years ago she converted to Mormonism and has found a wonderful home for herself in that Church. They've helped her to deal with her mental illness. She told me there are Sundays where she's so *down* that she can hardly move, but she's goes to service, and later attends classes where people just hug her while she cries. I'm not sure you could get that at every church.

"Many of the people who I've asked to interview have said, 'This is so important. It's so nice of you to ask.' Nobody has ever been interested in their story. Again, quoting Melvin Mencher, he used to say as a take-off on Thoreau, that '*most men lead lives of desperate quietness.* 'He would always say that 'Most people are just dying to tell their stories. It makes their life more real.'"

What would you like you're legacy to be?

"Oh Gosh, I'm afraid that whatever I say here will sound pompous. First thing I'll say is that I'd like to usher my children into a good adulthood: free, faithfully Catholic, relatively happy, and productive

"I'd also like to know that in some way I've helped to improve people's lives. I hope I've helped to give more people an equal shot at things—especially people who have personal problems. I'd like to give people greater freedom, an awareness of what God intends for them, and a larger vision of what's possible in their lives. I think *poverty of imagination* is one of the worst poverties for a person to have.

"All of us have a certain amount of freedom, even in the most restricted of societies or circumstances. Look at Victor Frankl, who, while a prisoner in a German concentration camp had a very significant insight. He became conscious that even in such a terrible place he had the power to choose his attitude. He recognized that prisoners who fared better than others, in large part had better attitudes toward what was happening around them. I believe that's one of the most basic freedoms we have as human beings. It's a cliché to say, 'Have a good attitude,' but I honestly believe attitude can sometimes be the difference between life and death.

"I know that I have to do what is mine to do without looking for specific results. The situation in Uganda didn't change because I wrote about it, and I really don't know how much attention my stories on Iraq got, but I had decided all those stories needed to be told. I was also fascinated by investigating and presenting the spiritual side of things in *The Soul of Recovery*, but I was also nagged by a sense that this topic gets short shrift, where dealing with addictions is concerned. We've got the same problem in treating mental health; it's even worse there. That's one of the reasons I'm writing this latest book. Many of the people being treated for mental illness receive lots of access to medications, but no one's ever asked them what kind of spiritual life they have, and if it's significant to them. All of this confirms for me the importance of writing these stories."

Postscript: In June of 2008 Chris was named editor of The Evangelist, the official weekly newspaper of the Albany Catholic Diocese.

Chris may be contacted at ringwc@sage.edu or at 518.292-1727

His books: *Faith in Words*; *The Soul of Recovery*: Uncovering the Spiritual Dimension in the Treatment of Addictions; and *A Day Apart*: How Jews, Christians, and Muslims Find Faith, Freedom, and Joy on the Sabbath" can all be purchased online from major booksellers.

Chapter 18
Intention
Jim Garrett

"I do a fair amount of backpacking and other outdoor activity, and I have a philosophy that says, pack out more than you pack in! What that means is that I will pick up little pieces of trash and litter that people leave along the trail or in a campsite in some remote place. I also view that metaphorically in how I try to live my life. When I leave this life I intend to leave it a better place than it was when I arrived..."

Jim is a 59-year-old Social Worker and interventionist, working in the addictions field. His professional work is focused on helping families that have been affected by the alcoholism or chemical dependency of a loved one. His passion for this work has motivated him and Dr. Judith Landau to pioneer a new method of Invitational Intervention, the Arise method, that assists families to get resistant loved ones into treatment at earlier stages than had previously been thought possible. Jim is also an avid sportsman whose spirituality and commitment to learning and his personal growth, inform every aspect of his life.

"I have a number of passions. Professionally, my passion is seeing families move from being captured and controlled by addiction, to becoming families in recovery. I've really dedicated myself professionally to that being my life's work. I marvel at the resilience, resourcefulness, and ability of families to pull together and help one another, as well as the individual in a family who steps up and begins to make changes and break cycles that have often gone on for generations. I feel honored that families trust me enough to work with them during one of their most vulnerable times, without knowing whether their addicted love one will 'make it' and whether they'll ever get that person back again.

"This work inspires me, keeps me energized, taps into my creativity, and allows me to go to another level of consciousness. When I'm working with a family to help get an addicted loved one into treatment I enter what I call the subconsciousness of the family. What I mean by that is there are often dynamics within a family that have been passed on from generation to generation, and if you can go to the subconscious of the family, you can actually get to the root cause of their pain—often an untimely loss or trauma. When you can show the origin of the pain to them, you can help the family members understand how the addiction, in the beginning, was meant to help the family heal from that pain, and to prevent the family from more loss and pain. Over time, however, as the family passes through the generations, the addiction becomes more and more imbedded. So, two or three generations down the line, no one remembers the original pain because no one from that time is alive. All they know is, *we have this dysfunctional, addicted family now,* and, with that comes a sense of hopelessness that the family can never get better. The family, at this point, has lost the knowledge that it did not always have addiction in it. I believe that by tapping into what I call that family subconscious, which leads back to the origin of the pain and the start of addiction, families are able to understand what has happened and, together, are able to invite the addicted person to enter treatment and recovery. That family, then no longer needs the protection of the addiction to cover whatever pain or loss it was originally shielding the family from. That's my passion, professionally.

"On a personal level, I'm a sports 'nut!' I've been gifted athletically and I love the inner challenge of athletics. I don't talk about this a whole lot, but I was a small college All-American football player and received a number of athletic awards while attending college. I've also been a bronze medalist in cycling, at the Empire State Games, here in New York. I've been blessed with those kinds of talents and I'm just tickled by being around people who push me, challenge me, and encourage me.

"I'll never forget the time when I got the medal in a criterion race at the Empire Games. Prior to the race, I warmed up with Paul Marcasi, a colleague from my cycling club. He was also a U.S. record holder as a speed skater and had been an alternate on the US Olympic short-track speed skating team. Today he's an Olympic coach. So I'm warming up with Paul, and I questioned him about how he was able to set his skating records. He told me about a process of visualization he uses, as well as how to finish what you start. He said that it's so easy to get caught up in finishing *well*, but not finishing up on the 'podium.' Paul and I had biked thousands of miles previously but I'd never heard him talk this way.

"He asked me to visualize a place and time where I'd felt my absolute best in a race, and then remember it in all of my muscles, emotions, strength, thoughts, and in my sense of invincibility at that moment in time. I was able to do that.

He continued, 'What I want you to do now is take that memory, go *inside* and let yourself know this will be what you experience in your upcoming race. Then, as you get fatigued, or doubt yourself, or start to waver, I want you to go to that place within you over and over as you need it. I want you to be totally focused on what you're next move is and to be mindful that you've got the strength, the explosiveness, and the conditioning in you, because you've used it before. You're not going to let anything get in the way of you finishing on the podium!'

"I used that visualization over and over again throughout the race. Going into the final turn there were five of us bunched so close together that as my bike leaned, my arm was touching the arm of the man next to me—we were all leaning into each other. It would have been so easy for me at that point to have backed off. Instead, I called up my memory and was able to tap into that feeling of explosiveness and have that final burst of speed that pushed me ahead and over the finish line. I used what

Paul shared with me that day and went on to win a medal. I just love that kind of sharing and support, along with the challenge that's part of sports. "

It sounds as if you'd created some kind of mind and body memory that your whole being reacted to at that moment.

"Absolutely, and I've used that process in other parts of my life as well.

"As I mentioned to you before our interview started, I was recently asked to chair a support group meeting of which I'm a member. I was asked about five minutes before it was scheduled to begin, which left me no time to prepare myself. It's quite a contradiction that I can be up in front of 300 people presenting confidently about my professional work, but put in a situation where I've got to talk about myself in a small group…it's very difficult. I'm actually very shy and, at times, quite insecure. What I didn't share with people that day was that I used visualization in those few moments before the meeting began to combat my anxiety. I create a mental image in which I allow my Higher Power to go first into the situation, while I follow. As long as I follow, I am allowing myself to be guided. So when I went up to sit in the chairperson's seat, I pictured my Higher Power leading me and, as a result, I was fine.

"I believe that most people don't understand that probably 80 percent or more of what controls and dictates their behaviors come from their subconscious. When I tap into what I call that *inner reservoir of wealth,* it's like being poor and finding a bank account that I didn't know existed, and thinking, *Wow, this is great. I didn't know I had all this!*

"That's how I've trained my mind, if you will, and how I've trained myself to deal with my recovery from alcoholism, or in working as a professional in the therapeutic context with families, or in doing something athletically. It's very energizing, but hard for me to describe accurately to you. These principles tie into all parts of my life. Sometimes people will say, 'Jim, you just don't seem to get tired! You seem to have lots of energy and enthusiasm.' That's true, you know, but it's not really a physical thing. This energy is as much mental and emotional for me. All I'm doing is simply availing myself of this energy-source, or higher power, which is an excitement and an enthusiasm and a passion for life. I believe that energy-source is in each of us.

"Sadly we disconnect from this source from time to time. When I disconnect, I sometimes experience an empty hole within me, where this dense darkness lies. That emptiness neither allows light in or out. Sound is dampened. There is no connection to my senses, no joy—just this dark senseless pit of emptiness. It's a horrible, horrible place to be!

"I get spiritually disconnected, locked up inside my fears, and then the fears can take me. Subsequently I can get caught up in negative, runaway thoughts that tend to build on one another. Often when that happens, I get so out of sorts that I don't sleep well, get anxious and nervous inside, disconnect from others, and might even become ill at ease with my marriage. This emptiness affects me on every level of my being."

How do you work your way out of that?

"To be a bit crass, this spiritual disconnection has taught me how my *ass is connected to my soul*! So often when I'm just *dragging my ass around* I'm reminded that I've lost my connection to my soul and that I'm functioning below that *God-line*. I know, through experience, that functioning above my *God-line* is so much richer and healthy for me.

"To move through that state, I first have to identify what the fear is that precipitated all this emptiness. Usually the identification of that will come to me in a dream that frequently will be disturbing and seem to make no sense at all. The next step is going to my recovery group meetings and being very quiet. Over time, I've found this process of inner reflection and listening to others reminds me over and over again of the principle that there are 'no coincidences.' When I'm *off* and I have this disturbing type of dream, I'll later be at a meeting and suddenly a topic will come up or someone will share something, and I just think *aaah,* followed by a wave of ease—very gentle, inviting, soothing, and warm—that washes over me. Something inside says, *Here's what it is!* Once I know what it is, I can use my spiritual principles to get past it; very similar to tapping into that whole body experience with biking that I described earlier. Then I'll usually share it with my mentor, my wife, and other friends in recovery. The slogan: 'Name It, Claim It, and Tame It' gives me relief.

"Sharing my brokenness is vital for me because there's part of me that wants to present myself to the world as being perfect or altogether. That tendency can keep me sick and cut off from that deeper spiritual truth and my healing.

"This process reminds and reinforces how important it is to continue to practice these principles. It's the same reason I will continually get on my bike throughout the year and ride thousands of miles. Why do you do something like that? Well, I do it to stay in shape and to put biking into my muscle memory, so that I don't have to think about how to do it. The same thing applies to my ongoing recovery from alcoholism. I've been sober since August of 1980, but I want to build these spiritual principles into my subconscious so that when I need to tap into them, which I know I will, they'll be readily available for me to use."

Would you expand on the idea you used earlier that spoke of *tapping into the family subconscious* as a way of helping individuals and families better understand the problem of addiction in their situation.

"My belief is that families are intrinsically healthy. Now that flies in the face of: *Oh, I come from a dysfunctional family.* That doesn't mean that families aren't sick at times or have dysfunction, just as our bodies sometimes need a doctor's visit and possibly a prescription to help regain its healthy state. I view families as being intrinsically healthy, but at times they get off-track and develop unhealthy dynamics that need to be addressed in order to regain that healthy state of being.

"With this belief comes the idea that a difference exists between a family with addiction, and an addicted family. It's incredible to me that a family, with an addiction, will come into the office, and let's say they have a 24-year-old daughter who's in trouble in school, not able to function well, has problems at home, and gets picked up for a DWI. The family steps in and will address the problem straightforwardly and guide their daughter right into recovery. There's no shame, no guilt, and it's all up front. They're able to say, *We have a problem here, and we're going to help you just as we would if you had another health problem.* That's a healthy family that has an addiction problem!

"On the other hand, an addicted family typically has multiple generations of alcoholism that they're not able to look at and understand there was a time when addiction didn't exist in their family. There was a time when they functioned as healthily as the first family I talked about. For whatever reason, this second family was unable to address the problem back where it started. As a result, the alcoholism then moves on into the next generation and the next.

"What we know, for instance, with families connected to the Holocaust, is that the generation of families before the Holocaust, experienced very little addiction—it was almost nonexistent. Just one generation later, the rates of addiction are the same as we see in the rest of the United States. So we know there's a direct connection between loss/trauma and addiction. The earlier we can intervene, the better the family can understand that things weren't always this way and that it can change. They can then understand and address the loss without having the addiction take the focus off the real pain.

"When I talked earlier about tapping into the subconscious of the family, I meant that I look at identifying the origin of the family's pain— what's not being talked about. I focus and I listen to what's *not being said* and that will guide me to the origins of the family's pain. When working with an individual, I will often create a family genogram, which is a written therapeutic tool for exploring family history and dynamics. As we explore the history, I might say, '*Oh my gosh, so your grandmother died in childbirth! She died giving birth to your father! Did your dad ever talk about your grandma? Who raised you dad? Who helped him with his feelings?*'

"*'It becomes understandable how dad's drinking would just take off given the level of pain and loss he must have felt back then, and it becomes very clear that dad would be sensitive to loss. As a consequence, (speaking to the daughter,) you leaving home as a 22—year-old is going to create more loss for dad. It's a natural and healthy loss, but a loss nevertheless. So your alcoholism would keep you connected to dad, but also keep you from attaining a healthy independence. You most likely will suffer failures that will keep you coming back home. So, on the one hand, all the trouble you're in causes dad pain while on the other hand he doesn't have to deal with the pain of loss which is connected to* his *original loss which has never been dealt with.'*

"That's the family subconscious that I tap into. That's where I go. It's not just an intellectual thing; it's a very emotional and spiritual process. It's part of the universal connection that I believe we all have and that's what I'm able to tap into—that's the family subconscious.

"Even as we talk I'm reminded of a recent tragedy in my family. I have 29 first cousins and one of them, whose father died from alcoholism, was recently killed in a horrible farming accident in which he got caught up in an augur, thrown around, and died. A week later, my mother and I visited his wife in a small town outside of Rochester, NY. As we sat around her kitchen table and talked, it became apparent that my cousin who was killed was clearly alcoholic. Whether alcohol played a part or not in the accident no one knows, but carelessness definitely played a part in the accident. It was at the end of a long work day. It had turned dark. The work crew was rushing to get a few things done and my cousin had shared previously with my mother that he couldn't wait to get everything on the farm wrapped up because he was going to have a month or two off. He told her, 'I can't wait to sit back and just drink for a month or two before I have to get ready for spring planting.' I felt so sad when I heard that.

"In talking with his wife, she told me they'd raised his brother's oldest son who has decided not to drink after seeing the damage it had caused in his family. So here's an 18-year-old young man who at least at this point is saying, 'I am not going to drink! As I look back I see what drinking did to my grandfather, my father, and his brother, and I just do not want to see it continue!' The impact of alcoholism on our family is so tragic."

The following passage is Excerpted from the book, Invitational Intervention by James Garrett and Dr. Judith Landau

Jim Garrett grew up in Rochester, New York in an Irish-Catholic family, as the oldest of four boys, with a large extended family system. He notes that family gatherings were frequently times when drinking would be an integral part of the social fabric. He remembers discussions between his parents regarding hiding bottles when certain family members would visit so that there would not be heavy drinking. He remembers his parents surprise when one of the individuals would end up intoxicated despite the bottles being hidden and no one having seen that person drinking. Nobody could figure out where he got the alcohol from, and when he could have drunk so much as to have become so obviously intoxicated.

This was Jim's first introduction to alcoholism, and the lessons he learned from this cunning, baffling, and powerful disease. Unfortunately, three uncles he loved died from complications related to alcoholism because the family did not know what to do. So, it only seemed natural that Jim would be interested in learning anything he could do to help families further their interest to get addicts into recovery. This led Jim to pursue a course of study in Social Work...go to work in the addictions field, and then in the early 1990's, with his friend DR. Judith Landau, create the ARISE Method of Intervention to help families effected by alcoholism and chemical dependency.

Over the years Jim has seen a number of his own family members get into recovery as the result of their families being involved in the treatment and recovery process.

Who were your heroes when you were growing up, Jim?
"Growing up and going through high school and college during the 60s, my hero was Cassius Clay, who later changed his name to Muhammad Ali. Like him, I was vehemently opposed to the Vietnam War, believing that we'd been misled by our leaders. Friends of mine had died over there, so I naturally had a lot of fear about being drafted myself. I became more active as an anti-war activist as I grew older. However, seeing a man give up his world boxing crown and everything that went with it; stand up and refuse to enter the draft because he

opposed the war; and then be sentenced to five years in prison; left me asking myself if I could have done that? I don't think I could have. So a hero for me is someone who's able to do something, and stand up for something—some moral principle—they believe strongly in, regardless of what their personal sacrifice might be. What matters for a person like that, is being true to their heart. Such people have a higher purpose—something greater than their self-interest—and they're willing to stand up for it, no matter what, even if it means a year in jail! Ali taught me something that I've never forgotten."

Is spirituality part of this great passion of yours?

"Without question! For me the whole concept of spirituality relates to goodness. I grew up a very conservative Catholic in a household where Mom was Catholic and Dad was not, and he didn't attend church. What that meant, according to what we were taught, was that he could never make it to heaven. So as a little boy, I was growing up and hearing about all of the great rewards in the hereafter, and thinking that my Dad will never get there. Somehow I was accorded this privilege of being able to enter heaven, while my dad, one of the kindest, gentlest men I knew would be kept out! It made no sense to me.

"I remember once when I was an altar boy, asking our parish priest, 'Father, can you explain to me how it is that my father will never get to heaven? Does that mean he's not a good man? What does it mean? Please tell me how that's possible in our church and how can it be justified?'

"I was really asking him to talk about spirituality—the difference between man-made rules and the spiritual life. I didn't know it at the time, but that's what I was asking.

"I'll never forget his answer. He said, 'You don't have to worry about your father getting to heaven; he's such a beautiful man!'

"So I said to myself, 'Oh good, I don't have to worry about that anymore! What he was really saying however was, *I have the same questions and I have to go to a place inside of me to answer that.*

"There was an interest for me in things spiritual, so I ended up entering (surprise, surprise!) a Catholic seminary to study and become a priest. A big part of that decision was to satisfy my mother. If you were a Catholic mom and one of your sons when on to the vocation of priesthood; boy, you were held in great esteem! My time in seminary lasted three years. My interest in sex got in the way of that. I realized that the *celibacy thing* was not for me.

"My belief, in terms of spiritual presence, is that there is some kind of unifying force and spiritual dimension beyond what we can understand, and it truly is present. I believe that unifying force is in all of us, and its goodness, its light, and its love allows us to connect with one another."

Have you experienced this unifying force in your work?

"Oh yes! In doing intervention work with families, it's normal that by the time they come in to see me, some pretty nasty things have happened. If you listen to what's gone down on only one level, it shuts off the access to what else is present within that individual. So, I listen to families and their stories to get a context, and then I challenge the *other side* to uncover the goodness and the positive. I view the spiritual aspect as the resiliency within them and within me. I see us all evolving and moving forward spiritually, and I believe we're *guided* in doing that.

"In that moving forward, it's not always pleasant; change is sometimes filled with turmoil, disappointment, and pain. When that's occurring, I have to step back and say to myself, *Well, this may be beneficial 5 years or 100 years or 500 years from now. Something may evolve from this that I will never even see.*

"I do a fair amount of backpacking and other outdoor activity, and I have a philosophy that says, *pack out more than you pack in!* What that means is that I will pick up little pieces of trash and litter that people leave along the trail or in a campsite. I also view that metaphorically in how I try to live my life. When I leave this life I intend to leave it a better place than it was when I arrived and I believe this is only possible if I maintain a spiritual presence. That means I must align my head, my heart, and my soul. When that alignment happens, I just know and feel it inside! I experience it in the way I function, the energy I feel, and in the possibilities I see. On the other hand, if my head, my heart, or my soul is off, I also know that! I get thrown off in terms of my sleep, my ability to focus, my energy, and my own happiness."

What do you do in order to achieve this alignment?

"For me it's a series of things. One of them is to put as much commitment, nurturance, and effort as I can into my primary relationship with my wife. If my home life is in order, that creates a foundation for me. As I'm saying this, I realize that it may sound contradictory that I don't begin with my connection to my Higher Power. Let me explain by saying that because of how I view that relationship, I know that if my primary relationships are in order, I'm comfortable with them, and have a high degree of honesty and openness within them, I'm then aligned with my Higher Power. So in an odd way, I guess that foundation provides me with the guidance I need.

"Another piece of alignment for me is my daily and weekly spiritual practices. Weekly I meet with my spiritual mentor. This is a cherished time for me where we reflect upon the guiding principles of working a recovery program. For me that's working certain spiritual steps or practices into my daily life. We do it every Monday morning, which is vital to me, because it puts the upcoming week into perspective and gives me a path or map for whatever may come my way. I also read a daily spiritual reflection, and do a meditation that usually focuses in some way on ego deflation. That means becoming less ego-driven, and more focused on what I believe are the more important areas of life. From that, I feel a sense of comfort that I'm going to be okay no matter what develops in my life. I also enjoy reading books, primarily ones that are focused on spirituality and recovery. The third leg of alignment for me is physical exercise—it clears my head and helps me to relax. I sleep better and my energy is boosted.

"The final thing is doing some kind of service that allows me to give back. By that I mean, I make sure that a certain percentage of what I earn, is given away. I'm a little reluctant to even talk about this. Not everyone, I believe, has been as blessed as I've been blessed. This is one of the ways I'm able to express my gratitude, which is something I do on a regular basis as well."

Jim Garrett may be reached at www.linkinghumansystems.com. or at zeke1@logical.net

Chapter 19
Listening
Connie Messit

"I knew something powerful had happened to me during that month's renewal. I had been asked on a couple of occasions to give homilies after retreats I'd led, because the retreats had been so powerful! I think I had touched a deep place in myself that I didn't know even existed! God certainly spoke strongly to me in those days."

Connie Messit is a Roman Catholic Sister of Saint Joseph who resides in Chestertown, New York, where since 1987 she has been Co—Director of the Priory Retreat House, an interfaith retreat/renewal center. A passionate woman, she sees her special gifts of listening and encouraging, as her avenue for making the world a better place.

"When I initially thought about this interview, I began to ask myself what it means to be a passionate person. One dictionary description for passion that struck me was 'a fondness or enthusiasm for music or nature.' That struck home because I have more than a fondness and even enthusiasm, for beauty, nature, good literature, art, and music. They all fascinate me and touch my emotions. Looking at a beautiful picture will do that for me. I then began to ask myself what my big passion is. For me, I guess it is about trying to make the world a better place, even though I'm just a 'small pebble on the beach,' so to speak. I do however see myself as more than a small pebble. I have the ability to listen and encourage people; and the more that I've learned about energy, the more I believe there is more each of us can contribute to the world then we think we're capable of. I believe we all have real power within us, and when we're able to tap into it, that power we can make big changes in the world."

"I see it happening here at the Priory when people come for programs or when I go out to facilitate programs. Sometimes I might be very tired and nervous before a program starts, but once the program gets underway, I forget about me and I get connected with the people. I also think energy is created when people are gathered in a circle during a retreat and that energy goes with them when they leave here. It spreads out from here. Maybe it won't last; maybe it will—but I don't know that!

"When I can help someone be in touch with their inner source, and strength, I'm doing what I love. It's important for me, first of all, to accept them where they are. Then I can possibly help them to recognize and trust that all of life is process, and although they may be in a tough place right now, they will not be there forever. I believe there are still points of peace within us and when we're able to experience them and see the beauty all around us, we can then find some serenity and happiness. For some reason, it seems that in order to feel the joy of life, we have to experience the pain.

"I guess listening is something I do pretty well. I seem to have the gift for accepting people where they are, which means that I can sit with someone when they're in pain. When it's called for, I'm also able to encourage them to move through whatever challenge they're facing at that time."

It sounds like love to me.

"I hope so! Some people see it as that but I've never called it love. I guess it is; some people have said they see love in my eyes. I think I'll be exploring the word love all my life long (laughing)…what does that really mean? What does it call me to?"

"I grew up in an alcoholic family; so when my mom was living with me, she was able to hit certain of my 'buttons' and I didn't always respond as nicely as I could have. I didn't feel good about that. At the same time, I was reading a book on love, and it motivated me to ask myself, why am I having my mother live with me? My answer was that I love her, at the same time realizing that my actions were anything but loving. So when I would say to myself, do this small act out of love for her, it became easier. This enabled me to do things for her with a different attitude. My gifts of listening and encouraging, as I mentioned earlier, weren't showing up with mom—I wasn't accepting her as she was. I was thinking it would never end. I didn't like her suffering and I wanted to take it all away! In this instance, love meant doing some things I didn't want or like to do—but doing them with a loving attitude nevertheless. Love became an attitude and a change in perspective for me. What is Love is a question that I can surely ponder for a long time.

"Love is probably what brought me here to the Priory even though I didn't understand it at the time. I guess part of that process was listening to that pull from within, which might sound a little funny.

"The two great commandments Jesus gave were: to love God, and to love your neighbor as yourself. I think most of the time we forget about the self part. We think that if we love God and take care of our neighbor, that's it. Yet there is this great struggle in learning to love our self. When I've treated someone well, I sometimes ask, Do I do that for myself? Do I listen to my own inner urgings? Do I take good care of myself spiritually, physically, and emotionally? When I'm answering no to those questions I am compulsed! I'm unable to listen to that voice within and like others in this society I get caught up in running and having too much to do in too little time. At the same time, here I am up on this mountain with all this gorgeous scenery surrounding me.

"When the indigenous people would move from place to place, they always had a 'fire keeper' who would keep the flame alive. I have pictured myself as a fire keeper… I get teary-eyed when I think about it…and periodically the question that recurs for me is how do I keep my flame lit and help others to light theirs? That certainly is a passion of mine even though I haven't given it a name. It's about being in touch with what is life-giving or what helps that inner fire to burn brighter.

"Being part of the Community of the Sisters of St. Joseph is one of the ways I keep my fire burning. Even though I don't see them a lot, I do know that I have their prayers every day and that means a lot to me. Once a year we also have what we call a Community Day, where as many of us who are able to, gather at our Provincial House. There always seems to be something that occurs there to rekindle my spirit whether it's simply sitting around a table talking, or reflecting on the themes of the day. We have a liturgy and usually end the day with a ritual, so that we feel energized and enthused as we leave. Our community is a very alive, passionate group of women and being in their company lights my fire. We catch the spark from each other. Unlike a number of religious communities that are dying, we're not, and I believe we do influence our world. In my early forties I left the community for about four years. I had entered way back when I was 18 years old. Today I can say that I feel very lucky that I'm a Sister of Saint Joseph!

How did your journey as a Sister of St. Joseph begin?

"I grew up in St. Bridgid's parish in Watervliet, New York, a very vibrant community, and we had our own grade school, which for those times, provided a very well-rounded curriculum. That included music in our classes twice a week and the parish itself had three different choirs in addition to pageants and concerts in which I participated. That's where my love for music began. I sang a lot, enjoyed piano, and later when teaching primary grades I played a little guitar. I enjoyed it so much that after I'd graduated, I'd come back, along with many others, to sing in the parish's high school choir. We also had a strong sports program for girls. I got to play softball and basketball. We'd have roller-skating parties. It was a well-rounded place and the sisters there were a big influence on me. They'd play sports with us and even roller skate! So when I was in 7th Grade, I started writing to various religious communities. My mother opened my mail one day, and seeing what my intentions were, became very upset because she didn't want me to become a nun. (Laughing)

"In High School, I attended Vincention Institute in Albany, and had

Sisters of Mercy as my teachers. The Sisters of St. Joseph however had a spirit that I really connected with and as I got older, I learned that each person has a unique spirit as does each religious community. That's why I was attracted to the sisters of St. Joseph. Their charism—the spiritual heart of our community—is Unity and Reconciliation, and that's a strong part of who I am.

"Now that can have a different meaning for each person. For me, unity defines my oneness with everyone, which means I don't look at someone who's not Catholic as being separate from me. That's a big reason why I love the work I do; People of all faiths and some without any faith come here to the Priory, and I trust that I'm one with all these people. When it comes to reconciliation, I realize that without forgiveness, I can not be in touch with that sense of oneness and unity.

"I'm not sure I can fully explain the attraction to the religious life, except to say, I think there's a certain amount of mystery in any vocation you find yourself being drawn to. There's struggle in it too. I remember when I was preparing for my Final Vows and thinking, *Sorry God, I can't do this—I really can't do it*—and then found myself saying the vows anyway.

"As I said earlier, I left the community for four years in my forties. At that time, I was teaching in a school that wasn't the healthiest place for me and I was thinking about leaving. Before I would make a change however, I wanted my future to be in 'black and white'—I wanted to know where I'd be going next and what I'd be doing. In the summer of 1981, I took a one-month renewal program at Mercy House in Madison, Connecticut and when that ended I realized that my life had changed, without really knowing how or why. When I went back to school that year, I told my class that our theme for the year would be 'Turning Points,' not knowing what a turning point that year would be for me. In the Fall I became sick. By Christmas I had an argument with the Principal and then refused to go back to work—I quit. In those days, women religious just didn't do things like that. If your Superior told you to go back, you'd go back; but I kept saying, 'No, it's an unhealthy place for me and I'm not going back!'

"At the same time I was in the midst of my mid-life crisis, which I didn't know anything about at that point—I was falling apart! During this time, Pat Black, an artist that I'd met at the summer renewal program invited me to come to Madison and do some silk screening with her, and also asked if I would co-facilitate some youth retreats. It was while leading these youth retreats that I became aware that I'd burned out from teaching.

"When the Superior said no to my request, I made the decision to take a leave from the Community, because I was unable to find any work that would be life-giving for me. So I left and lived as a lay woman for those four years, working part time, at home, repairing jewelry for various jewelry stores in the area while also working part time in the retreat house. During this period, I was becoming aware that I was being called to retreat work. We'd joined with a woman who was a holistic nurse and we began leading 'Mid-Life' workshops (laughing) while I was in the midst of my own! I then found that people at the retreat house were calling on me to do spiritual direction and more adult workshops. I also found that my art transformed while going through these changes. As a young person, my drawing was realistic and usually of a subject right in front of me. During this period, however, it became eclectic; my art now came from the inside out and was very powerful for me. I'd get very strong urges at times to create a drawing before I could do anything else! So this was both a painful and a creative time for me. 'The Agony and The Ecstasy,' the novel about Michelangelo's life, reminds me that without the pain there is no ecstasy! "

What motivated you to rejoin the Community?

"At the end of the four-year leave, which was coming up in August of that year, I knew I needed to decide whether I would rejoin the community or not. Having no real answer, I was very nervous about the decision. While on personal retreat in May of that year, the director asked if I was ready to decide. I said 'I'm not' and she said, 'Well let go of it then!' So I did. She told me that when I was ready to make that choice I would know. Now the theme that emerged and persisted for me throughout that retreat was to trust—trust God, trust myself, and trust the process I was in. About a month after the retreat, I went back to see the director and I told her I was ready to discern although I was unsure about my answer. She then presented me with a lot of questions to pray about, and the last one was, 'What will you do (if you return)?' Every time I'd write about this decision, I'd get to that last question and answer, I don't know! (laughing)

"In August I went to see my Provincial Director and told her I thought I still needed another year of living alone. She asked, 'Does that mean that you want another year away or do you want to come back to the community?' Without even thinking I blurted out, 'I want to come back to see if I belong; more than I want the year alone!' I never expected I would give her an answer that day but out it came.

"So I returned to the community in October and lived in a house in the Catskill Mountains. I have to tell you that I was still resisting what God was calling me to do. I kept saying, 'No, you don't want me to do this...you don't want me to!' Nevertheless, I did have a sense that I wanted to continue performing retreat work, so I kept on interviewing, but nobody was looking to hire a retreat director. I actually had the Priory at the bottom of my list because I knew little about it except that it was an empty building. The last monk had moved out in 1986. I continued getting negative replies but one day decided to give the Priory a try. I called someone from the board and inquired whether they would consider turning the place into a retreat house. I was told they were looking for a priest to come in and possibly create some kind of men's retreat house or community. At that time the idea of a woman religious running a retreat house on her own was unthought-of. He did offer to give my resume to the president of the Board, but I crossed the Priory off my list after I'd hung up the phone.

"The next day however, I received a call from one of our sisters who'd previously interviewed to be a retreat director at the Priory. She decided she was not interested, but thought that I might be. So I said, 'Alright, so you want me to go further!' I then called the President of the Board and he invited me to come up and talk with him. It happened to be during their Christmas tree decorating, So I thought I'll just go for a half hour interview and then I'd leave. But I got there for afternoon mass, stayed for supper and left after four hours. At the end of our meeting he told me that he couldn't hire a woman unless he got the Ok from the board. The board met in mid-January, invited me back in late February and hired me that very night.

"All during this process of interviewing I was also inquiring of myself if I wanted to be all alone on top of this mountain. I'd just come back to the community and now I was looking at living alone again. There were other job opportunities that presented themselves to me throughout this time, but I didn't take any of them. I remember sitting with two sister friends of mine one day, and they were both telling me, 'You know you're going there.' It seemed like everyone knew where I was headed but me. There was always something that was drawing me; that same sense of mystery that drew me back to the Sisters of St. Joseph. I'm amazed! At the time I didn't know what was drawing me to this place, but 20 years later, I'm still here.

"Trusting and letting go is so important. I used to do liturgical dance and I can still remember how I had to walk through my fear the first time I let myself dance. On the other side of that fear was a great sense of freedom that came with trusting God and then letting go."

The four year period in which you left the Community must have been an emotionally difficult time!

"It was! At one point I was ashamed of having left. The process of separating from the community for four years was called exclaustration which sounds like some kind of disease. It was also like a divorce emotionally. In those days the Community didn't understand what I was going through, nor did they understand 'mid-life' and what can happen to people at that time of their lives. So for a few years I was ashamed of having left, but later on realized that I needn't be ashamed because that event brought me to where I am today.

"That four-year break was actually a gift that allowed me to discover who I was. You have to remember I became a nun at 18, was a teacher from my mid—twenties through my early thirties, and then was named the principal of a grade school and later a middle schoolteacher. So I think I had to let go of being a sister, teacher, and principal and find out who I was as Connie Messit without a title! I'd also mistakenly thought, for better than 20 years, that I understood the everyday world, when in fact I really didn't! It wasn't until I lived in it for four years that I could really appreciate that life."

Where did you get the courage to make that decision and then follow through?

"I didn't think I had any choice really. There's a quote in Dueteronomy that says, 'Choose Life!' I felt that I was being stifled at that time. I'm not laying blame on anyone but the only life-giving situation or choice I could see for myself was to leave. It was hard! Even coming back was hard because there were some things that needed healing between myself and the Community."

I'd like to go back to your statement about seeing yourself as a "fire keeper." It seems that vision is very close to your heart.

"I'm not sure why it's so emotional for me except that the image is so very powerful! In any ministry or job that deals with people you can burn out very easily; yet at the same time you're trying to help others to enkindle their fire. So in being a "fire keeper," which the native peoples saw as their source of light, I don't want that light to die! When I'm in touch with that, as Deuteronomy says, 'I'm choosing life for myself and for others.'

I remember that during that period when I was burned out, the director at a retreat I was attending asked us what our dreams were. I realized that I didn't have any. I felt very broken at the time. I'm not sure when this work became my dream .but I know that something powerful happened to me during that month's renewal. God certainly spoke strongly to me in those days. I chose this new direction, but spirit was also working through the people who were calling me to do this work. I admired many people who had the vocation to lead retreats but didn't see myself having that kind of ability. So I was surprised whenever I'd be called to lead a retreat. The woman, who I worked with, Pat Black, however had this same dream for herself and I guess that somewhere along it became mine as well. I've been living that dream now for twenty years!"!

What keeps you going?

"It's a lot of things: sharing with people and listening to their stories; attending a concert; seeing a sunrise or sunset; playing with the dogs;

and being in touch with the God inside of me—that's really what the fire is that I'm carrying. Taking my prayer time before the day starts is very important for me. When I don't take that time, my day can be so fragmented! It's also essential for me to make room for play time and 'alone' periods. It's that search for a sense of balance. With all of that, there are still times where I can feel burned out. Recently I had two weekends in a row that were so filled up that I was thinking, I don't know if I can keep doing this! At the same time, I get excited through my contact with the people who come here. Their excitement becomes my excitement—it's life-giving for me."

What would you say to someone who says, "I want to feel passionate about something, but nothing moves me"?

"That's a hard question! I remember a couple of people who said they'd never had any 'God-experiences,' which I'd say is pretty similar to a person not feeling any passion in their life. So I'd ask them if they'd ever seen a beautiful sunset or sunrise, or been surprised by a deer on the path, and how did that feel? Did a good friend ever surprise them with some act of kindness? Were they ever touched by watching a child play? Did they ever see a movie that excited them? Then I would say, Delve into what it was in those events that touched you. Sometimes we believe we have no passions, when in fact, we really do. I think in various ways we cover them over or numb them out. I sometimes ask those who aren't feeling anything, if they would just be open to happiness, joy, anger, etc., over the next week and see what happens.

"Years ago I wouldn't cry, at least in front of anyone, and one day a psychologist asked me, 'When you go away next week would you be open to crying?'

"I said, 'no way!!'"

"She replied, 'Just try it.'"

"Finally I relented and said I'd try it. When it happened I was surprised because I thought it was something that only occurred when I was sad. Then I saw that I cried when I was touched by the sunset, the birds, and many other things. It was like the Agony and the Ecstasy; it opened me up to my senses, which I so needed to be in touch with. When

I'm not in touch with my passion, it's because I have these layers blocking it, and they can only be removed by paying close attention to my feelings.

"There are times when, although I strive to live passionately, I do not, and I ask myself, OK, what do I need do to be in touch again? It could be just sitting here and being fascinated by the light coming through the trees. I don't always allow the time for that to happen and as a consequence I miss a moment of beauty. That little cat on the beach came to me for a reason—I was open and receptive. I can be on the beach and be in my own movie any time I choose—it can be ecstasy! It takes me out of myself and transports me to another place. I just have to allow the time and space for that to happen."

So living in the present moment is a major part of keeping your fire lit?

"Definitely, and living in the present moment is a challenge for me, even though I've lived on this mountain now for twenty years and have a sense of connection to all of creation which I can feel when I stay in the moment. I went to Mercy Center on Long Island Sound last month, and while there I had the opportunity to be creative. I drew a mandala and there was a strange shape in the bottom of it which I couldn't figure out, except thinking it might be a dog or cat. So I took it to the beach with me and while sitting there and reflecting I heard a jingling sound which I didn't appreciate since I wanted solitude and silence. I felt very annoyed and thought, Why doesn't this person go somewhere else! Suddenly I looked down and a cat was rubbing against my leg and eventually lying down beside me. So I thought, OK, there has to be a connection to this animal shape I'd drawn on my mandala and this cat who's decided to come and spend time with me. Sometimes, when I can be in the present, I let the animals in our house or in the woods speak to me and give me lessons about life. I also love Julian of Norwich's mantra: All shall be well, all shall be well, all matters of things shall be well." Simple mantras like that can bring me back to the present moment with all of its peace and beauty."

What has your journey taught you about what it is to be human?

"When Fran (Sister Francis Anne Gilchrist) and I came here to live as Community, we made it a goal of ours to be emotionally honest with each other. That's something I've learned that I need to be. That's what helps me to move through whatever process I may be in the middle of. As human beings I think we're always in process. I'll never be finished learning. When I'm with another human being I'm also in the midst of mystery, because I can't completely understand them any more than I can completely understand myself. I do think, however, this mystery will guide us if we're willing to listen and follow."

Connie Messit may be reached at www.prioryretreathouse.org/ or at conniecsj@yahoo.com

Chapter 20
Passion as a Way of Life
Cary Bayer

"There's nothing wrong with you that need's fixing, but something great in you that needs awakening. And when that something great wakes up, life becomes more than just doing what we have to do each day; instead life becomes a passionate, joyful experience we can't wait to wake up to each day."

Cary Bayer is a Life Coach, meditation teacher, workshop leader and author of *Prosperity Aerobics*. He coaches people all over the world, and teaches classes such as: *Finding One's Purpose*; *Breakthroughs*; *The Inner Journey,* and *The Healing Power of Laughter*. Cary's mission is to spread the word of new possibilities for our lives, using his humor, playfulness, and wisdom. He currently maintains residences in Hillsboro Beach, Florida, and Woodstock, NY where this interview took place.

"My earliest incident of passion would have been at about five years of age. My father, whose name is Sam, and his brother Dave, both of whom had a terrific sense of humor, were at one of our family get-togethers and they just clicked with each other, and got everyone laughing uproariously. In fact, they were so funny that my father had tears coming down his face. My experience was that I was filled with tremendous feelings of joy and happiness. It was one of those *Kodak moments* where time stopped for me; I looked around the room, saw all this happiness, and thought, 'I want to do that!'

"That became a strong interest in wanting to make people laugh and to make people happy. So later I wrote and performed a lot of comedy. Then I discovered the Chinese proverb that says, "If you give a man a fish you can feed him for a day, but if you teach him how to fish you can feed him for a lifetime." So, it got deeper for me. I learned that you can give a man a laugh and he'll be happy for a short time, but if you can teach him how to be happy, he can be happy for a lifetime.

"For quite a number of years I was very much into being the 'comic.' I was very funny and made people laugh. When I became a teenager, however, I added an *"s"* to the comic and I became cosmic. I became very interested in spiritual development; starting meditation at 17, and teaching meditation by the time I was 20. I was suddenly teaching hundreds of people, and as that evolved, I became more interested in other forms of personal growth, until my career eventually morphed into what I'm doing now, which is being a life coach, author, motivational speaker, and workshop leader.

"You know, we live in a world where every time you turn around, the front page of our newspapers are screaming about how dangerous life is. Most people are very scared a lot of the time. For example, somebody called me recently to talk about how, because of the fear of identity theft, they were afraid to give out information over the telephone while applying for a credit card.

"So, my work is about helping people find out who they are in the greatest sense. I help them realize a deep sense of inner safety, so they're able to express themselves through the creativity, and talents that God gave them. I give a variety of workshops like: learning to communicate clearly, creating meaningful relationship through changing the ways we relate to others, or engaging in activities a person loves, and be paid for doing them. I also present a class for people who want to learn how to work through procrastination which can prevent them from being fully alive."

What does teaching do for you?

"That's a great question! Years ago, I began practicing transcendental meditation and eventually studied with Maharishi Mahesh Yogi, who said, 'The teacher always learns more than the student.' So in the act of teaching, you're always going to get more out of it than you're giving out. That's the nature of the teaching process. Every time I teach some principle or value, I grow in that value myself. An example of that would be when I teach a course called 'Prosperity Aerobics.' In the classes I teach people how to heal the dysfunctional attitudes they've learned around earning, saving, investing, and spending money. As I teach it, I sometimes have a deeper insight into things that I learned from my parents that were dysfunctional. As a result, there will often be another level of freedom for me in that area. Sometimes I'll be asked a question and I'll say to myself, *Shucks, I don't know how to answer that.* Almost immediately, though, an answer will come to me. I think one role a personal growth teacher plays, is to be an instrument through which the Higher Power, God, or Cosmic Intelligence if you like, can present itself. Often the information or wisdom that is offered through me is more than I knew that I knew— it's fascinating! So the really provocative questions can be where my greatest learning takes place, because I've got to have answers for my students. These answers, I believe, often come from somewhere beyond my conscious awareness. My ego cannot come up with this information. (Laughs) I think most teachers will tell you that some of their richest learning experiences occur when they're being challenged by their students in some way.

"So, questions are a challenge just like any other kind of event or issue in life that I might not know how to deal with. There are times, for example, when I need to make a specific amount of money in a certain length of time, or I must be in a certain place at a particular time, and I don't see how that can happen. But, if I'm fortunate, from somewhere a solution comes. It might mean that I must reach out to others for support; reach into my higher self for support; reach out to God for support; or experience some intuitive insight. These are the solutions to the challenges. I've also learned that challenges, although taxing at times, can bring out the best in me, in the same manner as questions can bring out the best in the teacher. In answering your question about the benefits to me of teaching and being challenged, I initially didn't have the answer. The answer came from the challenge your question presented to me."

Where were you born and brought up Cary?

"I was born in a little town called New York City (Laughs) in May of 1953. I believe I was brought into the world as much by my brother's wishes as by my parents' desire. He came home from school one day in tears and when asked by my parents what was wrong, he said 'I'm the only kid in my class who doesn't have a brother or sister!' He was five at the time, and because finances were rough, my parents were not planning on having another child. In fact for the first four years of my brother's life, they lived with my grandparents in the lower East side of Manhattan. My grandparents were both immigrants from Hungary, coming to New York through Ellis Island. They met in New York and eventually married, having four kids of whom my mother was the youngest. Since my family didn't have a lot of money, when my father returned from the war in 1945, they lived with my grandparents for the first few years, then moved to Brooklyn, and eventually settled in Queens. So it was my brother's desire for a brother or sister that brought me into this world. Initially they wanted a girl, because there were three Bayer's—You can say it like *bears*—and they figured a little blond girl would make us 'Goldilocks and the three Bears,' (Laughs) but I didn't come out a girl.

"I grew up quickly. I had an instant love for sports, and my brother, six years older than me, and his friends, saw that I had talent and could hold my own, so they nurtured it, which was great for me. My childhood love for baseball, football, and basketball was one of God's great gifts to me for which I'm very grateful. I hope this doesn't sound too immodest, but I was also gifted with a certain degree of intelligence which made school very easy for me and I did quite well there. As I grew into my early teens, I used that intelligence to try to find the answers to the great existential questions like *Who am I,* and *Why am I here?* I didn't really see answers that were very satisfying in what I was studying, so I started looking elsewhere. This search led me, at the age 15, to Carl Jung, Hermann Hesse, and Joseph Campbell. They seemed to be addressing the bigger questions of life, within a context that led to moral answers that were more convincing to me than the answers that were presented by the world's religions, many of which I had studied at an early age."

What is your religious background Cary?

"I was born Jewish and was Bar Mitzvahed, but my involvement was not much more than that. So, by the time I was 16 I was reading a lot of Jung, Hesse, and even the *Upanishads* which are very sacred Hindu scriptures."

It's interesting that at the age of 16 you were pondering such questions!

"That's right, but when I was 16, it was 1969 and it was a very unusual time in American history. The world was changing very dramatically!

"At sixteen I was at the Woodstock Rock Festival, in Bethel, New York, for a few days. That was a dramatic experience, especially for a 16-year-old. My parents were not there. I was with my friend who was 15 at the time. That was such a remarkable confluence of factors and energy coming together. I could see a half a million-people could live together in harmony. It was amazing! We had insufficient toilet facilities, rain, not enough food or drinking water, hot August temperatures, and instead of a riot, which most people would have predicted, we had something that was extraordinary—a level of peace, harmony, love, and compassion that I certainly had never experienced. Then, out of that emerged the concept of the 'Woodstock nation.' The energy of the place and the event was so dramatic and powerful that I came to Woodstock in 1971, just to check the place out. I loved it, and in 1989 I moved here.

"So at 16, I was exposed to many things that my brother certainly wasn't in 1963. His music was Chubby Checker and the Four Seasons, while I was listening to the Doors, Dylan, and Jimmy Hendricks. In the space of six years the world changed quite dramatically for me.

"In 1970, while attending the University of Buffalo, I saw a poster, with a picture of Maharishi, announcing a lecture he would be giving on Transcendental Meditation. Immediately I thought *That's for me*! You've heard of 'Love at first sight': well this was 'spiritual direction at first sight!' So I took the course and there was this amazing shift in my consciousness, almost immediately. TM (Transcendental Meditation) was great! The techniques worked for me right away. I practiced regularly and it became so helpful to me that I dropped out of college after that semester. What I had been looking for at school, I was finding in meditation.

"I decided I would work, save enough money to buy myself a Volkswagen bus, and then drive across the country to find my 'deepest self.' I moved back with my parents and made some money by selling incense on a street corner in Manhattan. In the end, I didn't raise enough money to buy the bus, but I did get enough together to enroll in a one-month class that Maharishi was teaching in Amherst, Massachusetts. I got to see him every day. The class was fantastic. In fact, this experience got me back to college because now I discovered, that, while previously school could not give me what I needed, once I already had what I needed, college became really interesting and exciting. The 'self' that I was looking for was awakening! Now I could enjoy the insights of all the great thinkers, poets, and philosophers that I would study in college. I was attending school in a whole different context now, and I saw that it had so much to offer me. When I graduated from Buffalo, (Cary graduated summa cum laude) I went on to a year of graduate work at Maharishi University in Fairfield, Iowa. It was one of the greatest years I've ever spent. Mostly I studied the Science of Creative Intelligence, which is the perennial philosophy of life as applied to our existence. I taught a freshman class that year, graduated, and then moved on to start my career."

Who are your heroes or the people who have motivated you on this journey?

"Well, people like Maharishi, Hermann Hesse, Jesus Christ, Walt Whitman, Alan Watts, Carl Jung, Groucho Marx, and on a very different note, Superman, Batman, and Zorro. The super heroes are fun for me. They represent, in their mythic embodiments, what is possible for a human being to become. I give two workshops on superheroes. One is called 'Zen Teachings of the Super Heroes,' and the other is, 'Christ, Superman and You.' The focus is on what spiritual attributes the upper heroes embody, and the potential that they invite us to awaken in ourselves. Their dual identities, like: Clark Kent Superman and Bruce Wayne Batman, have always suggested to me what Christ said, which is, "*You can be in the world, but not of this world.*"(paraphrased) In other words, we all have a visible role that we play in the world, such as janitor, author, workshop leader, etc., but there's something invisible inside all of us, which if you play your cards right, so to speak, you can begin to awaken to. Then you really lead a dual life: an outer world that everybody sees like being a car mechanic on the outside, but a Buddha on the inside, or like Clark Kent, a *mild-mannered reporter* on the outside, but a super hero on the inside. Dual identities have always fascinated me."

You mentioned Carl Jung earlier. How did he inspire you?

"What I saw from Jung was the recognition that the myths, religions and stories from around the world, whether they were true or not, were significant in that they were psychologically true. They represented archetypes of what he called the Collective Unconscious. This means that within all human beings, culture to culture, and throughout time, people continually create similar stories that speak to a greater possibility for mankind. So whether he was talking about the alchemists of the Middle Ages, or the yogis of a bygone era, he began to see similarities in the stories. That became very significant, because it suggested that the psyche had a motivation, and the motivation was toward wholeness and growth. It wasn't just a collection of pathologies that Freud and a lot of other psychiatrists had talked about. Abraham Maslow, years later, spoke about self-actualizing people, but for me, Jung talked about the psyche and the urge toward growth in a way that was very deep and wise in many ways."

Has ego challenged you as you follow your passions?

"Sure! I think, for me, one of the great challenges has been in my passion for food and eating. I have to be conscious daily of how I eat, or I'll lose my balance and gain weight. That's a lifetime challenge for me! I mean something as beautiful as wine is a good example of this. In the first miracle recorded in the bible, Jesus turned water into wine at a wedding so that people could have a wonderful time together. For some people however, drinking a glass of wine can be dangerous, just as having an ice cream cone for me can become a problem.

"I also believe there's always a tendency or temptation for the human ego to distort where knowledge comes from. In my work as a life coach and teacher, I could be making a presentation to a small group of 20, while at other times, such as next month; I'll be speaking in front of a group of 2,000. In the latter situation it's easy to think, *Oh look how great I am!*

"I see the ego as the *small-self,* who can be deluded into believing lies about its importance, and the *higher-self* as a larger self, able to see that we're just instruments in something much greater. When I step out as a teacher, my *higher-self* is aware that I'm that instrument and the knowledge or wisdom comes from a higher source. The ego, however, tries to convince this higher-self that *it's* the source. That's why people go on ego trips and why we often see people 'fall from grace.' It's something that I have to be conscious of every moment. It's not like, at one point I can say; 'Now I'm past that and it's gone forever.' A perfect example is the story of Christ in the desert, where this very great soul is about to step out to the highest calling in life, which is to serve God and bring people to enlightenment. He spends six weeks in the desert preparing himself, and suddenly he's confronted with temptations from Satan, or his ego, or whatever you want to call it. He is tempted with dominion over all of mankind, which is what every king or emperor has always wanted. If Napoleon was offered that, he would have said, 'Sign me up!' (Laughing) The story of Faust or even 'Damn Yankees,' the play about baseball, has been about someone giving up their higher nature for temporary success in the world. I believe that will be a challenge for all of us as long as we're alive."

Have there been sacrifices or losses for you in order to live this life you live?

"That's a good question. I noticed it once with regard to a friendship

I had with a guy who was very, very funny. We had a ball together and as long as we related on that level we had great fun. At other times he would project some very powerful negative energy that could come out as sadistic humor and anger. Although he was a very good friend, I grew uncomfortable and got to a point where I decided I didn't want to be around it anymore. At this stage, we pretty much only connect by e-mail, sending funny stories to each other from time to time. I love him, but I don't care for some of what he stands for and I know he doesn't like some of what I stand for. I stand for a belief that people can live in peace and harmony, so I don't want to be around someone who is expressing nasty energy. If I find myself laughing at cruel jokes about earthquakes, tsunamis or 9/11, my heart doesn't like that and I feel terrible. So I have to make sacrifices in situations like that."

You're speaking here of spiritual discipline as part of the framework for the work you do, and the life you lead.

Yes! I believe that discipline leads to freedom, and enlightenment is the greatest freedom that exists. It's interesting that the people, who ultimately achieve that, do it through discipline. I see a paradox, in that positive discipline creates freedom. An alcoholic, for example, achieves freedom through the discipline of not picking up a drink. A parent who teaches a child how to positively discipline herself, ultimately shows that child how to be free, while a parent who provides little healthy discipline, prevents that child from growing into the adult they could be. Gandhi said, "Everyone who will, can hear the Voice, it is within everyone. But like everything else it requires previous and definite preparation." Much of that preparation includes a measure of self-discipline.

"I believe discipline is best if it's enjoyable, otherwise tension can be created and that could create difficulties. If, for example, meditation was really laborious and a big strain on me, it would eventually defeat the purpose for which I practice it. Some people will discipline themselves by embarking on a very austere diet in order to get the payoff of losing weight and looking good, but if it's too difficult they will eventually be defeated.

THOSE WHO WALK WITH FIRE

"I use that idea in my coaching work. I believe that growth is natural, that it should be enjoyable. God blessed me with the gift of humor, so I use it a lot when I'm working with a client. My experience is that a person often grasps something faster and makes it more memorable, when I use a little humor, than when I teach them in a more serious way. I think levity lightens the way and speeds up the process by which a person learns."

How have you profited by living your passion?

"Well, it's great to wake up in the morning and know that I'll be doing things I love to do, and at the same time I'll be making a difference in peoples' lives. Most of the work I do is one-on-one private coaching, and a good part of that is over the telephone, just because of the world we live in today. So, I have clients in Bermuda, France, and all over the United States. So in a day's work, I'll hear people say things like, 'Thanks Cary that was great!' Or 'That helps a lot.' It's a thrill to be part of seeing people grow. I'm not a gardener, but as a gardener, you set up the initial conditions for growth in your garden: You plant the seeds; you water it, you love it and nurture it in whatever way you do that and then it's out of your hands nature takes over. As the gardener, it's exciting to know that you've contributed to the creation of that wonderful garden. In the same way, it's exciting to know that I've had something to do with helping people to grow."

How does spirituality integrate with the work that you do?

"My coaching work, which is called Breakthrough Coaching, is a way for people to make breakthroughs that represent ongoing growth. A belief of mine is that *We're all spiritual beings having a human experience, and the reason we're here, is to awaken to that great potential within us as quickly as possible.* When that awakening happens, we can live life more fully on a daily basis. So my work is about helping people to awaken to that reality, so they can allow the very challenges that can sometimes overwhelm them, to instead become important life lessons, which will empower their lives. I like to think that this spiritual belief of mine becomes manifested in me, in the form of my work, which helps people to learn how to become enlightened to this wonderful, inner spiritual power they were born with."

What is the legacy you'd like to leave through the work that you do?

"My ideal legacy would be that I came into this world and made it a more fun place for a lot of people; a more awakened place; that people had a chance to see that life is bigger than they realized, and that they were able to unfold more of their abilities than they even knew they had, as a result of my having worked with them. Hopefully I did all this with a sense of wit and play and tried to do the best I could to embody some of God's qualities of play, joy, and wisdom.

"I think all the great dreams that humanity has ever had, about living in some kind of heaven, may be available to us after we're put in the ground; but it's also available to us while we're walking the earth. As soon as we recognize that possibility, and work inside ourselves to waken the fantastic beauty within and around us, and begin living with each other in such a way that harmony and peace prevail over its opposites, the faster we'll make the lifetime we have available to us, something really *heavenly*. I know it's not only possible, but it's in the process of happening. How quickly it happens is every person's choice."

How do you know that Cary?

"There's a word—*noetic*—which means a kind of inner knowing, and for me it's that deep inner knowing that tells me this is true. Christ said the Kingdom of Heaven is within us, but I've also heard it described as amongst us, suggesting that maybe part of what he was teaching us was about life on this earthly plane. Everybody knows Christ was teaching us to love each other, but all those things about 'heaven' may also apply to our time here on Earth. I believe this world is more than just another "rainy, gloomy, gotta—go-back-to-work" Monday morning like today, that we simply exist in. I think we all have a *spark of the divine* in us, and as that inner 'pilot light' gets lit, it begins to light up the whole person, bringing with it the possibility of creating what's been called Enlightenment. Again, this is my belief for why each of us is here. The sooner that more and more of us can realize and live within this greater reality, we can create something on Earth that has never been seen before. In fact the name of my publishing company is Heaven on Earth."

What would you say to someone who says, "I don't know what I could be passionate about?

"I would say, 'It's actually simpler than you know.' For instance, if you have some free time, on a Saturday afternoon and you're puttering around in your workshop or maybe baking some cookies, notice that this may be something you love to do, but you don't very often get a chance to do it. You may call it a hobby, but you can transform that hobby into a livelihood that you can enjoy doing 20 to 40 hours a week. Then it can become a '*lovelihood.*' When you do what you love to do and you're paid for it, your life shifts powerfully! That's the work I help people to do. Everybody has something that excites them and its different for each person. Some people love to tinker with car engines for example. It's not my talent, but boy, my brother can do anything with a machine. He loves it! That's God's gift to him. People are happier when they can turn those passionate hobbies into an activity they do more than just a couple of hours a week."

What do you think prevents people from making that shift?

"People fear that if they do what they really love they'll not earn enough money, to sustain themselves. As children, most people are told to make enough money so they 'have something to fall back on,' and the truth is that *falling back* can break your ankle or hurt your back (laughs); it's just not good for you. People are willing to settle for safety. At the same time, safety or the comfort zone prevents them from living in the *real zone.* Some day I'm going to do a workshop called, *From the Comfort Zone to the Zone.* The zone I speak about is the place we live in when we're open to the grace of the Universe. You can't get there if you try and control everything by staying in that comfort zone.

"Most people go to a job and know that every week or two, they will be paid and their salary may even be deposited directly into their checking account for them. I live in a world where a lot of the time when I wake up, I have no idea where my next bit of income is coming from; But as the day unfolds, sources of income show up for me."

It sounds like you have a lot of trust and belief in a benevolent Universe.

"That's a requirement if you're going to be self-employed. Finding safety in being employed by a single employer throughout your work-life is more and more becoming an illusion within the reality of today's constant corporate downsizing and business relocations. The self-employed person, on the other hand, can have multiple streams of income. Courage and trust are needed to be able to do this however. I haven't had a 'job' since 1983! I have nothing to fall back on!"(Laughter)

"My connection to the Higher Power of the Universe energizes my mind with creative ideas and a power to attract opportunities to me."
A Cary Bayer affirmation

Cary Bayer may be contacted at his website **www.carybayer.com** or by E-Mail at **RLINK "mailto:Successaerobics@aol.com" Successaerobics@aol.com,**

Chapter 21
Unfolding
John Anthony Frederick

"I want to allow this life of mine to continue to heal and unfold so that I can make a difference in the world. I'm English major, and I remember a quote from Montaigne, the great French essayist, which best illuminates my passion: 'I am myself the subject of my text.' For me, whatever I'm doing, great or small, is important in the way that it impacts the world about me. I want to make a positive impact. At the same time I believe I must first save myself before I can have any part of saving the world."

A photographer, musician, poet, former county legislator, and most importantly, a spiritual seeker, John was born on Long Island, brought up in Johnstown in the Mohawk Valley, and today resides in Albany, New York. He is the proud father of Nicole, 30, and Robin, 26.

"I'll be 50 on October 10th of this year. It's a big birthday but so was my 30th. With this birthday however I'm going into it with my eyes more wide open than when I was 30. Back then I didn't know what was about to happen.

"To answer the central question of this interview, I first must say that I don't have a passion for just one thing, which at times is strength, and at other times can be a weakness. I have passion for a lot of things, and sometimes my energy gets scattered in many directions. So in thinking about this interview with you, it's helped me to clarify that my 'great passion' is really to discover myself and who I am: in this body, on this planet, *this time around.*

"Through my healing I want to become who I really am—my Christ-self, or God-self, or Buddha-self—however you want to say it, and be free of attachments. That's where I long to be.

"My passion has ultimately come by way of my recovery from alcohol and drug addiction, which started right after my 30th birthday in October of 1987. On New Year's Eve of 1988, I met a guy named Wesley(Not his real name) at a party and would run into him again at a Valentine's Day party in February, at which point I fell head over heels in love with him. At the time I was married to my wife Patty, and had two young daughters. I knew I was gay but I was still *in the closet.* I was a real desperate guy—heavily into drugs and alcoholism along with a pretty dysfunctional sex life. My relationship with Wesley eventually brought me *out of the closet,* completely against my will, because I had no desire to do that at the time.

"I ended up having an affair with this man, which filled me with great shame. In time, I left my wife and children, which was extremely painful, and moved in with him. My relationship with Wesley contained a lot of alcohol and drug abuse behavior. In fact at one point, he stole money from me to buy drugs. When I discovered what had happened I felt devastated and betrayed.

"Someone suggested I go to an Ala-Anon meeting, which I did. I attended a meeting in Gloversville, New York where I was the only man, in a room full of women who were mostly talking about the problems that alcohol created in their relationships with their husbands. Although I felt very uncomfortable, since I was in a gay relationship, and living in this very small town, I stayed, bought some literature, and went on to attend a wide variety of support group meetings there, and in Albany, when I later moved there.

"I knew that to get out of my pain, I had to do something different.

During this period, Wesley and I had an apartment that was close to the Sacred Mountain Healing Health Center run by a man by the name of Jack Allison. Here I am, a man who grew up in a small mill town, and suddenly I'm at Jack's Center, wanting to try his sensory-deprivation flotation tank! I figured this might be a *good trip.* (Laughing) Then I realized I couldn't afford the $30 hourly rate. At the same time he was also offering Course in Miracles classes, so I took a class, just to check it out. To continue however, I needed to purchase the book, which I couldn't do because my car had just been repossessed and I was in deep financial problems—again! When I attended that one class, I knew that I really could use a miracle, but I couldn't grasp what they were talking about nor could I understand the text book they used. Despite my confusion, however, that was when the Course in Miracles came into my life and it's been a great help to me ever since.

"My relationship with Wesley eventually fell apart and ended. He passed away in 1991; in fact, last week was the anniversary of his death. When he and I broke up, I moved in with friends and was living out of a spare bedroom in their house. By the time Wesley died I was homeless once again, and was sleeping on a friend's couch. My belongings were stored here and there in boxes, while my cats were temporarily living at my brother's house. My life was a real mess!"

"Wesley's death was really tragic—he had just turned 26. He had AIDS when I met him, but kept it a secret until I became suspicious about how often he was seeing doctors. AIDS was still very mysterious during the late 80s and early 90s, and drug companies had developed the drug, AZT, which was often over-prescribed in dosages that were later found to be more toxic than the virus itself. He had also never told his family of his illness, so it was a terrible shock for them. Since they couldn't blame him, they became angry at me for not telling them. I felt I couldn't tell them because Wesley didn't want them to know. It was a terrible time for everyone.

"One of the things I recognized about myself during that time was that I was extremely loyal. It never would have occurred to me to leave him. Loyalty can certainly be strength, but by not considering what was in my best interest, it became a weakness.

"Within two months I was in another relationship, and within two months we had moved in together. Once again however I was using a lot of alcohol and drugs, and the two of us were doing a lot of acting out with others. It was chaotic, and within a year our relationship careened out of control. He left in 1993.

"I now hit a *bottom* that was lower than any I had previously experienced, and it left me feeling hopeless, desperate, and totally lost. I was alone. I had no career because I'd been fired for my crazy behavior. I was also in school at the time trying to finish a four year degree. It had taken me from 1975-85 to get a two-year degree, and then it would take from '85 to '93 to finish my bachelor's degree. Now I must tell you that all this chaos seemed normal at the time, because I saw myself as a victim, and everything was just happening *to* me. *I didn't have any part in all this.*

"To back up a bit: after Wesley died, I needed something to do, so I volunteered to be a staff person at the Gay Community Center in Albany on Sunday afternoons. I figured I could watch the football games on TV and do some homework. I was told that staffing had been inconsistent in the past so they had stopped staffing Sunday afternoons. I told them I would be staff during those hours and I would be consistent and committed. Another guy spoke up and said 'I'll staff with you.' It turned out that the person who volunteered with me was Tim, who would become, and still is, my very best friend. Now, as I look back, I can see that I was being *led* by some 'greater power' but I didn't know it at the time. For the next three years, I staffed at the community center every Sunday from 1:00 p.m. to 7:00 p.m., serving coffee, watching football, studying, and talking to people.

"As I was finishing my shift each Sunday, I was aware that people were coming in and heading up to the third floor where a meeting for recovering addicts was held each Sunday night. So one Sunday evening, feeling lonely, hopeless, and helpless about my life, I came to the center to return Tim's car, and decided to literally *crawl* up those stairs and attend that meeting.

"As time passed, I went to meetings, put together six months of sobriety, but eventually relapsed with marijuana. I then proceeded to smoke weed while abstaining from alcohol for the next 13 months.

"During the six months I had been clean and sober, I was in school, and I had been given an opportunity to apply for an internship at the New York State Assembly. This was something I'd always had a desire to do because I was fascinated by the workings of the government. I was accepted for the internship and ended up working there for 13 years.

"These positive events were all working together for me. I was *being cared for*, despite myself. I was also being put in situations with people who were in one way or another helping me to get to the next level of spiritual awareness and growth. Looking back, my ex-wife—I love her—got me out of my parent's house; Wesley got me out of the closet; and my last relationship brought me into recovery.(Laughing) At the time, I was completely unaware of the journey I was on, and how all these pieces were coming together.

"In 1995 I really hit a bottom with my drug of choice, which was marijuana. I had smoked pot daily since I was 15. In the beginning it seemed harmless, but by 35, I was hooked physically, mentally, and psychologically. It had taken over my life. Each day I was obsessed with getting high. At first it would feel wonderful, but once I was stoned, I'd think *Oh my God, I don't want to be stoned! I can't do anything about it, and I'm going to be stoned for the next six hours!* Then I would think, *I don't want to live like this*; but at that point it was too late. Such despair! It was a vicious cycle that went on for months. Finally in January of 1995 I surrendered, got into recovery *full-time,* and have not had a drink or a drug since.

"At that time, I had started another job in the Legislature, so the timing was perfect for me. Audrey Hochberg, the Assemblywoman I worked for, was one of the healthiest and hardest working people I've ever met. I loved working in the legislature. I love the process of government and making legislation, and I'm good at it.

"In August of 1996, something happened that could have thrown me for a loop. The month before I'd become very ill with food poisoning. After a couple of days of being very sick and weaker than I realized, my friend Tim took me to the hospital, where they hooked me up to an IV and kept me overnight. In the morning the nausea had subsided and I was feeling better, so they agreed to release me the next day. When I went for my follow-up visit, however, my doctor asked if I'd ever had an HIV test. I answered, no, but I felt numb when he asked me, because who wants to deal with that? I'd been avoiding it for months. He suggested I have the test, which I did. Three weeks later I went back to the clinic for the results and found out I was HIV positive. I was at first scared and apprehensive, but eventually was able to accept it. I guess I would have been surprised if I wasn't HIV positive.

"When I shared the news with a close confidant, he suggested I find a sober person who was HIV positive so I'd have someone to talk with who could better relate to this problem. The man I eventually chose to talk with sometimes *kicks my ass* in a harsh but really loving way. One of the questions he asked me was: 'Why did you invite this disease into your life? '

"With that question, I realized this disease did not just *happen to me*—I wasn't a victim. It didn't just fall out of the sky and hit me in the head! Something in me brought this experience to me, and I invited it in. *Why did I do that?* The answers to that question are still revealing themselves to me, but I'm aware that I needed to hit some kind of a *bottom* with how I was living my life, and I needed to more diligently seek spirit in my life. In that respect the disease has been a vehicle for my healing, and given me a real sense of direction. My healing, I hope, has also shown others they can do it, too.

"My confidant introduced me to a couple of therapists who were doing spiritual healing work with people with HIV, and they encouraged me to attend a retreat in New Jersey that Brother Bill Stevens, a Catholic Brother, was facilitating with Chrysalis Ministries, a group from that area. At this retreat I was able to do some very important spiritual healing. The retreat, presented by John Calvi, a Quaker who works with people with AIDS as well as torture victims, lasted for four days, during which we formed a beautiful, healing community among the 60 people who attended. I was completely *opened up!* At times I just cried my eyes out. (Tearing up) We also honored people we knew who'd passed away as a result of AIDS. We grieved and healed, and even have some fun. We ended one night's work with a big ice cream party! So when I think about it, I realize that HIV brought me to this spiritual community so that I could begin to heal my life. I attended those retreats for the next couple of years until Brother Bill retired and they were discontinued.

"As far as how the disease has manifested itself in me physically, I can report that I'm in the best health of my life right now.

"Looking back like this is a gift. It shows me that once again I'm being *carried* and I'm meeting the people I need to meet, and I'm doing the things I need to do to carry forward this unfolding of my spiritual journey. It's similar to the Buddhist image of the lotus blossom, which continues to open, petal by petal. I think life is like that—continuously unfolding and revealing something new. It really helps when I can keep that image in my mind, in the midst of another transition or change in my life, such as I'm in at the present time.

"In 1995, everybody in my little community of sober people was talking about going to the *Roundup,* a weekend gathering of sober gay and lesbian people in Provincetown, Massachusetts. Although kind of broke at the time, I attended and shared a $45-a-night room with another guy. While there, I was attracted to a very nice-looking, tall African-American guy named Vince (Not his real name). I assumed he was way too gorgeous for me, but I introduced myself to him anyway. We danced, spent time together, and I ended up inviting him to come visit me in Albany, New York.

"He took me up on my offer and came to Albany for a visit. We hit it off beautifully and from that point on started dating. Our relationship, however, was on-again, off-again and our connection was sometimes tenuous at best over the next couple of years. I learned a lot about letting go which was a big change for me, during our relationship.

"I remember that one year when his birthday arrived I bought him a beautiful card. But, wanting to make a point of doing something healthy and different: at my next therapy session, I told the therapist what I had done. I also said I was really annoyed, because I'd been doing most of the work of keeping our connection alive. So I said to the therapist 'It would be doing something really different if I didn't send him the card, wouldn't it?'

"The therapist said, 'Yeah…it would be something very different.'

"'On the other hand' I said,—I'm a Libra and I'm always doing *on the other hand*—'it would be really thoughtless if I didn't acknowledge his birthday.'

"Oh no, you're not being thoughtless at all—you're putting a lot of thought into this,' replied the therapist.

"This gave me a different way of looking at this situation. I was only thinking of *his* feelings and leaving my own welfare out of the equation. As a result, I decided not to send him the card and, in fact, stopped contacting him until three months later when he called me. Vince and I subsequently resumed our relationship, and shortly after, he moved to Albany and into my new home. We lived together as a couple for the next nine years.

"We were married last July in Canada, and despite having issues that we had to work out, I was confident that our relationship was on solid ground. Shortly after the wedding, however, Vince began to relapse with his addiction. He couldn't stop and ended up moving out. He's now living in another state.

"That's where the relationship is now. I really miss him, but I am determined to heal from the dysfunction that I contributed to our relationship: my sex and love addiction, and my codependency. I really regret that I was not able to tackle those issues before they poisoned our relationship. But a person's *not ready until they're ready*. Today I am ready and working hard at this phase of my recovery.

"I liken this process to the branches of a tree being pruned, *or* silver being burned in a crucible and the dross being skimmed off. It's dam painful at times, but this process of moving forward through the events and the pain of my life, to uncover the real me that God created, is my greatest passion. Without this passion I never would have survived all I've been through.

"I want to allow this life of mine to continue to heal and unfold so that I can make a difference in the world. I'm English major and I remember a quote from Montaigne, the great French essayist, (1533-1592) which best illuminates my passion: 'I am myself the subject of my text.' For me, whatever I'm doing, great or small, is important in the way that it impacts the world about me. I want to make a positive impact. At the same time I believe I must first save myself before I can have any part of saving the world."

In all the trials you've been through, have there been times where you've wanted to give up?

"Yeah, it's occurred to me, but I haven't so far. I really want this life of mine to come out right and not just for me. I want Vince and Wesley's life to come out right. I want my kids' lives to come out right—they're so important to me. I want my mother and father's lives to be healed as well, even though they've passed on. Part of me believes that I am helping to heal them, as I make new, healthy choices.

"Throughout this journey I'm describing, I've done many things that have negatively affected the lives of the people I've mentioned. I'm happy that recently I've begun making some amends to them, and it was done in the midst of this despair I've been going through in my personal life. When things get difficult for me I seem to step up my recovery and my spiritual searching."

"My daughters, Nicole and Robin, were pretty wounded by my leaving in 1989. They were quite young at the time. We've always stayed in contact and, despite a few struggles along the way, have maintained a relationship. There's never been any real estrangement between us, mostly owing to their mother and me never playing any emotional games with them. After I left she wanted full custody, which I agreed to because I didn't want to fight and create more tension that would have further hurt the kids.

"Recently I was with my daughters in Long Island, where they now live, and my older daughter was really angry at someone she dislikes. Robin, my youngest, told her that she should realize that people can change. She said, 'Everybody can change, look at Dad and how far he's come from where he was. Whenever I think about the possibility of people changing I think of him.'

"I became very emotional. I thought, *Oh my God, I'm an example for my kids!*

"Nicole was recently diagnosed with MS, so she's on a healing journey, much as I've been with HIV. She's really taking charge: creating her own way of dealing with her illness; and I'm being helpful to her where I can. I'm proud of her.

"Nicole's health crisis has also been a gift in the sense that I've had to be honest with myself about where my daughters have fit in my life. Because I've had this obsession at times with romantic relationships, my kids have often been in the background for me. They're always there and I care about them, but they've often been secondary in importance to me. I cringe, hearing myself say that, but it's true. With Vince not in my life at present, I'm able to be more conscious of that. Their place in my life deserves more importance than I've been giving it! Because of that awareness, I've taken steps to amend and change my relationship with them. Recently I've been doing some healing work around my relationship with my parents, and I've become keenly aware that by putting my girls secondary to my romantic relationships, I've been following in the footsteps of my parents whose attention to us kids was secondary to dad's relationship with the bottle, and mom's attention to her romantic affairs. So this is a chance for me to let Robin and Nicole know they are very important to me. I want then to know they have a place at the center of my life, and that we are truly a family."

It seems that your passion seems to show itself as this inner well, so to speak, of positive, spiritual energy that you're able to tap into at the worst of times.

"Yeah—it's there. I could have gone out and gotten high when I tested positive for HIV—many people do. I chose instead to use it as a springboard to get healthier in various ways. I stopped smoking. I stepped up the search for God in my life. I got physically healthier. I gave service by sharing my story with groups and in my political life as a county legislator. I figured it was good if people could see me as an example of someone who was openly HIV positive, yet was healthy and making a positive contribution to society.

"While I was working in the Assembly, there was anti-HIV testing bill that was coming before the Legislature and getting a heavy push by certain people. At the same time, the issue was getting a lot of press. I couldn't do anything on my own to stop it, so I became very angry and got inappropriately upset with some people at work because of my feelings of helplessness around this issue. At that point I asked myself, *what can I do?* What came up for me was the idea that I could run for office and have more say in issues like this. I then saw that the woman who was the county legislator in my district wasn't really working very hard, and was beatable.

"I then made a decision, which for me was very powerful. After making a lot of preparations, I decided that I wouldn't run for election that year. Running against her would have been right, but it would have been for all the wrong reasons. At that time I truly was not ready, and I was being motivated by my arrogance and my anger. If I had run, I would have created a lot of animosity and problems for a lot of people. Spirit was not in the mix of what I wanted to do, and that wasn't the way I envisioned my political involvement.

"I bided my time, planned well, and in the end won election to a seat in the Albany County Legislature. I served for three years until I chose to resign in order to take a new job, which required me to have no involvement in politics.

"Looking back on that whole chain of events, I'm happy that I was able to discover more of myself; gain confidence in my abilities; accomplish something; and most importantly, inject my spirituality into another area of my life. When I did finally make the decision to run, people knew I was involved and wanted the job because I cared and wanted to make a difference in our district."

"I'll tell you of an achievement that was both my high and low point. I introduced a piece of legislation that would give lawful protection to transgendered persons in Albany County. In the process, this legislation brought people out in droves to oppose it. Many of them were homophobic, hateful, and prejudiced. They spoke at our committee meetings and spoke out during the public comment meetings, and generally stirred up so much controversy and fear among my colleagues that I ended up withdrawing the legislation because it would have been defeated miserably.

"Although the legislation was not passed into law, it was a high point because I really stepped out and fought for something I believed in, and in that process advanced the issue. There's a whole community of damaged and victimized people who need healing in the sense of being able to be who they are in the world, and not have to endure having doors slammed in their faces, being refused the opportunity to rent an apartment, or being fired from their jobs simply because they're trans-gendered. They constantly live under that kind of oppression. To be able to introduce and get the legislation out, bring some visibility to the issue, and to do some coalition-building among transgendered people, gays, lesbians, and straight people who allied with us, was certainly a high point for me. I know that even when you get a setback on an issue like this, it doesn't mean that it's dead. Others will try again in the future."

"By facing up to adversity when it comes, and staying on this path of spiritual-seeking, I'm able to step back and see a coherency to it all. In hindsight I sense a purpose to all these events of my life: *coming out of the closet,* becoming an alcoholic and drug addict, entering recovery, my spiritual search, my time as a legislator, and joining my church. The picture of my life as a tapestry is clearer when I can stand back and see the interconnectedness of all the events."

How would you describe passion?

"For me it's an ever-present, underlying energy that's very powerful, like the fuel underneath a huge rocket that lifts the *behemoth* into space. It's more than love, more than infatuation, or desire, yet it has elements of all of those.

"In the past, people would often ask me if I was passionate, and I'd reply that I didn't know. I mean I was an old 'stoner' who'd sit around on the couch in my house, get high, and think about what I'd do someday—maybe!(Laughing) I'm envious of people who have spent a lifetime engaged in writing and performing music, which I also feel passionate about, but my passion is present throughout many areas of my life. Today, I'm passionate about my recovery, my spiritual journey, and the various vehicles that help me to grow spiritually like politics, music, photography, and my job.

"I recently read a story about Christopher Wren, a renowned 17th century British architect, who was in charge of rebuilding the Cathedral of St. Paul in London after it had burned to the ground. He happened to be walking by one of his workers one day and inquired as to what he was doing. The man replied that he was building a wall. He then asked another worker who was working with wrought iron what his assignment was and the worker answered that he was creating a piece of iron grating. Further on he asked a man who was sweeping a floor, the same question, and the man said 'I'm helping Christopher Wren build the greatest cathedral in the world!'

"Now that's a great story for me because I'm currently working on what appears to be a *minute* piece of legislation for the Education Department, but I choose to use my '30,000 foot vision' and view it as me helping to build the *greatest educational system in the world,* by simply doing my little part."

I hear the passion in your voice as you talk.

"Yes, it's there, but it's something I really have to work hard to stay in touch with. To get to that consciousness where my passion is, I meditate whenever I can. Still, there are days when I'm nowhere near where I want to be. On those days I just seem to be trudging along, feeling ungrateful and sorry for myself. I want my next 50 years to be less of a struggle. I'm tired of struggling. I really want to live and work with more confidence and joy."

What would you like your legacy to be, John?

"My ego says, *If I could bottle my recovery and spiritual journey, and give it to everybody, they'd be just fine. (Laughing)* Ego aside, I would simply like people to be able to think, *gee, if John was able to do it, than I can too. He was a real nut!*

"A while back I was encouraged, to perform a song in front of people at my church. My fear and shame had such a hold on me that I had avoided it for a long time, never believing that I could pull it off. But I practiced and finally got up there with my guitar and sang that song. I made some mistakes, but I didn't run off the stage or wish that a hole would open up so I could jump in. That was a *big deal for me* because I had this terror of making a mistake in front of people—I've been told I'm a perfectionist. (Laughing)

"I guess if a person can look at me and say 'Wow, he got sober, I can get sober; he quit smoking, I can quit smoking; he can get up there on stage, I can get up there; he survived losing a significant relationship and didn't drink; he came *out of the closet*, I can do that; he has HIV and he's still alive and doing really well; and he got involved in politics and worked for change—I could too.' The Course in Miracles says, *You will do miracles and you'll never know who will benefit from them.* I'd like to know I've made a positive difference in someone's life. I'd like to know I've performed a miracle."

John Frederick may be contacted at janthony10@yahoo.com

Chapter 22
Living Life To The Fullest
Stephen Anderson

"I remember Susan often saying that she wished she had done this and done that. I thought to myself, 'I don't want to be wishing at the end of my life: I want to do the absolute best with my life now!'... So, as odd as it sounds, her death was a gift because it woke me up."

Stephen Anderson is presently employed by IBM as a project manager, specializing in developing information systems for clients. Steve's deep desire to be of service to people, mixed with his ever-evolving spirituality, and his love of travel, has motivated him to join the Peace Corps. In the week following this interview, Steve will begin a two-year leave of absence from IBM in order to use his skills to help government and nongovernmental organizations reduce poverty in Africa. This interview took place in Steve's near-empty apartment in Albany, New York, as he made final preparations to begin his Peace Corps training.

"Next Tuesday, to be exact, I will enter the Peace Corps. My passion is to use my mind, skills, and heart in service to other people, and to explore and experience other parts of the world. At present, I'm a project manager with IBM, developing information systems for clients.

For 15 years before that, I developed projects in both the environmental area and in business systems, for an electric utility.

"My spiritual background is that I grew up in the Unitarian Church. My late wife, Susan, however, opened me up to more of a heartfelt orientation to the world than I'd ever known. Later I would discover and experience Unity Church, as well as the Dances of Universal Peace, which over the past 15 years, have opened me up to another level of spiritual experience."

Can you say a little more about what you mean by this other dimension?

"Well it's a whole other way of *knowing*. Before meeting Susan, I was very logical and looking back at it, I might even say cold. I knew things at a distance, but now I can feel and know things with my intuition and my heart, rather than only with my mind. I think intuition and the connection to my insides and to those around me was what I was missing before. That's been a grand gift from my late wife. As I continue to explore all this, I've growing stronger and more self-aware. This has led me to bring my professional and spiritual life together in a really heartfelt way, to better work with and serve people. That sounds kind of bland as I say it, but I feel it very deeply.

"I guess another way to look at it is that I've spent basically all of my life, up to this time, addressing self-needs. Some of them were really selfish: me, my work, my education, my health etc… Some of them were broader, such as supporting my family: caring for my wife in her final days; and then caring for my four children—three step-children and one of my own. All of this was loving in its own way, but my love and caring was confined to me and my own family. Before I die, I want to experience reaching out into the world around me, and opening my heart and eyes to other people. I want to connect and serve.

"As I look at the world about me, seeing all the needs and opportunities that are there—environmental, justice, and economic issues—it seems there could be a need for people like me, who know how to manage work and projects with sensitivity to business and environmental constraints. As I've networked with other people, they've confirmed my plan to offer my talents in this way. It truly feels like the right direction for me.

"Susan died in 1991, and I spent the next year mainly working my way through all the grief. After that year I entered counseling, attended some retreats, and I began creating a mission statement for my life. I also read Steve Covey's book, *The Seven Habits of Highly Effective People*, which has had a great influence in my life. He suggested having a perspective on your own death, which was kind of appropriate, because at that time I was helping my wife through the final stages of *her* life, and simultaneously contemplating my own mortality.

"So I went through Covey's exercises: identifying what really matters to me, what I want to accomplish, what really energizes me, what I'm good at, what's exciting for me, and what kind of work am I drawn to and how can it be used in the world? I mapped all this data out on big pieces of paper, using crayons and drawing colored lines to connect the various elements. This was accomplished over a period of four years. I even spent a whole New Year's retreat by myself, working on these questions."

So it was a process?

"Very much so! It didn't necessarily provide me with clear cut answers, but it did put me more in touch with myself. Year, after year, I would come back with largely the same answers. Eventually, this vision of mine became strengthened, spiritually and emotionally, by my participation in Unity Church along with other dimensions of learning. This process of creating and strengthening my vision brought many positive experiences into my life. There were even times I would intuit something and it would happen! I knew I was headed in the right direction.

"There are many dimensions to my *mission statement*, if you will. There are relational, personal, spiritual, health, and educational dimensions, and my core dimension, which combines living a heartfelt life of honest, open expression, with my interest in people, my intellectual curiosity, and a commitment to service.

"From that, I asked myself, *How can I best serve*? I looked at the answers that I had already mapped out regarding what I am good at and what excites me, and then married those elements into a kind of project management—information system service to the world about me. How I would actually do that, I didn't know at the time. Later, however, after I had mapped all this out, the steps pretty much revealed themselves. I decided I would get a second masters degree, and work for some international corporation which turned out to be IBM.

"How this next step manifested itself was amazing! I had graduated, and during that very time, I was working for New York Electric and Gas, which was going through a buyout and was offering 'early out,' voluntary lay-off packages to their employees. Right after I got my master's degree, I accepted a buyout, and they actually doubled my severance package. I then began looking around for a job, and was eventually hired by IBM. So everything fell into place—doors were just effortlessly opening up for me."

How did the idea of the Peace Corps come to you?

"It came through exploration, because I didn't know how I would manifest my vision. During my first five years at IBM I was totally focused on IBM. I wanted to do a good job and build a solid reputation, so I focused on learning all there was to know, and earning whatever certifications I needed. I would sometimes work as much as 70 hours a week throughout that period. When I got home, however, my heart would prod me to read journals and papers and cruise the internet for NGOs (Non-Governmental Organizations), to see how they were exploring and meeting the world's needs through various types of projects. I attended conferences, some of which I paid for myself, during my vacation time. I attended conferences, for example, in New York City and Toronto on climate change, during which I handed out my business cards to everyone I could. I assumed the nature of addressing the climate change problem would include developing projects, which I saw as a good fit for me.

"It never panned out! I spent six months networking, e-mailing, attending classes, taking correspondence courses, and going to meetings. I pursued climate change and it just didn't work out. Even though they said, 'There's a big need out there,' I didn't get a job. Then I thought that if I couldn't work for an NGO, then maybe I could work for a corporation that's doing work in those same areas. So I sent my resume out to half a dozen consultancies that were doing work in developing countries, but again it was a no-go. I had pushed and pushed, but the door just wouldn't open.

"Then I thought, *I'll do volunteer work.* I was taking a correspondence course in climate change at the time, and one of the instructors worked for the UN. I volunteered to work with him in his consultancy for six months in exchange for the experience. In the end that door was closed on me as well.

"I couldn't understand why no one was interested in giving me a chance. Whenever I traveled down to New York City to see one of my medical providers, I'd schedule my visits to coincide with the times that the UN had meetings on issues that were open to the public. I would attend my appointment, afterward head over to the United Nations, and then during the breaks, hand out my cards, talk to people, and find out what opportunities were available. I tried all of these routes but I wasn't getting anywhere and I was becoming very frustrated.

"Basically, I was working 70 hours a week at IBM and scanning for opportunities at night. After I hit five years with IBM, I began to drop back on my work hours somewhat. I then increased the intensity of my search.

"I was in a relationship at that time, and I had told the woman I was going with about my dream. As our relationship progressed, however, I became aware that she was more interested in me being home-oriented than she was interested in my going out into the world. She was a college professor; very intelligent and loving. I learned a lot from her, but when it got down to a choice of my going out to the world or my being home every night at five o'clock for dinner or out working in the garden, we were unable to reconcile those differences. In fact, I would not apply or even consider joining the Peace Corps while we were together. Although I loved her a great deal and still care for her, our differences were too much to overcome.

"Right after our breakup, there was a great soul shift within me, and surprisingly a lot of things started to open up for me. I made more contacts and finally connected with an NGO in a bank in Bangladesh that had a worldwide reputation for micro-financing. My contact at that bank, a woman named Jennifer, accepted my offer to work for them as a volunteer, after spending many hours on the phone with me over period of months, helping me understand their mission. She also understood why I had been so frustrated at not being hired. This was such good news! Today I realize that NGOs have their pick of employees, because so many people want to make a change in their lives, and offer their time and services to the world.

"Early on, my egotistical, self centered perspective was, 'Now that I have two master's degrees and I'm certified by IBM and I have all this experience, they'll roll out the red carpet for me. They, however, were saying, *That's not good enough—plenty of people have education and plenty of people work for big corporations. What they have, and you lack, is overseas experience and a background of working with people in need.*

"That got me thinking about where I might get some field experience. Now, I had been thinking of the Peace Corps for probably 15 years (pointing to a file cabinet in the corner of the room) and the idea came back to me again. Jennifer, my friend in Washington, had been in the Peace Corps. She said that the Peace Corps experience would not only provide a service to others, but it would open up this whole other network to me. Jennifer was so important to me.

She helped me to understand the reality of what was going on around me, and then gave me guidance on how to respond to it as a way of achieving my dream. I actually got a chance to meet her in person and have lunch on a day when we were both at the United Nations.

"I studied all the books I could on the Peace Corps. I then asked my accountant if I could really do it financially. With the guidance of my minister, Jim Fuller, I explored the spiritual side of this decision, and with my therapist, I explored the emotional angle. I then discussed my idea with friends and family. When I discussed it with my accountant I thought that he would say, 'No Way,' but basically he said that I could do it. I wouldn't be rich, but with what I had in my kitty I'd be OK. If I didn't work until I retired and didn't touch my savings, I would have enough money for a minimal living allowance to take care of my necessities. I fully expected to work again, so I said, 'Let's do it!' The way everything opened up for me was amazing!

"So, I sent in my application. It took about two months for them to process it, and complete the security and health screenings."

What role, if any, did your spirituality have in your decision-making?

"My inner spirit knew this was the path for me, but my logical self didn't quite believe it and still had to double-check it. I know this path is right for me but sometimes I get a related message that is influenced by my ego or something else, and I get confused. My mind will sometimes focus on the risks: *Two years of IBM salary going out the window, and the loss of friends, family, material goods, etc.* At the same time, I've also learned to trust the spiritual voice within me that tells me my decision is the right path for me."

So fear was a big part of the negative messages that were telling you not to take the risk?

"Yeah, the fear was about the loss of lifestyle, certainty, routine, money, etc. My 'inner child' was part of that: wanting to know what was going to happen each day. I usually get up each morning, ride my bike down this road, and I go to work; Then I go to my French class at school, or I go kayaking. I enjoy listening to the kids playing in the street, and looking out my window, and seeing this glorious pond. Part of me still loves this!

"This stronger voice, however, was saying, '*Yeah, you can do that some other time, but for now you're joining the Peace Corps.*' Too much was lining up for me. My health was wonderful, I have no dependent kids; my finances would allow me to do this; and my current relationship, Regina, is very supportive as opposed to my relationship with my ex-fiancée, which was confining. Recently Regina and I cried together and made that poster (pointing to a poster in the corner) identifying who we are and what we want from life as individuals and as a couple. In some ways this decision to enter the Peace Corps and go to

Africa is difficult and sad, but we are also strong in the rightness of what I'm doing.

"Some of my friends turned away from me as I pursued this. My ex-fiancé and some friends of mine, for example, thought I was crazy. When those friends turned away, I asked myself how it felt. I realized I felt OK. So be it! I felt strong in my direction."

So your feelings in pursuing this passion were stronger than the feelings you had about the losses?

"Yes, and I had losses. The 'inner child' in me would want to give up at times. As a matter of fact, during my negotiations with my ex-fiancé, I had an office in the corner of the house and I used to look out at the street cleaner when it would come up the street and think, *I could do that job and be home at 5 o'clock each night for supper. Then I could mow the lawn and help her with the garden. She'd like that and she'd be very satisfied. That would keep me here.* But I couldn't do that. That's an extreme example, but I looked at many jobs that were safe and predictable. Each time I'd get close to taking one, though, I would realize that I couldn't do that to myself. Whenever I considered *caving in,* I would feel constrained, strangled, and drained. I knew it would kill me if I gave up my dream.

"Although this path is occasionally unnerving, in a greater sense it also feels very comfortable."

It sounds like this process has increased your tolerance to being uncomfortable?

"It has. Speaking of discomfort, I'll share a couple of experiences that have had a profound impact on me. When I was eight years old, my father brought me to the YMCA in Rochester, New York, and enrolled me in a learn-to-swim program. Dad, as I remember, was the only person in the bleachers beside the pool. So the instructors lined up all of us kids along the deck of the pool told us to march one by one to the diving board and jump in. I was terrified! The pool was 10-12 feet deep and I didn't know how to swim. It was like *Chinese water torture* for me because I was at the back of the line, watching them jump in, one at a time. Some of them could swim but I didn't have a clue. I was just about to step out of the line, as a couple of other kids before me already had, when my father gave me some hand motions that told me he wanted me to see it through. So I remained in line, and then jumped in, terrified as I was. Down below the surface I sank, until some force magically lifted me back up to the surface. I felt wondrous and very proud of myself. I think of the buoyancy of life, like the buoyancy of that water. It brings me back up to the 'surface,' and gives me the trust and confidence in myself, allowing me to 'breathe' and feel that sense of wonder. That memory has helped me to step into many unpredictable situations in my life. I'm the oldest of four children and my other siblings are still living in the Rochester area. So something has influenced me to continually step out onto the 'diving board' in my life.

"I think my mother, as much as I love her, has had an impact in creating this fearful *child* in me. When I invited my family to my second college graduation, she came to Syracuse and she said something like, 'I hope you don't go to any more schools; it's such a long trip to get here.' Her discomfort seemed to mean more to her than any pride in what I had accomplished. I felt sorry for her, but at the same time was aware of her negative influence in my life.

"My step grandfather, George, who grew up in the Canadian woods, was also a real positive influence in my early life. He and my grandmother owned 100 acres of woods and farmland. As a little boy, I would go out into the fields with him carrying buckets of saplings, and we'd plant Christmas trees. From him, I also learned how the natural world works, and how to nurture and care for it. He'd tell me wild animal stories, and that I should always respect these creatures as individual beings. He said, 'If you come upon a bear in the woods, you stand and be respectful and strong in your own right, but also honor the bear's right to be there. As a result, I didn't have a lot of fear or sense of separation in the natural world."

"I took the Meyers Briggs test years ago, and found that I was introverted, intuitive, thinking and judging. As I get older, however, I find those character traits have moderated and I actually appreciate and find it nourishing to talk with other people—but generally in smaller groups. Through meeting people from other cultures in my travels, I find there are differences, but the most amazing realization is how similar we are: we're all just people!

"Looking back, I had spent 15 years with New York State Electric and Gas, bought my first house in Binghamton, and lived in the same house until I left. My kids grew up in that house and my wife died in that house. I was so comfortable there that I felt scared when I left to go to work with IBM in Albany.

"Once I got to Albany, however, I actually flourished! I grew exponentially. My reputation within IBM got to such a point that I had important people in the work world offer me exciting job opportunities because of how I related to people and to the world. I was getting this wonderful feedback that said, *Steve's way of relating to the world has a positive influence, and it makes people happy.* That was such a gift! I mean this was relatively late in my life. I grew up in this closeted family, that didn't share emotions. But then I met my late wife when I was 27, married her at 29, and she helped to open up this whole other dimension in me which has continued to grow ever since.

"As I grew, emotionally and spiritually, I found myself collecting little toys and trinkets. Sometimes I'd even put on silly glasses, which embarrassed my daughter but helped me. I had been so serious all my life, so I'd wonder, *what does this mean? How could I play more?* I then discovered that Hudson Valley Community College in Troy had a 12-week class in clowning, so I enrolled. Even though I really wanted to do it, I was scared. I mean people *laugh* at clowns and I'd been protecting myself from that all my life. You have to stand up in front of people and do crazy things. It was unnerving but something was calling me to do this.

"The clown class was incredibly spiritual. After they gave us all the clowning 'tricks of the trade,' they told us we had to pick our clown character. They told us we had to look inward, find elements of ourselves that we want to play with, and then give those elements a name. We actually studied ourselves in the mirror, making faces at

298

ourselves, so that our makeup would be as unique to our facial characteristics as our costume was unique to the character we chose."

"As I looked inward I discovered a side of me that was funny, free to express itself, and, amazingly, was loved by other people. For our graduation ceremony, I came up with an idea for a skit, which our entire class worked on and refined. After we performed the skit, my fellow clowns told me that their friends and parents watched the video over and over; laughing uproariously each time they watched my character. Wow!

"Today, I am able to work with IBM, do serious things, give of myself through service, and make people laugh. I also know that I can go to foreign lands, pick up elements of that language, and relate to people so they can feel comfortable with me. I'm feeling very energized. Joining the Peace Corps is a huge leap for me but in a few years I believe I'll look back at this time of my life and see it as another *jump into the swimming pool.*

"Throughout my life, it seems that whenever I would read that someone had died, death had always been *out there* and not related to *me.* My father was killed in a car accident in the early eighties, and as close as my father was to me, my internal self was still saying, *that's somebody else, I won't die.* When my late wife, Susan, died, however, that mindset all changed. She was such a part of me. I had been with her and knew her intimately for 13 years. Our relationship wasn't always perfect, but Susan brought so much into my life. Then suddenly she was gone. She died in our home in Binghamton, where our children were brought up and where we had our Christmases and many other gatherings. I was by her bedside when she took her last breath; She was just 47 and I was 39 at the time. Through the long process of her battle with cancer—the doctors, the hospitals, the many ups and downs—I had no idea what it would be like when she took her last breath. When she did pass, I experienced grief, deeper than any pain I had ever experienced. And for the first time, I knew that I, too, would die someday!

"This shook me more deeply than anything I had ever experienced in my life. At the same time, her death reminded me what Stephen Covey had been saying about viewing your life with the end in mind. Now I was asking myself, *how do I want my end to be? What do I want to experience in my life?*"

"I remember Susan often saying that she wished she had done this and done that. I thought *I don't want to be wishing at the end of my life. I want to do the absolute best I can with my life, now.* She was a vivacious, sexy, musical, creative, loving, laughing and smiling person, and suddenly she was dying—just wasting away. As odd as it may sound, her death was a gift to me. It woke me up. I still feel her presence from time to time, so I know she's with me. In her Being and her non-Being states she has given me the willingness and courage to leave things behind, as I move toward achieving my purpose.

"I have two medium-size suitcases and a backpack that have to hold everything I'm bringing to Africa with me. Scattered about the house I also have many boxes that will hold what I'm not taking. Choosing what will stay and what will go with me is kind of how my life is. I'm continually challenged to decide what I will focus on, and what will I give my time, money, love, and energy to?"

I think it's very easy for passion to cross over into obsession, and cause a person to lose their sense of balance. How can you tell when that's happening to you?

"The first word that comes to mind when you say obsession, is control. There were times, like when I thought climate change work was going to be my direction that I tried to control my outcomes. After all, it was just so obvious to me! I *knew* there was a need out there and that was where I was headed. I spent 9 to 12 months driving toward that, even though things were happening that told me this wasn't the way for me. That definitely became a period of obsession. Everything felt hard and *effortful*! When I'm trying too hard, I'm obsessed.

"I continually used force to try to get what I wanted. It was like herding a bunch of cats into one place. Since I'm now on the right path, it feels *effortless* and sort of like being on an escalator or floating down a stream. I'm going with the flow now. What a difference!"

As you go forward, pursuing this passion of yours, what would you say is your greatest challenge?

"Not going into fear. I've picked up fear from my parents as a child, but it comes from my own personality when I'm impatient and I want to control things. When I do too much of that it can stop the creative flow of ideas and insight, as well as healthy relationships with people. The Unity perspective on life includes a 'deep knowing,' without knowing the specifics or outcome of a situation. This outlook allows me to be confident and to freely move into a process while maintaining my creativity, confidence and love. The life discomforts like no electricity, little water, excessive heat, and possibly sickness, that I will face in Africa, will definitely challenge me to not let myself be overwhelmed. I can't let those challenges become the prominent influence on my life while I'm there."

As a last question, how would you like to see people benefiting from your talents and what you are about to do?

"I want to do what I can to make possible the poverty-reduction work of both government and non-governmental organizations. Then I want to watch them achieve their objectives. That would be so exciting! I love to collaborate and be around other people who have similar ideas, interests, and passions.

"When I share what I'm doing, I've been astounded to see how excited people are for me. I think it strikes some inner desire that most people have down deep in their souls. That reaction was totally unexpected. I can't ever remember making this many heartfelt and honest connections with people before. It's all so amazing to me!"

Postscript—Steve's two-year tour with the Peace Corps ended on 9/14/07. He spent most of that time in Mali, in Africa, the 4th poorest country in the world. Among the his experiences there, he said he really enjoyed,

"—The friendly people who smile and wave, whether they know me or not,

—being invited to share a meal with friends as well as strangers,

—children running up to me with big smiles and out-stretched hands in order to shake my hand,

—having the opportunity to make a difference in people's lives."

He said he will not miss lack of quality medical care, sleeping under mosquito nets, and 115-120 degree temperatures.

During his two-year tour Steve worked and consulted with small and medium businesses and supported the Ministry of Economics and Finance in their microfinance program. He also worked with a jewelry maker in Kibera, Kenya, to develop marketing ties with a retail business in New York City. Before finishing his tour he also created a partnership between Jigiya, a Malian group of people with disabilities, and Self Advocates of New York, a similar American group, for the purpose of ongoing cultural exchange and funding support. This exchange culminated in the organization of a videoconference in collaboration with the Public Affairs Division of the U.S. Embassy in Bamako.

Since returning, Steve has made presentations to many business, civic, and church organizations, about his experiences in Africa with the Peace Corps. He's continued, as well, to be active as a volunteer in many organizations that support development of small and medium sustainable businesses throughout Africa, and is continually exploring new avenues where he can make a difference in the world.

In May 2008, Steve presented a paper titled "Can Project Management Support Poverty Reduction in Africa?" at Project Management International's Global Congress in Malta.

"I was personally touched by the rich culture and friendly people of

Mali. My mind was also opened to the conditions that 80% of the world's population lives in. This experience has been profoundly moving in so many ways and I will always feel privileged to have spent two years of my life living and working among the people of Mali."

Steve Anderson may be contacted at steve_intj@yahoo.com. For his peace corps experiences,—http://peacecorpsonline.org/messages/messages/467/3213925.html

Chapter 23
Making Dreams Come True
Steve Holmes

"I'm a soul on a journey like you, trying to do all the things I can do
With the help of a few friends like you, we could build a new world
or two.
I can dream, I can dream, I can dream."
From the song, "I've got a song in my heart," composed by Steve
Holmes

Steve's life-passion is working with, and empowering people who
live with physical disabilities. Steve is a musician, songwriter
extraordinaire, and the Director of the Self Advocacy Association of
New York State. He is the father of two adult children, Matthew and
Stephanie, and lives in Albany, New York with his wife Cathy.

"I came to be involved with people with disabilities, 37 years ago. As
I look back I see that it came out of the peace movement of the 1960s
and '70s

"I was born in Somerville, Massachusetts, just outside Boston, 56
years ago. I joined the Navy at 19 to basically avoid going to Viet Nam,

I suppose. I had been attending Northeastern University where I was involved in the ROTC program, and while I wasn't against the war at the time, I did not want to be shooting and killing anyone. I thought that the Navy or other type of service would be better for me since I didn't want to be drafted and end up in the Army. I subsequently dropped out of school after a year because I couldn't afford the tuition, which was another reason I joined the naval reserve. I did however enroll in a writing course at Boston University during this time. The Navy program, in which I had enlisted, required that I complete Basic Training, attend weekend drills, and then complete a two-year active tour of duty, which most likely would be Viet Nam. Following that I'd be on Reserve status for another four years.

"So here I was studying the writings of Bobby Kennedy, Gandhi, and Martin Luther King at Boston University, in a writing course called *Radicalism in America* during the week, while attending training on a Navy ship on the weekends. Being trained as a Communication Specialist, I wasn't worried about having a lot of day-to-day experience with guns. One day, however, I realized the time would come when I would be on a Destroyer and the crew would be firing 35 MM cannons that could cause many deaths. I couldn't see that would be much different for me than pulling the trigger on a gun myself. This reality shook me and got me thinking, this is not what I want to do!

"I must also admit that I enjoyed certain things about the Navy. I was a young kid and I liked the fun of: partying (They partied like crazy!), the camaraderie, and the people. The knowledge that this life was not for me, however, just burned inside me until I finally had to drop out. I just stopped attending drills.

"After a little time passed, I began receiving notices from the Navy letting me know that the U.S. Government, through the FBI, was looking for me, and unless I came in and had a good reason for my absence I would be prosecuted.

"During this time, I'd also started my involvement with the peace movement. When a friend of mine began talking about being a conscientious objector and heading for Canada, we headed down to Harvard Square in Boston to talk with some people who were offering draft counseling. While my friend was in an office talking with a counselor, I was approached by another counselor who said I was next, and invited me in to his office. I told him it was too late for me since I'd already joined the Navy. He still insisted that I come in. I did and told him my story after which he said, 'You sound like someone who has a deep personal and religious belief about the war.'

"I said, 'I do but it's too late, I've already joined.'

"He then pulled the manual of Navy rules and regulations off his shelf, opened it to a chapter on conscientious objectors, and told me that I could apply if I could prove that my beliefs about war had changed since I'd enlisted.

"At the same time, I'd received a letter from my naval unit advising me to either show up on the next Monday or be arrested. So on Monday, dressed in jeans and an army jacket, and sporting a scraggly-looking beard and longer-than-normal hair, I went in and talked to my commanding officer who questioned me about my absence. I told him that I'd discovered I was a conscientious objector. He said, 'Bullshit there's no such thing!'

"I then told him what I had learned about naval rules and regulations. At that point he left to talk with another person in the office. When he returned he said, 'Well this is bullshit, but you do have the right to do this. I don't think there's any way that you'll get it though. It never happens!'

"Once again he left to confer with someone. When he came back he said,, 'Shave that beard, cut that f...g hair, get rid of that army jacket, and start going to unit drills again!'

"So I began attending drills again. At the same time, however, I was also going through the process of being separated from the Navy. To make a long story short, I did get out within a year; but throughout that time I continually received orders to go to Viet Nam, which I refused despite a lot of pressure from the commanding officer. Their logic was that I should take the assignment until my discharge papers came through. In fact, I was just about to be arrested and put into Portsmouth Naval Prison when my discharge finally came through.

"Once discharged, I was required to perform some type of civilian service. It just so happened that during this time I happened to have a friend, whose cousin was a resident at Fernald State School in Waltham, Massachusetts, an institution of 2,500 people with developmental disabilities. I applied for a job there and was hired. When I showed up for work the first day, I was assigned to a ward of 28 men who were all confined to large metal cribs. They were lined up in four rows; seven cribs to a row. The terminology used to describe these men was that they were considered *profoundly retarded and physically disabled.* My job—without any training—was largely custodial and limited to feeding and bathing these men, while generally keeping the place clean.

"So on that first day, I'm a 19 year-old-kid, and they hand me a tray of food, and tell me to spoon-feed people one after the other. The meal was primarily ground food, out of fear people would choke, from their lack of activity. I would feed only eight people, because we had some help from 'worker boys' who were considered higher functioning residents. They were capable people who lived in other buildings on the grounds of the institution. We'd give them quarters for helping us. A few years later, these fellows would be among the first to move out when de-institutionalization occurred. That was my introduction to this work.

"As an aside, the terms I use here—'worker boys' and 'higher functioning'—are terms that I would not use to describe men and women with disabilities today.

"During the year I worked there, employees would come and go all the time. I would train new hires in the morning, they'd go to lunch, and never come back! (Laughing) It was a very challenging job. I didn't really understand at that time how we as a society could be mistreating people like this. But at the same time, it seemed like such a common thing—all these people crowded into these large buildings."

It almost sounds like a warehouse.

"It was exactly that—a warehouse. The injustice of what was happening to these people hit me very hard.

"I was also developing relationships with some of these folks, especially among the 'worker boys' who'd come in and help. They were very capable and interesting people. Like me, they loved the Red Sox, so I'd take them to games, movies and, because many of them were the same age as me or a little older, we'd *hang out* at times. I didn't believe that any of these guys belonged there; in fact, I didn't think anybody belonged there.

"As difficult as it was to work there, I loved it! I loved being of service to these men—the custodial care, bathing people, feeding them, and even having to change the diapers most of them wore. There was just one old wicker wheel chair there for the entire ward, and I remember bringing tools and parts in to repair it when it would break down. One at a time, I'd get people out of bed; strap them into that wheelchair, sometimes with old sheets, so they could sit up. I just tried to give them a bit of enjoyment. I experienced a connection with all of those men, despite the fact, that with the exception of two men, nobody knew my name. I just discovered that it was something that I really, really enjoyed!"

Talk a little more about this connection you felt to them.

"Well, I was 19, had narrowly avoided prison, life was kind of *at my doorstep*, and I had to make some very intense decisions. Would I go to war, indulge in some form of escape, or just drop out? I'd become very politically aware, and by this time was also an activist, so I was shocked that we as a society would be warehousing people like we were.

"Regarding the connection I experienced, I can now understand, 37 years later, that when I see people like them, I'm seeing them as souls who are on this journey with me. I don't know if I'll ever know why these folks are unable to communicate like us, but they do communicate, and they do have an *earthly experience*. That I'm sure of! I no longer try to judge what that is any more; I just trust they're here for a purpose, too.

"These people were treated inhumanely because they couldn't speak or stand up for themselves. I'll also add that caring for them was a very difficult job that contributed to *how* they were cared for. Some workers just did not view them as fellow human beings. In large part I see the institutional setting as being responsible for that attitude.

"I'll give you an example. Once while I was working in a different building, the 200 men who lived there and were divided up into six different wards would be stripped down at the end of the day and marched downstairs, naked, to the shower room, which was one big open area. There they'd be showered and dressed from clothes that were packed in big bags. Workers would put clothes up against the person to see if they'd fit them since they didn't own any clothing of their own. They'd dress them in 'johnnies,' one-piece garments that resembled a mechanic's coverall with zippers or buttons to close them up. We shaved people with electric razors that belonged to the institution. These men didn't have a razor or even their own toothbrush. It was incredibly impersonal and inhumane.

"I eventually left there and was hired as a nurse's aid at another institution in Massachusetts called The Paul Dever State School. That was pretty much a repeat of the conditions and experience I'd had at Fernald.

"That was in 1973, and the first group homes were opening up in the community as part of the de-institutionalization movement. Eventually I was hired to work in a group home and later ran an apartment program in Massachusetts. So I became part of the de-institutionalization movement and as people were moved out of the institutions, I was able to get a job in the Watertown group home. Watertown had residents who'd lived in Fernald State School, and were intellectually and cognitively capable, but severely challenged with Cerebral Palsy and other physical conditions that necessitated their using wheelchairs.

"I absolutely loved that job. I got to hang around with and support these folks, and in those days the environments were largely unregulated; we *made it up* as we went along. Because of lawsuits that had been filed against the conditions in the old institutions, there was now a lot of money flowing into these new services. I was able to develop my management skills, because I was running the house, and I had people working for me. My passion however was for hanging out with these folks; we'd go to ballgames and lots of other activities.

"One of my favorite stories from that era involves a painting of a golden urinal that hung in my office and was given to me by one of my friends when I left that job. In those days, the residents would have a planning meeting every six months. They'd develop plans for themselves, which involved identifying goals and the support they'd need to accomplish them. Now one guy, John, had a dream to go to a Red Sox game, and sit up in the right field bleachers, instead of in the handicapped section. He wanted to watch the game from there and get drunk. I told him I could get him into that section, but if he was drinking a bunch of beers I didn't know how many times I could get him back and forth from the rest room. He told me not to worry because he had that part *covered.*

"He said, 'I'll bring a bottle and a blanket, and you can empty the bottle every once in a while.'(Laughing)

"I said, 'Okay. That works for me.'

"Since my parents were acquainted with some of these guys, my father agreed to go to the game with us. At the game he and John both drank some beers and John ended up having one of the best times of his life. Later on I would relate the story to people as a way of telling them that they have to develop relationships with these folks, and not to be afraid of their disabilities.

"Needless to say, John was the friend who gifted me with the painting of the Golden Urinal.

"I just loved introducing these men and women to my friends; meeting their families; and doing things with them. I also loved serving and supporting them. Many of them became my friends. All of us who worked with that group had a feeling that we were doing something unique: we were helping these folks to live lives like everyone else. That theme remains, but in the '70s it was very exciting because we recognized that these people had come out of these institutions with incredible spirit and a burning desire to fully experience life. At that moment in time, I knew this was what I wanted to do! At the same time I never really expected, that in 2006, I'd still be doing this work in some way. In fact if you'd asked me back then what I'd be doing today, I would have told you that I'd most likely be working for the American Friends Service Committee or some other activist organization.

"So I remained in this field and, over the years, I've been the executive director of an agency in Massachusetts, ran group homes and programs here in New York, and over the last 13 years I've been working for an organization called the Self Advocacy Association of New York State. I've always thought of myself, even while running group homes and programs, as working *for* the people I provided services to. Now I actually do—the board of directors I work for are all people with developmental disabilities.

"I'm more of a coach than a director, because the board as a group speaks for the organization. I'm more in the background: administering, grant writing, and helping people prepare to give speeches and presentations. Best of all, I get to hang around some of the most interesting people you'd ever want to meet. Talk about passion; these men and women have a tremendous passion for what they're doing and I love being part of their lives. I consider it to be a real privilege.

"I'm not a person with developmental disabilities, but no one would ever question whether this is my passion. I think that's something that just comes with being around these folks so much. When I first got the job, our organization had very little money, so when we'd have board meetings, people would stay at my house. I'd carry people in; bring in their wheelchairs and basically do whatever had to be done. During this time, our theme became "Whatever it takes." If we were attempting to influence someone or change somebody's heart and mind, we'd do whatever it took to accomplish that.

"Today, on a macro level we're working to change the way money is spent for people with disabilities. So we're developing this thing called Self-determination and Individualized Service, which means that instead of living in group homes, many people want to live in their own apartment, and have control over the kinds of support they receive. They want to create their own life.

"Once, while managing a group home, I read a lot about the importance of people being part of a faith community. I realized that people who live in institutions don't often get the opportunity to attend and be part of a church, so I started to encourage my staff to do what they could to help and support people in attending church. Later I got a call from the minister of a Quaker Meeting House who told me that eight people from our group home had showed up his service and *silence had gone out the window.* I had good intentions but didn't really give people good directions. So I got the group back together and said, 'We really have to figure out what churches everyone wants to attend, and then do what we can to support their choices.' Supporting the desires of people to be citizens and part of their community is our goal, while the practicality of accomplishing that can sometimes be a difficult challenge.

"We also advocate politically and with policy makers, on a regional level, and work at collaborating with other organizations to reach our goals. Right now we're working on legislation to change the name OMRDD (NYS Office of Mental Retardation and Developmental Disabilities) because the word *retarded* is so stigmatizing.

"Telling people what you want, can do, and dream of, is a primary part of Self Advocacy. We also open people up to possibilities and options by telling stories, creating books, and creating a lot of information. Because some folks have been institutionalized or in group homes for a long time, they may have very little response when you ask them, 'What do you want to do with your life?' They'll say something, but even considering that question may not be an option for them. Some people may advocate having relationships, including sexual ones. If they live in a group house they might advocate changing the food that's purchased for them.

"What's most enjoyable about my work is being part of encouraging and helping people to express themselves: then watching how passionate they are in speaking out about what's important to them. The leaders of our organization are incredible people! They have no problem getting out and speaking in front of a crowd of thousands. Watching them develop is a thrilling part of this work for me. These people can work, contribute, volunteer, and they bring an unbelievable spirit that comes out of their life experiences. It's almost trite to say that people who've overcome some of the challenges these self-advocates have, bring a tremendous spirit to any community.

"There's a spiritual element to this also. A while back we were looking at the institutional past and we found that many people were buried in institution cemeteries, without any names on their gravesites. We went to our commissioner and said we we'd like to put names at these sites and acknowledge that these people existed. He said we couldn't do it because of privacy and Mental Hygiene laws. Instead of *getting in his face* about it we asked him to come and visit the cemetery with us. He's a good person so he approved our proposal. We went to his house in a van, picked him up and drove for a couple of hours down to the cemetery in Wassaic, New York. Once there, he got to meet people who formerly lived there, people who were concerned, and another person who actually dug some of the graves as punishment, while he lived there. On the way back home the Commissioner said, 'We've got to do something about this!' At that point there was no longer a need to push him."

You seem to have had the ability right from the beginning of your career, to see beyond someone's disability. Why is that?

"I don't know. When I go back to being 19, I recall that I was feeding a few people as part of my first job in this field, and this one guy said *"Thank you"* to me—it freaked me out! I didn't realize he could speak at all. I looked in his eyes and I saw another human being…a man…a soul! The staff people, who were teaching me how to relate to the patients, were teaching me to be detached. I realize today that patients treated this way will grow more distant themselves. At that time of my life I was probably more atheistic in my thinking so I wouldn't have mentioned *soul;* but looking back at it today, I know that's what I saw. One of the young, more capable guys whose name was Dave, just loved to play wiffle ball. Some days I would bring four or five of the guys home, we'd have dinner and then play wiffle ball for hours. One of the personal gifts I've received from this work has been in finding ways to have fun with these folks. I think they have fun with me too."

What have they given you Steve?

"They've given me a lot of friendship. I'll give you an example. The first song I had written since the '60s was about 10 years ago. It was about self-determination, but I thought it was kind of a stupid song. Tony and Chester, two of the wonderful men I work with, were sitting around my kitchen table with me one morning and I decided to tell them about the song. I said, 'I have a song I'd like to sing to you guys.' I proceeded to sing the song and they loved it. They told me that we should sing the song at our next presentation.

"I immediately said, 'No way, I am never going to get up in public and sing a song! Let's try and find someone who will sing it.'

"At that suggestion Chester said, 'Steve, you push us to do things all the time and now we're doing it to you. You're going to sing this song!'

"So I did, and it went real well—people liked it. That was my beginning of using music in this work. Within six months we created a dozen songs that I would perform at our presentations and conferences.

"This work has given me the opportunity to stretch, and to use so many of my skills. There have been times when I've thought about leaving this job and trying other things, but I'm always drawn back to it because of the relationships I've developed. I have a tremendous amount of friends in New York, who, with me, are on this team to help people with disabilities to be viewed differently".

Where does spirituality come into the picture for you?

"As I got older and began to recognize that I had spiritual thoughts, I began to consider my soul; it's in a lot of the songs I write. I think there's a soul in you and me, and its part of something much bigger than us—maybe a *spark of the divine*. It's not easy for me to describe but I do believe it's there. If I remember, when I'm sitting across from somebody, that our souls are connecting, it's hard for me to get my ego involved and then become angry or defensive in response to something they might say to me. I think of the people I work with in that way, but I also think of the people who we're trying to persuade or who may be in opposition to us. At times we're attempting to change the system to a more person-centered one, so the flow of money could be altered and people's jobs could change. Some people perceive change as hard and not everyone who works in an organization wants to look at people with disabilities as their 'bosses.' When I speak I'll often say, 'What a different world it'll be when all of us who work in this field can look at and accept these people with developmental disabilities as our bosses. I mean these are the people we work for, not the other way around!'

"Rudolph Steiner, a latter-day mystic, and I'm paraphrasing here, said that the people with severe disabilities are advanced souls having an easier life—taking a break." (Laughs)

Have there been obstacles in your own life that help you to relate to people with developmental disabilities?

"The answer is, yes. I've had obstacles and I think they've helped me in this work. After I entered this field, I discovered I had challenges with alcohol and with depression. I have been able to overcome those challenges, so I'm very healthy today and have been for a long time. Facing those challenges, however, have helped me to understand and be a better coach for people with depression and learning disabilities. What I always say to everybody is, 'You can do it!' You can overcome this! You can deal with it!' I know this to be true from my own experience. This year I got an award from our board that I really cherish. In part it reads, '…for inspiring people to advocate for themselves through your dedication and your music.' I love to motivate and inspire people."

Who are the people who've most inspired you?

"I was really drawn to Martin Luther King's humanity and activism in the sixties. I loved the respectful way in which he opposed others. He never vilified people he was opposed to; but he was an incredibly *hard-assed* advocate. I mean he was in people's faces when he needed to be, but he was also willing to love his enemies. I also admired Bobby Kennedy. In the two years before his death, he brought great passion to his politics.

"My biggest inspiration in those days however was Daniel Berrigan, the activist Jesuit priest. He actually played a big part in how I now think. After the peace movement of the sixties died down, he began working with people with AIDS, and started facilitating retreats, many of which I attended at the Pyramid Lake Spiritual Life Center in the Adirondacks Mountains of New York. At one retreat where I believe the theme was something like, "Transforming the Empire," we discussed our frustrations with Father Berrigan about trying to make changes within the system in New York. After listening to each of us he said, 'One of the things that strikes me about this, is that all you guys have your eyes on this prize and what's going to happen at the end. You're going to be fighting this battle forever, so let me give you a little insight. It's the work you *do* that counts. It's the interactions! It's the friendships you build; it's not what you accomplish.'

"That was 15 years ago, and those words altered my life and my whole approach to what I do. I realized that trying to change a policy or an organization was very important, but it was also where my ego can get in the way and try to take control. The ego, to me, is all about fear. Berrigan was saying to more or less live in the moment and enjoy the journey. My whole way of thinking changed after hearing that.

"I really am passionate about changing systems that don't work, and I would argue that people, including me, who want to vilify state policy makers, leaders or congressman have to remember there's a little bit of them in all of us. I believe the way to get them to see things differently, is to help them see their own humanity and what connects us, rather than to view us and them as separate and different. That's why I love to help people sit in a room like this and be across from a policy maker so that they can interact. That can be terrifically empowering for everyone.

"After my encounter with Berrigan I began to observe my work and ask myself, for instance, *What am I experiencing in this meeting; what should I be getting out of this interaction, and what do I really know about these people?* I then began to read a number of spiritual books like the Course in Miracles, the Kabbalah, and many others, which spoke to these questions. Although I'm certainly not perfect at this, with my altered attitude, I'm more and more able to keep this perspective, despite some very difficult times.

"Another hero of mine is the musician, Neil Young. I like him because of the way he expresses his beliefs through his music. I also appreciate him because of the passion he brings to what he does. I don't know if you've ever been to a Neil Young concert when he's playing mainly rock and roll; but he's very intense and he just gives and gives. It seems that he's always right at the edge of explosion, yet still able to sustain an incredible energy throughout. Once in an interview, in response to the interviewer's question about how he maintains such an intense level of performance, he replied that he sees himself as a new candle at the beginning of a concert and he's not satisfied until he's *burned up every single bit of that wax.* I've always felt that's how I approach the work I do.

"An important question for me, which you asked earlier, is: *How do I find balance between passion and obsession?* That balance for me is right where that candle burns down. If I go beyond the end of that candle, I can go into obsession very easily. I know because I've been there. Actually I've crossed that line a lot! (Laughing) Some of the times I've crossed it I've ended up emotionally drained.

"One of my challenges, which is also one of my gifts, is this tremendous, sometimes *manic* energy I have. There are probably a lot of us who do this work that have it. We want to use every opportunity to make a point or a connection. The downside of this great energy is that I sometimes fail to recognize my limitations. That doesn't happen to me as much now, because I'm getting older, I'm more aware of it, and my wife Cathy, who is very astute, will sometimes point it out to me. I'm also fortunate to have enough friends who will sometimes say to me, 'Hey are you over that edge now?'

"Getting back to heroes, I'd say the most influential heroes I have are these people with disabilities whom I work for; they're real leaders. There are thousands of people with disabilities, around the country, who are incredibly passionate leaders. They may have cognitive disabilities and some limitations, but they also have charisma and the ability to inspire and lead."

Where does music fit into your passion Steve?

"Well, it fits in unbelievably! Many of my songs are 1960s-movement-type songs for people with disabilities. At a conference, my friend, Chester Finn, will often introduce one of these songs, as music of the Disability Rights Movement. If you think about the peace movement, the women's movement, and the Civil Rights movement, there have always been songs that have been created or adopted to energize and support those causes. So I'm composing songs that celebrate the heroes of this movement—what they said, did, or dream about. Here's part of one: (Steve sings)

I got a song in my heart, won't you help me sing it
I've got a gift to offer, won't you help me bring it

I'm not asking for much, just a chance
For a home, a real job, and romance
And some friends who will not look askance
At my dreams.
I'm a soul on a journey like you, trying to do all the things I can do
With the help of a few friends like you, we could build a new world
or two.
I can dream, I can dream, I can dream
I can dream, I can dream, I can dream

"I believe this is the essence of what people with disabilities are saying: *Hey I'm a soul too! Help me to be all I'm meant to be.* These people have a lot to give. They're not charity cases; I never want people to view them in that way.

"I once had a guy I worked with, who never knew what meeting we were going to, because he had short-term memory problems. Yet he always had the knack of saying something very important during the meeting.. We used to call him *Mr. Quotable*. At a meeting he would listen very intently and say the most amazing things. On one occasion, we were trying to persuade some budget officials to spend some money differently, After listening to the haggling that was going on, he said, 'I'm sick and tired of listening to these people thinking *we're dollars with no sense!'* At that point everybody present got it! (Laughing) His profound message was, *don't think of us as slots in a program, or as units of service.*"

How has this work changed you Steve and what have you learned about yourself in the process?

"I've learned a lot about myself. It's helped me to understand the role that ego plays in work and in system change. I've really had to confront that in myself. When I got this present job I went from being an executive director, running an agency, to being an administrative director who largely stays in the background as much as possible, because I'm coaching these guys to be good leaders. At the same time, I'm out there interacting with people from the state system and I think there were times when I wondered how they viewed me. I've also learned over time to get comfortable with my own ability to get through any situation by letting go of control, trusting the people I work with, and then simply watching where the process leads.

"In addition, they've taught the *go-go guy* I am, to be patient. Working with people with disabilities and doing the kind of work I do means that I'm usually organizing some kind of an event. Because of physical limitations, it might take a person 10 minutes and my assistance, in order to use the toilet, and with some one else I may have to take time to get them into my car. I can get really swept up in what I do, so I've had to learn to keep that *go-go guy* at bay from time to time. When I can't get everything accomplished in a day I've learned that it doesn't really matter. It's more important to look at what we've done together, what fun we have, and what difficulties we overcame."

What would you say to someone who claims they don't have any passion in their lives but would like to?

"The first thing I'd say is to be present, pay attention, and try to listen a little more.   pay attention to the needs that people have. I think when someone is not feeling passionate they're probably not in touch with their spirituality. I'm most passionate when I am drawn to something for a higher purpose."

How would you like the world to have benefited from what you do?

"That's an easy question. I guess I would like it to be said that people who knew me, in relation to the work I do, would say that I helped people to get acquainted with other people, in a way that emphasized what was similar about each other instead of what was different. As a consequence, friendships and connections were engendered, rather than conflict. I like to think that the work I'm engaged in now is a little bit of the work that needs to be accomplished so that we don't engage in more war. I believe resolution is found in people-to-people dialogue and through offering respect to each other. We need to build bridges, so

I hope when people look back at the work I've done, they'll see I helped to build those bridges.

All the people I work with want folks to look at them and say, *"Hey, how ya' doing? What's happening? What do you like? How's your life going? Who's you're favorite team? Have you got a boyfriend? Are you having sex? (Laughing)*

They don't want people to look at them and say, *Gee, it must be hard to be you? How do you deal with that wheelchair or it must be a bitch that you don't speak well?*

"The world will be a much better place when *every* person's gift is present and is part of the mix, and people aren't labeled because of their differences. I believe that each of us is truly part of one big community."

Steve may be reached at—seholmes@earthlink.net or at www.sanys.org

Chapter 24
Passing It On
Steve Rock

"I think of passion as a fuel that fires my furnace and life without that is just a dry, dull shell of a thing. Life with passion is vibrant and energetic. For a human being it's like the hydrogen in a star; without it I don't think I can ever be fulfilled or be a fully alive person. We can end up being drones who nothing more than keep the economy moving. That's really sad and a waste of life to me."

Steve lives on the east side of the Lower Hudson Valley in Mahopac, New York. He works as a technical writer, is married to his sweetheart Margaret, grooves to the music of Santana and Gato Barbieri among others, and can wax poetic about his passion for hunting, researching, and sharing his love of wild mushrooms and the connection that has created to his family ancestry.

"Mycology is my passion and a nice word to use when putting a respectable spin on my passion for going into the woods to hunt for wild edible mushrooms. I mean when I tell people that I'm an amateur mycologist, they'll probably think this is a pretty respectable hobby. (Laughs) I'm a mushroom man!

"Actually mycology is a very young science. There's an awful lot that's unknown about mushrooms or fungi, and mycology in general.

What they're discovering through DNA studies is that mushrooms, which seem to have no connection to each other are really almost like brothers to each other. On the other hand, mushrooms that seem so similar that experts thought they had to be from the same genus or family, have turned out not to be unrelated. There might be a *puffball* in North America, for instance, that's a spin-off from something that happened millions of years ago, and then you've got a *puffball* somewhere in Asia, and people think it's from the same species of mushroom, and it's found not to be. So the science of mycology is constantly evolving as the experts increasingly find out how little they really know. Although it can be rather confusing at times, it's also fun because when I get together with other mycologists, there's so much we can talk about. We can talk the old words, the new words, the transitional words, or the latest science discoveries of today.

"Our club get-togethers are called forays. We have a club foray, a regional foray each year that I try to attend, and we have an annual national foray, which I will take part in this year in Pipestem, West Virginia. It's been organized by a fellow by the name of Bill Moody, author of *Mushrooms of the Appalachians*. It'll be fascinating because some of the authors of books I've read will be taking part."

What is there about this process of hunting, seeing, and recording wild mushrooms that so grabs some people's passion?

"There are a lot of people in the club who have the inclination to try to find as many species as they possibly can. They know certain species exist and they'd like to be able to say, 'I found it and I identified it.' So some of this is for status and then for some people its pure curiosity. Some folks really get into the identification while I'm much more into the hunting and foraging so I can bring home mushrooms to eat. That's my primary intention in going into the woods. Nevertheless the science part of it is a nice add-on for me because it's something to think about, discuss, and do some research on during those times when I'm not out in the woods.

"The whole idea of finding something that you've never seen before and then finding out what it is, is just plain exciting. There's something about it that gives me some satisfaction or feeling of completeness. I want to be able to say, 'Oh, I've seen that one, I know it!' It's a way of saying, 'I didn't know what it was but I've identified it and I'll know it the next time I see it.' That's a big thing for us; we want to be able to know what we see when we walk in the woods.

"When we go out in April and May looking for morels there are five or six different species of them, so you end up rehashing the same information: 'Okay is this the grey one or the black one, etc., etc.' You want to know what they are so that when you're out there with other people you know what you're talking about. It's also real nice to be able to pass on this information to newcomers. We get newcomers to our club every year, and their fascination and interest is always high. So it's nice to be able to say to them, 'Yes, this is a ____, and this is how you identify it, and these are the characteristics of this mushroom.'"

You get to act as a mentor.

"Absolutely; I enjoy it! Part of my passion for mushrooming is being able to pass it on to others, inspire them, and get them passionate about it. If you can get people thinking about it in a way they haven't thought about it before, they will pursue it more actively, take a bigger interest, and be inclined to keep it in their lives as they go on. A hobby like this is something I can carry into my old age and will actually facilitate better health for me at that time of my life. I've seen members of our club who are well into their eighties and still *sharp as tacks* because they're doing this all the time. When people keep learning, their minds don't shut down as they can when they prop themselves in front of a TV and their brains turn to *mush*. If a person has curiosity and a desire to learn they'll stay energized and vibrant..

"Our mushroom 'guru' for the Northeast is Sam Ristich, who lives in Maine and celebrated his 90th birthday at last year's COMA (Connecticut-Westchester Mycological Association) foray. He's still giving lectures, sharing new information with us, leading walks, conducting laboratory research, and writing—he's unbelievable. He's one of the people who have really inspired me to learn properly. I was so excited at the first COMA foray I attended that I couldn't sleep. I got out of bed at 3:00 a.m. the first night I was there. I went into the collecting room where there were over a hundred species of mushrooms and reference books laid out. I walked around the table, and eventually selected a field guide to read. I laid down on a couch to read the book in an effort to learn, when Sam walked into the room and asked me what I was doing. I told him I was trying to learn about these mushrooms by reading this book. He said (raising his voice),'That's no way to learn!' He got me off the couch and directed me to the laboratory where he had an assortment of microscopes set up. He clears the desk off, brings the books in, lays them out, turns the lights on properly, and says, 'Now that's a proper learning environment!' Then he walked out and left me there. This man knew how to learn; it's what he does best. He's a fascinating man. I love him."

When was the seed for this love of mushrooming first planted in you?

"It probably started as a kid, although I never did it then. I was born and brought up in the mill town of Cohoes, New York—a bit north of Albany—right at the confluence of the Mohawk and Hudson Rivers. My father, John, who's a second generation Carpatho-Rusyn (his father emigrated in 1892 from a village called Wola Cieklinska, which is now in the southeast corner of Poland) would, at certain times of the year, go out into the woods or down to Lansing Park in Cohoes, and bring home big shopping bags full of these large aromatic mushrooms.

"Many of the mushrooms were well past the point at which they should have been harvested for human consumption. They'd be infested with larvae from bugs that had already been inside the 'shrooms and laid eggs there while eating what they wanted. I would discard any such mushrooms but my dad didn't.

"You see, he did something with mushrooms that I never do with mine—he boiled them. He'd put on a huge pot of water and cut the mushrooms up into it, and bring them to a boil. The whole house would stink from it, and the smell would linger for days. He once told me that his dad would hang his mushrooms over the wood stove to dry, and all night long you'd hear the sound of maggots dropping and sizzling on the top of the stove, as they burned. *Yuck!*

"Anyway, dad would boil them, strain them, and put them aside. Then he'd really get to work. He'd break out all the animal fat he had stored in the refrigerator (usually in an empty coffee can), heat it up and render it down if needed. Into this fat he'd cut up onions and peppers, mostly grown from his own garden. Then, he'd add copious amounts of onion and garlic salt—his two staples of cooking. Into this he'd add the pre-boiled mushrooms, and let that mixture simmer until he was satisfied with it.

"As young kids, this was the last thing in the world we'd choose to eat. None of the younger kids wanted anything to do with these mushrooms, which Dad would usually serve up (mostly to himself) over noodles. As I got older, I would sample them, and eventually grew quite fond of the dish, despite knowledge of what it was and how it came to be. After I moved out, I'd count on Dad gifting me some of his frozen mushrooms whenever I visited. I'd bring them home, thaw them out, and enjoy them wherever I happened to be living at the time."

What drives you Steve to pursue this passion of yours?

"One day about 10 years ago, my wife and I were out walking in a wooded area in Pawling, New York, close to where we live, and I spotted a mushroom growing on the lawn, on the edge of a hemlock stand. Not knowing how many species of mushrooms look alike, I said, 'Hey, that looks like one of the mushrooms my father picks.' I took it home, but didn't eat it. It deteriorated into a nasty smelly mess pretty quickly. But my curiosity was piqued. As luck would have it (if you believe in luck), Margaret found a notice in the newspaper about a lecture on wild mushrooms being given the following weekend at a library in a nearby town. So I attended. The lecture was given by a woman named Marge Morris, who was nearly 80 years old at the time. Her slide show and lecture hooked me! She did a very basic presentation for us but I think part of my original interest was thinking, *This is a way of going out in the woods and finding free, healthy food that I could take home and cook up.*

"As I looked at the slides and photos it also connected to something very deep in me—something I had only just begun to get a hint of the week before when I'd seen that mushroom growing in that hemlock stand. I had thoughts of my father, thinking that he'd brought that kind of mushroom home, so I believe it was genetic. My interest connected me to my ancestors who foraged for mushrooms and any other edible foods they could find in the woods. Mushrooms were a dietary staple for those people and helped them to survive.

"I spoke with Marge after the show, and she handed me a registration form for the local mushroom club, COMA. Marge was one of my original mentors. I love her very much.

"As I left the lecture to get into my car, I noticed another one of those mushrooms right in front of it. So I picked it and brought it back into the library where Marge was still talking to some of the attendees. I handed her the mushroom and asked her if it was edible. Having heard my story about the 'shroom I found up in Pawling, she asked excitedly, 'You found this in Pawling?'

'No' I said, 'I just found it right outside in front of my car.'

"Then the truly unexpected happened. Like a priest with the host during the celebration of the Eucharist, Marge held the mushroom up high and declared quite loudly 'King Bolete! King Bolete!' Her excitement was infectious. I pressed her for more details, and she told me I'd found a specimen of *Boletus edulis*, one of the most highly sought-after mushrooms in the world; also known as "porcini" by the Italians and "Cep" by the French). It was one of the choicest edibles one could find.

"I joined COMA, but it wasn't until the third year I really participated: attending lectures, going on most of the club walks, attending all of the lectures, and enjoying the people I was meeting. My wife Margaret and I attended our first COMA foray that year. This is a three-to four-day gathering of folks who love wild mushrooms and are dedicated to collecting, identifying, eating, and discussing them.

"My interest in mushrooms was also piquing me intellectually in a new and exciting way. I'm not stupid. I'm a pretty smart guy. I did well in high school but never attended college because there wasn't any money for that in my family. I came from a very large family and don't ever remember any discussion about going to college. When I graduated from high school, I recall my father handing me $100 and saying, 'There you go; congratulations.' That was it—the rest was up to me. I worked wherever I could make a buck—mostly bakeries and restaurants—to earn a living and get out on my own. That didn't leave much room for intellectual stimulation. This new interest of mine, however, was something that played a significant role in the universe, and it was something I could grab onto and learn about. I was very excited!

"I've learned that fungi are responsible for almost everything on earth. In fact there would be no life on earth if it weren't for fungi—no plants, no animals, nothing. Even in the dry parts of the earth, fungi have prepared the land for the plants. Fungi are at the root of everything, literally and figuratively. They play a huge role in supplying plants with the food and water they need to reproduce. When you see a mushroom growing on the ground you can be sure that it has a relationship with at least one plant in that area. The mushroom is really a fruit of the fungus which is hidden in the ground. It's a fascinating subject matter."

What is passion to you Steve?

"I think of passion as a fuel that fires my 'furnace and life without that is just a dry, dull shell of a thing. Life with passion is vibrant and energetic. For a human being it's like the Hydrogen in a star; without it I don't think I can ever be fulfilled or be a fully alive person. Without it we can end up being drones who nothing more than keep the economy moving. I think that's really sad and a waste of life.

"It's great to know that I have something I can use or participate in whenever time allows. In my everyday existence, my job as a technical writer makes it possible for me to enjoy this passion of mine. Hopefully a person has more than one thing they feel passionate about. I am passionate about music, mushrooming, literature, and my relationship with my wife, which is the most meaningful thing in the world to me. It's important for me to give time to that relationship. If you don't allot time to what you're passionate about you'll lose it. I have to stoke the fire every day in some way."

Have there been sacrifices in living this way?

"My first reaction to your question is to say, *No none at all;* but when I think deeper about it I'd say I've probably given up a formal education. Most likely, I could have a pretty good college degree right now if I truly wanted to apply myself to that goal, but that's not how I want to use my energy. In fact I don't think of a degree as critically important to me, although many people have tried to convince me otherwise. I grew up in a time when if you were a fairly smart, honest, hard-working and industrious person you could be successful in the world—and I was. I was never afraid of hard work.

"I watch very little TV. What Margaret and I want to see, which is not much, we will often record and watch on the weekends. I really spend very little time in front of the television. I guess you could say that's been a sacrifice, but I really don't think so."

Does your ego present challenges for you with your passion?

"I remember a time when I was working for a software company in White Plains and there happened to be a woman who worked for me as one of my writers. She came to work one day and described a mushroom she'd found in her yard, and the description sounded very much like a mushroom we refer to as the "hen of the woods." This was still early in my work with mycology, but I encouraged her to bring it in the next day, which she did. I told her it was the mushroom I'd thought it was. So she decided she'd make a vegetarian dinner for her sister using the mushroom. She cooked it and cooked it, and the mushroom became tougher and tougher, and as it turned out it wasn't very tasty. I had wrongly identified it. Fortunately no one got sick because it is an edible mushroom. When I discovered my mistake I felt terrible about it. It was a rather crushing blow to my ego that told me I was no expert and I shouldn't try to be. It was quite a lesson in humility, but that's how I learn! This person is still part of my life (laughing) and she's now my boss. Whenever any discussion or mention of mushrooms comes up she never hesitates to tell that story. I don't know that she'll ever let me forget that one.

"Hunting for mushrooms helped me to discover that I could be passionate about something. Before mycology came along, I didn't know that. The only thing I'd ever felt similar about was music. I was fortunate to be introduced to a different caliber of music from what I'd heard on top forty radio in my early teens; something I attribute to my friend Andy and his older brothers from whom he learned. I was listening to Pharaoh Sanders, Rahsaan Roland Kirk, and Gato Barbieri when I was 16 and 17—talk about infectious passion! I developed a passion for music, but because of my lack of confidence, it was always tempered by other people's tastes. I shared my favorite music with anyone who'd listen, but it was never a source of personal pride for me.

"Mycology, on the other hand, is something I'll have forever, and it can be discussed, but not really disputed by those who know nothing of it or by those who know 100 times more than I do. There is still so much that is unknown, that even the greatest experts are on a fairly slippery slope. I'm content with what I already know and confident that as I continue to pursue this passion my knowledge base will continue to expand."

Please explain how your spiritual beliefs impact this passion of yours?

'My spirituality began to evolve when I got involved in a personal recovery group 18 years ago. That process continues. Right now I'm an atheist. I believe in the universe, I believe in love, and I believe that the two are somehow connected. I believe there are an infinite number of powers greater than myself, but feel no need to define one in particular, assign it human characteristics and appeal to it or even believe it can be appealed to. I just don't need that in my life. The only knowledge I really require is that I am NOT the higher power. That perspective can save me an endless amount of trouble and heartache; but because it goes against my childhood training, it doesn't always come easy.

"My spirituality enables me to take what the world offers and be content with it. Although I go out at certain times of the year to hunt mushrooms that grow in that season, I try to be satisfied with and enjoy any fungi that happen to find. Mushrooms make great photography subjects, so I take hundreds of photos each year, but I don't pray for rain to *bring up* the mushrooms."

When you describe what you do, it reminds me that in order to really see what you're looking for, you truly have to be *in the moment* and not easily distracted. Is that true for you?

"That's a big reason that I do it. When I'm out there in the woods looking for mushrooms, that's all I'm thinking about. I've taken myself out of my normal, everyday life along with all the concerns that go with that, including the noise that's usually going on in my head. I'm just there in the woods, enjoying what I'm seeing and doing, and feeling grateful to be there, no matter what the day's effort might bring. There are days when two or three hours might go by without finding anything. It's easy, then, to think, *This sucks, this is a waste of time, I could be doing something else. I think I'll go home…blah, blah, blah!* What turns that thinking around for me is the knowledge that I'm doing something I really love: I'm out here in the woods; I'm getting fresh air; I'm getting exercise; and I'm connected to the Earth. The mushrooms themselves are really a bonus on top of all these other benefits.

"One day I was out in the woods in a group, and we crossed paths with three strangers coming from another direction. As we passed, one of our guys said out loud, 'Oh man can you believe how many different kinds of mushrooms we're finding out here?' Someone from the other group overheard us and said, 'we haven't seen any mushrooms but can you believe how many different species of turtles there are around here?' They were searching out and studying turtles. So you see what you're looking for, and, if you don't look, you don't see.

"I'm always looking. When I'm in my car and driving, I'm *'shrooming*. Whenever I'm in transit or at a picnic I'm observing and I'm *'shrooming!*'(Laughter) Last year at my father's 80th birthday party, I was able to show and tell my brother Danny about various mushrooms I found. It's great fun!"

Is there beauty in a mushroom?

"Yes! They're gorgeous. Mushrooms have evolved over centuries and they're still evolving. The kingdom of fungi is the most adaptive kingdom on the planet; it has to be. Mushrooms are constantly battling parasites, mold, and the plants they interact with. There are many different ways they evolve. So when I think of how long it took for a particular mushroom to evolve in this particular way, I'm amazed and fascinated by that process. When I look at two mushrooms that appear to be very much alike, side by side under a microscope, I see the variations in the structures between the two and I wonder, *How did this happen?* You can theorize all you want, but it's a mystery. I'm so touched by the beauty that at times I attempt to capture it by taking pictures just to be able to present it in all its varied beauty."

"I've been delighted in the past year to discover that I have nieces and nephews who have some interest in mycology. I'm nurturing this interest by sending them links to sites and articles, offering to take them on walks to find and study mushrooms, and stoking the fire of what I hope will become a passion for them. I hope they can find in it some of the fun and personal connectedness that I've found, as well as being more in tune with their ancestry.

"Being more connected to my ancestry helps to answer some questions for me as well as giving me a source of pride about my family. I started doing genealogical research about five years ago, but I must say that this search to find our nationality, roots, and family line has taken a much longer time to evolve. When we were kids, I remember we asked my father what nationality we were and he said we were Ukrainian. Years later he told us we were White Russian. My mother told us we were German and French on her side, but we later learned that we were German and French Canadian. My father never found out where his father had come from because of the language barrier between them—his dad had never learned English. Although dad knows a lot of the language, he never truly had a connection with his father, so was unable to find out much about his ancestry. So I never really knew what nationality I was.

"One day dad and I were talking on the phone, we were about to hang up, when I decided to ask him one more time about his father's birthplace. He said there was one town his father used to mention in regards to attending church. He pronounced the name of the town as "Pelegrrimka," which was located in Poland. I checked out the name of towns on a website, and found there were three different towns with the same name (spelled Pielgrzymka). I did a lot of Google searching and eventually connected with a woman who had records from one of these towns. Luckily she responded within 20 minutes and informed me that I was on the right track. In fact, she was in possession of some of the records of my father's family that she had obtained from a genealogist from Poland by the name of Ivana. I contacted Ivana and within a day she found my grandfather's birth record. It wasn't until I'd contacted my cousin Connie however that I knew we'd found my grandfather's records for sure, since there are many people with the name Rock in that area. One day in a phone conversation with her, she told me that she'd been named Constance after her great-grandfather, who was Constantine and Theodora (middle name) after our Grandmother. I was shocked and exhilarated to say the least. I was now one hundred percent certain that I'd found the correct family line (back to 1774), and that our nationality is Carpatho-Rusyn, not Polish, Ukrainian or Austrian. Our people were basically the people who populated the northern and southern slopes of the Carpathian Mountains, which ranged from Slovakia, through southern Poland and down into Romania. "

This sounds like a very soulful experience for you.

"Absolutely! In doing this research I began to take a lot of pride in my new-found heritage, and experienced respect for these people, that I'd not known before; and not because I found them to be of nobility or anything like that. These were dirt-poor people who lived and breathed dirt, and shared their homes with their animals. My pride was in knowing that I was part of these hard-working, industrious people who survived a very difficult existence. That's me too! I've been a hard-working industrious survivor who's done quite well with my wit and my ability to work with people. My ancestors were people who labored hard till the day they died! This information has become very meaningful to me in my life. It's part of what I'm attempting to pass on to my nieces and nephews when I discuss the tie between mushrooming and our ancestry. This genealogical search also connected me big-time to my dad; we were talking on the phone every day during this time period and he totally supported me in this research."

"I frequently share what I forage with friends, family, and neighbors, so that more people than I can enjoy the bounty of nature. It gives me great satisfaction to put in the efforts required to locate, harvest, and bring home these treasures, and to provide those who don't have the time or inclination to do it themselves with some of what I've acquired. Maybe it's a *Santa Claus or Robin Hood complex* or something, but I relish spreading the wealth and letting people know what's out there if they care to go looking.

What would you say to those who desire more passion in their lives?

"Well, part of me just wants to wake people up to the potential that lies outside of the comfort zone of their everyday routine and encourage them to be healthier people by investing some of their energy into exploring new things, ideas, and places. I would say, 'Get out of your comfort zone. See where life leads you. Discover something that kindles your interest and inspires you to pursue a healthier way of living. Find out who you are, from whence you came, and what your ancestors enjoyed—these things are in your blood and have great potential to lead to passions in your life. When you find something you are passionate about, consistently devote energy and time to enjoy it and to keep the flame alive. Find others of a like mind and enjoy or just discuss it with them whenever you can. See yourself as being worthy of having this passion in your life and give it to yourself as a gift. Remember that life is short and that as you age, your ability to enjoy that passion may be seriously depreciated—go for it now!"

Steve Rock can be reached at **steve_rock_0916@yahoo.com**

Chapter 25
Perseverance
Amy Hart

"…I've been at this long enough to know that I don't give up; even in the moments when I experience being down and my heart hurts. I know that because I've proven it to myself many times when I was sure it was absolutely over. I'd see myself get back up on that horse and ride it."

Amy currently lives and works in New York City. This interview was conducted in Albany, New York, where she resided at the time. Amy sees her core passion as the desire to make a positive difference in the world through her filmmaking and other forms of storytelling. She's the proud mother of Jay, currently a college student.

"I think everybody has the capability of being passionate about something in their life. My central passion, however, is a burning desire to make a difference through film and other forms of storytelling. This water documentary project is my latest passion, but if I look over the course of my life there have been many ways that my core passion has manifested itself. Its intention has always been to communicate something in a way that wakes people up.

"I'm a global filmmaker. My latest project is entitled *Water First.* The intention of the film is to raise awareness of the need for clean water for everyone on the planet. At present, more than *one billion people* do not have access to clean water—primarily because they cannot afford it.

"My background is in theater. When I was 16, I got into a professional mime troupe; Friends Mime Theater based in Milwaukee, Wisconsin, and toured with them for a summer. It was a real highlight for me during that period of my life. We were able to draw attention to important community issues, through our show, *This is Our Neighborhood.* We actually helped to stop the scheduled demolition of a predominately black neighborhood in Milwaukee for the purpose of building a super boulevard to speed traffic in and out of downtown.

"I saw that theater could make a difference, so I continued working in theater for a long time, performing in an original children's theater, and writing and performing one-woman shows, which I performed at UN conferences and at various world social summits. I would continue to do theater except it's a very difficult field, financially speaking. That's why I moved on to film.

"I'm presently working on a trilogy of themes: water, women, and children. Right now I'm working on the documentary *Water First.* Then I'll be filming *Mother Maroon,* one of my one-woman shows that I presented at UN conferences and other venues. The central characters are four women who come from India, Haiti, Sweden, and America. Each has a different maternal issue affected by culture, and national or international turmoil. After *Mother Maroon* I plan to produce a piece called *Where Do the Children Play?*

"One of my major influences has been Whoopi Goldberg's one-woman show, *The Spook Show,* which she performed about 20 years ago. In that show, she tells stories, and takes on the persona of many different characters. I watched her performance over and over. I loved it! It inspired me and I thought, *I can do that!*

"I'd always wanted to do theater on a big scale but it was difficult to pull the financial resources together in order to get people to commit their time to it. For a seven-year period when my son Jay was young, I worked with the Enchanted Circle Theater, an educational theater company, in Massachusetts. It was a wonderful experience. The company was one of the few like it to survive; but it was still hard to make a decent living. So I moved on to film and TV for a more viable source of income.

"Now I'm a professional producer and director. I produce programs for the SUNY Albany School of Public Health and the Center for Public Health Preparedness. I've produced more than 100 shows in four years, covering a range of issues from bio-terrorism to AIDS. In fact water issues go right along with all this.

"I've always looked for *day jobs* that would give me something back. My advice to a person who must have a steady income stream is to always find a job that in some way feeds into your passion project, directly or indirectly. I believe there's always a job you can find that will do that.

"I also think there's a bit of collaboration with the universe when you're intention is right. I moved upstate from New York City because my son's father was here, and sharing a child together was a lot easier while living in the same area. At the same time, I didn't think upstate would offer me any opportunities to work in TV and film as I had in New York City. So I began my own freelance commercial production company because I saw there was a need for that. I had a lot to learn, but things gradually progressed for me to the point where I got my present job at SUNY, where I've learned a great deal about public health and the many ways it relates to people's lives.

"When I said earlier, *collaborate with the universe*, I meant that when you're willing to be in touch with some kind of universal flow, and that may be God, or spirit, or whatever you may call it, gifts come along. It's important to seize those gifts and opportunities, and expand upon them. I would have never thought that I'd end up in this field."

How do you go about being in touch with that universal flow?

"For me it's mostly in listening and in determination. The words for me, spiritually, have always been *universe and collaboration*. I do use the word God sometimes, but I'm more likely to use the word *universe* because it resonates with me more. I see myself as part of the universe—I'm just one little energized cell—but what I do has an effect on this whole planet and can also change my life. I have a belief that when you have a good intention and it's in line with your destiny, the universe will conspire to support you and further you on your path. I've experienced great challenges on that path: times when I worked in theater and had to go to the food bank to get a bag of groceries, and years of not having any medical insurance. At the same time, I strongly believe the universe responds to perseverance."

"When I decided to move to New York City in 1994, it was with a sense of determination. I'd been in theater in Massachusetts, but hadn't been making a lot of money. I decided it was time to move to New York to further my connections with people in the television and film business and to expand my possibilities. So I decided that on November 15th of that year I'd be moving out of my apartment!

"When I made that decision I was divorced, didn't have a dime saved up, and no idea where I would live. Nevertheless, I had a plan that I would pack all my possessions into my sister's basement, take a backpack and move to New York. So, on November 15, 1994 I moved everything into my sister's basement and then drove back to my room to sweep it and unplug the answering machine. When I got there, there was a message on the machine from a friend saying, 'Amy, I need to leave the country, would you like to take over my apartment?' It was a rent-controlled one bedroom apartment in a nice neighborhood of Park Slope, in Brooklyn. It had a panoramic view of the Manhattan skyline and the Verrazano Bridge, and it was just a block away from the entrance to beautiful Prospect Park. I ended up living there in that apartment for seven years. The universe had conspired to support me!

"Next, I decided I would work in films. Because I knew very little about that kind of work, I set out to find out what I could, and who the 'players' were in the film industry. I visited a video store, pulled out 10 of my favorite films, and in reading the back of the cases, I saw that seven of these movies had been released by Miramax films. I found the address of the main office, went there, and sat across the street. I remember telling myself, *I'm going to work there*! (Laughing*)* So I

337

wrote a cover letter and sent them my resume, which I also sent to 20 other TV and film companies. I heard nothing from the other 20, but I did hear from Miramax the next week. This was nothing short of miraculous since I later discovered they receive roughly 4,000 resumes a month. For some reason they called *me*!

"They started me in the mailroom, but by the end of the week I was the head receptionist in charge of the mail room, the receptionists, and the floaters. In time I got a position in the international marketing department, where I learned a great deal about the business.

"With all that I was learning, I became aware that I really wanted to write screenplays and make films myself. I didn't want to answer phones and market other people's films forever. Eventually I got a contract to write a screenplay based on a book. It became one of those nightmarish Hollywood stories where you think your *ship has come in* and it turns out to be an illusion. Thinking I had this deal in the bag, I left the job at Miramax. The big promise of a contract didn't really turn out as it was supposed to. I was told that I would get my contract next week…next week…next week, and it just never happened. I eventually came to a point in 2000 where I thought, *forget this screenwriting business—this stinks! If I'm going to write films, I'm going to be the one making them.* Because the feature-film world is so hard to break into, I decided to focus on creating documentaries."

What gave birth to this idea of raising awareness of the need for clean water?

"I'd heard a talk about global water issues in the year 2000. In researching the subject I discovered how this issue was interconnected with so many other social issues. We can live without oil, but we can't live without water.

"There are some countries that are facing severe water scarcity and there are states in this country that have huge political, economic, and financial disputes about water rights. Water is a huge issue because civilizations have always been centered near water. People have always settled along streams, lakes, and harbors because we can't live without water. Today we're using water at twice the rate it's being replenished by nature."

"I believe that we will not solve a single *Millennium Development Goal without making sure everyone has clean water. Secondary education can't be provided to young girls in underdeveloped nations if they're spending five hours each day hauling water to their homes. You can't empower women if they're spending their days hauling water and getting raped at the well at four in the morning, when they need water. This lack of education for women also prevents any level of gender equality.

"I've been highlighting a group in Malawi named the Freshwater Project and its run by a wonderful man by the name of Charles Banda, a man of great passion."

Your face lights up when you say his name.

"He's an angel! Charles is the central character in the film, *Water First*, which lays out the message of how water relates to all of our other goals to help civilization. When you talk about passion, that's a man with passion! He's been a fireman, a preacher, a taxi driver, and the father to several children, and truly a man of his community. But one day he went into a village to preach and discovered many people there who were violently ill from cholera. He was so moved that from that point on, he put aside everything in his life and set out to do whatever possible to help the people of his country have clean water. Charles has been working on this water project for 10 years, living basically hand-to-mouth. Over that time he's drilled about 800 wells and provided water to roughly a million people.

"He sacrifices so much to do this! He also has a singular vision, which creates great power. I've sacrificed a lot in my life, but he sacrifices more than I could ever bear. This has been a particularly hard year because their drill rig, which is used to dig the wells, is very old and constantly in need of repair. It costs money to make these repairs and their financial resources are beyond empty. When I talked to him this morning he was still filled with faith and hope, despite his kids not being able to attend school because he doesn't have the school fees right now. For Christmas, they'll have nothing. It's heartbreaking to me just how much they give up...and they do such great work! I hope they get the help they deserve through my film.

"I'm also working to get financial support for this film. In three years, I've gotten mostly small donations. Just recently I received a grant, the largest donation that I've received so far, from a Parks foundation which will go toward paying for the sound track. I love and appreciate that people are giving in any way that they can, both for the film project and for the well project, which are two separate entities.

"While I'm making this film to open people's eyes to the global need to prioritize the water problem, I think all of my work in theater and film, has the goal of raising awareness of the underprivileged and the underserved in this world. One day in Malawi, we followed a young girl as she set out to get water at the well at 4:00 a.m. I asked her if she would attend school that day. She told me that she couldn't go to school because she didn't have a pen and her parents couldn't afford to buy her one until they got paid. There are challenges that poor people around the world have that we don't even think about in this society. I was doing public relations work for Oprah Winfrey a while back and we would get letters from students in the south asking for pens and pencils. So where are we in this country? How do we just ignore dire need? Why isn't it our concern as a human race to be certain that we have all the basic needs covered for all people?

"I believe there's a blindness that prevents people from seeing the truth. I think if people really saw the need and understood it, they would naturally open their hearts and their wallets to help, as they did when Katrina hit. My mission, as I see it, is to tell the story. I don't think that people are cruel. I think they're just not aware. That's why I believe story telling is so important."

When and where were you educated, Amy?

"I graduated from Bennington College in Vermont. While there I met and befriended an amazing woman by the name of Lilo Glick, who today is 92 years old. She has been a true role model for me. She was in my graduating class and we did our senior concert together. As a young person growing up in Germany, Lilo was a very talented musician. As things got serious there during the war, she escaped out of Germany and came to the United States.

"Although she'd become a concert violinist, and had taught as a professor, she'd never got her college degree or even a high school diploma for that matter. In her 60s, feeling a sense of incompleteness, she proceeded to earn a GED and then attended Bennington as an undergraduate student. We ended up classmates, attended the same drama class, and since we were the only two inter-divisional music and drama majors, we decided to do our concerts together. We were good friends over the course of our time there, and we still keep in touch with each other.

"In this country, we're very much youth-oriented and when you asked me my age, I sort of cringed because I don't want to tell you that I'm going to be 45 next month! (Laughing) I look to Lilo as a role model because she had the *chutzpah* to go back to school at 60, and never let that be an obstacle for her. She's never let anything stop her. She always looks for the goodness in life. She's a real inspiration and a hero for me. Whenever I get to thinking I'm too old for something, I remember Lilo Glick and I think, *Are you serious, look at Lilo!*"

Where did you grow up?

"I was born in 1962, in Racine, Wisconsin, where my parents, Sylvia and John, had met while both were involved in theater I have a sister Jenny and a brother, Nick, both older than me, and a younger sister, Emily. We're all within five years of each other.

"My parents were divorced after 10 years of marriage. Mom decided to move back home to Hawaii with the children, and my father remained in Wisconsin. So we ended up with this enormous 5,000 mile cultural divide in our lives.

"Because mom was an actress, we kind of grew up backstage. It was a lot of fun. My sister was named Emily because mom portrayed the character, Emily Webb, in the play *Our Town*. By the time I was seven or eight years old, I was acting on stage. Mom worked a secretarial job during the day and filled her weekends and evenings with theater. Every once in a while she'd say, 'Oh, I shouldn't be in a play, I should be spending more time with you kids.'

341

"We'd say, 'No, no, no, you got to do this, it's your passion! You're unhappy when you're not doing it.'

"We knew that about her, and although it did take away from family time in a traditional sense, we had this vibrant, crazy theater community that was a lot of fun to be part of. We were all on stage at times. In fact we once played the kids in *The Rose Tattoo*. As an eight-year-old kid I was performing before a full house in a 500-seat theater, so I guess I always felt that I would be on stage.

"When I was 16, I joined a theater group. Later, after college, I joined an educational theater group, and eventually was performing one-woman shows in various venues. I always expected I'd be performing, until I became a mother myself, realized it would take too much time away from raising my son, and I made the decision to stop."

So you struggled with the conflict between theater and parenting as your mom did?

"I did, but I chose a different road. I was still passionate about my work, but I realized I didn't need to be on stage to express my creativity. I also believe in filling a need and, quite frankly, I don't think there's a need for any more actresses on this planet. I thought, early-on, that I wanted to travel the screenwriter's road, but I ended up directing, really by default. I didn't plan on being a director. It was just that I didn't like a whole project being taken away from me, which is what happens when you're a screenwriter. It's like giving birth and having your child ripped out of your arms! As a producer I bring all the people, resources, and technical needs together to galvanize the projects; and looking back, I'd been doing it for years in theater without really calling it that.

"Going back to my childhood history—we grew up memorizing my mom's lines with her. It was like *household music.* For instance, if mom was doing Shakespeare that season, we'd be speaking 'Shakespeare' around the house. If it was Pinter—that was a completely different style. We'd learn the nuances of each playwright, and that language became part of the household while she was in that production.

"At the same time, there were other things I wanted as a young person. I'd seen all the swimming trophies that one of my aunts had, so I became a competitive swimmer. When you're a real outcast, like I was in Hawaii, there's a desire to gain recognition and to win at something.

"It was very painful growing up in Hawaii as a little white girl who felt like an outcast. The local children called us *haole,* which meant stranger, but it was mainly applied to white people and was derogatory. I remember one day there was a house down the road with a big birthday party going on, and my older sister noticed it was her classmates who were attending the party. Every single girl in the class was invited except her! That wasn't uncommon for us. I recall that being the last kid picked for the kickball game was daily fare for me. Getting beat up became such a serious problem that at one point my older sister needed a police escort to attend school. We all got into physical fights. It was commonplace. Consequently, I understood what it was like to be the minority.

"I've thought about this dynamic in relation to the ease with which I get along with people of color. I have an immediate affinity and rapport for those in the minority because I understand that existence and what it feels like. I felt ugly and ended up hating my pink skin! I wondered why I couldn't be brown like the others who had that beautiful Polynesian/Asian brown skin. I also hated them for hating me. I felt it at the swim club, at school, and at my sister's baseball games. When the people you love are being ostracized, you feel it too!

"In the theater world, however, which was predominately white, there was a sense of camaraderie. It was a very loving and open world. There were locals who participated, but they were loving, fun people to be with. The world of creative people tends to be more accepting of cultural, sexual, and racial differences. So this was a world where I felt more comfortable.

"In the more traditional world, however, I was always striving to gain acceptance. I think that might be why I fight for minorities and why I know that the difficulties of being a minority are compounded by financial difficulties. I'm fine now, financially, but it's still difficult to get funding for my 'passion projects'—so they can take longer to come to fruition, and that can be frustrating.

How do you keep going when you feel this frustration?

"Well sometimes I feel defeated…sad! I definitely have some frustration about timing as it affects my projects. At the same time, I've been at this long enough to know that *I don't give up*; even in the moments when I experience being down and my heart hurts. I know that because I've proven it to myself many times when I was sure it was absolutely over. *I'd see myself get back up on that horse and ride it.* I can ride through that experience as a feeling and not as an existing reality. I don't *live* in the feeling—I know that I'll get up the next day and be working again. I'm an active person, so whenever I have a day when my heart's not in it, I know that if I take one action, that effort can regenerate the motion of the *wheels on the train* and get me moving again. You can always physically set your intention back in motion, even when the weight of your intention feels unbearable and hard to lift.

"I believe that physical, spiritual, and mental maintenance are keys for the survival of the passionate person. For me, that includes: physical exercise, yoga, meditation, not using drugs or alcohol to excess, and maintaining balance in my environment and financial world. A person can burn themselves out at 36, or accomplish a lot more by being slow and steady, and living and working passionately till he or she is 80! There's a balance between wanting things to happen, and the patience and faith that things will happen as they should.

"I also had a coach by the name of Loren Beller, whose number one principle for success was to *give energy to that which you want to see grow.* You do that by cultivating the things you care about. Prior to her coaching I didn't have a production company, a full time job in production, or a film. Now I have all of those things. So much of that success comes from the power of my thoughts, and where I decide to place my energy.

"One of those *keys-for-success* books I've read, talked about how you may be working a job that is not your passion, but how you choose to use those eight hours when you're not sleeping or working is vitally important. For a person has who desires to manifest a passionate life, those eight hours are their greatest resource. Sure, you still have laundry, dishes, and shopping to do; and those eight hours may have dwindled down to four, but you still have four hours or maybe just two hours and that's a lot of time if you use it well and focus during that time. I'm acutely aware of how I allocate my time; even more so than how I spend my money. If I'm spending my time out drinking, or talking on the phone, or sitting in front of the television, those are choices I'm making about how I use those valuable hours.

"I think passionate people are easily inspired and that can be our greatest gift as well as a fault. I believe it's important to choose something and stay focused and committed to it. I've had to learn to say *no* to many of the things that I'd like to do. If I try to do 50 different activities I'm not going to get very far with any one thing. I believe you have to *burrow in* and use discipline to accomplish anything of value.

"For a passionate person, I also believe that maintaining balance is very important. I had a theater teacher years ago who said, 'Your most important task is to ask the question, *Why does art destroy its practitioner and what can you do to prevent that from happening to you?*' The creative spirit is meant to *sweep you away.* There's a joy and beauty to that, but there's also a danger and a risk to it. The challenge for the highly creative person is in remembering that life is more important than one's creation. For example: the number one thing that's kept me on track has been my son. He's such a delight and so real. I realize that parenting isn't just about the *big event.* For me it's about Jay and I each doing our own thing, then coming together and doing something together, and then being apart again. Jay means more to me than anything in the world. My passionate projects will be there if I maintain balance in my life, which for me includes being with other people in a peaceful way.

"If I were to put into one sentence what I would like my legacy to be or my impact to have been, it would be that I raised compassion in an artful way. I would hope that I helped audiences to get inside another person's shoes, or bare feet, and know what it is to walk five miles to get dirty water each morning, or to be the only white kid in a class, or the only poor kid, and to know that we have the power to help each other out. I see the world as a community; and I believe if we understood each other better, had more empathy, and gave compassionate and material support to each other on a personal level, it would be a better existence for all of us.

"I also want the world to recognize that every woman, whether she's a mother or not, is a *mother* of some sort and is an equal whether she has the money to support a child or not. All mothers are equal; all children are equal. One of the most challenging things I see in this world is the plight of poor children."

Could you say a little bit about your future project, *Where Do The Children Play?*

"The idea for *Where Do the Children Play?* was born when I was in Egypt in 1994 for the World UN Conference on Population and Development, where I performed *Mother Maroon*, my one-woman play. While walking down a street I literally tripped over a baby in a box and had to step over children sleeping on bare concrete. I had gone to that conference as a performer but I attended one of the large meetings with one of the delegates and decided to speak to the assembled delegates. I said, *Here we are, delegates from around the world, gathered to talk about population and development, and there are children sleeping in the street just a mile down the road from here. What are we doing about that?'*

"I remember the response of a delegate, who was a woman from the United States. She said, 'We don't have time to talk about that in this conference!' I thought *That's wrong! Who deserves and needs support more than a child? If we have the resources to put on a UN conference which costs a bundle why don't we have time to talk about a kid sleeping on a sidewalk or a baby lying abandoned in a box?* I was very upset and frustrated.

"In realizing that life *is* longer than thirty years, I feel like I can actually work on these issues. In accepting that life is relatively short, I think it's very important for me to choose a point of focus. It's vital to find my mission and give my attention to that. So *'Water First,' 'Mother*

Maroon,' and *'Where Do the Children Play?'* is third for me. That's plenty for a life's work."

*Millennium Development Goals were developed by the UN in 2001, recognizing the need to assist impoverished nations more aggressively.

Amy Hart may be contacted through her website: www.WaterFirstFilm.org

Chapter 26
Finding My Mission
Carol Sue Hart

"Growing up we never hugged or expressed our love to each other, so this has never been easy for me. In the clown outfit, however, I feel safe to learn how to do that. Now I'm a hugging person. When somebody's hurting I just give them a hug; it's so comforting and I don't really have to say anything."

Carol Sue, 64, lives in Saratoga Springs, New York with her husband George. She's mom to three adult children: Dirk, Tammy, and Vickie, and grandmother to seven. Carol Sue is also proud to be known as *Sonshine the Clown* or *Miss Piggy Sue*. She's brought healing and joy into her life, and to those she comes in contact with through her passion for clowning.

"Recently when I had no clowning work for a couple of months, it was very hard for me, because growing up, work was the only thing I was ever recognized for. For many reasons there were just no clowning opportunities for me during that time. Then I said, 'Okay God, I want you first in my life!' So, when I came back to clowning I was so much more passionate. It really became God doing it rather than me doing it alone. I think that time where I had no work was also God's way of saying, *you've been putting this before me and I want you to put me first and let me bring you joy.* Now I feel great joy in doing clowning. It changed my whole outlook.

"When I'm clowning in a hospital, I've got to be *up* for four hours at a time. One day, while driving to a hospital to clown, I had a difficult personal conflict going on in my life, and tears were coming from my eyes as I realized that without God I'm just not going to be able to do it. So I said, 'God, you're going to have to help me! I just can not do this nor can I pick myself up.' At that point, I saw some contractors standing on the side of the road while I was waiting at a traffic light. I put some of my clown face on, rolled down the window and waved to them. When they saw me they jumped up and down, waved, and laughed, and then I began feeling happy. (Laughs) Another time I might be clowning at a hospital and someone tells me that I made their day, or that I look cute. I often think that *I* get more out of it than do the people I'm clowning for. As a clown, all I want to do is just touch people's hearts."

Where did your desire for clowning begin?

"I guess I was always *my kid's mom, and then my husband's wife;* but I had no identity of my own. Growing up in an alcoholic family, many negative things happened to me, so I was constantly trying to be the *perfect kid* and then the *perfect daughter* who did whatever my parents expected of me. As a result I was never really me. It wasn't until I became involved in my 12-step recovery program that I was able to begin expressing my own truth—I'd always kept everything inside.

"My mom was 92 when she passed away in 1992. She accepted the Lord when she was 90. She had gotten married when she was 40, and gave birth to my brother at 42 and then me at 43. She seemed very old to me—as I remember it. She seldom left the house after I was seven, except to plant her flowers. The story goes that someone had said something very hurtful to her when I was about seven or eight years old, and from that point on she stopped going out of the house. Mom didn't: go shopping, to my high school graduation, or even attend my wedding. I think she felt funny, because in those days people in their 50s were considered old and *didn't have little kids.* I think that's part of the reason that I always had a desire to visit, and later do clowning in nursing homes as a grown up. It was easier for me to relate to the elderly than to kids.

"I'm unsure how the idea of becoming a clown eventually came to. I wasn't really around a lot of clowns, but I think what attracted me was, that as a clown, I'd be under makeup and no one would recognize me. That way I could be myself. Someone once told me that when you put on your clown make-up, you transform into who you really are.

"What happened for me was that one day I went to a Methodist church to attend a 12-step meeting, and saw that the church was having a magician come in to entertain at the same time. I thought *the heck with the meeting; I'm going to see the magician*! (Laughing) Now I have to tell you that I'd been unsuccessfully looking for a clowning class at all the local community colleges for quite a while. At the magician's show I asked if anyone knew where a clowning class was being offered, or if they knew of anyone who taught clowning. I was told there would be a one-week summer camp offered, on clowning, through the church. I thought, *"Wow, I can go to this, learn clowning, and then I'll be' perfect' at it*! I felt I'd have to be perfect in order to ever do this before the public, which was similar to how I felt about dancing in public."

That's a pretty limited existence!

"It sure is; but thank God for breakthroughs! So I called up the contact person and I was told the classes being offered were for grade school students but I could volunteer and learn everything the clowns do. Before the camp took place, however, Schenectady Community College offered courses on clowning. There I learned to do the three faces: the white face, Auguste (two colors), and the tramp or hobo. I also learned how to put on makeup, and did a little juggling, played with balloons, and performed a skit for the rest of the camp. So I learned some things and then was able to teach that to the kids at the camp. A while back I attended a Christian Clowning Class in Atlanta, Georgia where I picked my name 'Sonshine.' I chose that because Jesus, the "Son" of God, gives me joy. I'm presently taking new classes at Sears. The education of a clown goes on forever, so I'm forever learning.

"There was also a woman in the area by the name of Marie Beck, or

Mischief the Clown, whom I consider my mentor. She was teaching Christian clowning. That ignited a spark in me! I thought, *This is something I'd like to do!* Marie's the head of 'Joyful Joeys,' a clowning ministry that performs one-hour church services for any religious denomination. I've been clowning now for about 14 years, and a member of the 'Joyful Joeys' for eight of those years.

"The first year I was with the Joyful Joeys we went to a summer camp in the Catskills where there were roughly 500 kids from the inner city of New York. These kids just love to talk, but when we were performing you could hear a pin drop. It was truly amazing! We've also performed at camps where there were only kids from Community Reformed Churches—not reform schools. (Laughs) At the end of the service, we have clowns who portray the Father, Son, and Holy Spirit. They begin a handshake and a hug in the center aisle and then the kids pass the hugs and handshakes from the ends of the aisles through every pew. When we do that it seems that God is sending down his love on them and us.

"Sometimes my intuition will tell me to hug a particular person who really needs it. Growing up we never hugged or expressed our love to each other, so this has never been easy for me. In the clown outfit, however, I feel safe to learn how to do that. Now I'm a hugging person! When somebody's hurting I just give them a hug; it's so comforting and I don't really have to say anything.

"When I entered counseling 20 years ago, my son Dirk was still a teenager. I'd never told him I loved him or hugged him because I'd never got any of that myself. I remember asking my brother Lee, 'How come you hug your kids and tell them you love them?'

"He told me that he was friends with this large Italian family down the road and they'd be hugging and expressing love all the time   it was what they grew up with. So after this discussion I went and gave Dirk a hug; it was like *holding a board!* (Laughing) I remember that I was crushed! When I next spoke with my counselor I said, 'I'm never going to be able to do this!'

"He said, 'Just do it and don't expect anything in return.' I worked at it and now Dirk and I hug freely.

"There's another story involving my mom. When she was 89, I'd accepted the Lord in my life, and one day I was moved to just go over and give her a little kiss on the cheek. She looked at me and said, 'You're only doing that because I'm going to die.'

"Once again I said to myself, *I'm never going to do this again.* But I did keep doing it and soon she began to kiss me on the cheek. That was so tender and so touching.

"I was also working on forgiveness, with my counselor, and I wanted to ask my mom's forgiveness for not having expressed love to her throughout my life. I fantasized that when I did, she would take me in her arms and she'd say, *You're forgiven Carol—I love you.* It didn't happen. She had Alzheimer's and was in *blank-out* stage, so there was little reaction. Once again I felt crushed.

"She passed away at 92, and that week following her death we did a memorial service for her. A day or so after the service I woke up in the middle of the night and I heard her voice saying, 'Carol, I love you.' (Lowers her voice) I just laid there and thanked God. Mom couldn't do it here, but she was able to do it now that she had passed on and was in heaven.

"Currently, there are 12 of us, ages 15 to 75, in the 'Joyful Joeys,' and each of us has made a two-year commitment to the group. The lady who's 75 is so energetic you'd never know how old she is. She's has more energy than many of us. We've also have two singers and a person who handles the tapes for us. We're a local group, but we've traveled as far as Long Island and Rochester and even down into New Jersey. It's very touching when you look out at the congregation and see tears streaming down their cheeks. That's been a big part of my personal healing.

"Each part of my act has healed something in me. When I started, I was looking for a costume, and when I finally found one I liked, it was a little big on me. Wearing that dress however, became healing for me, because when I was young I was skinny, gawky, and not nearly as developed as other girls my age. So I always felt very different and not as good as the other girls. Acting out anger as a clown has helped to heal and release some of my own anger. I had no idea how much anger I held inside. It's the same with the sadness and tears I've acted out—it's all helped to heal me. In growing up in an alcoholic family, I'd suppressed all my emotions just to survive. There have been times while clowning, where the tears have just flowed from my eyes and I knew they were from my past. When I'm able to do that, I feel healed and so connected with everyone else; sort of like being a leaf on the vine of the human family.

"While I was still employed part-time by the State University of New York, where I'd worked for 30 years, I also became involved with a group called Clowns on Rounds, who dress up as doctors and nurses, and visit patients. About eight years ago, they asked me to do some clowning at Our Lady of Mercy Life Center. Where I'd felt safe in the Joyful Joey's because it was a group, I was now being asked to work alone which was much scarier. I kept thinking I wouldn't know what to do when I got to an assignment. So the first person I encountered at the nursing home was a retired GE executive who was unable to speak, but he'd start laughing each time I walked into his room. I'd go home at night feeling terrible and think, *Oh my God, he's laughing at me.* (Laughing) Eventually I came to this startling realization, *That's why I'm here*! Weeks later, I happened to be in the hallway of the same nursing home, out of costume, and this same man heard my laugh which got him laughing. I was shocked because I wasn't trying to be funny at the time and I wasn't in my clown costume. I guess it was my *God-laugh* that he recognized. It was amazing and gratifying to me to see how people responded to what I did as a clown. In fact, after my four-hour assignments would end, I found myself not wanting to leave, and would often stay another couple of hours.

"My next assignment was at St. Clare's Hospital in Schenectady where I'd work with people who were undergoing one-day surgeries. I loved it. One person I visited, happened to be a friend from my 12-step group, and she said, '*Oh My God!*' when she realized it was me. One of the little jokes I played on her was to say that I had come in to take a stool sample. I told her I would demonstrate how, at which time I took a tiny wooden three-legged stool out of a little plastic case, and told her this was a *hard stool*. It got a big laugh. She later told me she felt very blessed by me.

"There was another person I clowned for who was about to enter bypass surgery. When I was done he said he couldn't remember why he was at the hospital that day! (Laughing) I find that even when they don't laugh a lot, they'll say something like, 'Thank you for making my day a little easier.' One person said, 'You're so cute.' My husband will tell me the same thing, but I wish he'd say it when my makeup is off. (Laughs)

"When I first started clowning I had Mischief, who had been clowning for 15 years, and Loretta who was the head of Clowns on Rounds and had taught us how to go into the hospitals, as my teachers. I would just follow them and attempt to do exactly what they were doing. I thought I had to be just like them. Today, much of what I do as a clown is really *me*. I think that transition happened, as I mentioned before, when God took my clowning away for a while.

"Part of my act is wearing big, floppy shoes. I tell people (in clown voice), 'When I was a little girl my mother bought me these shoes so that my feet would have room to grow. She saved a lot of money that way. When I got older they were perfect for my bunions and corns—lots of room!'(Laughing) Then I tell them, 'When I was young, I wanted to be a cheerleader but I was a *klutz*. When the other girls would go up, I'd be going down. This is why I became a clown.' Then I'll dance for them using my little clicker that I bought from Pet Smart. Seeing people laugh is so rewarding for me.

"I don't see a lot of children when I'm clowning in the hospital, but one day I entered a little girl's room and she happened to be lying in her bed. I said 'Hi,' and asked if she'd like a little company. I got no response from her. Sensing she was not feeling very well, I asked her if she'd like to see my magic coloring book. This got her attention. She sat up and really enjoyed what I was doing with her.

"Another young girl, 6 or 7 years of age, who hadn't eaten in three days and wasn't feeling well, didn't want me to leave after I'd been clowning with her for a while. She kept saying, 'Don't go! Don't go!' So I stayed a while longer. Later while helping another clown clean some artwork off the hallway windows, I happened to look into the little girl's room and saw that she was eating ice cream along with some other food. Eventually the little girl came out into the hallway with an IV in her arm and asked if she could help me. Over time I became truly amazed at what a little bit of laughter could do!

"I have a friend who is part of a laughter club and she was able get her daughter laughing in between *two* brain surgeries she was having in the same day. The doctors were amazed at how positively the laughing affected the second surgery.

"When my daughter Vickie was ready to deliver her second baby, she called me and asked me to come to the hospital. I was all dressed up as a clown when she called, so up I went in costume. The doctors later said that she laughed so hard, and was so relaxed, that the baby just slid out!"

"In my heart I believe God is going to use laughter to heal a lot of people. I don't know how, but I truly believe there's so much in people that can be healed by laughter.

"People, including my kids, used to make fun of my laugh earlier in my life, so I'd stopped laughing for a long time. If I did laugh at all, I would really tone it down so no one would be offended. I really thought something was wrong with my laughter. There was also a time in my life when I'd laugh because I didn't know what to do or say; like when a dirty joke was being told. Today I laugh because it's in me and it's real. I think, *This is me and I hope you can accept me as I am.*

"Recently I went to a woman's 80th birthday party at Applebee's. I came in dressed up as *Piggy Sue,* who's one of my characters. She has a pig nose, a Boa, pink glasses, and a flip-up wig. When I walked into that place people began laughing out loud. I told the lady who was retiring (in character), '*Oh my God, I'm sorry I'm late, I just had my hair done!*' (Laughing) She was breaking up!

355

"Another time I was on a bus trip and for some reason that I don't remember, I connected with a woman who was sitting on the other side of the aisle from me. I would look over at her and she would break up laughing and she would look at me and I would break up. At the end of our trip she said, 'I have to tell you, my mom died a year ago and I have not laughed since, until we connected today.' It was very healing for her and healing for me to hear that.

"When I do my clowning in nursing homes, hospitals and other places, I know it is God working through me. It's not me alone. When I'm able to touch people I'm also aware of what a privilege it is to be doing this. It's overwhelming for me sometimes to think that Jesus died on the cross for me, and now I'm able to give something back to Him.

"I want to educate myself all I can about laughter and about clowning so I can keep improving."

Have there been people who've motivated and influenced you?

"Marie, *Mischief the Clown,* taught that first Christian class I took, and has now become a best friend. I can call her any time of the day and she'll answer my questions about clowning and she'd let me borrow anything I needed. She's been such a blessing in my life. Her caring for people, and her desire for them to be the most they can be, has inspired me

"I've also been greatly influenced by Rick Warren's book, *The Purpose-Driven Life* and another book, *Battlefield of the Mind* by Joyce Meyer."

Carol Sue here goes on to discuss some aspects of her spiritual journey.

"As kids we were brought to church by my father and dropped off for Sunday school Mom and Dad didn't go. Later when I was married, George and I, in an effort to provide religious education for our children, were Sunday school teachers, even though I didn't really know the Lord yet. In 1989, however, when my husband and I were having troubles in our marriage, I began attending New Life Church in Schenectady. I was invited to attend a woman's retreat there, and accepted, even though I was very scared to go. At the retreat, a woman asked me if I would like her to pray with me. I said, 'No!' On Saturday night, however, while in the circle, I said that I wanted to accept the Lord in my life. It was like I put my hand up, and He reached out and forgave me all my sins. I was really at a *bottom* in my life at that time. There had been times when I even wanted to hurt myself. I was not living the way I wanted to, and not being the person I knew God wanted me to be. After I accepted the Lord, it was as if the weight of the world was lifted off me. I had a new beginning and for the first time I experienced unconditional love—no matter what I'd done in the past. Although my relationship with my husband has improved greatly, my relationship with God has become my priority.

"I also experience great freedom and relief by being part of a 12—step group. God's presence is *so there*! Sometimes I walk into those meetings feeling as if I'm carrying a big heavy brick on each shoulder. When I leave they've been lifted; they're gone! The folks there remind me of the importance of putting God first, as they share their experiences. I think we need that so we can have examples, hope, and inspiration for our lives. When I began this journey I didn't know who I was. Taking baby steps, though, I have been able to walk through my fears, and discover who I really am.

"Getting back to clowning, here's another story I can tell you, and it's about money:

I performed at a birthday party for 22 six and seven year-olds. Marie had told me I would be paid $150 for this job and that I should take no more than an hour for what I would be doing with them. I thought, *$150—how can I do this to these people?* I wasn't taking into consideration the hour of preparation, the learning, and practice it takes me to get ready to do a show. My effort and preparation didn't seem to count with me. So I performed a half-hour show for the kids and then did face painting that lasted at least an hour by the time I was done. I didn't want to leave without painting every kid's face. So when I was finished the father handed me a check and off I went, still thinking that charging $150 for what I did was outrageously high. When I reached home I happened to look at the check and was shocked to see that he'd included an extra $50 as a tip for me. I just couldn't believe I was worth that much money!

"During that party I was aware that I was having a lot of fun as were the kids. In the clown classes I'd attended, they had put a big emphasis on that and said that if we weren't having fun we should not do it.

"When my grandson was in kindergarten, I performed at a class party they were having, and I remember those kids laughed so loud that you could hear them from one end of the school to the other. They had such joy in their eyes and I was so in tune with them. I wondered, *Who is this person who's putting on this show?* You see I always seem to have this 'devil' that sits on my shoulder and wants to tell me that I can't really relate to kids. But I now know that I have a kid inside of me—I really do have it! I'll never forget my grandson's party. Whenever I start to doubt myself, I remember and think, *OK I can do it. I can do all things through Christ, who strengthens me.*"

What would you say to a person who wants to be passionate but just doesn't feel passion for anything?

"That's really hard. I think everyone has something they could be passionate about, but the challenge is to find it. I feel that God found it for me. I trust God has a purpose for each of us and that's where our passion lies.

"I remember that I wanted to visit nursing homes, but I didn't know how to do that. I was afraid to go, just being myself. I'd think, *What impact could I make? I don't have anything to share and, besides, I don't talk to strangers.* Now you can't shut me up! George sometimes will say, 'Can't you go back to the way you used to be?'

"I'll say, 'Nope, too late!'(Laughing)

"I think when kids are young and in school, even college, they're trying to find what they want to do, without having had much exposure to the world. That's very difficult and I think that's why it's so important to give yourself permission to try different things throughout life. I think I'm signed up for four different educational courses this year.

"When my life is over, my greatest hope is that my kids, grandchildren, and husband would have seen God through me.(tearfully) It hasn't always been easy for us, but I hope that through the laughter they get to know that God can always bring joy into their lives, no matter their circumstances. That extends to all the people I come in contact with. When I go to the hospital, I am…I can't even put it into words…I am so blessed being able to go there and touch the people there…to make them laugh…to help them talk. I want to be there. When I go to the hospital, I'll pray, 'God lead me where you want me to go' and someone will come up to me and request that I visit a patient who needs to laugh. When that happens I know I'm being directed. I just follow, never really knowing how I'm going to affect a person.

"I remember an occasion I was told ***not*** to go to room 222 and later, while walking through the hallway, I was asked by a man to please go to room 222. I told him I couldn't, but if he checked with a nurse and she okayed it, I'd gladly visit. He obtained permission and when I came into the room, I saw four visitors in the room, and decided to come back in a little while so as not to disturb them. Later, when I returned, there were six people in the room, so I decided to just go ahead and do some clowning. The patient and the visitors all got laughing and had a great time. After a while, I left and the people thanked me so much. I think those moments when I was clowning and she was laughing, were within the last couple of hours of her life. Her laughter was mixed with tears so it was kind of like a *laughing good-bye*. She was going out in joy! What a wonderful way to leave this life."

It sounds like this passion of yours is continuing to evolve?

"Yes and sometimes when it's evolving I say, 'Are you sure Lord?'(Laughing) Recently, I've felt a calling to become involved with the Prayer and Healing center in Albany. This is a clinic created by a local doctor who's mission it is to provide medically and spiritually for those who need healing regardless of their ability to pay. I've felt for awhile that Nurse Sonshine, (laughter) and God could be part of healing people at that center. At the same time it scares me. I don't know if my praying would be good enough my prayers are very short and sweet— but in the end, this will is all about God's timing, and my *not* missing it, like I sometimes do."

Postscript: April, 2007—Carol Sue continues to expand the reach of her clown ministry. In the coming months, she will be presenting talks on the importance of humor to nursing school graduates, and to staff at a nursing home.

She is also honing her speaking skills by joining Toastmasters International.

In Carol's words: "God is go-o-o-o-o-d all the time. I'm learning to trust God. Sometimes that is hard, but I've learned it's all in how I set my mind and heart."

Carol Sue Hart may be reached at nursesonshine1@aol.com

Chapter 27
Risking
Steve Carty Cordry

"All those things that make me comfortable and safe are the things that keep me from being totally alive and passionate. It seems as though safety and comfort would bring me life, when in fact, what they bring me is zero possibility for any worthwhile change or growth. After all, did Martin Luther King, my hero, have a certainty about how his life would go? Did Jesus Christ or Gandhi live risk-free?"

Steve, 56, lives on Cape Cod, Massachusetts with his wife, Ellen. He's presently the pastor of the Unity Church of the Light, in Hyannis, which is the culmination of a journey that has taken Steve from the corporate world, where he'd been a successful but unfulfilled hospital administrator, to ministerial school and into the rewarding work of serving others. This journey parallels to Steve's spiritual passion for discovering who he really is and for helping others to do the same.

Maybe the most intriguing aspect of this interview is that Steve had forgotten our interview appt. in August of 2007, so it was rescheduled for October instead. As Steve would later tell me, "If you had interviewed me in August you would have gotten an entirely different interview from what you will get today." In September 2007, while at a conference in Kansas City, Missouri, Steve was stricken with angina, an acute restriction of the blood flow in the coronary arteries. Following open heart surgery, a near-death experience with post-operative congestive heart failure, and a period of recuperation in Kansas City and at home, Steve was back at work for just a few weeks when we met for this interview.

"As I pondered the question of the passion in my life, I recognized that my main passion is a spiritual one. I guess if I had to describe it specifically it would be the passion to know or to remember my wholeness and worth, and to help others to know it as well.

"The first story that comes to mind, although I'm sure there were earlier ones, was that of my first heartbreak and what it *drove* me to. *(Laughing)* It happened right after college graduation in 1973. I had in the preceding couple of years been passionately in love with a girl, who in my high school days was someone I'd thought to be out of my reach. I was just so in love with her, and we'd gotten engaged against her parent's wishes. My spiritual philosophy in those days was very different from what it is today, so her parents were very averse to me. Actually, her mother slapped me when we announced our intention to get married.(Laughing) In looking back, I guess I should have known by my fiancée's reaction, that it was the beginning of the end of our relationship because her reaction was not at all to rush to my side, come to my defense and say *I don't care what you say or do, this is my man, and I'm standing with him!*(Laughing) Since we were at a distance at that time—I was training to be a medical technologist and she was student-teacher training—it was pretty easy for us to just fall apart.

"When the full reality of that hit me, I had an intensely, emotional reaction. In retrospect I see that it touched all the feelings of unworthiness, abandonment, and rejection that I'd ever experienced in my life. I remember listening one morning to Beethoven, my favorite composer, and experiencing what I describe as an *epiphany* and a breakdown at the same moment. Tears were streaming down my face and I made a commitment to myself that I would leave my medical technologist training in Pontiac, Michigan and drive to California to do

THOSE WHO WALK WITH FIRE

therapy with Nathaniel Brandon, the author of 'The Psychology of Self Esteem,' a book I'd just read.

"He was affiliated in many ways with Ayn Rand whose writings awoke me to the possibility there was something beyond Catholicism. I had grown up Catholic and in fact was attending seminary in the 9th Grade. I guess I'd had always had some degree of spiritual calling from the very beginning of my life.

"So I drove all the way to California with very little money. Before I left, I did a brake job on my rusted out Volkswagen. By the time I reached St. Louis, Missouri, however, I'd completely destroyed my brakes again and gave what little money I had left to the Volkswagen dealership for a brake job. I was fortunate that they kindly accepted what money I did have as payment.

"I lived on my credit card until I reached Oklahoma when my card was revoked. At that point, I was forced to trade some tools I had for my next tank of gas. To conserve the gas, I actually turned my engine off when driving downhill and just coasted, which at times was on the freeway. My car eventually ran out of gas very close to my destination, where I bartered my pocket watch for enough gas to reach the house where I would be staying and to where my last paycheck of $200 had been mailed. I had nothing. I pulled into Los Angeles at six o'clock on a Saturday night looking for a place to camp and eventually found a campground north of LA. To make a long story short, the question here is: what would motivate me to risk driving from the wild woods of northern Michigan where I grew up, across the country to this sprawling, multicultural center on the far west coast of California, where I knew no one, and had no job or home? *I mean what was driving me? What was calling me?*

"In looking back I do see that it was a desire to recapture, or remember, that I was safe! I was OK! I was worthwhile! I was lovable and I was loved! As I look at my continuing journey from being a professional hospital administrator, all the way to being an ordained Unity Minister—in fact it was 7 years ago yesterday that I showed up here for my trial as minister—I see this journey of mine as a quest to know who and what I really am, and to help others know that as well.

"One of the questions you asked me to consider in this interview is whether personal woundedness was a motivating force in what I have a passion for. I can tell you that is totally true in my case. As a child I was overweight, not athletic, kind of bookish, and *pretty holy;* and that combination of characteristics did not make me a popularity winner! (Laughing) Even in our little town of Iron Mountain, in the Upper Peninsula of Michigan, with a population of 6,000, I was picked on, not chosen, and often bullied. I think a piece of my passion, and probably true for many others as well, who identify with being the underdog, or the *frog who turns into the prince,* is facilitating in some way, a transformation or victory over fear, self-doubt, and feelings of worthlessness. That's what ultimately called me from a very successful, but non-soul-satisfying business career, into the profession of ministry. The ministry allows me to be present to, and connected with, human beings in ways and in moments that are both profound and challenging. It's a rare privilege to be allowed into people's lives and to be asked to support and help them to move through the joyous and the challenging moments of their lives."

Were you always aware of wanting to help others as a result of what happened to you?

"No. No. As we were talking earlier over lunch, I think that much of what has driven me in whatever career setting I've been in, has been just the opposite. I was never clear about *what* was moving me; I just always had a strong desire to have my worth and lovability validated by an external source, because I couldn't do that for myself. So I was really being driven by fear. Underneath that however was a desire to really be of help to another human being. So it's not black or white, or good or bad.

"I had open-heart surgery 6 ½ weeks ago, and in the aftermath of that, I was completely stripped of any sense of personal control or power. I was forced to surrender to Spirit or God, or whatever you call that power. It was only in that surrender that I became conscious of how driven I had been to find acceptance, esteem, competence, and love through achieving certain external goals, positions, or successes. Being conscious of that drive, has handed me a sense of freedom, and opened up the opportunity to be present with people, in a way that was not possible when I was unaware. That's very powerful for me!

"Today, in a very personal way, I know that I am cherished regardless of what I've ever said, done, or thought. For me, that knowledge has allowed all the fear-based, mental machinery in my head as I call it, to shut down. The way I put it to my congregation is: 'I've created a lot of mental machinery to keep me emotionally safe and to feel loved and worthwhile. Today I am at peace in my life. I no longer worry about whether you love me or what you think of me because today I know I'm loved and I'm cherished, which gives me the potential to love and cherish you."

It sounds like you're saying that you're motive in giving to others has changed as a result of this life-changing event.

"My motive has changed to the degree that I'm now more conscious. My old motive as I'm sharing it with you was largely invisible to me prior to my illness. I also wouldn't say that my old motives were my whole purpose in what I did but to the extent to which they were at work I had no idea of how deep they went.

"These days' people tell me: 'You're different. You look different. You're *eyes* are different.'

"It's wonderful to be at peace and not be concerned with what I have to do next in order to be sure I'm OK? That gives me the space to be with people in any entirely different way.

(Laughing) "You're getting *this interview* due to the fact that I missed the first interview, and the interview that's happening now is very different. I think the way things happened with us is no accident. It's just another example of the *universe* at work.

"That's another part of the change. The *controller* or the part of me that wants to be sure that I have everything under control and knows how everything will turn out has now become *unplugged*. Today it's more that *I don't know—I really don't know what going to happen in my life or my ministry.* I really don't care. I just know that as I show up in this peaceful space, whatever I need to know will be revealed, and it will be perfect.

"When, for example, I first walked into a Unity Church, or any place where truth is being spoken, for that matter, I can feel a *yes* rise within me. Something within me resonates with what is being said, and it makes perfect sense to me. My journey which has spanned 21 years now has been, I guess, about how that understanding deepens. My experience has been that with greater understanding comes a gradually stripping away of the need for any notion of personal power or control.

"When I lay in that hospital bed, thinking that it was over for me and believing that I would die, there was no sense left that I was actually doing anything. It was all a part of something so much bigger than Steve Carty Cordry. I experienced that I was just a part of something greater unfolding. That's much different than my being the *driver* in my life. I see myself as truly a part of the *sweep of Divine expression.* This belief allows me to surrender in a way that I think is foundational to the core of my life's purpose. I'm sure that when Jesus prayed in the garden, he knew what he was facing and that he thought, *I don't really want this; but I'm not in charge of what's happening here. If this is what it's going to take for me and for our world to wake up then 'Thy will be done.'* I don't think there's any other prayer that speaks more directly to the core of what I believe spiritually and feel passionately about.

"When I look at the lives and challenges of St. Francis of Assisi, Jesus Christ, Mother Teresa, or Martin Luther King, I trust that none of those people said, *well this is what I would like to do today! This is the life I have decided would be best for me.* Each of them in some way probably said, *Oh Great Mystery, do with me what you will. I just want to be with you and to serve you.* My intentions are not so much about me today as they are about knowing God's will for me, so I can direct my intentions toward that end."

In your little corner of the world?

"Exactly! When I came back from my illness, my intention was no longer about growing the church, which can be seen as the bottom-line for a minister. My intention had become helping to deepen the sense of community within our church and then within the greater community in which we exist. That's what I'm interested in now. If we don't ever have more people than we have attending services now, or if we only have enough money to sustain us as a community of love, that's fine with me. On the other hand, if we quadruple in size that's OK with me too."

One of the reasons I was attracted to interviewing you is because I've seen the positive effect you have on people when you passionately express your love and emotions. At times you almost seem childlike: that is the child who hasn't yet learned to be cautious and protective of his emotions. Am I imagining that?

"I hope not! (Laughing) I think that's heaven on earth; everything else is created from the mental machine. When my love flows freely all the time, to everyone; and when I'm attuned to others and know that nothing can hurt me at the level of my spirit and soul, that's the *Garden!* Whether you accept me or not I can't be hurt; I can only love you, and see that you may be suffering in that moment, as you're directing anger at me. What I can offer at that moment is compassion.

"What you've observed in me is exactly the feedback that I've been getting from people since I've come back from my heart surgery. As I think about what you said, it may very well go back to that child, who knew only love before he was introduced to the world of rules and propriety. I cry publicly and I kiss!

"One Sunday our guitarist, Jack, sang 'It's a Wonderful World,' and Jack is this wonderful character who pretends that he doesn't want to be loved, (Laughing) so after he finished and was receiving a thunderous applause from the congregation, I was so moved that I snuck up behind him and kissed his head. Later, while I was giving my talk to the congregation, the clip, which holds my ear mike in place, came off my collar, and I wasn't able to fix it. Jack saw me struggling, walked up on the platform where I was, and fixed it for me. I turned to him and jokingly said, 'give me a kiss,' and he gave me a kiss. (Laughing) Now this is a guy who would say, 'don't touch me!' I also kiss the ladies in a non-romantic way. I just let my humanity sort of 'plop out.'

"Not that long ago, Ellen and I took a cruise to Mexico. At the time I'd grown whiskers, and weighed about 245 pounds—which was 23 pounds ago—and she took a picture of me sitting on a beach, looking like an albino sea lion. (Laughing) This past Sunday, I showed that picture at service, and I can't remember what the purpose of my talk was, but I posed this question to the congregation: *what in me would create this level of protection for myself?*

"I think part of love is to let people see that I have my warts and I'm no better than they are, and that we're all together on this path of learning, discovering, and healing. I get the biggest blessing because I get to do this for my work!"

Earlier in our discussion you described yourself as *holy* when you were a kid. What did you mean by that?

"I grew up in a house that was across the alley from a Catholic Rectory where the priests lived. Back a little further was the Catholic Grade School, and then 'catty-cornered' from us was the convent where the nuns lived. So we were surrounded! A case in point is that one day I was walking to church for confession and the Monsignor was driving home to the rectory and stopped to ask if I was going to confession. I said I was, at which point he motioned me over to the car, and while half in and half out of the car, he heard my confession right there in the street. That's the neighborhood I grew up in.

"My parents were very devout Catholics, as were most of the people in my neighborhood. I was an altar boy right up to high school. In ninth grade, I entered seminary, intending to be a priest. Alas puberty struck (laughing) and suddenly celibacy didn't seem like the right path for me.

"I recognize today that a prime motive behind wanting to be a priest back then was to please my parents, and to be loved and appreciated. Underneath all this religious striving and pleasing others, however, I believe I always had a deep longing for connection to my spirit.

"Unfortunately, how all this would show up to my peers, was that I was seen as this 'holy boy,' which didn't make me very popular."

Have there been people along the way who have 'lit your fire' or been heroes to you?

"Oh yes—so many! My wife Ellen is a hero. She is fearless in her generosity, her spiritual journey, and her insistence, in a positive way, for clarity in her relationship with me and others.

"My son, Michael, is also a hero to me. He's 24, and in the past five years he's gone from being an average young man struggling in school, and just trying to get along, to being a heroin addict and a felon, and today he is a credentialed pastor, and, I think, a very humble servant to those who are caught up in the grip of addiction. He was forced by his addiction to find a path where he learned that we are all children of God, no matter where we've been or what we've done. I'm very proud of him.

"Another is Maria Nemeth, an author and coach, whom I first met at a conference at Unity Village. Ellen and I have done a lot of work with her. She's committed to supporting people in knowing their authentic selves. She helps them to see how they've become snagged in that 'mental machinery' I mentioned earlier, and how that machinery has driven them, as opposed to them making positive, authentic choices in their lives. I love her, she's masterful!

"In the larger-than-life category of heroes, Martin Luther King stands out to me for his: vision, courage, and willingness to surrender to what he felt passionate about.

There's also a fellow Unity minister by the name of Bob Wasner, who I believe now has a church in Australia. He's the first Unity minister I had any relationship with. My introduction to Unity took place on the island of Oahu, Hawaii. As a member of the church there, I took part in the search process for a minister. That minister turned out to be Bob. He greatly inspired me and gave me a firm grasp of Unity principles. He also supported me with compassion and optimism as I moved through a very painful divorce; and much later, when I married Ellen, Bob officiated at our wedding. When I was ordained, I wore Bob's robe which he had given to me for the occasion. His relationship meant so much to me.

"Another mentor from the ministry is Steve Colladay who introduced me to Unity in Hawaii. I hired Steve as a consultant when I was a hospital administrator. We became friends, and I became aware that he had real peace of mind which was a commodity I was very short of at the time. (Laughing) He eventually left his consulting practice to become a Unity Minister. I moved to Danville, Virginia to take a new position, while Steve finished ministerial school, was ordained, and subsequently chosen to be minister of a church at nearby Chapel Hill, North Carolina. I then hired him again as a part-time consultant, and I in turn was the Finance Committee Chairperson in his church. Later he trained me as a lay minister. Our relationship just flowed back and forth over the years."

Was there a precipitating event or moment that told you that your professional career in the business world was just not working for you any longer?

"I'd say there was a kind of *divine discontent* going on for me. Even though from a professional perspective, my job, developing new business was exciting, I was not happy in my soul. I wasn't excited about going to work; I wasn't *feeling it!* I found myself getting depressed, so I decided to take a little time off to give my creative self-expression a chance to reveal my next move to me. Consequently, I took a week, wrote poetry, and did some free drawing. One of the things I drew during that time was a little church by the sea, and here I am today as minister in this church on Cape Cod. That's amazing! I decided at the end of that week that I was going to pursue ministerial work which I loved, and had been doing as a volunteer lay minister. Earlier, at my graduation from that lay ministry program, my wife Ellen told me that she believed we would end up at Unity Village, for ministerial school some day. I didn't disagree. My wife is very intuitive.
"

What is Passion to you Steve?

"I don't know that I can define it as much as I can give some characteristics of it. For me passion is hooked up with purpose. When passion is present there's a clarity that says: *this is who I am, this is what I love, and this is what I'm here to do*! Another aspect of passion for me is the emotional fuel of fire and excitement, which has the potential to be consuming as well as nurturing at the same time. There's an intensity and aliveness which goes beyond the commonplace of everyday existence.

"Seeking passion, however, for only the sake of the experience can become another means of distracting myself from fear, and, in the long run, can leave me burned-out, and emotionally, physically, and spiritually depleted. When, however, I'm engaged with something that revolves around my true purpose and higher intention, I experience a sense of peace and joy. How and where I direct my efforts while being conscious of the presence of God makes all the difference.

"The way this has come to me since my heart failure has been: I *am in my Father's world.* In other words, all is well! It's not the gender aspect of the word *father* that grabs me, as much as the idea that it's not my world to control and to manipulate events the way I think they should be. It's for me to live in it as my *Father's son,* which means I love myself first. Jesus said 'love your neighbor as yourself.' That means I love *me,* and when I can love *me* and take care of *me,* I can love others to that same extent. I used to worry about how many things I could get done in a day, where now I'm more interested in the *quality* of the time I have. Right now, I'd rather sit here with you. In fact I could sit here talking with you for hours John and I wouldn't worry about anything. I'm not worrying right now about what's going to happen to my church in the future or if next Sunday's sermon will be acceptable.

"I'm no less productive now with my change in attitude, than I was when my to-do list ran me, or when I sometimes ran from it. What's been altered is the quality of my existence. I can't help but believe that my connection to the people in my life has vastly improved. I experience more authenticity and real joy in my relationships. I have a greater interest in listening to *your* contribution to our conversation than I previously had been."

What would you say to someone who says, 'Steve, I envy you— I wish I had the kind of passion you have.'

"In order for you to say, *I envy you,* you must first see something in me that you recognize at a soul level. What you don't see is that you have that same potential within you; otherwise you wouldn't recognize it in me. Jesus said 'all things are possible.' There's nothing that you can't create. It's more a matter of what are you going to let go of, in order that you might live in the way your soul wants to live. Are you willing to be uncomfortable and be in the place of *I don't know, or I need help, or I surrender,* which are places the 'fear factory upstairs' wants to totally avoid because it wants to be safe. "

You say that with a lot of energy.

"That's because it's true for me. All those things that make me comfortable and safe are the things that keep me from being totally alive and passionate. It seems as though 'safety and comfort' would bring me life, when in fact what they bring me is zero possibility for any worthwhile change or growth. Believing, for example, that I don't have the possibility of equaling the passion you have for life is first of all a misunderstanding, but is also my fear's way of keeping things risk-free and pretty much the way they are. That in turn makes living a passionate life impossible. That's the tradeoff! It's hard to be passionate about something if you insist on being safe and comfortable. Did Martin Luther King, my hero, have a certainty about how his life would go? Did Jesus Christ or Gandhi live risk-free?

"I believe that the *great unknown* we're called to step into if we want to live a passionate life is also in the end benevolent. The universe is really designed to support us in our passion and in our quest as opposed to the common idea that the universe will *get us* in some way. The person who stays insistent on being comfortable collapses the possibility down to: *if I go out into the uncertain, here's the possibility—I'll be penniless, I'll lose respect in the eyes of others, my family will leave me, etc.*—instead of seeing the unlimited possibility for good that might happen if I step out beyond my comfort zone."

You like to use humor in your talks and in your interactions with people. Would you talk a little about the importance of humor in your life?

"I do an annual Humor Sunday at church and on just about every Sunday, I will use humor sometime during the service. I do a takeoff on the 'Father Guido Sarducci' character from the old Saturday Night Live show that comes right out of me and out of my youth. It's also a blatant rip-off of a rip-off. (Laughing) One of my teachers at Unity Ministerial School would often do that character and I liked it so much that I learned it.

"I think that at the core of humor is our common humanity. To be able to look at our humanity, see its absurdity, and embrace it is healing. It tells me that everything is really OK. People sometimes view spirituality as so *heavy* when truly it's not. I believe it's important to be able to look at ourselves and our mistakes at times, and laugh. I also think it's essential to a way of walking in the world that's light and part of the experience of living authentically."

Steve may be contacted at either **steve.ucl@verizon.net or www.yeahgod.org**

Chapter 28
Self-Discovery
Bonnie Kriss

"I'm not sure of all that I found out about myself on this trip, but I do know that these people are now part of me and that I'm more connected to my brothers and sisters throughout the world. Before visiting South Africa, I was somewhat aware of the situation there from listening to and reading the news. I can honestly say that at that time, I had a feeling of them being different and separate from me. Now I feel a part of them and they're a part of me; we're all connected and we're all children of God! I intellectually knew that before I went, but now I feel it deep inside of me."

Bonnie lives in Clifton Park, New York, with her husband Ted. She works as a Coordinator of Volunteer Services for Community Hospice Inc., the largest hospice program in New York State. Bonnie's passion, in her words, "is to fully experience who I am." She has been able to glimpse a clearer picture of that reality through her work, and most recently through her trip to Port Shepstone in South Africa's KwaZulu Natal Province, where Community Hospice has partnered with South Coast Hospice, to help them deal with the HIV/AIDS pandemic which has swept through sub-Saharan Africa in recent years.

"When I came back from South Africa, I had my first stab at writing because the experience there was *so big* that I couldn't accurately describe to people how I was feeling without first putting it down on paper. I just couldn't articulate my experience in one or two sentences. People would ask me to describe my trip and my standard reply went like this: 'Oh it was incredible! It was both heart-wrenching and heart-warming and now I am seeing through different eyes.' The truth was that I needed to *sit* with it and have the opportunity to process the whole experience. In fact, the group I had traveled to South Africa with was planning to meet two weeks after we got back, in order to process our thoughts and feelings about the trip. I told them that I wasn't sure if I'd be ready to do that. That's how unsettled I felt at that time.

"As time passed, I realized that I needed to do some work with this. As I began writing down my thoughts, it occurred to me that, *Yeah, I really am seeing through different eyes*. I am a changed person. So I titled the description of my trip, 'Seeing through Different Eyes.' It was an account of my experiences—physical, emotional, and spiritual, and I planned on using it as a guide for any presentations that I might have the opportunity to do. A big reason for volunteering for this trip was to support our partner hospice in Port Shepstone with fundraising and by raising awareness of their needs, so I've done two presentations just this week, using my writing as a guide, along with a slide presentation of my pictures, complete with African music. I'm very thankful to my husband Ted for helping me to put this presentation together. I never could have done it without him."

What is your passion Bonnie?

"I'll be at the 'speed-limit' (55 years old) soon and my passion at this stage of my life is to fully experience who I am….(Chokes up)…

"Wow! I didn't realize that identifying this passion would bring up such emotion for me. This has been my goal for quite some time. I guess I thought that God would tap me on the head some day and then I'd be fully enlightened, or a switch would suddenly be flicked on, and I'd say, *Aha! I am now an enlightened being*! Today, I know that's just not going to happen. It takes time, daily spiritual practice, and the unraveling of the *stuff* within me that got built up over the years and made me forget who I really am. I'm learning how my belief system, which was formed in the past, influences me today in my daily life. I'm also experiencing that I can change it as I grow more aware of what I'm thinking and doing, and why. I came into this world as a beautiful innocent child of God and my task is to recapture that."

"Humility comes into the picture as well. I have to remember that I'm not creating this change or reality on my own; I'm co-creating it with God. My job is to become willing to let go of the layers of guilt, fear, and unreal expectations that I learned from my parents and society. I don't mean to blame anybody, but this is how I learned to be in the world. I've had false beliefs like: 'I'm inadequate, I have an awful voice, and I'm too fat,' but through my spiritual work and with the assistance of my mentors, I'm slowly undoing that belief system. In a sense I'm letting go of the darkness to embrace the light."

What have you found to be the truth about you so far?

"Well, I've had glimpses of that *light* inside of me. I can see myself as an extension of God. He created me and as such I'm beautiful, powerful and a spiritual being! That's the reality I want to live in…He bolsters me so that I can be that.

"When I first began studying A Course in Miracles, the class facilitator, Ray Newman, went around the room and asked each person what their goal in life was. Almost everyone, including me, said their goal was to find peace. So, that's been my journey and I've had brief moments of real joy, peace, and even bliss at times."

Where did this journey begin for you?

"Well, I grew up Roman Catholic and brought my two sons up in that religion. I divorced their father in 1989 and my goal at that point in my life was just to find some peace. I searched around some for a spiritual path and then met my present husband, Ted, who suggested that we try the United Methodist Church, which we then attended for about 10 years. During that time, I was reading various spiritual books and all the authors kept referring to A Course in Miracles. Being curious, I visited our local library and did some research. At the same time, a woman at my workplace asked if anyone was interested in signing up to take A Course in Miracles. So I signed up for an introductory class.

"I struggled with the Course at first because it's very intense; but the way of life it laid out was how I wanted to live, and was the path to becoming who I wanted to be. As time passed, I began to see that the theology and perspectives of the Methodist church were increasingly at odds with what I was learning through A Course in Miracles. Coincidentally, through these classes, I had met Marti Breyer, a massage therapist whom I began having body work sessions with. She mentioned that she attended Unity Church and thought that it might be a good fit for us. That was about three years ago. We've been attending Unity Church ever since.

"It's really nice to look back at all these incremental steps I've chosen and realize that I'm designing the life I want for myself. I've gone from full to part time in my work life. I coordinate volunteer services for The Community Hospice, where Ted and I have been volunteers since 1993. Prior to working for hospice, I had worked at GE for 25 years in an administrative capacity until my husband, also a GE employee, was recruited away to a more lucrative job, which necessitated our moving out of the area and my leaving my employment at GE."

Where did this desire to be involved with hospice come from, Bonnie?

"It grew over time. Unlike many volunteers who have had loved ones on hospice at one time, I had no experience with hospice. Ted and I were then at a point in our lives where we wanted to give something back to the community, so we were searching for something we could be involved with. We didn't want to just send our money to a worthy cause or be on a board of directors. We had a desire to physically contribute something and to connect with people. I must add that at this time, Ted was employed at GE in Schenectady, and when hospice came there as part of a fundraising campaign; he volunteered to be a coordinator. One day he called me up, saying very excitedly, 'Bonnie! Bonnie! I've found something we could do. We could volunteer for hospice.'

"My first reaction was, *Hospice! I don't even know what it is or what a volunteer would do.* When I did find out what hospice was, I wasn't sure if I could do that kind of work. My parents had never talked about death and neither had I. It was a topic I gave very little thought to and, frankly, it scared me.

"But we did attend an informational meeting where I learned more about hospice volunteer work. I then decided to take the training program which was totally a leap of faith for me. Although it was in line with what I wanted to do with my life, it was also far outside of my life experience and comfort zone. I guess this was one of the many times I would step out and follow that *still, quiet Voice* inside me.

"The volunteer training seemed like a big commitment because I was driving from Pittsfield, Massachusetts, to Rotterdam, New York, each day after work, to attend a total of 36 hours of training sessions. But I found hospice work to be a wonderful gift. It's an honor to be part of a person's journey at the end of his or her life and I receive so much more than I can ever give.

"Initially I feared the emotional impact of giving so much of myself to a dying person. I imagined that I would be unable to handle my feelings when someone passed on. Well, the reality is: there is sadness, but the effort is also very rewarding. I get to hear their stories, their life lessons, their wisdom, and, I get to experience some great connections with them. It's important to say that not every person has what I would call a good death. Some people die as they have lived, which is not always positive.

"So that's how we became involved with hospice. When we moved away again, this time to Maryland, we wanted to continue to volunteer and we did until eventually the opportunity arose for me to become the full-time office manager at a hospice there. When we eventually landed back here in the Capital District, I returned to the hospice where I was originally trained, and was hired to be the part-time coordinator of volunteers.

"Because the Community Hospice has a now five-year partnership with two hospices in South Africa and one in Zimbabwe, I was able to become involved in a trip to assist the program in South Africa. We provide financial assistance, a staff exchange, medical supplies, education and information to the program there. I had thought that only the clinical staff were eligible to volunteer, and never thought it would be available to me. In talking to our office coordinator for the trip, I learned that I didn't need any special skills to be part of the program. She explained that if I went, my role would basically be that of a volunteer: visiting and sitting with people, holding their hand, or maybe just offering a Kleenex.

"She told me that if I was interested, I would be required to write an essay describing why I wanted to go and how that would benefit the partnership between the programs. In reflecting on my own spiritual journey, I knew that I wanted to further connect with all people. At the same time, my inner voice was saying, *Get out of the box you're in and step out!* So I applied for the trip and ended up being one of nine people selected: three would go to Zimbabwe and six to South Africa.

As I was preparing myself spiritually and psychologically for my trip it came to me that I'd like to write a letter to my husband that he could read while I was out of the country. The letter was about how I was feeling about our relationship, the trip, as well as thoughts I had about myself that previously I had been unable to share with him. In evaluating where I was in my life, as I composed the letter, I thought, *Okay, I study A Course in Miracles and do my best to practice it throughout my day; I'm more connected than ever with the people in my life; I have a couple of good, close friends; I am enjoying my church; and I walk and spend time alone.* It seemed that I was doing all the right things yet the peace and easy flow that I wanted to experience in my life seemed to be eluding me. I didn't want to only work at *gaining* peace; I wanted to *be peace.* So I began to wonder if a Greater Plan, so to speak, wasn't at play here in this opportunity I was given.

"As a side-note, a couple of weeks before I left, I began getting a little fearful, wondering if I would be overwhelmed by what I might experience there. Many of the Zulu people live in pretty harsh circumstances, aside from the debilitating effects of the AIDS sickness itself. I was frightened that I might get hung up on these conditions, forget my intentions for being there, and not be as totally present to the people as I wanted to be. So I meditated and prayed that I'd be able to see people for the spiritual beings they are, and that I could let go of any judgments of their outer circumstances. The end result was awesome— the fears just fell away.

"I'm not sure where all this is going to go. I don't fully know the reason I went to Africa, but it's important for me to keep the experience alive. So I pray and ask for spiritual direction. Recently I shared my experience with our staff and volunteers and soon I will be sharing it with a group of volunteers at the Saratoga, New York Hospice. I'm also beginning to get involved with the African partnership, through fundraising and whatever other ways I can help."

Would you talk some about the work you and your group did while in South Africa?

"Our group was hosted by a hospice program in Port Shepstone, a small city on the southeast coast of South Africa, on the Indian Ocean. We had three registered nurses, two volunteers, and me, a coordinator of volunteer services. Among us we had an excellent mix of backgrounds, expertise, personalities, and senses of humor. Mary Lou, our leader, who had taken this same trip four years previous, insisted that we come up with a name for our group. We knew that with time, a common thread or inside joke would lend itself to an appropriate name for us. Eventually the name, 'Six (or Sick) Sisters' (depending on how you say it), attached itself to us once we discovered that the term for nurse in South Africa is sister.

"The supplies we brought with us to Africa included rubber gloves, hand sanitizer, face masks, gauze pads, band aids, children's vitamins, anti-fungal medication, clothes, and even some children's toys. Some of these supplies we personally purchased, some were donated by family and friends, and some were given by hospice. Since these people have very limited financial resources they were delighted to receive these items for use in their in-patient unit, and for home care patients and their families.

"The program in Port Shepstone serviced the Afrikaans (white people) as well as the Zulus (black people), with teams created along racial lines to service the population they were attending to. While apartheid is officially gone, the races are still separate in a lot of ways, and the Zulu people suffer from extremely high levels of unemployment and poverty.

"Once we arrived, our local host arranged for us to take part in outpatient visits, accompanied by their local staff. So I would often travel in a team of caregivers made up of me and two or three of their staff. The Zulu population we served lived in shacks, 15 to 20 minutes outside of town in the countryside. While the countryside is beautiful, the roads often do not extend to people's homes and where they do, they are sometimes impassable because of weather conditions. Many of these caregivers get up at 4:00 a.m., walk a long distance to reach a bus stop, and then wedge themselves onto a bus that is designed to hold 10 people, but often crammed with 20 to 30; all this to reach work by 7:00 a.m.

"At the hospice office, the caregivers gather for a song of prayer which was a very powerful experience for me; music is a very strong element of their culture. They would break out in song, even between patient visits. Hospice provides them with toast for breakfast, but with the exception of a little bread and boiled potatoes, they don't have much food for their lunch while on the road. Some of the female caregivers— with beautiful names like Happiness, Gladness, and Charity—work in exchange for their monthly sanitary supplies.

"Because of their knowledge of the road conditions during bad weather, management often defers to the recommendations of the Zulu caregivers to decide if it is safe to drive in order to make their visits. Then they break out into teams and are sent out to visit patients and families. I normally traveled to the rural areas with a Zulu care giving team, making visits to Zulu patients whose diagnoses were primarily AIDS-related. Another team supports the children who have been, or will be affected by a loss of a loved one who was, or is, on the hospice program. These children are followed for several years by hospice. Another team, which consists of the Afrikaan staff members, visits Afrikaan patients and their families. These patients primarily have cancer diagnoses.

"There is also a 10-bed hospice inpatient unit where the overall census consisted of 95% AIDS patients and 5% cancer patients. In addition, a drug-resistant strain of tuberculosis often compromises the already weakened immune system of the AIDS patients, and to further complicate matters, poverty leaves them without proper nourishment.

"Zulu people live in either the traditional adobe hut or in corrugated tin shacks. The dimensions of these homes are comparable to a small room in an American home. Most homes have no running water and only a few had the most rudimentary form of electricity. Most Zulu homes have dirt floors with maybe some worn linoleum or old rugs on them. For sleeping, the mattresses are laid on the floor. A small bench might serve as a counter with a lantern on it. That would be about it. Families live in a cluster of these types of homes and I believe they might all share a common kitchen in one of these huts. With all that, the huts were as neat and clean as possible, which really impressed me."

You mentioned previously that one of your fears was that you'd be overwhelmed by the conditions you saw these people living in. What was your actual reaction while you were there?

"One of the first amazing realizations I had was that I could make a connection with people whether I spoke their language or not. They were warm and welcoming to me. When I asked permission to take their picture, I could tell, even though they were speaking in their tongue which I couldn't understand, that they were touched and very humbled. They were 'tickled pink' to see their faces show up on my digital camera. The adults weren't big on eye contact but the children were, and that's how we were able to make a connection.

"These people were warm and open to us, very grateful, and just loved hospice coming to help them. On home visits the people were always inviting to me, despite me sometimes being the only white person there. Zulu people usually would walk several miles to get to a small clinic except when they were really sick in which case hospice might drive them to the clinic or take them to the hospice inpatient unit. They don't have the medical care or doctors to give them what they need. It's very sad!

"I was expecting to see grief and terrible strife on the faces of these people because of the disease and the conditions in which they live. But much to my surprise, what I saw instead was a peace and serenity they had about them; you might even say a joy for life. I was very inspired! I saw families sticking together, helping each other and for the most part, having an acceptance of what they were going through. One exception to this occurred when we visited a very young boy and girl who'd lost their mother and were being cared for by the grandmother. An aunt visited and she was crying and deeply grieving the loss of her sister. That was the only real despair or stress that I saw while I was there. What did *I* do for her? I handed her a Kleenex, which was the extent of what I could do.

"To support the children, South Coast Hospice developed a memory box program for those who have been or will be affected by a loss. Inside this box, they keep special memories such as photographs, birth certificates, letters, and other mementoes. The children then paint the tin box to their liking. One little girl I visited kept a puppet of her mother that was made out of a paper bag inside her memory box.

"We also visited an orphanage, which housed approximately 36 children (ages 3 months to 14 years old). This was another moving experience for me. When we arrived, the children, craving attention, literally burst out of the door to greet us, latch on, and hug us

"I was happy to see that the patients who tested positive for the HIV virus and were receiving the anti-viral drugs, were for the most part up and functioning quite well. Their hospice program works with the clinics and doctors to facilitate the patients receiving these medications.

"I'm not sure of all that I found out about myself on this trip, but I do know that these people are now part of me and that I'm more connected to my brothers and sisters throughout the world. Before visiting South Africa, I was somewhat aware of the situation there from listening to and reading the news but I can honestly say I had a feeling of being different and separate from them. Now I feel a part of them and they're a part of me; we're all connected and we're all children of God. I intellectually knew that before I went, but now I feel it deep inside of me."

"I'm not able to relate to or completely understand what they're going through, and I haven't experienced the loss of a parent or child.

But I did discover that I'm able to reach out more and extend myself beyond my own comfort level. I think I've unpeeled another "layer of the onion" within me and found that I'm capable of sharing more love than I ever thought possible. There's more depth to me. I no longer think we're here only for ourselves. I think we're here to connect, join, and share with each other.

"Something I haven't talked about is that my *feelings* are changing also. The 'Tectonic Plates' around my emotions are shifting, as a spiritual friend of mine recently so aptly described. Instead of my emotions being way down inside, they're barely below the surface, so that when I do feel my emotions, good or bad, out they come. There are times, for example, when I feel exhilarated after a good workout at the gym. I'll have tears of joy, thinking, *Wow! This is cool! I'm so glad I'm doing this.* Just recently I was sitting with one of our hospice trainees, crying together over something that was sad, and I felt happy I could cry with her. It hasn't always been fine with me to cry like that. So this emotional change that's been bubbling inside of me for some time now is moving up and out."

Earlier you talked about seeing your world through 'different eyes.' Can you talk a little more about that?

"Well, different things matter to me now. In Africa I observed a world in survival mode and then I came back to all this *stuff*—the big house, big car, and big stores. It took me a while before I could even go to the market or Wal-Mart. Our lifestyle is so far removed from how the rest of the world lives. I no longer want to get caught up in all that *stuff*! I want to live simpler.

Being judgmental and over-busy are two of the biggest obstacles I face in staying on this spiritual path of fully experiencing who I am. On my trip I was also able to step back at times, get quiet, and find my peace, truth, and joy amid all that was happening around me. As a result, I was able to stop and perceive who these people really were instead of allowing my judgmental mind to paint a negative picture. That's a big change."

How do you hope the world will benefit from what you do Bonnie?

"If I shine my 'light,' then someone may receive some of the rays. I think we're all teachers for each other, so if I really share my gifts with the world—and sharing my Africa story may be part of that—others may benefit."

"I let go of the illusion that I am separate in any way, and I experience my oneness with You and with all of your creation. Everyone is my sister, everyone is my brother. In this I find my peace."
Excerpted from a prayer Bonnie included in the summary of her trip.

Bonnie may be contacted at **tedandbonkriss@hotmail.com**

Chapter 29
Self-expression
Paul Ehmann

"In a way, writing is showing me who I really am. This person, who operates with honesty and integrity as a writer, is the man I've always wanted to be.

Paul Ehmann has a passion for creative writing. His work is witty, poignant, thought-provoking, and quite often healing for him. A real estate broker by day, he has found his true voice and a vehicle for self-expression through his writing. The desire to be heard and understood motivates Paul to create essays, poetry, and memoir about subjects he feels deeply about. He lives in Loudonville, New York, with his wife Diane and their two cats, Stella and Pearl. Paul is also a proud father to an adult son, Sean.

"Passion for me is driven by a desire to be heard and understood. I find that I'm just not able to express myself adequately with words unless they're on a page. When I can put the words in the form of a story to describe an experience I've had, or witnessed, my feelings become identified, and on that level my writing becomes therapeutic for me. Like almost every person I know I like to be heard; to hear someone say, 'I got it, I understand what you're saying and how you're feeling.'

Sometimes I can't do that unless I write it down, turn it into a story, and read it to somebody or ask someone to read it."

So value for you lies in the process of writing?

"That's right. My passion is in the process. I hate deadlines, but I have to have them or I won't write. I guess you could say I have a reluctant passion. I know for instance when I told you today that the newspaper will print an article of mine that I sent them, I felt like a little kid who wants everyone to know—'*Look at the Times-Union on Monday, there's going to be an article I wrote!*' That hasn't gone away. Although I've had a fair amount of my writing published and I've been fortunate to have people willing to consider my work, I'm still a neophyte. So the passion for me is in being heard, and writing is a tremendous vehicle for that purpose.

"It's also a great outlet. When I'm unable to adequately verbalize my feelings in a conversation, I can write it all down, and after looking it over, I'll sometimes say, *That doesn't actually describe how I feel; there's got to be a better word*! Then I go to the Thesaurus, find better words, and think, *Ah—now that's a better word, that's how I feel.* Before someone let me know it was okay to use a Thesaurus I thought you actually had to have the vocabulary; that it wasn't acceptable to look it up. I grew up, believing I inherently needed to know everything.

"I wrote poetry for a brief period as an adolescent, but the real passion for writing began about 20 years ago while I was in a rehab, being treated for alcoholism. During treatment I just started writing poetry. Then I recalled that I began writing poetry when I was seven or eight and continued until I was about 10, when I stopped because you just couldn't be a poet in my neighborhood. (Laughing) Most of my artistic bent, I think, got *slammed* right around that time. As a victim and survivor of sexual abuse, I experienced that my poetry and many of my other healthy outlets ceased when the abuse began to occur.

"I do remember, however, one writing incident from my high school years. It occurred in my English class. I wasn't a good student, but I did fairly well in English. I remember that we had a class assignment to write a true story about an incident or event drawn from our life experience. So I decided to write an imagined account of my father's death. The teacher, Cynthia Gallivan was her name, later took me aside and with tears streaming down her face told me how touching my story was. But I was quite flippant about it and told her he wasn't dead—that I had made it all up. She was *pissed* at me because she had been so taken in by the story. So I didn't write again nor did I think about writing until I entered rehab many years later.

"During my early years of recovery from addiction I wrote some poetry, and from time to time would think, *Well, maybe I should really take an English Literature class.* But generally I would get to thinking so hard about it that I ended up taking no classes at all. About six years ago, however, an old friend told me there was a person who taught a writing class at the Rennsselaer County Council for the Arts in Troy, New York. This time I checked it out, and signed up for the course.

"I had no idea what I was getting into at the time. The name of the course, which was about writing personal memoir, was: *Writing What You Know.* When I began the class I was very scared. There were 10 of us and most were woman. The teacher, Marion Roach, asked each of us on the first night to tell why we were there and what our writing experience was. I answered that I had written poetry. She told me not to worry about that, because they were going to slap that right out of me. (Laughing) She has turned into being one of my closest friends as well as my writing mentor. She helped me to understand that my *voice* is important. I wouldn't have known that without getting some of my thoughts down on paper.

"My sense is that anytime I had written something that I thought was important, and it got put in front of someone, it turned out to be meaningful to them or to me in some way. Marion and others kept encouraging me to write things down that I felt were important to me. About 12 years ago I was invited to testify before the New York State Legislature to advocate for the New York State Teachers Moral Conduct Unit, which at that time was badly in need of operational funds. This same organization had previously helped me to investigate a teacher who had sexually abused me when I was just an adolescent.

"As a result of this invitation I had to write a prepared statement that told my story, and told why I believed the organization deserved more money. At the hearing, while reading my statement I was aware the legislators were busy reading papers or doing other things. The aides were running around delivering bills and papers to the legislators, and it appeared that no one was really listening to me. I stopped reading, at that point, and asked for their attention. When I did that, many of them looked up at me like I was some wise guy or something, but they did give me their attention. As I proceeded, I had to read my story; I couldn't tell it. When I finished, a couple of the legislators and a few senators came down to where I was sitting, to talk with me about my testimony. In those moments I became aware that I could actually do something to help others and myself through my writing. That was a very powerful moment for me.

"I like the sense of myself and my purpose that writing gives me, even if no one else ever sees it. If what I write is good, and most importantly true, it brings a big smile to my face when I'm done. It feels so great! I'll always ask Diane to read it. She's a little biased for sure, but I can tell whether she thinks it's any good by how she reacts. That's my process. Writing is a great vehicle for me to express my truth.

"I don't have any delusions about being the next great author or memoir writer, but I write because I love to do it and because I like to have my stories told. My mentor says that if I have 75, one-thousand-word essays written about my life experiences, I'll find a way to get them into memoir form and maybe a book will come of that.

"A lot of my writing is about suffering and redemption because that's what I know. For instance, a kid is abused, but later as an adult is able to come full circle, and resolve it in some way and in the process creates a measure of change. This child is lost because of what happened to him and he increasingly becomes more lost as he runs away from the reality of what took place. At some point he makes a decision to change the destructive and avoidant way he lives, and suddenly the continuum he's been on shifts, and begins to take the shape of an arc: At least for me it did. Then, somewhere, there comes a divine intervention, and he begins to find his voice. I found my voice by way of the written word, in testifying about my childhood abuse before the legislature. Now the circle is complete. So this *bad thing*—sexual abuse—happened to me, but redemption came from speaking my truth to those who would listen.

"This theme of suffering and redemption drives and weaves its way into a lot of what I write; but I like to write humorous pieces too, and like my last article, I also enjoy writing things that lean a bit in the direction of politics. My last piece, which ended up in the *Albany Times-Union* was about how wrong it is to box people in with certain political labels like *bleeding-heart liberal* or *staunch conservative,* when in fact most people are more often a little like me and somewhere in the middle. I might lean to the liberal side of many issues, but when it comes to abortion, maybe I'm pro-life *and* pro-choice! I like to write pieces like that."

Where do your writing ideas come from?

"They sometimes come when I'm asleep. A thought will enter my mind, and I'll get right up and write it down. I've been told to always carry a notebook, which I do, since you never know where or when ideas will come. Most of my ideas for subject matter come from my own experience. A lot of times an experience or memory gets stirred up as I listen to someone tell a story. Because I attend some 12-step meetings each week, I get to hear people telling stories of what's happened to them, which brings to mind my own memories, which in turn jars loose ideas for writing. Very often my original thought isn't what a piece of prose or poetry actually ends up being about. It's sometimes only the start or the spark that shakes loose a writing idea. When my dad died, for instance, I thought my feelings were about this tremendous sadness of loss. What I discovered, however, while writing about his death, was that I was actually having an amazing spiritual experience. Besides the sadness I felt, there was real joy and even some laughs in being able to go through dad's final days with him. How great is that?

"If I tried to simply remember it all, the details and the positive facts would fade very quickly and be forgotten. My memory might be something like, *I watched my poor father die, and I was so sad—poor me*. It wouldn't have included the wonderful experience we had at hospice and some of the people we met there. So, writing the events and details down as they occurred allowed me to see the richness of that experience.

"I believe writing provides a clearer vision of events to the reader as well as the writer. When I began writing, it opened up a little bit more of the universe to me. I've also been able to see the commonality of life experiences, which helps me to feel less alone. When something I've written about *my* life is read, I'm able to see how others can relate to it. I'll hear them say, 'Yeah, I understand that' or 'Yeah, that happened to me too.' That feels great to me.

"In my heart of hearts I'm a *ham*, and I want to be seen; I want people to know who I am, and I want to be able to say, 'Yeah that's me, I wrote it! That was my life and that's how it was for me.' I guess that's the selfish aspect of my writing—but why not! (Laughing)"

Where does that drive to be noticed and to be recognized come from?

"When I was a kid I hated being the center of attention or singled out in any way. I did a killer of a "crazy Guggenheim" (a character from the old Jackie Gleason show) imitation when I was young and my parents, when entertaining their friends, would sometimes wake me up and say, 'Come on out here and do your "crazy Guggenheim." I'd usually say, 'I don't want to.' So I really didn't want to be seen or singled out

"Then I was sexually abused for the first time when I was eight and by the time I was 15, I had been abused by four different men. While it was certainly bad and had a powerfully negative impact on my life, it also had a positive impact. Instead of retreating further into myself, I went the opposite way and coped by being more outgoing. I would be the clown and take any dare that anyone suggested. The drinking and drugs also helped me to be more *out there*. (Laughing) I'm thankful that I didn't retreat further into myself. Even though I no longer have the chemicals to give me false courage, I don't mind putting myself out there for people to see and hear today.

"I guess, like many people who are artistic, my passion came out of the pain of my abuse."

Who have you heroes or mentors been Paul?

"My dad's a hero to me. He was a reader; not so much of books, but of magazines and newspapers. He was forever pulling out articles, saying 'You ought to read this' to get a certain point across when he knew I might not listen to what he had to say about a subject. When I look at that, I realize I'm the same way. I don't know if you noticed when you came in the house, I had cut an article out and left it on the table for my wife to read. (Laughing) It seems that what was most annoying to me when my father was alive, I now do. It gives me a lot more compassion for him today.

"He *turned the corner* a few years before he died. I got to see that even at 78 a man could change. He was the focus of a lot of my writing during the couple of years before he died. His name was Jack or 'Big John.' Like me he was a real estate broker, but he was known as Albany's largest real estate broker and that wasn't because he sold a lot of real estate. It was more about his prowess with food and drink at the summer clambake. At his biggest he went about 360 pounds.

"His change seemed heroic to me because I never thought it would or could happen. He wasn't a hugger or a 'feelings' guy. As an example, when my nieces or nephews—his grandchildren—would leave the house after visiting, they would say, 'Love you pop,' but he would never say, *'I love you'* back to them.

"One day I walked into my parents' house and they were sitting in the parlor in their *matching lounge chairs* watching an Oprah Show, where the topic of validation was being discussed. He turned to me and said, 'What's this validation crap?'

"This was during the time when I had gone public with my childhood sexual abuse, in the local media. I replied, 'Dad, if you were to tell me that what happened to me, should never have happened; that you would have done anything to prevent it; that you might even have done physical harm to the perpetrator; and that you love me, that would be validation for me.'

"He said, 'You know *we* would have done anything to prevent it. It shouldn't have happened, and I would have beaten the guy to a pulp.'

"And I said, 'and…'

"He said 'what?'

"I said, 'and…' Three times I *went to the well* but he just couldn't say he loved me.

"A few years later, when his age and bad health really caught up with him, he began changing a little bit. He and I both have a sarcastic bent, but he was very caustic. One day he was very sarcastic and I just couldn't take it any longer. I said, 'Dad, if you keep up the sarcasm I'm going to leave.' I was someone who visited mom and dad almost every day, so this was a big thing. He said something sarcastic in reply so I left, and progressively over time my visits occurred with less and less regularity. He and I became more distant. What I began to sense, however, was that when we'd be together, he wanted to be emotionally closer to me. One day we were discussing the subject of sarcasm and I told him 'Sarcasm comes from Latin and it means to: cut flesh. So when you're sarcastic with me that's how it feels.' He was never sarcastic with me again, although he was still sarcastic with others.

"So I began to see a change slowly take place. The next thing you know, I'd lean down to hug him and he'd hug me back. Then he'd tell me he loved me. People around us would look at dad and wonder *who is this guy?* So as I watched all this happening, in my eyes what he was doing was heroic. When I started writing and had a few things published, dad was the proud father of a *third-grader* again. Everything I wrote went straight into his scrapbook. That felt great to me. It was a great change, a major surprise, and dad went right to the top of my hero-list.

"My wife Diane is also a hero because I know what she's been through in her life, and survived. She's also been a real mentor for me as has Marion Roach, who I mentioned earlier. Friends of mine in recovery are also heroes because they go through everyday life without falling prey to their addictions. That's an act of courage. I guess my heroes tend to be the folks who have showed me how to grow my own spirit, as opposed to those heroic people who would run into a burning building to save someone. The more personal the experience, the deeper I feel it."

How can you tell if your healthy passion is becoming an obsession?

"If I feel a sense of satisfaction and peace when I'm writing, I know my passion is healthy. If on the other hand, I'm feeling guilty or fearful because I'm embellishing the truth in order to make a point or impress someone, I'm in obsession. I don't want that because I know how rewarding it feels to be writing from my truth. If it doesn't reflect my truth in some fashion then it's got to go. There's no real risk or reward in being false; telling the truth can be risky. "

When you do write a piece that is truthful and maybe a bit risky, what is the reward for you?

"When I get the sense that I've done something as well as I can do it, a smile will crack my face, and I feel good. I rarely get that in a lot of places in my life, and that includes my job. If I sit down at my desk, though, write something that's honest, and finish it, it doesn't matter if it gets published or not. It doesn't make any difference if anyone other than my wife ever sees it, although I might push it around a bit among my friends. (Laughing)

"See, I never knew what joy was. I had no real barometer for it nor could I recall any joyful times from my childhood. I had to *actually ask people* what joy felt like: 'Is it a physical feeling? Is it just something that you know? Does it make you smile? Does it make you get loud?' I just didn't know.

"The first time I could put words to joy was one day when I was in the parking lot of a Home Depot store in my brand new red pickup truck, and I saw a man and his wife struggling unsuccessfully to secure a big piece of fence on the roof of their little car. I approached them and suggested they put it in the back of my truck and I would follow them home and drop it off?'

"When we were done, these people were very grateful and I was *beaming*. I never knew their names nor can I remember where they live, but I'll never forget the joy I felt at lending a hand to them. When I got home, I wrote down a few words about the impact of that incident on me.

"When I finish a piece of writing I get the same sense—I'm giving something away that's worthwhile. The other night I finished a piece and I felt real good about it. I showed it to my wife and she gave me a high-five which let me know she really liked it. Diane doesn't give out high-fives easily. I then brought it to my writing class where it was critiqued by 20 other writers. They liked it and thought it was publishable, so I submitted it to the *Albany Times-Union,* and have been told it will be published as an op-ed piece in the near future. Some regional publications have printed my writing and I hope in the future to have my work published to a wider audience.

"For me, the fear in writing seems to be most pronounced when it comes to submitting a piece of mine for publication. It just kills me and I'm so reluctant. I'm always looking for someone to tell me a better way of going about this process, but the advice I get is generally to select who you would like to publish your work, and just send it out to them. Marion will tell me, 'Stop editing, leave it alone, and send it to somebody!'

"I'm very grateful that fellow writers keep pushing, guiding, and teaching me. Someone once told me that I write like I talk. At first I was taken aback—I didn't know they'd given me a compliment. (Laughing) What they meant was that if I can put my thoughts on the page the way I talk, it could be pretty good. Today, I accept that compliment. If I have that gift, I'll take it and I'll be grateful for it."

You mentioned earlier that you sometimes become *frozen* and just aren't able to put another word down. How do you work through that?

"There are times I freeze up and I get stuck. My mind will tell me I'm never going to find another word to write or I'll never again have anything worthwhile to say. What I do to work through it are things that take me totally away from writing, for the moment. I might make myself a sandwich or clean my desk. I also have a ball of soda stone that I'll roll around in my hand, sort of like a meditation. I also have a stone shaped like a heart that I'll hold and say, 'Come on, come on, come on,' like a mantra, and then I'll look around to see if anyone's watching me. (Laughing) Of course no one ever is with the exception of my *judgmental self.* After all that I'll again sit down, grab my pen, and just make myself write a few sentences. My writing teachers told us that author Thomas Hardy use to tie himself to a chair as a way of getting through his blocks.

"There are times where my fear and my critical self will get the best of me. When that happens I run away from it and procrastinate for awhile. There's no joy when that's happening. I hear every sound, whether it's the cat scratching or the heating system making noises. My passion for writing, however, always draws me back. Before long I'll start thinking about it and then I want to write again. I have to say that although my critical self is strong and may never completely leave me, I also don't want to lose it because there's something about the victory over the fear and pain that feels very powerful and even joyful for me. I've found my voice so I intend to keep on honoring it through my writing.

"For me, the major requirements of living this passionate life are honesty and integrity. It's vital for me to be honest about who I am, what's important to me, and how I'm going to communicate that. When I finish writing a piece, I will usually read it out loud to hear how it sounds and how it feels—are the words coming from my gut and are they authentic? Am I building up a story to make it something it isn't, or am I eliminating certain elements of a story because I don't want you to see it? If I answer yes to any of those questions than I'm undermining myself.

"Writing with integrity also affects the rest of my life in a positive way. In a sense, writing is showing *me* who I really am. This person, who operates with honesty and integrity as a writer, is the man I've always wanted to be."

Getting back to how you evolved as a writer, when was it that you decided you were ready to put some high energy and commitment into writing?

"Well, the poetry I was writing, in all honesty, wasn't very good in the beginning. Later, however, as language began to intrigue me, and my writing got better, I wanted to learn more.

"I also have an old dread of being in a learning situation where I don't *get it* and I end up looking stupid. Nevertheless, I kept thinking *there's got to be a way for me to learn. There's got to be someone out there who could help me and encourage me.* I didn't put a lot of energy into finding that person but it was a yearning that stayed with me.

"I then started writing little pieces I called *Paulisms for Diane*. I would send her one every day by E-mail. They were sometimes poetic while other times more prose. Here's an example:

"experience the present.
be available to it.
watch your past
through your heart's eye.

anticipate.
listen to your scout.
choices
are not goodbyes.

listen to your present.
feed your soul.
lost children are cherished
in God's eyes."

"I could see my writing was becoming more intelligent and I realized something was happening for me. At the same time my friend Angela Doyle, a writer, told me I should definitely take a writing course that was being offered by Marion Roach. I realized this might be the avenue I'd been looking for. It could help me learn more about writing. After much procrastination I enrolled. Then I found out the course fee was $235. I thought *$235—I might not even last a week!* Well, despite my fears, I signed up and I've now attended that course three times a year for the past five years. That's my place! I've found safety in the company of Marion and my fellow writers, many of whom come back repeatedly as I do. I've discovered I can learn and grow as a writer. As a mentor, Marion has the knowledge I seek and she knows how it is to be a learner. She has passion for writing and teaching, and com-passion for the student, which has been so important to me. Her interest lies in helping me discover what *I* know, rather than telling me what *she* knows.

"It's worked out well for me and I don't know if you can ask more than that from someone you choose as a mentor."

You seem to be saying that being with others who are passionate is powerful for you.

"Absolutely! It's no different than playing golf with guys that love to play golf—I get better. The people who I attend writing classes with, help me to improve because they love to write like I do.

"I also can't raise my level of writing unless I practice; similar to how my wife plays guitar every day so she can improve over time. It's work, but there's a sense of fulfillment as a reward for that work. I never had that in my life prior to this experience.

"I believe that when you can find ways to fulfill yourself, in even very small ways to begin with, you can find what you will ultimately feel passionate about. *All or nothing* just doesn't work for me—there's never any sense of accomplishment. My journey with writing began with not-so-good poetry, then a little better poetry, progressed to my *Paulisms,* then to my writing classes, and today my present style of writing. These were all *little bites* that have given me satisfaction and fulfillment—the energy that has fueled my passion and kept me going.

"The thousand-word limits on my writings are also *little bites*. For me that's much better than driving myself to write the next great American novel. I'm not Mark Twain—that's just the way it is! I'm very easily discouraged, so small pieces that I can accomplish are more encouraging and rewarding than failing at much bigger writing projects. Accomplishing small projects then opens me up to attempting something a little bigger the next time. I'm much more a step-by-step guy than someone who suddenly goes *full-tilt boogie.*"

What has your passion for writing taught you about what it is to be human?

"I think a person's daily state is predicated chiefly by where that person is spiritually. In my writing I've become conscious of just how frail the human condition really is. On the other hand, I've also seen how heroic and graceful it can be. When I see someone who feels beaten down in every way by life, yet doesn't pick up a drink or a drug to escape or medicate himself, it tells me that the human condition is not all about failure.(Laughing) The possibilities for benefiting others and yourself are endless if you don't throw in the towel. The most painful parts of my journey are also what have given buoyancy and meaning to my life. That's where the 'bagel' is, as they say in writing; it's where everything comes full circle."

Paul may be contacted at **etrain@nycap.rr.com**

Chapter 30
Strength of Character
Debra Burger

I got to meet Pete Seeger and Tom Paxton. I never got to meet Joan Baez, but I got to sit up close. They are all people who continue to sing and speak their truth and hold their moral ground regardless of what's going on. They've all done it at least in part through singing. Martin Luther King was my hero. Bette Davis was a hero to me growing up. That might sound surprising but she had the strength of character to hold her ground even when other people didn't think she was so wonderful.

Debra Burger, 55 years old, lives in the hamlet of Clarksville, New York with her life partner Carole Fults. She is also the mom to her 22-year-old daughter, Casey. Debra is a musician, composer, psychotherapist, and spiritual seeker, all of which she is passionate about. Deb, self-admittedly, has a big presence and unafraid to speak, perform, or live her truth.

"My mother tells me that when I was a year old, I stood up in the crib and started singing like Ethel Merman. I never stopped. I remember, early on, pretending that I was on TV, singing in front of the mirror. I loved the cowboys and Broadway shows, so some of my greatest joys came from watching Gene Autry or Molly Bee, who sang and yodeled, and listening to my collection of records before the other family members awoke. Music was a way to detach from the violence, anger, and depression that pervaded my family. Perhaps too, I knew who I really was when I sang or heard others sing."

Do you remember what records you listened to?

"Oh yeah! I remember the Teddy Bears Picnic! (Sings): *'Today's the day/ the Teddy Bears have their picnic.' / (Laughing)* This would make me happy. It was here and now, and happy. I remember another one. My grandmother Sophie, whom I've written a song about, loved me…really loved me. She was my main loving presence. She would come to me with these *tragic* love songs (laughs) that she would sing to me and then we would sing them together. It was a connection—a real loving connection. So music meant getting to know myself and it meant real (human) connection.

"My family was not musical, so when I asked to learn an instrument, they thought I was weird. I saved my babysitting money and, at 14 years old, I bought a $25 guitar. There was a TV show on PBS that taught folk guitar, and from that I learned how to play. I'd listen to Joan Baez and wished that *her* voice would come out of me when I opened my mouth. But I loved Judy Collins, Pete Seeger, and Joni Mitchell, too. I also learned every song Bob Dylan and Tom Paxton wrote. Music gave me a way to express what I believed, and a way to feel united with others who also thought about who they were in the world. As soon as I could change chords on the guitar I began singing in hospitals and with children. It became a way of giving that I never stopped honoring.

"When I was 16, I would go to the Lincoln Center Library in Manhattan and take out records of songs that were new to me, so that I could discover what music I really liked. In many ways, I did not know who I was. So much of my life was about being what I thought others wanted me to be or did not want me to be. Music helped me to connect with what I really liked and did not like, and taught me the process of knowing myself beyond others' expectations. My preferences in movies and music helped me to understand how to engage in a process of knowing myself in other areas. I discovered Irish and Scottish music and learned that I loved listening to Maria Callas, the great opera singer, sing *Carmen.*

"I performed often, but my real hope was to be an actress. Singing was an enjoyable way to earn money while I pursued my passion to act. I studied at HB Studio in New York City and was on my way to what I wanted. When I was 18, I hired an agent and was singing regularly at weddings and Bar Mitzvahs, where I was the specialty folk act. Folk music was very popular then. In the summer of my 18th year, I had a full-time job working Catskill mountain hotels, making $350 per week plus my room and board. I thought my 'ship had come in.' Fortunately, however, I discovered that professional acting and singing was not a good path for me. So much of professional acting and singing was really about pleasing others and trying to make them like me. There was too much focus on the ego and not enough on being the best of who I am. It was not healthy for me.

"At the same time, while singing in the hotel day camp for the children and teens, I found that I loved talking with the young people about their struggles and dreams. It was then that I decided to be a psychotherapist.

"Through the years, I've learned to find the proper place for music in my life. I write songs, for and with, the children I provide services for in school. I am a school social worker for children with special needs. I use music in my private psychotherapy practice, as well, to communicate at a level different from just talking. I sing and play regularly at Unity Church, in Albany, New York. I particularly enjoy singing songs I've written about how spirit works in our lives. Aside from singing and guitar playing as performance, I have also done workshops at retreats on songwriting and chanting. Chanting is a meditative practice for me, which uses my musical inclination to experience connection with God. I'm also president of the board of Old Songs, an organization that is dedicated to keeping traditional music and dance alive. Music is a central part of my life today, and I am grateful that when I open my mouth, it is *my voice* and my love that comes out.

"When Arthur Wells was the pastor at our church, he led an exercise that helped me understand the importance of music in my life. He asked that we think about a problem we were having. He then suggested that we close our eyes and become aware of the first idea that came to us. That idea, he told us, would ultimately be the solution to the problem. As I closed my eyes, a voice within me rang out loud and clear. It said, 'Sing!' Indeed, as I stumble along on my journey, I sometimes get confused or sad or scared, but the one thing that always brings me back is singing. It is my most direct path to feeling connection to the Divine."

I know you touched on this a little earlier, but I'm wondering who your mentors or heroes have been?

"When I was a kid growing up in Brooklyn, as I said previously, I loved cowboy movies and the Broadway shows, but as I got older and became a teenager it was very much Joan Baez and Tom Paxton and Pete Seeger who influenced me. They knew who they were and what they stood for. People would say to me, 'You're so idealistic, but you'll grow out of it.' Those performers touched me then and they touch me still. I got to meet Pete Seeger and Tom Paxton. I never got to meet Joan Baez, but I got to sit up close. They are all people who continue to sing and speak their truth and hold their moral ground regardless of what's going on. They've all done it at least in part through singing. Martin Luther King was my hero. Bette Davis was a hero to me growing up. That might sound surprising but she had the strength of character to hold her ground even when other people didn't think she was so wonderful.

"Here's another thing I struggled with that's related to the Bette Davis. Like her, I have a big presence. (Laughs). I grew up with a mom who was very uncomfortable with that. She wanted me to be a *smaller* person; not to stand out and embarrass her. It was interesting that Bette, on her tombstone, wanted inscribed, "She was too much." So I think I gravitated to people who were not afraid to be bold. I don't have a Joan Baez sweetly high voice. I have a booming voice and if I try to hold it back it doesn't sound good. I have to sing *my* voice."

You said you've used music in your psychotherapy practice.

"I've got to make a disclaimer here. I don't do it with a lot of my adult clients, but sometimes, I'll share a lyric that has touched me or one that I have written, if I think it can be helpful. I'm more apt to use music with kids. The kids and I have composed songs about how it felt being in foster care or how it felt to be a kid to be in a difficult family situation. They were able to talk about their experiences in a way that actually took away some of the shame and gave them a sense of pride. Sometimes I have kids writing a song together. It gives them a way to say what they feel, express it, and have some joy in it."

"I'll tell you a funny one. There was this one kid who was getting on another kid's nerves. So, in order to give him a way to express that it was driving him crazy, we wrote a song that went like this:(*sings)*— *'You gotta say it and let it go baby / say it baby and let it go/ your driving me crazy / you're driving me nuts/ stop repeating yourself/ we've all had enough.'* It gave him a way to find some humor in the situation. It also gives kids a connection and a chance to be proud about saying a thing in a deeper way. It's been an incredible therapeutic tool.

"I've not found it easy to use music with adults. I get nervous because I have to be present for them and not as able to concentrate on the music. I have had a couple of occasions where some wonderful healing has been able to happen for adults through music, but generally I have a difficult time."

What kind of challenges has Ego presented in sharing your passion?

"Huge ones! I described myself as having been caught up in a lot of 'people pleasing' when younger, so I think it's hard to perform without tapping into the desire to have everyone be happy and like me. I think it also kicks in to what the Buddhists call, the *'comparing mind'—I sing better than her, but not as well as her*. I think those things trip us up and they prevent the connection with God. So, I continue to struggle with that in my singing. One of the reasons that I love to sing in Unity Church is that it comes up less there, than anywhere else. If I make a mistake or forget the words I know I'm in a *loving family*. I think it's very hard in other venues. I pray before I perform and try to bring myself back to my higher intention, which is, *My performing is an expression of something that's real and true in me. It's not a way to get people to like me."*

There is a line between healthy passion and obsession and I'm wondering what that line is for you and how you know when you've crossed over?

"That's such a great question! Years ago I heard a well-known folk singer and guitarist at a concert and later got to meet him. He said that music was all he ever did from the time he woke up till the time he went to sleep at night. He just practiced all the time to the exclusion of everything else. I realized I didn't want success that bad. So it leads me to think that whatever we do has to be in some kind of balance with everything else in our lives. I think it also has to be connected with who we are on the inside so we don't lose our connection to God. If we put all our eggs in one basket we lose the sense of who we really are. For instance if I'm in love with someone, that's great, but I can't let that person become my "everything." If I have a passion, that's also great, but it can't become my whole life."

How do you know when you're over that line and into obsession?

"I start to get fearful. If I'm in a relationship I'm passionate about, and I get fearful that I'll lose that person, I'm headed down the wrong road. If I'm choosing my music to please people and get them to like me I'm not truly being me. If I sing and play my truth, the right people will gravitate to that music. In the end, what I have to express may be really unique and it may impact only a few people. I've sometimes sung a song that I wrote and had someone will come to me and say how much it meant to them. For a hundred people that same song may not mean anything, but if you write something that's true, it's going to hit some people profoundly. To do that, you have to be unafraid of speaking that truth. What better thing is there in the world, than to touch a person or two deeply with your truth, and help them have a healing experience?"

Have you experienced losses along the way in order to follow your path?

"I'll tell you what does come up for me when you pose that question. I'm very theatrical! I have an actress and a singer alive and well inside me; it's definitely my karma. But I made a decision not to go that route. Some of the kids I work with tell me I'm crazy that I chose to work with them instead of being an actress. They say, 'You're out of your mind to give up the possibility to be famous in order to be with us.' I tell them, 'I love working with you guys.' I never regret my decision. I'm very grateful for the choices I've made.

"Sometimes, though, when I watch the Oscars I still remember the speech I wrote for the day I would win the Oscar. (Laughing) If I see a not-great actor or singer I sometimes have regret that I'm not doing that instead.

"Sometimes I wish that I had an extra life so that I could have done these things. My work as a therapist has required that I work at night, so Community Theatre is out for me too. But you know if I had chosen acting back then I wouldn't have survived. I would've got caught in that trap of needing the acclaim and never getting enough. Doing theatre here at church occasionally has been just right for me. It's been fun, it helps to build community, it's a chance to express myself, and it's been a chance to say something to the congregation, instead of Debra always needing more acclaim."

What have you gained from following your passion for music?

"Jim (the church pastor) and I got a chance today to talk about his topic for his next week's talk, and I got an opportunity to think of what songs would support him. That's such a spiritual exercise for me. Then I come home and begin to write verses that fit for what he wants to say. I'm very blessed to be able to live my life this way.

"Humans are just amazing. When I express my gift, I discover the *amazing-ness* in me and in all people. This keeps it out of the Ego. I'm not hiding my light under a bushel basket—I get to feel it, express it, and act on it. When I'm able to come from the place of Spirit, I'm able to see it in others too…it's not theoretical, I truly know it!"

What do you hope people get from your work?

"Early in my development as a psychotherapist—you notice I can't separate myself from my work as a therapist—I thought that if one person's life was better because of what I did with them; if they said, 'I get it,' then what more could I possibly ask? When I can surrender to spirit and give of myself through my work, it comes back to me, many times over. The magnitude of this process blows my mind, and it's not there for me any more than it is there for everyone else."

Debra Burger may be contacted at dburger3@nycap.rr.com

Chapter 31
Surviving Fear
Bob Blood

"I was afraid at school: afraid I wouldn't perform well; afraid my playmates would ridicule me—you name it, I was afraid of it. I found that sculpture was a safe place where no one could disparage me. It was also a place where I could feel positive about myself. That's how it started, but then it became for me a way of looking at things, feeling about things and people, and discovering a dimension of myself that I liked."

When driving along Regent Street in Schenectady, New York, and approaching Bob Blood's home, a stranger would have no difficulty in knowing an artist resides there. Situated on the lawn surrounding the home are strikingly large and uniquely shaped metal sculptures that alerts one to the presence of an exceptionally creative spirit who has given his life to his art. Despite a serious back injury that occurred a few years previous, at 82, Bob is energetically creating new work and redefining himself as an artist.

"These days I am working quite differently than I have in the past. I've needed, for professional reasons and because of physical limitations, to create a fresh way to approach an old idea that has gone on since the dawn of man: that is, to make something that has a symbolic use rather than a physical one. Now I'm in what I call an interim period, and I'm finding that many things are getting in the way: rearranging my studio for instance, and then, of course, my fear. I have a lot of drawings that are indicative of the direction that I'm going, but I'm also scared. I generally work being frightened about the outcome of what I'm doing. My fear, however, also means that I'm searching. I'm looking at my art differently today. It's exciting and frightening at the same time. Both elements are important parts of creativity. If I'm not excited, my work's not going to go anywhere, and if I'm not pushing myself and being somewhat demanding of myself, it's not going anywhere either. I was familiar with my old approach. It's very easy to keep going back to the same old routine, technique, and correctness, but I'd rather do something that has passion, depth, and personal involvement.

"So, I'm in the process of redefining my work, and how I see life. I'm asking myself: *How much time do I have left in my life; How much energy will a piece of work require of me; and, Am I capable of doing this?* When I was younger I just did things, but now I'm asking myself what each new piece of work will ask of me. I made scaffolding in order to work on a 15—foot-high piece when I was sixty-eight years old. Up and down, up and down I went while working. I didn't even think about it, but I do now. This is not unique to me. I think it happens to everybody. Breaking my back (falling from a roof while clearing ice) a few years ago is also a facet of this need for redefinition of my work. The aging process is a way of helping me define my limits physically but not necessarily mentally. Looking at life differently is very important. It beats doing things the same old way."

Can you say a little more about this fear you have mentioned in connection to your work?

"Part of it, I'm sure, is my upbringing and the abuse I suffered. I was afraid at school: afraid I wouldn't perform well; afraid my playmates would ridicule me ¯ you name it, I was afraid of it. I found that sculpture was a safe place where no one could disparage me. It was also a place where I could feel positive about myself. That's how it started, but then it became a way of looking at life, feeling about things and people, as well as a new dimension of myself that I discovered I liked. Sculpture eventually grew to a point where it became my profession. In a weird way, I guess I have my childhood abuse to thank for that. It's too bad that something so painful was needed to discover that aspect of myself. That's what got me through in the beginning of my journey. It also gave me a focus so that I was able to discover the best of me.

"There was a time when I felt I was a sculptor first and a human being second. That view was an exaggeration of how I saw myself at that time in my life. Today I don't think that way. "

How would you define passion, Bob?

"I find it's somewhat difficult here to express what I want to say when my chief medium of expression is my art. I guess I see passion as deep involvement and caring about what you're doing. As such, it can become very consuming. I have to be always sure that I have something of myself in reserve, so that I can go on to my next piece. To be deeply involved is very rich, no matter what it is that you're doing. I also think that when you have something you're passionate about, you're able to get more insight into your humanness. I discovered that I've been able to find out who I am and what I have to contribute in this world that through my work

"I think that many people are so intent on gathering material goods that they have no idea what their passion is. What's ironic in my case is that my creative self is looking to get rid of possessions. Many things that have been important to me in the past are now being passed on to good friends who I know will appreciate them."

When you're deeply involved, as you just said, it must also require a great amount of physical and emotional energy?

"Yes, that's true. At 82 however, I don't have the same amount of physical energy that I had at 40. Emotionally, I use to have a lot of energy around what my needs were, while today I get great satisfaction in a job well done.

"When I look at my past work, I realize that was the state I was in then, and I'm aware I may have been putting demands on myself that might have been beyond what I could do at the time. This is why, when I get three-quarters of the way through a sculpture, I begin to realize my limits with that piece. Hopefully with that next piece, I will be able to reach through this limit into a new possibility. I mean that's what life is about: extending ourselves into or even beyond what's possible. I think that's what has made some humans so outstanding. I think Lincoln, as President, reached beyond what anybody else in that office had ever demanded of themselves. The more I read about him, the more remarkable he becomes to me."

In a biographical video of your life I viewed earlier, you talked about your faith in human beings, and what they are capable of. Could you say a little more about that?

"There are individuals whom I admire enormously like Hesse, and Frederick, and Johann Bach who accomplished great things. There is Abraham Lincoln who stands out so much today because we have no one on the horizon who even comes close to having his passion and compassion. He cared about people and he carried out his plans to help them: He didn't just talk about it. I admire that.

"We all have something unique to offer, and our mission in life I think, is to give that gift to the world, and give it willingly—not holding back but giving with our spirit—without asking *what's in it for me*? I think it was Einstein who said we use about fifteen percent of our brain capacity in our lifetime. It's very easy to live on this *treadmill* in which we just live day to day, without ever challenging ourselves to create something that can contribute to the betterment of the world. As a society, we're very good at destroying things. At present I'm very disappointed in human beings. I see this glorious planet—unique in the solar system—and we're destroying it. I'm really sad about this."

You've said you have a great curiosity about life and what's 'around the next bend.' Could you say more about that, Bob?

"I'm interested in discovery, and in not being restricted by concepts. That's why I have a difficult time with organized religion. I tend to trust science much more. Religions seem to be more vested in preserving concepts, which goes against creativity. The whole idea of the *unending universe* boggles my mind. I want to push concepts and see where they go. I want to be open because we are always creatively changing.

"I think most creative people go through a process or a period of time where they are blocked. I'm aware personally, that my road blocks are often self imposed. But eventually, for whatever reason, a road block will break open, and all kinds of possibilities reveal will themselves. My former wife once told me that my being too tense was the cause of my migraine headaches. She said that when I would relax they'd go away. It's probably the same reason for a lot of my creative blocks."

I was touched by what you had to say about this quest for the *surprise* in life?

"Well that's where I am right now. It's frightening in a way because I don't know yet how the redefinition of me and my work will come out; so there's both fear and excitement present. I think this is true for anyone who is reaching into an unknown aspect of themselves.

"When I was young I was told that my mother had programmed me to fail. I say she didn't program me enough, because, to hide from her, I would go into my little bedroom at five years of age and play with clay. As a result, over time I discovered something that would come to mean a great deal to me.

"The effects of my abuse still go on. Depression still comes, but I've learned over the years how to deal with it. I think most abused children think they're at fault. Some are very angry and some just retreat into themselves. In my midlife, I was in denial about it: I was so buried in my work that I didn't think about much of anything (laughs)."

Was there anyone during your childhood who gave you any positive feedback or encouragement in your work with clay?

"Not really. That's the amazing thing. But in high school there was an art teacher named Helen Mier who was very supportive and encouraged me to attend art school.

"The art school I attended was very conservative. I remember I did a carving of a seated monk with a cowl over his head. One of my friends named it 'the constipated Capuchin (laughs).' It was very abstract and nobody else was doing anything like that in that school. The college, The Pennsylvania School of the Fine Arts, was a good school, but it didn't really challenge me in my interests. I decided to leave and come back to this area.

"Here, there really wasn't anyone who could have been a mentor for me at that time, so I kind of *mucked about* for awhile until I discovered *my way* of approaching sculpture. I did my first welding, and it was very powerful for me. It's nice to look back at my work from time to time and see how I've grown.

"I also think it's amazing to be privy to the creative process and be able to see the continual changes taking place in a piece of work. I have a film of Picasso at work in which he is creating the head of a goat, and repeatedly changing the form. At the end of it he asks, 'Do you think someone who views this will know that I spent over six hours on it?'

"People, who experience art, often interpret it in a way the artist may not have seen or intended himself. Sometime a person, in viewing a piece of mine, will make a very insightful comment that I didn't perceive, and I take that as a great compliment. For whatever reason, that person's imagination was stimulated to see that work in a way I didn't see it myself."

So that really speaks to the subjectivity of the viewer, to determine meaning, rather than the effort of the artist to get the viewer to interpret art in a certain way.

"Oh yes! I can't anticipate how an individual or audience will view what I've done. I have to be reasonably certain that my idea for a piece is what I want to do, and then go ahead and do the best I can. How they perceive my work is up to them."

Much of your art appears to be emerging from a chrysalis (the pupa of a butterfly). Can you talk a bit about what this form says to you about the human condition?

"In a sense, I think we're always emerging. I'll give you some background on the chrysalis. One time, one of my models climbed into a cotton tube and began moving around in it. I photographed her from many different views and eventually ended up creating some of these shapes in welded steel. In some cases they were open, and one of the models said, 'Why don't you think of it as a chrysalis?' She came up with the idea. I thought, *that's right, when the chrysalis opens it's like a portal opening up into a different existence.*

"If you think about it, this shape connects with all life. When we're born, we all come out of a sack. I also think adults are looking for this child-like quality in themselves in order to feel alive, excited, and curious about life. Picasso had that sense of awe and curiosity. Frederick Back, the illustrator and film maker, has this child-like quality as well. His work is very sophisticated, but he hasn't forgotten the child in himself."

Is this true for you?

"I try. I recently saw a child who must have been a year-and-a-half old. He was sitting under a rose. He saw a petal fall off the rose, and tried to put it back in place. It was amazing that at his age he could make this association. I keep learning from children and the fresh way they look at things."

Would you speak a little of your own childhood?

"My father was Frank Blood and he was an electrical engineer in Kenosha, Wisconsin. When he decided to travel to Schenectady, New York, he did so on a *one-speed* bike, mind you, and no paved roads at the time. He had $10 in his pocket to pay for whatever he needed on the way and he once told me that if he paid more than 50 cents for an evening meal, a night's lodging, and a nice breakfast that he was being overcharged. Fifteen dollars was a good week's pay. He never caught up with the *present day*. He just couldn't believe that in the final five to six months of his life, we would have someone come in to take care of him during the day. He died at almost 103 years of age and he was still living in his own home. My father was an amazing man. He was remarkably healthy in body and mind, curious about things, kept up with current events, and would get very ticked off about how we acted toward one another. He was a Democratic Socialist, which I am myself.

"He was the best father he could be, but he did have limitations. He never confronted my mother's abuse of me, and I realized in a therapy group exercise a few years back that my father was terrified of my mother. My mother's sexual and physical abuse of me was really torture by a woman who was mentally sick and taking her anger out on her child. Because I was in such mortal fear of her, I learned to retreat and become invisible. When mother would rail against Dad he would get this look on his face that told her he was off in space somewhere. She would become even more enraged and I, as an innocent child, would take the brunt of her rage.

"Mom's name was Ethel. She was the oldest of six girls, four of whom were mentally ill. One of her sisters lived in her car after burning down her house. Another sister lived in a mental institution for 40 years. I'm glad that mother was the only one who had children. Thankfully, I was able to discover something in my life to make it meaningful and worthwhile. If there had been others, I don't know that they would have been so fortunate.

"I did not do well scholastically, athletically, or even socially in school. In my art, I had found something that was important to me, and I really didn't care about anything else. It was difficult, however, getting to that point, because like any kid I wanted to be successful at something that others would appreciate. As I got older and matured, that desire became less important to me.

"A wonderful period of my life was when I was living in the Schenectady Museum—where my archival work is stored—with my wife, Esta, and my son, Peter. The first seven of Peter's eight years were spent in that museum. I was truly the artist-in-residence. I've never heard of another situation like that. I was sort of a custodian, doing whatever was needed, while at the same time I had a very large studio where I could teach and begin to get some public commissions.

"Teaching for me has been a way to give to others and fill in the gaps for what I didn't get in my training when I was young. It became a very refreshing experience for me and a chance to pass on to my students and later my apprentices, all the dimensions of my creative process as well as my experiences. A young girl who visits me on occasion, has told me that one of her teachers is interested in having me come and speak to her students. That kind of opportunity is very exciting for me. One of my former students, became a professional artist, teacher, and now has become a school principal."

Have there been sacrifices that you've had to make to pursue your work?

"Well, that's probably the reason why I'm single today. My marriage to Esta worked well for 38 years, but in the end, I think the amount of attention I paid to my work, left her wanting someone who would pay more attention to her. Consequently she chose someone to be in relationship with, who had been a friend of mine, and she eventually moved in with him. Fortunately, we still relate on pretty good terms, which says something positive for both of us. What is more important or more difficult then maintaining an intimate relationship?

"Esta is a composer— a very creative person— but she's not now, and I feel very sad about that. She was involved in a project of mine, in 1989, which was the installation of a Portal at the Unitarian Church in Schenectady. She wrote some beautiful music to accompany that installation. I hope to get her involved again, but I'm not sure that it will happen.

"Being an artist is not a practical profession. You can't justify entering this profession if you're looking to make a good living. I was very fortunate that my Dad had left me three houses, one of which is this house I'm living in. I've sold one and I'm holding a mortgage on another one. So, I depend on social security to live on. At the same time I feel very fortunate to be doing work that is fulfilling, and living my life simply, without the demand for an excessive level of physical output from me."

Two gifts you've given to people are: the idea that being creative has little to do with age, and, that creativity is not limited by having had a difficult early life. That's quite a contribution!

"I think some have looked at me and said, 'Hey here's this older guy who's got something going!' There are two young students from Scotia-Glenville High School who visit me regularly as part of a program in which high school students visit the elderly (laughs). We have great conversations and they actually enjoy it. I feel very privileged. I have the gift of my art and they are giving me the gift of their time. They even sang carols to me last Christmas. That's what gifts are all about: giving without expecting anything in return. If anything comes back its *gravy*. I had a chance last year to share bits of my experience and some encouragement with a student who was moving on to become an architect. That was also very satisfying to me."

What is it that you hope that others would get from your art?

"Stimulated! Hopefully, no matter what their present situation happens to be, they'll come away from my work feeling a little fuller and more positive about their lives than they did before they viewed my art."

Bob may be contacted at **www.robertblood.com/**

Chapter 32
A Thirst for Meaning
Matt George

"When Matt George taught social studies at Draper Middle School, his eighth-graders knew they could expect extended blocks of instruction on the Civil War. His passion for this subject once led a colleague to say, 'You take more time to teach the Civil War than it took to fight it."

"I could talk all day about this stuff if you'd let me."

From an interview by Rick Clemenson, Staff writer, Albany *Times-Union, May 30, 2006.*

Matt's deep desire for a meaningful life, and a wish to make a difference in the world, is obvious in the passion he has for sharing his knowledge of the Civil War. As a longtime student of Civil War history, Matt feels a responsibility to pass on what he knows, and to help people see the reality of that terrible war—the nobleness as well as the darkness—which threatened to permanently sever the Union. Part of how he instructs is by presenting *living history* as he dresses and acts out the part of a Civil War soldier. From 2005—2006 he served as the President of the Capital District Civil War Roundtable.* Matt retired from teaching in 1998 and resides in Rotterdam, New York.

"I don't have any trouble talking once I start. I present a lot of *living histories* and people will often ask me how long I'll talk. I'll usually answer them by asking, 'Well, how long do you have?'(Laughing) People, whether they're 7 or 95, are always responsive to what I do, so its fun for me. I live off their responses.

"The youngest group I've ever presented for was made up of five-year-olds who were taking part in a summer recreation program here at Mohonasen Central School. We gathered together under a pine tree on the school grounds. Once I started, it took me at least a ***half hour*** to get them to understand I really hadn't fought in the Civil War! As far as these kids were concerned, I'd fought and just recently gotten out of the Civil War. (Laughing)

"No matter who I present to, it's always rewarding for me.

"Probably one of the nicest things that has happened to me…actually two nice things happened to me in one week…was in early winter of last year. I retired as Capital District Civil War Round Table President and was given a beautiful bust of U. S. Grant as a symbol of the chapter's esteem. That was very nice.

"As satisfying as that was, in the previous week something happened that touched me even deeper. I was asked to give a presentation to fourth and fifth-graders that was part of an area program for young, advanced scholars in our area. As soon as I walked into the room in which the presentation would take place, a little guy with big brown eyes by the name of Ben, noticed a poster I was carrying that displayed a drawing of Joshua Chamberlain charging down Little Round Top at Gettysburg. He got very excited and said, "Wow, Joshua Chamberlain at Gettysburg!" Now, he was only a fourth—grader but I knew this little guy had a lot of knowledge. I thought, *this is going to be good*. As my talk progressed, he asked a lot of great questions as did many of the other students, and the teacher later shared with me that Ben loved to talk about the Civil War. When I finished my presentation, I was packing up my assorted props and Ben approached me and asked if he could help. I said 'Sure,' and I handed him some items to carry out. With that we headed down the hallway and during our walk he said, 'You know, my daddy taught me everything I know about the Civil War.'

"I said, 'That's great, I'm glad he has an interest.'

"I happened to have some historical sheets on the 134th New York Regiment, so I told him he could give those to his father. I told him the 134th was a regiment from our area (Schenectady and Schoharie County) and his dad might find them interesting.

"Well, Ben was thrilled and then he turned to leave with me. As he reached the door, I told him that because it was so cold outside he didn't have to carry my materials any further. So I took the articles he was holding, thanked him, and opened the door to leave. Just as I was about to walk through the door, I heard this little voice from behind me and I turned around, '*Mr. George,*' — (at this point Matt demonstrates Ben's crisp military salute). I was touched very deeply.

"The following week at my retirement dinner, upon receiving the bust of Grant from my chapter, I told the audience that this moment and the salute I got from Ben the week before were probably the two best things that had happened to me in a long time.

"In college I read *Man's Search for Meaning,* one of Victor Frankl's books, and an idea of his that I remember so well is that a prime motivation or drive for human beings is this *thirst to find meaning in their lives.* Beyond getting out of bed to get a cup of coffee in the morning, I believe this *thirst* is what motivates most people and probably separates us from what motivates chimpanzees. I read it back in the 60s, and that idea has stuck with me since. I guess you could call it a guiding principal for my life.

"The other motivation for me, which I always passed on to my students, was to make a difference in whatever you do. I don't care if I'm coaching baseball or teaching kids or seniors about their heritage, I try to convey this message. I love the game of baseball because there's a lot about it that is much like life. It's a team game yet it's a game played by individuals; you succeed if you sacrifice, whether it's by a sacrifice bunt or by hitting the ball to the right side of the infield to advance a runner. You give yourself up for the betterment of the team, and that's the same task we have in real life at times.

"There's a great pleasure in what I'm doing because it's for the purpose of keeping our heritage alive and making young people more aware and curious about a period of history in which I've always had a deep interest. It's a great thrill for me to see these kids sitting there with their eyes wide open and their hands in the air to ask questions. It reminds me of the expression—*"when the lights go on in the eyes."* I can almost see that at times.

"I didn't read about the war as a young child but it seems I always had my toy Civil War soldiers to play with. Somewhere in the time I was a student in Middle School, my family visited some relatives in Maryland, and during our stay we visited the battlefields at Manassas and Bull Run. Seeing those places at such a young age really had an impact on me. Civil War board games came out during that time period and I got to know more about the war from playing with them. My interest just grew over time.

"My mom and dad valued education, although dad had to quit high school before he graduated in order to go to work and support the family. It was the time of the Great Depression, so he went to work for Montgomery Ward and then later joined the military. Mom worked for Traveler's Insurance while he was away; in fact, was at work when she received the notification that he'd been injured in battle.

"He'd been wounded in the knee by a German artillery round that exploded close by him. The good news was that he survived, but the bad news for me was that he never wanted to talk about what had happened. All he would tell me was that he'd been in France for a few days; he'd been shot, flown back to England, and then returned home. After he'd passed away, I found out from an uncle, who by the way had been a B-24 pilot, that the concussion from the exploding shell that landed near him had been so great that it blew open his kneecap *without making a hole of any kind in his uniform!* I can only imagine the strength of that concussion.

"At a birthday dinner, one of my uncles told me the real story of how my father had been wounded. He said, 'Your dad was in a line of soldiers crossing a field when a German shell exploded near him. The men to the right and left of him both died but your father survived.'

"I would never have known all this, had my uncle not told me. That's an amazing story. It also helped me to understand why dad spoke so little of the experience. He was wounded just before the battle of the Bulge and I often thought that had he not been injured, he might have died in the battle of the Bulge, and I would never have been born.

"When I graduated High School in 1963, I recall that the post-Sputnik panic about falling behind the Russians in science was still very much in our psyches. In college, everybody was being pushed into science programs. I did fairly well in science but I just barely scratched by in math. While helping me apply for college, my high school guidance counselor urged me to choose chemistry as my major. I agreed, because at that point I wasn't sure what I wanted to study. Well, at American University I was chemistry major for exactly one-and-a-half years! I ended up with an F in calculus, a D in the chemistry coursework, but an A in the chemistry lab—figure that out. With the support of a fellow student by the name of Romero, I changed my major and everything, figuratively and literally, *was history*. I was able to maintain a solid B or better average the rest of the way.

"Beginning in college, the Civil War became an interest of mine. Later, in the mid-1980s, I began attending some Civil War Roundtable meetings. I thought it was *really neat*. I increased my activity in the group to the point that I served as secretary. I also felt strongly that educating younger people about the importance of land and historic preservation would help insure that historic organizations like ours survive, and at the same time would maintain public interest in our history and culture."

Why do you believe it's important to keep history alive?

"Kids will often look at me like I'm crazy when I tell them that the color-bearers in a military unit during the Civil War were out in front and if they were shot and fell, the first thing the other soldiers would do is pick up the flag, so that it never hit the ground. These were the regimental colors and about the only thing a soldier could see through the smoke of weapons-fire was the flag. Now that caused many flag bearers to be shot because the enemy knew that if he shot in the direction of the flag he would hit somebody. Kids will sometimes say,

'That was stupid. Why would you die for a flag?' This is a different generation today. People had some very different values back in 1860s America. It's important to me to do my best to pass these values on.

"Abraham Lincoln is a personal hero of mine and there are revisionists who are critical of some racist remarks he made when he was a younger man. He *was* somewhat racist in modern terms when he was younger and, admittedly, the Emancipation Proclamation did not free all the slaves, but for his time, he was far more progressive than most of his political peers. The truth is that Lincoln changed as a person as he grew and matured. He altered his thinking and became more conscious of social equality as time went on.

"For a back woodsman his writing was extraordinary. It's been said that he wrote the Gettysburg Address on the back of an envelope on the train taking him to Gettysburg. Actually, the truth is that Lincoln agonized over every word of that document, as he did with many other famous speeches he gave. Lincoln thought mightily about each word and how it would be understood by those who heard him speak it. For a farm boy he became a great intellectual—he was an amazing person.

"Another hero for me was General Joshua Chamberlain, who was a college professor at Bowdoin College in Maine when the war broke out. He was a man of letters, spoke several languages, and as a very young man, had attended seminary with the intention of someday becoming a minister. Fortunately for him, he survived the war and was later able to write brilliantly of it with the skill of the college professor he was. Some of the words he wrote after the war are just beautiful. Here's an example:

"In great deeds, something abides. On great fields, something stays. Forms change and pass; bodies disappear; but spirits linger, to consecrate ground for the vision-place of souls. And reverend men and women from afar, and generations that know us not and that we know not of, heart-drawn to see where and by whom great things were suffered and done for them, shall come to this deathless field, to ponder and dream; and lo! the shadow of a mighty presence shall wrap them in its bosom, and the power of the vision pass into their souls."

—From a speech given by Chamberlain for the purpose of

"Dedication of the Maine Monuments," given at Gettysburg, PA, on October 3, 1888. In it, Chamberlain talks of the heroic service performed by Maine troops at the battle of Gettysburg, July 1-3, 1863.

"That's great stuff! Although the movie, and later Ken Burns' documentary on the Civil War, glamorized him, when you read his books and the books written about his life, you see that he was just a college professor who chose to *pick up the sword,* and, only later became a national hero. He was tough too. He led a famous charge of Union forces at Little Round Top in the Gettysburg Campaign and later was severely wounded at the battle of Petersburg. He was fortunate to survive."

Have you taken part in Civil War reenactments?

"My knees, which are in pretty bad shape, could not stand up to running across a battlefield. I would like to do re-enacting, but for me doing the *Living History* work, whether I'm presenting to kids or a senior group, is much more rewarding.

"A lot of the stories and how I present them make it all come alive for people. Very often I come into the presentation in character—(Matt then goes into character)—"I'm Private George of the 134th New York. Colonel Ryder has requested my presence here for attached duty from Colonel Custer. I'm here as ordered by Colonel Jackson." (Laughing)

"I then do about 15 minutes of Living History. I tell them for instance: *'I worked in the mills here at Mohawkville. In '62 I went off to fight the rebels because they were going to destroy the Union. My best friend Sam Swales worked with me in the mills and another friend Jacob Trask and Alonzo Van Arnum were good buddies. They gave the final sacrifice and were killed at Gettysburg.'* I really act it all out and after 15 minutes, I usually will remove my hat and say, 'Ok, now I'm really Mr. George and some of you probably know me from baseball or school.' Then I'll go on to explain the intricacies of the musket, my food, and my uniform. That's a lot of fun for me.

"Some of the questions that folks ask really make me think. I had an educational deferment during the Vietnam War and one of the toughest choices I ever had to make in my life was in 1969. I was doing graduate work at American U., but I didn't quite get my master's and decided to withdraw. As a result, I lost my 2-S deferment and had to go to a pre-induction physical. If I was drafted, I wondered if I would fight in this war that I thought was morally wrong? In the end I didn't have to make that decision. Because of my extreme nearsightedness. I was declared ineligible for military service. I later took part in the big peace march in Washington D.C. and throughout, was against the war. During this time I promised myself I would finish my postgraduate work someday. I did finish at St. Rose College in Albany, New York in 1988, graduating with a Master's in Science, in Education and American History.

"People will sometimes ask me, 'How can you have that kind of leftist background and be celebrating the Civil War?'

"I answer that by saying, there's part of me that's very interested in history, but there's also part of me that is fascinated by the *dark side of our nature* that motivates us to participate in war.'

"Lincoln has wrote about the 'better angels of our nature.' I find it remarkable that Americans were able to kill Americans—600,000 worth—while at the same time, there were countless examples of sacrifice, goodwill, and mercy. The Civil War was the most destructive, dirty, vicious war that you could imagine. I think, *How could human beings play cards with their enemy one night and then turn around the next day and try to kill that same man?* Sometimes it was brother against brother or even father against son!

"I still deal with these questions. I'll ask myself: *How can you be studying war if you were against war?* There's something to be said about what was, and I believe, always will be, our '*mark of Cain.*' Yet what appeals to me in a man like Chamberlain, is how knowledge and reason will always win out in the long run. I guess I'm idealistic. I believe this better part of our nature will triumph over the purely animalistic side of us that wants to kill people.

(Pointing to a picture)—"Here's Chamberlain who was a hero during the war‾ the two armies have been killing each other for four years, it all comes to an end at Appomattox, and the Confederates are marching in to surrender their weapons. The Confederate officer, leading the rebel army, had his horse make a bow of salutation to Chamberlain and his troops, after Chamberlain had ordered *his* men to salute the Confederate troops—the same men they've been trying to destroy for the last four years! There's something very noble about this whole surrender. These men are honoring their former enemies as if they were all brothers."

Doesn't this somehow speak to a higher nature within us all?

"Well, however you want to say it. As I get older I become more aware of my own mortality and I get to thinking there's got to be something longer-lasting and more worthwhile in this life, for humanity's sake. The good side of our nature has to win out or there is no hope.

"I think it's important to provide kids with a chance to look deeper at life even though what I'm sharing with them is about war. It makes me think of a famous quote which I'll paraphrase here: *People who don't pay attention to history are doomed to repeat it!* I believe that's true, because those darker parts of our nature that we don't admit to; will continue to commit terrible atrocities just as people have been doing over and over again for centuries. The spiritual points I'm making here don't just come from organized religion because more people have been killed in the name of religion than you can ever imagine! I'd like to think we each have a noble side to our nature, but when I get depressed about the state of the world the best I can do is *hope* so.

"I'm not sure of its veracity, but here's a story that has been handed down. In the midst of a battle, a mule that was being used to carry ammunition had gone down, leaving the ammunition lying on the ground in *no-man's land.* An officer then looked for a volunteer to go out and bring the ammunition back to the Union lines. According to the story, a peach-fuzzed young soldier who was built rail-thin, raised his hand and said, 'I'll go sir.' The story goes on to say he stripped down to his trousers so he could move quickly, and with that his fellow soldiers provided covering fire and out he ran. The Confederate soldiers then commenced to fire at him, but he was able to secure the two ammo boxes with some rope, and then began to run back to his lines dragging the boxes behind him. The confederates then increased their fire in an effort to stop him while the Union soldiers were encouraging him from behind their lines. Suddenly he stops, **(with Matt, standing and demonstrating how he transported the boxes),** rearranges the boxes and then resumes his run backward to the Union lines. The question everyone had for him when he got back was, 'Why did you *ever* stop in the middle of the field?'

He said, 'Well sir, I thought I was gonna die, and I couldn't have my body sent home to my mother with a hole in my back.'

"He didn't want his mother or others to think he'd been a coward on the battlefield. Today, kids will hear me tell that story and they'll say, 'what are you talking about?' It doesn't make sense to them. (Laughing) If that story didn't happen it could have happened. The point is that was part of the mindset of people at that time.

"Here's another tale I thought *never* happened, but I've since found to be true. It came out of the battle at Antietam when the Irish Brigade from the Union forces made a charge at Sunken Road. The story goes that the brigade attacked the Confederate unit in a straight line formation and was taking heavy casualties as might be expected. Meanwhile a young, very thin, Irish lad wearing pants that were far too big for him had joined the charge. He was a recent replacement, so this was his first action. Each time this young soldier would take three or four steps his pants would fall down. Then he'd drop his rifle to pull his pants back up and an officer would yell at him to charge. Then he'd run a few more steps and down would go his trousers again. Finally the commanding officer in frustration with the young soldier begins waving his saber and screaming at the young recruit to charge. At that point the young man just threw his pants away and continued to charge!

"It's a great story for the kids because they can picture him running across the field without his pants. Sometimes the kids will laugh hysterically when I tell it.

"About 10 years ago, I visited Antietam and while there I began talking with a Park Ranger. I mentioned that 'ridiculous story' about the Irish kid running *bare-ass* across the field during the battle. The Ranger said, 'Don't laugh; we have collaborating letters from the families of

Confederate soldiers attesting to that *crazy Yankee soldier.* They didn't
want to shoot him because they figured the boy had enough problems
already!'(Laughing) So as improbable as the story seems, it's most
likely true.

"In the battle of Spotsylvania, which is in close proximity to
Chancellorsville and Fredericksburg, in Virginia, there was a place,
where by all accounts, a vicious battle was waged that went on all
afternoon and night. The men who survived said the ferocity of the
fighting returned men to their animal instincts—hand to hand and fist to
fist! They were even axing soldiers as they attempted to climb over the
walls. Men were strangling each other with their bare hands! It's said
that any trace of civilized humanity disappeared during that battle.
Many of the survivors described it as *being in hell.* The dead were
stacked so high in the mud in front of that entrenchment that some were
discovered still alive under the pile of bodies when the battle was over.
The savagery of that day was *horrendous.* It is unmatched in any battle
of the war. Accounts of the fight are still scary to me—to see what
depths of violence man can sink to. For five hours the worst darkness in
these men took over.

"I think many people don't understand how something like the
Holocaust could happen. They don't understand how this dark side,
which exists in all of us, can take over. I mean how could German
citizens know full well what was happening in the concentration camps,
yet still allow it to happen? I don't know the answer, but this inhumane
treatment of our fellow human beings happens over and over
throughout history.

"My Uncle Paul, who's in his 70s now, gave me some differing views
of WWII. He's probably *as* patriotic if not more so than most people.
He was born in Germany and when he was 12, he became a member of
the Hitler Youth, which was mandatory for youngsters his age. He's an
expert on military history. Though he does not have a positive view of
Hitler, he's very proud of German technology and their ability to
manufacture tanks, planes, and military hardware. He has a family

photo album that depicts his family history; and in that album you can see that out of seven brothers his father was the only survivor of the war. All 6six of the uncles died on the Russian front. Atop the picture of each of them is the German Cross.

"My uncle remembers that the day before the Americans entered his village, toward the end of the war, the American commander met with the Mayor and, through an interpreter, told the townspeople to put a white sheet in their front window signifying their surrender. My uncle was about 12 at the time and he remembers that he went to school the next day and during the day the American tanks, trucks, and jeeps filled up the school soccer field. The children were then ordered to assemble on the field and my uncle remembers that he was very frightened. With memories of what had happened to his uncles on the Russian front he envisioned them all being executed. Well, eventually the tanks and jeeps left and the trucks remained. He was still afraid they would be machine-gunned or taken away.

My uncle then said to me, 'You know what they did then Matty?'

I said, 'No Paul, what did they do?'

"'They opened up the trucks and they gave us all Wheaties and milk!'

"That, again, is about goodness in the middle of the insanity and violence of war. I love that story!"

How has your involvement with Living History benefited you??

"Part of what I do is very rewarding to me personally, so there's definitely some self-gratification to this work. I feel good when the folks who attend my talks are enjoying themselves, so I guess you could say it's ego-building to some degree. There's also, however, a desire to leave a positive legacy behind. I want to leave *part of myself* to the next generation. I'd like to exist somehow, in a good way, when I'm gone. Although the Civil War was horrifying and cost us 600,000 lives, at least there was some good that came out of it. I think the story of how we ended the terrible evil of slavery while preserving the Union is a story that I'd like to pass on to future generations. It was, I believe, one of the few *just* wars we've ever engaged in.

"I once presented to a cub scouts group, ages 7 to11, in Rensselaer, NY, and though the 10 and 11 year-olds were sophisticated enough to know better, the 7 and 8 year-olds probably still thought I actually fought in the Civil War. When my presentation was over, the kids wanted to continue asking questions rather than attending the other activities planned for that day. I felt honored that the kids wanted to keep asking questions rather than play nerf-ball in the gym. When I told one of the younger kids that I really hadn't fought in the war, one of the 11 year olds asked me how old I really was and I told him I was 59. But then one of the little '*midgets*' piped up from the back of the room and said, 'Did you ever get shot when you were fighting?'

"I didn't want to go through my denial again so I just said, 'No I was very lucky. I didn't get shot.' (Laughing)

"When I was finally done there were some kids and parents lingering; and one of the fathers approached me with his little 'midget' whose head was down. Urging his son on he said, 'Tell him who your great, great, great grandfather was.'

"The *little guy* picked up his head slightly and without looking at me replied, 'I don't know if you'd know him.'

"'Go ahead and tell me,' I answered, trying to encourage him.

"'He was a general and his name was General Hooker.'

"Now I'm knowledgeable enough to know that General Hooker was not highly thought of as a commander; but one good thing he did when he became the Commander of the Army of the Potomac in 1863 was to have insignia's designed for each of the various corps in an attempt to increase their esprit d'corps. These insignias would then be worn by the individuals in that corps, on their hats. The insignia would certainly help to create pride in the unit they served, but would also help to identify by glance, which unit a soldier was attached to. This would be especially helpful in the smoke of the battlefield.

"So I said to the little Cub Scout, 'What does that neckerchief, you're wearing, stand for?'

"He replied, 'that's for the Webelos.'

"I told him that his great, great, great grandfather decided that he should divide the Army of the Potomac into groups just like the Boy Scouts decided to divide up the scouts up into different groups— groups like the bear clan and the Webelos. Realizing the connection between his great, great grandfather and his scouting clan, he let out a big smile, and that made me real happy. We also didn't have to go into any of the negative stuff I know about Hooker. So you never know who you will be presenting to.

"When I teach kids, especially middle school students, there has to be a certain degree of entertainment in what I do so that I can keep their attention. When I talk about southern soldiers for instance, I'll talk in a southern drawl and the kids just love that. Other times I might ask one of the kids to try to hold the rifle or musket so they can get an idea of what these soldiers carried around with them. This makes it all the more real for them. Then I have their attention.

"I always tell the kids that the Civil War was horrible! When I visit Gettysburg, which is very special to me, and I walk out onto the battlefield or into the cemetery there's a special feeling that comes over me. I'm very aware that, including wounded, missing, and those killed, there were roughly 52,000 casualties here. The reality of the slaughter that took place when these two armies squared off against each other for the *glory of their causes* was not fully appreciated by the public until Matthew Brady's photographs of the war dead began appearing in art studios in New York City. Then people began saying, 'This is horrible!' You have to remember the *glory* aspect of the Victorian age, and the popularly held fantasy of soldiers charging across a field with raised sabers, while trumpets blared, and somehow *no one got killed*—that's not the truth of how that war was fought."

Have you had to make any sacrifices to do this work?

"The main sacrifices for me in doing this work are time and money. These days I'm working on firming up a date with a teacher-friend of mine to go up to Johnstown to present to a seventh grade class. I will also be doing my Living History bit for a historical society in the Lake Placid area. In all the time I've been doing this, I've only taken money twice, and that's when the organization I was presenting to had to pay me. Both times I turned the money over to the Round Table. Financially my cost for purchasing the uniform, musket and shoes is probably somewhere in the neighborhood of $750 to $1,000. The bottom line for me is that I do this because I love it, and I love sharing this information with the kids and the grown ups."

Matt George may be contacted at **jbuford63@aol.com** or through **www.albanycivilwar.org**

Chapter 33
Awakening
Jim Fuller

"We started singing a chant based on the prayer of St. Francis, and the line, "as I awaken the living Christ inside of me" caused me to tear up. As I repeated the chant, I seemed to be pressed back into my chair as if I was a passenger in a speeding automobile!"

Jim Fuller, 55 years old, is the pastor and spiritual leader of the congregation at Unity Church, in Albany, New York. With his can-do approach, wisdom, compassion, and excitement for life, Jim has created a loving and highly energized environment within his church community. He and his wife Kay reside in Delmar, New York.

"My passion at this time in my life, and I suspect has been my passion throughout my life, has been discovering who I am as a spiritual being. I'm also discovering what God is in relation to me. It's my relationship, with God that seems to live in the back of my mind continuously, and can even confuse and excite me when I get little glimpses of it. Working as a minister in a church helps to facilitate this search process, but at the same time it bumps up the bar for me. Previously, I could be in my job and do my spiritual search "on the side." As a minister I find that now I have to do my spiritual and personal search much more out in front of people. I think that's part of why at this point in my life, I've been led to the ministry. This work puts me in touch with many people walking this same path, so my faith and what I know and don't know, is being challenged all the time. This seems to fit perfectly for me right now."

Where did you grow up Jim?

"I like to say that I was born in Oakland, California and grew up everywhere else. My parents were both Californians and met at the University of California at Berkeley as part of the Christian Science group there. Both were veterans of World War Two and were attending school on the GI Bill. They had been raised by mothers who were Christian Scientists. My father eventually took a job working with a military contractor, Western Electric, and my early childhood was spent living one year here and two years there, traveling around the country. That was pretty unstable for me. As an only child, it was like that until I was about 14 years old, when we moved to a small town just outside of Winston-Salem, North Carolina. I attended High School there and then went on to the University of North Carolina at Greensboro. I stayed in North Carolina for the balance of my life until about five years ago when I left to attend Unity ministerial school in Missouri."

So you were determined not to repeat the travel patterns of your childhood?

"Yes. (Laughing) I like community and stability even though I didn't know anything about it in my formative years. The only community I knew was my father, mother and me and that was not all that stable for me. My parents' relationship was not particularly easy or rewarding for them either. I was frequently moving to a different town; living in a new neighborhood; having to make new friends; adapting to another school; and like my parents, not being very socially adept. That was a difficult experience."

Always the new kid on the block?

"Yes—always the new kid on the block and not talented academically or athletically, and not possessing great social skills—it stank! When we moved to North Carolina, my parents moved to a rural area outside Winston-Salem where there were very few kids. There was no way to become part of any community there, and I didn't really have the chance for that until I went off to college and began developing friends in Greensboro, North Carolina.

"As far as my spirituality was concerned, my interest during my college years was focused on psychic phenomena: things that would tend to give one a sense of personal power. I was reading a lot of Carlos Castaneda and his magical journeys."

And probably smoking a little pot?

"Actually I had a psychological addiction to pot for about five years. It began in High School and ran through 1974, the year after College. It helped me get through some difficult times but it was also part of that era of rock festivals, drugs and such. I attended a few rock festivals, hitchhiked across the country, and had long hair.

"I was reading Carlos Castaneda, Edgar Cayce and looking at people who were searching for, or had some kind of power. It was interesting intellectually but I realized there wasn't much in that for me. I guess there was no map about how to find that power. The books seemed to be about other people and their experiences, but in no way related to my life and my reality. While I was fascinated by these subjects, and had experimented with the altered state by taking LSD a few times, my search didn't seem to be going anywhere except for the entertainment value of the experiences. I wasn't particularly interested in churches, but I was fascinated by the stories, and the sacred art and philosophy of the Eastern Religions like Hinduism and Buddhism, which I was exposed to through art classes in college.

"When I enrolled in college, the logical question for me, who didn't know what he wanted to do, was, '*what am I going to study?*' Eventually I ended up going into the art program. I really enjoyed working with my hands, and, because I believed I was stupid, the easier academic requirements attracted me. After a while, however, I could see that I did not have the talent or skill needed to become a successful commercial artist.

"My girlfriend, who later became my wife, had started off as journalism major and then switched to psychology. I followed suit. I started taking elective classes in behavioral psych and found that I was gifted in that area and best of all very interested in the subject matter.

During the end of my junior year and the beginning of my senior year I discovered something remarkable—I was smart! I could be motivated and even make A's if I was really interested in a subject. A different Jim had appeared on the scene.

"I dated my future wife all through college, and then married in 1974. We were both happy "hippy" students who knew nothing about ourselves or about life, but were having a good time together. We got married at the end of my junior, and her senior year and I basically got busy working and raising two sons.

"Following graduation, my wife and I became employed in an Episcopal group home, as house parents to children, ages 6 to older teens, with delinquency problems, as well as kids who had been taken away from their parents by the courts. So I went from being the long-haired hippy, Jim Fuller, to being "Mr." Fuller to the kids and staff. Under the tutelage of Scott Cutting, a consulting psychologist, and his wife we developed our skills and were able to help these kids to learn, develop, and grow past some of the difficulties they had encountered in their young lives. It was very satisfying work.

"My wife became pregnant after we had worked there for a year, and we became apprehensive about having a newborn child while living in a group home, with kids who had acted out against their own siblings at home. The potential for danger concerned us, so we decided to leave that job.

"Over the course of the next 10 years, I would come up against many challenges in my work and personal life; each one significant in the lessons I would learn, and the doors that would then open to me. These lessons had an element of pain but consistently kept me moving forward, even if I wasn't conscious of that at the time. My marriage dissolved after many years of trying to make it work. But then after leaving, re-establishing myself as a single father, and following a long period of grief, I met my wife Kay who has been a true partner in my spiritual search. I lost a job running a group home because grant money ran out, and years later I was asked to resign from directorship of a program I'd run successfully for seven years in Charlotte, because my inability to adequately relate to my staff and Board on an emotional level, prevented me from resolving some very difficult conflicts within our organization. Growing up in a pretty uncommunicative family with few social skills, presented me with some real hurdles to get over in that area. This latter event was occurring at the same time my marriage was ending. Each of these events however presented a chance for me to stretch and grow, emotionally and spiritually."

. **The aftermath of those events had to be very painful for you.**

"That time of my life—the early eighties—was a definite "bottom" for me. Within one year I separated from my wife and later, would resign my job. It was a terrible time, *but thank you God;* it was the best thing that ever happened to me! I just didn't know it then.

"This had been the best job I had ever had; making more money than I ever thought possible; had a wife and two kids, and a house in a very nice neighborhood. On the surface, things looked very good for a young man with poor self-esteem. When all these difficulties came down in 1984, however, I realized that I had to start all over again. I felt devastated.

"So I'm living on my own, as a divorced man, in a small apartment, close to where my wife and kids lived, and I discover that I'm very depressed and had been for quite some time. Now I knew enough about depression to know that if I allowed myself to experience it rather than avoid it, I would be able to move through it. So I gave myself permission to just be sad and sometimes I would just lie on my bed and cry. Then I would have the energy to get up and do what I had to do. For days at a time I would cry for a good portion of each day, and then the sadness would pass."

I've heard it said that grief can sometimes be a pathway to the Divine or to God, if you will. Has that been true for you?

"Absolutely. In facing my emptiness, I awakened to a deep longing to be connected to something greater than myself.

"Just by coincidence, which I no longer believe in, I'm sitting in my little apartment one day, spending some time with my children, and I happen to see this crazy little man by the name of Leo Buscaglia, whom

I had never heard of, speaking on television about this very same topic. I was moved and very inspired by him and what he had to say. I mention this because a year later when I met my current wife, Kay, she has just finished reading one of his books, while she was going through a divorce. She then passed it on to me. He was very instrumental in my healing, and helping me to connect to the desire for family, and for something greater spiritually.

"During the following year I had another serendipitous experience. I was living a hand-to-mouth financial existence; helping to support two households—my ex-wife's and mine—living in a very small apartment, and not making a whole lot of money. A man named Larry, who directed an agency that operated community homes for people with mental retardation, called me one day to tell me that he was leaving his job and that I should apply to replace him. It was primarily out of desperation that I decided to apply, because this was an agency that I swore I would never work for. Subsequently, I was hired for the job and I stayed there for 15 years. In looking back I can honestly tell you that it was the best job I'd ever had. I was given the opportunity to do what I wanted to do professionally. We hired some wonderfully talented people, our office staff expanded, and the agency became an outstanding program. That shows you how much I knew. As time passed and my spiritual path continued to evolve we began attracting people to the agency who were spiritually grounded. We would often have these great conversations in the office about spirit and religion and how that applied to the work we were engaged in. It progressed to the point that before I left, we were having once-a-month prayer meetings in the conference room where we'd eat our lunches, and offer prayers for each other and for the work of our agency.

"It seemed that 'angels' were constantly coming into my life now. The first angel was my wife Kay. As we began dating, we were each finding ourselves again, after the painful ending of our marriages. We found we were both interested in spiritual studies and the spiritual search, so we would listen to local speakers who were talking about anything from astrology to ancient Egypt—anything that was a spiritual topic. At this time, we were both attending the Unitarian church, which we found interesting intellectually, but not spiritually. Shortly after we began dating in 1987, there was a Harmonic Convergence, a cosmic event of some great meaning where all the planets line up in some kind of order. I pooh-poohed it, but what I did see was that when a number of people believe something is going to happen, a tremendous energy can be created. So on the actual date of the Harmonic Convergence, which we were oblivious to, we went to visit a little "new-age" church we had heard about called the Brigade of Light. We attended that church twice a week for the next five years. The church had been founded by a woman who in her forties had a vision in which she was told to start a church. She was intuitive, some said a psychic, and had explored a whole spectrum of spiritual beliefs and encouraged her congregation to do likewise. This was a wonderful time of growth and learning for me..

"Sometime in 1988 or '89 Kay and I were spending some time at a friend's cabin up in the mountains and I found a little book called '*A Journey Without Distance.*'…" (Tearing up)

It's apparent that this memory has a lot of emotion attached to it. That book must have been of great importance to you.

"Yes, reading that book was a turning point for me. It's the amazing story of how the set of books that make up A Course in Miracles came into being. I was very moved by it."

"Also at my friend's cabin was the three-volume set of *A Course in Miracles.* As I looked at it on the shelf I could see that the three books together were about six inches wide and I felt very intimidated since I was still a pretty slow reader. Despite that, and being pretty broke, I had the desire to buy a set of these books and miraculously, within three months a complete set turned up on the shelf of my favorite used bookstore, at a price I could afford—coincidence?

"Well that got me started. I attempted to read the text and do the workbook. I later visited a couple of *Course in Miracles* study groups but they never seemed to resonate with me. I may not have been quite ready at that time. I also tried to read the material, but I found that between my bad eyesight and lack of focus, I was not able to remember what I had just read. "

Jim, I'm drawn back to a point in your story where you talked about books in the cabin. Would you elaborate a bit more on why finding A Course in Miracles that event was so profound for you?

"I believe we human beings have each created a *story* of a separated self that is attractive in some ways, but painful and very damaging to us in other ways. We've created a false self. Reading about the experiences of Bill Thetford and Helen Schucman in receiving and writing down *A Course in Miracles* was part of awakening my Real Self. It was saying to me, *"Hey Jim, I'm in here."* I knew, in a very visceral way that something was moving in me that was not my intellect or personality.

"Here I was, just clueless about who I was and where I was going, but I can tell you, as an example, that as I began to grow spiritually and let go of some of the *old Jim,* my kids had a much better father than they did when they were little. Although I wasn't physically abusive, I still had a lot in common with the abusive parents of the children who lived next door to the group home in which I was working at the time. The way in which I reacted emotionally to my children when they were misbehaving often added fuel to the fire and made the situation worse. Now, however, as my spiritual self emerged, I found myself increasingly loving, nonjudgmental, and less angry.

"As I continued to work with A Course in Miracles, I made another attempt to get through reading the text and doing the workbook. To support that, Kay and I announced there would be a *Course in Miracles* study group that would meet at our house. This time a number of people were drawn to study with us. That group continued to meet for the next nine years until we eventually left the Charlotte area. That's how we actually got through the Course for the first time. We and our friends supported each other and then we found that the Course was changing us.

"At about the same time, realizing that we had to find a church that better spoke to where we were on our spiritual journey, we attended and enjoyed the local Quaker Meeting a number of times, and then decided to explore Unity Church in 1992. We initially attended Unity because we were taking a friend named Allen, who was looking for a church. We thought he would benefit, even though we really knew nothing at all about Unity. The minister was an African-American gentleman by the name of Randolph Wilkinson who preached the Unity message in a Southern Baptist style. I still remember the affirmation he taught us that day. It was: *'Right now I have everything I need to do God's will for me today.'* My friend Allen never returned to Unity, but we did.

"We attended that wonderful church for many years and found that Unity's message, for us, was in complete alignment with A Course in Miracles. The underlying message was very similar to the religion of my youth,—Christian Science—although I never saw Christian Science as a practical application of these principles. At Unity, however, it seemed that people were learning and applying these spiritual principles to their daily lives. At Unity, it also seemed that people were very alive and that excited me. Since that time, my path has been a combination of A Course in Miracles and my involvement in Unity Church.

"In that same year, in another important development, I met a spiritual teacher by the name of Paul Tuttle, who happened to be visiting our area. I found his work extremely helpful, but I was really moved the most by him: his story, his deep spiritual connection, and the spontaneous, spirit-led way in which he taught. At a retreat Paul led in Vermont, in 1994, I experienced a spiritual healing which really got my attention. I'd previously had some brief moments of awakening or clarity in which I felt loved and at peace; but here at this retreat, while sitting in a conference room and listening to Paul speak, I suddenly had an inner guidance in which I knew with certainty that I could forgive people. I suddenly began to recall all the people who had harmed me and who I had felt victimized by. I could now see that my perception of myself and others had been inaccurate. I forgave each of them as their faces flew through my head. At the end I felt a physical lightness as well as an amazing sense of well being that just cannot be described in words. I think I could have floated out of my chair!

"I then heard a voice within me saying, *"You don't have to have allergies anymore."* These were the first words I'd ever heard coming from within me. I then opened my eyes and realized all of this had taken place in just seconds—time had stood still. After the session ended, I rushed upstairs and threw away all my allergy medication, which I had been taking for over 20 years. I'll admit that I still was frightened because being sick and taking medication was part of the *story* of who I was.

"I spent the next couple of days at the retreat trying to make sense of all that had happened. It was good but scary. I had a wonderful time for the rest of the retreat and felt better than I had ever felt in my life. It was a life-changing event comparable to the first time I had heard Leo Buscaglia speak. When I prepared to leave the retreat and return home, I began to get really sick like I had Flu. I realized it was my fear and not physical sickness. The first two spring times after the retreat, the allergies returned, but only for a few hours or a day. I would see all the trees in bloom and become afraid that the allergies would return. To combat this, I learned that all I had to do was be still, and they would go away.

"I was left with a feeling of wholeness and wellness, and a new-found ability to see others as just like myself. One of the people who did not come up for forgiveness at that time was my mother, who was the dominant person in our family, and with whom I had butted heads throughout my life. Within the past year or so, however, I was at a retreat, and was encouraged during a meditation, to put in my mind the person who has always been there in my corner, and been an advocate for me, so to speak. When I thought about it, the first person to come up for me was my mother. So my *story* about my mother has changed. That event tells me that my relationship with her has also been healed. My forgiveness of others is really about accepting both myself and others at a deep spiritual level, regardless of what dramas we have acted out with each other."

How did the idea of you becoming an ordained Minister come about?

"In October of 1997, I was attending Unity Church in Charlotte and a meditation teacher by the name of David Now was invited by our minister to come in and teach us meditation by using chanting. That was a very powerful meditation experience for me. As a result, Kay and I traveled up to Virginia to take part in another meditation workshop he was facilitating. Prior to the meditation time, I jokingly said, "I'm going to sit right in front of this guy so that I can see his *third eye.* (Laughter) So I sat right down in front. We started singing a contemporary chant and the line, "as I awaken the living Christ inside of me" caused me to tear up. As I sang this chant repeatedly I seemed to be pressed back into my chair as if I was a passenger in a speeding automobile. The bottom part of my body suddenly began to vibrate while I continued to sing this chant. Other participants took breaks or came and went for different reasons, but I continued on for about an hour and a half, with my body vibrating and my mind absolutely at peace and very still. At the end of all this my mind said to me, *It's time to quit my job and start my ministry.*

"Now the idea of becoming a minister left me unsure of what to do. My former minister, Marion, from the Brigade of Light church, advised me to start my own church as she herself had done. That didn't feel right for me, so I checked with my Unity minister, and was encouraged to apply to Ministry School. That would mean two years of schooling, which would actually be a retreat of sorts for me, and something I really needed in order to be deeply grounded in what I wanted to do. I also needed the challenges that I knew would arise in being a student there."

"So my passion for this journey was now asking me to walk away from the best job I'd ever had, where I'm making lots of money, and had lots of close friends, and to go off into this great unknown of ministry.

It seems that trust has been a big part of your journey?

"That's true, and I think it developed through my willingness to step out—despite my fears and difficulties—and risk in those directions that I felt moved to follow. It's only when I've gotten through the difficulties I've gone through and can look back at what's been accomplished, that I'm able to say, 'It was good to have trusted that impulse even though part of the path was difficult.' I'm then more willing to take that next risk, because I have a greater sense that there is a benevolent intelligence—call it the Christ within, God, or my true self—that is attempting to move me forward to my greater good. This idea is at the core of my passion for finding out who I am, and how God and I relate to each other."

"As Kay and I got ready to leave, it seemed as if everything was falling into place in a very orderly way. Selling our house went smoothly and our friends were very supportive. As we were excitedly moving toward a new future in a new place, though, we had to face the grief of the friendships we'd left behind. Although we were traveling in a new and positive direction, we were also moving away from our old life and all the close relationships we'd had. It was very painful at times!

"I went through a spiritual crisis the first fall I was in ministry school. The day after my birthday I began to develop a liver disease. Because it was painful I couldn't sleep, and I also had to limit my diet. I kept praying and asking what to do because I was terrified! I spent two months praying, just asking what to do and the word I kept hearing was *wait*. That definitely was not the word I wanted to hear. Two months and a week later, however, the pain and the sleeplessness mysteriously left me. Charles and Myrtle Fillmore, the founders of the Unity movement, called this kind of violent reaction "chemicalization." This was their explanation for the inner *civil war* that often shows up in one's physiology when you mix together new healing ideas, a fresh sense of who you are becoming, and your old 'story.' During this time I was told by doctors that this would be a life-long condition and I would be fortunate if it did not progress. After my healing I decided not go back for follow-up tests, but years later my physician here in Albany said that I should really do some blood work. I did, and the result was that my liver functions were all found to be perfectly normal.

"Ministry school was a mixture of learning, study, time spent in prayer, and time spent interacting with the Unity school administration and staff. During my time there, I was confronted by the staff with issues they felt I needed to address. This led me into some very good spiritual counseling that helped me to explore where I was spiritually, my beliefs, and my *childhood baggage*. I also had an excellent experience in forgiving and healing resentments that I had held against the faculty of the school for the manner in which they had confronted me. That was probably why at the end of the two years of school, my 28 classmates were given full ordination, while I was ordained provisionally. This meant I had to continue returning to the faculty for additional interviews, in addition to requesting that my ordination be made permanent. Graduation week was very tough because, despite being told I was progressing well and was on track to graduate, I was told at my final interview that I was not doing well and that I would be provisionally ordained. This was noticeable during the ceremony. It was difficult for me because many of my friends and family had come to support me and see me ordained. Kay and my son Nathan were remarkably loving and supportive of me throughout this process. In about a week's time I was able to do some healing around this whole issue and then I experienced what I can only call the overwhelming love of God. I knew I was loved, despite what had transpired.

"While I was at school, a fellow student and friend by the name of Morgan Barclay, who previously had been a member of the Unity Congregation here in Albany, encouraged me to apply for a ministerial vacancy that he knew existed there. So I did that mainly as a favor to him (laughs), because I really didn't want to be this far north. At the same time I was talking to a church committee down in Hilton Head, South Carolina which is very close to where a lot of my family still lives. So, we had to make a decision! Kay and I used a prayer, which usually she initiates that goes like this: 'OK God, take away what isn't ours.' Eventually the Hilton Head opportunity was taken away. The other thing that happened was that in visiting the church in Albany, we not only loved the congregation, but also the way the area felt to us. We knew we were being guided and that it was right for us."

So coming to Albany has been a continuation of this passionate journey toward discovering your spiritual self.

"Exactly. One of the frustrating things about this spiritual journey is my inability to be in any kind of control of the speed with which it progresses. Ten years ago I would have said you were nuts if you ever told me I'd be a minister at this point in my life. So, this journey of awakening and finding myself spiritually seems to be one in which I can only be present, and willing to take that next step as Divine Guidance reveals itself to me. For me now, that means doing things like making time to get together with other ministers, attending retreats, and taking the personal time for my daily study, prayer work, and periods of quiet in addition to my job as minister. This is how I can continue to move deeper on this journey. I can't lead others to a deeper spiritual place if I haven't went there myself."

It has always interested me in how the ego can get into this passionate process, and to use your words, *we get lost again*. Have you experienced that in your journey?

"Often, but I usually only become aware of how my ego has worked itself into my process in hindsight. I will notice how I'll have some great idea and within a day or two I'll realize that it was simply my ego wanting to inflate itself or trying to deter me from taking a step forward. My initial impulses are sometimes led by my ego that says, "Jim, you're a great human being." or "Jim, you're just a human being and you can't do that." So that's very much a part of the ongoing dialogue. Sometimes I'll catch it in the moment when it's happening and sometimes I'll catch it later when my decision just does not feel right to me."

What effect would you hope this passionate path of yours would have in this world?

"That's actually an easy question. I'd like to see this world as it actually *is*, whether that's through my eyes or through some other way of perceiving. I don't think in our day-to-day lives we really do see ourselves, each other, or this world as it truly is. The Apostle Paul talks about 'seeing things through a glass darkly' and the Bible speaks about viewing things as a 'dim reflection' rather than seeing the beauty, truth, and potential of our existence. What I'd like to accomplish is to help others so that we can all see it together. If I can do that, I know that it follows that many of them would then become teachers and eventually we could all awaken to a greater reality of who we are. That possibility has so much to offer us."

Jim Fuller maybe contacted at fullyjim@yahoo.com and at www.unitychurchinalbany.org

Chapter 34
Yearning
Darci Der'cole McGinn

"I still remember a time when I was sitting on this couch, fully aware that I was angry and very bitter. I saw that I woke each morning filled with resentment, and this resentment was eating me alive. In that moment I asked myself, 'Is this the way I want to be and live the rest of my life?' The answer was overwhelmingly 'no!' I knew that if I wanted to change my life so that I wasn't walking around bitter and depressed all the time, I had to pick up these teachings I'd learned, and internalize them in a way I'd not yet done."

Darci Der'cole McGinn is a single, working mom with two children who lives in a comfortable home in Delmar, a suburb of Albany, New York where this discussion took place. She has a thoughtful and enthusiastic demeanor when discussing subjects she cares deeply about. Her great passions are: teaching the "Origin Teachings of the Delicate Lodge," an ancient Native American-based spiritual wisdom; and her own spiritual quest, which are most often one and the same.

"Describing my passion is difficult because it's a spiritual quest that encompasses my personal journey, as well as the path I want to lead others on. This mission of mine has awakened me to a new level of personal and spiritual consciousness that is much like a flowering blossom that gradually opens and continually expands. That's how I view the process I bring to other people as well.

"The actual spiritual teachings I use are called the *Origin Teachings of the Delicate Lodge,* which come from the Native American peoples of both North and South America and have a lineage dating back to the ancient Mayan and Pre-Columbian cultures. They come down to us through the medicine people in those civilizations, and through the generations and tribes who have migrated up into North America and Canada. These teachings are currently in the hands of my teachers, WindEagle and RainbowHawk, who have brought them to a wider range of people by creating the Ehama Institute about 15 years ago. So they, along with WhiteEagle who studied with them, teach this body of knowledge to others. The tradition is to educate individuals or groups or communities, which is how I learned. Part of my journey or mission has been learning how to be part of this community, and then to create that same sense of community for others within which we can teach this spiritual path.

"I've been on a number of spiritual journeys in my life, but this particular journey began back in April of 1999 when I received a brochure in the mail announcing that one of my professional affiliates would be co-hosting a four-day ceremony with WindEagle and RainbowHawk. Being initially interested but not knowing anyone who'd be attending, I read the brochure and put it down many times before finally deciding I'd better get more information before deciding if this was right for me. I called, and after speaking at length with a wonderful woman, decided to attend all four days. Coincidentally, this was a crucial time for me because my then ex-husband-to-be and I had just agreed to separate and he would be moving out within the next two weeks. I thought, at the time, this event could be a loving safety net for me.

"The four-day ceremony was like stepping out of time and entering a new dimension. I cried often as memories and flashbacks of my life came pouring in on me. I also made some meaningful connections with people I'd not previously known, but who now felt like they'd been my brothers and sisters for eons. It seemed like we'd all made some agreement in our past lives to be together at this point in time so that we might experience this intensely powerful awakening.

"When I returned home after the event, I just knew that I'd been deeply impacted and that something profound had moved through me and monumentally changed who I was. As a result, the first things I did when I got home were to unplug the phone and turn off the TV and radio. So much had happened that a shift had occurred within me. I needed time for integration.

"At the ceremony the leaders asked if anyone would be interested in coordinating an event in New York, where the teachers could come and have a gathering with the idea of creating a community there. I immediately thought, *Yeah, that's something I'd be willing to put my energy into.* Ever since then, I've known this path is part of my *calling.* It was not an intellectual thought; rather it was more of an inner knowing that this would be my path and a part of me for the rest of my life. Since then I've been organizing and coordinating people to come together in community, where they can learn more about these teachings. These days I'm a guide (someone who informally teaches) in addition to gathering the people to come. Over the past few years, it's been a transition for me to reach a point where I now believe that I can *gift* people with this knowledge.

"RainbowHawk, WindEagle, and WhiteEagle, our three teachers, are known as *keepers.* To become a *keeper* you must make a commitment of anywhere from 7 to10 years of study as an apprentice. As a *keeper* you then dedicate your life to passing the teachings on to others.

"When, in 1999, I experienced this teaching for the first time, I knew it was calling me in a big way, but I didn't know why nor did I really understand it all. I certainly didn't know what lay ahead of me on this path, but as the process of my divorce moved forward, I experienced very painful and difficult times, and at several points I felt defeated, angry, and even victimized by my lot in life. I would ask myself why this was happening to me and lament how this wasn't the dream I envisioned. It was probably the most painful time of my life.

"I still remember a day when I was sitting on this couch, fully aware that I was angry and very bitter. Each morning I awoke with resentment. I just knew it was eating me alive. In that moment, I asked myself, *Is this the way I want to be and live the rest of my life?* The answer was overwhelmingly *No* and I knew that if I wanted to change my life so that I wasn't walking around bitter and depressed all the time, I had to pick up these teachings and internalize them in a way I'd not yet done. I had to release all my expectations of whom or what I *should* be, along with all my old dreams of how I'd envisioned my life would go. That decision truly began my journey of inner healing."

Please describe the awakening you've experienced through this spiritual quest of yours?

"This spiritual journey has awakened me to a pathway into myself that is very connected to the earth, to the natural world all around me, and to the people who are sharing this process with me. I also experienced that when I'd talk to God as I understood God, I was really speaking to this power that isn't separate from me and whose love I was able to sense in a very real way. The initial ceremony weekend with my teachers left me with the experience of being completely loved by not only the people who were there, but also by Mother Earth, the trees, and the spirits that came to me.

"Another thing that happened involved understanding beauty in a way I'd never experienced it before. One of the basic tenets of the Origins of the Delicate Lodge teachings is to live in the Way of Beauty. In other words, everything we create; every action we take; and every word we speak, is carried out with a sense of beauty or love. For instance, during one of my days in training, a beautiful, natural space was created where we could sit and talk and be in conversation with our teachers. They took willow branches and bent them over, and made these huge arching hoops that were then decorated with colorful ribbons, which all had meaning and significance. They also made a patterned stone ring around a tree and took ferns to create a beautiful altar by the tree where we could all sit and *be a part of.* Energetically and aesthetically, they had created an entity of beauty and being. I believe that when you create beauty you're creating love and at the same time expanding the *circle* and the connection between all living things. That was very much the essence of being with RainbowHawk and WindEagle and all the others. I think it was the first time that I'd ever been present with somebody creating something so beautiful, natural, and special, out of simple things like pine cones, ferns, or rocks. This was a revelation for me. As a kid I loved rocks and wanted to be a geologist, but people would tell me that collecting rocks was stupid, so I let go of that dream. When I became reacquainted with the natural beauty in rocks as an adult, it opened up a relationship between me and the spiritual essence of the rock, the trees, and all the other beings that exist in the world. I truly experienced being at home and grounded. I understood this connection deep inside of me in a way that defied words.

"This great bond with the natural world offered me the opportunity to meditate and open myself to what messages might be coming to me from the trees, wind, rocks or whatever I feel connected to. I was very open. The loudest message that came to me that weekend was my *medicine name, Gentle Song*, which was an answer to the question: *If you wanted to create a community that you could embellish, or foster, or grow in, what would it be?* I became aware that to fashion a loving community, I would have to hold and nurture the people like a newborn baby, while singing a gentle song or lullaby. Although I didn't comprehend all that at that time, I did know that being the *gentle song* would be part of my journey. That was my first image of who I was becoming.

"Gentle Song is manifested today when I create community with people at the Medicine Wheel we've constructed at the Priory House in Chestertown, New York. I invite folks to come; we give them a little information about what our group is all about; and then when they arrive we gather as a community within the teachings of the Origins of the Delicate Lodge. As part of our ritual for the weekend, we build a sacred altar together with articles such as a feather or a crystal that each person has brought with them. Then we start to see the weaving of the individual into the collective or community that we're forming. It's very exciting to watch this happen. The process builds a strong sense of safety, so that we can begin to teach people about the Medicine Wheel, which is a map of the human consciousness, used in many cultures. We first show them what it looks like and then we explain the various energies the wheel holds.

There are two basic wheels we start with. One is called the Four Daughters of Beauty, which are the four elements: the fire in the East; the water in the South; the Earth in the West; and the air or the wind in the North. Another layer of that wheel depicts the human elements: In the East is the spirit; In the South, we have emotion; In the West is the body; and in the North is the intellect or mind. When you put these two wheels together and start to overlay them, the richness begins to grow and the wheel has the capacity to create a depth of understanding and self—knowledge, as well as a greater appreciation of our connectedness to all things—both the *seen* and *unseen*.

"When people enter the wheel and want to know how they can acquire more balance in their lives or in a certain situation, we'll physically lead them into the wheel, move them around it, and ask them how it feels to be in each element. As an example I might ask, 'How does it feel to be here in the south where there's lots of emotion?' As a result, that person gets a chance to experience getting closer to his or her feelings. Then we might engage in some conversation to help them get clearer with their truth. Some folks will say, 'I'm very intellectual and I can really *think a problem to death* but please don't ask me to feel anything because I don't know how to do that.'

"What we're doing is teaching people the highest *art* of being themselves. To be that, you eventually need to stand in the center of the wheel, which means you're centered and balanced. That would mean I know my emotions as well as I know my intellect. I can walk between the two, or I can balance them in any situation, or I can diagnose how I am out of balance and what's needed to bring me back to a centered place.

"When we create a wheel, we also call on, and honor, the Creator and Creatrix, and all the ancestor spirits and guardian spirits of that land to be with us and guide us in whatever needs to be created."

It sounds like intention and purpose is integrated into each step in the creation of this wheel?

"I think that's very true. In the beginning of building the wheel at the Priory, we performed all this work, but began to experience some resistance in various ways. What came to me with the help of a woman, who was a spiritual counselor, was that the guardian spirits that exist on that land are extremely protective. They wanted to be sure we were coming there with good intentions and not walking away anytime soon. To convince the guardian spirits of this, I made a decision to spend an entire day alone within the wheel. During that time I *fed* the wheel and the fire, and I talked with the spirits and sat with them all day. Throughout that day I truly became clearer and focused on what my intention was in this work; what my heart's commitment was in being there; and what I was really willing to do. Since that time I have become even more open and expanded in my spirit."

What do you think is required to live a passionate life Darci?

"That's such an important question for me. It's only as I'm learning about living my passion that I'm beginning to understand what is required to do that. As a continuing student of the *Teachings,* I'm learning more about what it is to be who you truly are. What is your truth, and how courageous and how *big* can you be to passionately stand up and choose to be your authentic self? I'm also learning that it's not always so easy. I think it is until something new about me is revealed, and when I try to let go of that piece, I find there's some healing that I first need to do. Each time I can do that, however, I find I'm able to step out and become a little *bigger* in my life. Then I find myself on a nice *plateau* until I realize that I want to be a little *bigger* in some area of my life and subsequently I have to enter that healing process once again.

"As an example, I'm seeing recently that when we schedule these gatherings at the Priory House, I will first very casually call people together by sending a flyer out along with an e-mailing and announcing what our theme will be; maybe something like, *Putting Your Dreams into Action.* What I've become aware of, however, is that my passion has not really been present in that announcement process. I'm still holding back a bit when it comes to offering my gift in its full potential. So, the reoccurring question for me is: *What's holding me back from being bolder?* And then saying, *This is what I really want to be and this is how I want to do it!* The question I always have to answer is, *what is this fear that holds me back from being big and bold?* It usually comes down to a question of how much am I loving myself, because when I am, I increasingly heal and release my old wounds and fears that hold me down. Then I am *my champion,* and a great cheerleader for myself. Rainbow Hawk, one of my teachers, told our class that if we don't love ourselves enough, we'll forever find ourselves *on the road* to our dreams—always approaching but never truly arriving.

What's it like for you to know you've had a part in another person's growth?

"I've intuitively known for a long time that I'm on this earth to create a *container* for people in which they can do their healing work. My whole life I've pulled people together: in circles and support groups, as a therapist doing group and family counseling, as an educator, and now as a medicine woman bringing people Every time we close a gathering and perform our final ceremony, as everyone shares using the talking stick, I say, 'my heart is full.' It's full because of the beauty of the experience that happens with these people, and because I'm able to be present for it, not because I did something.

"The feelings I have are very similar to the bliss, peace, and contentment that fills me when I experience being close to God; the moments where I understand there is no separation between me and others, and that all is well. In those moments, I'm aware I am a channel through which spirit can move and heal people. That's when I know this work I do is truly right for me."

In the Delicate Lodge Teachings, the literature pointed out that "within community one could explore and be present to the greatest yearnings of the spirit." What have you found to be your greatest yearning?

"*The greatest yearnings of the spirit* sounds a little like the question, 'What does my spirit cry out to express?' which we sometimes ask.: For me, creating more beauty in the world is one of my great yearnings. Recently I've been drawing and creating mandalas, and allowing the colors in the mandala to speak to me, without trying to understand or rationalize what comes to me. I've always wanted to do art work, but in High School I didn't because of many painful things that had been going on at that time of my life. Now I'm just beginning to swing that door open and explore my talent.

"This past year I've stepped up and volunteered to be one of the lead dancers for the Sun Dance which takes place in Wisconsin this coming summer. In years past, I was a dancer, but wasn't required to dance every round, and I could eat and drink. Last year I did not dance, choosing instead to stay home and vacation with my children. After that, it came to me that I had a desire to make a commitment to the Sun Dance in a deeper way. As a lead dancer I'm required to dance every round, from sunrise to sunset, for two and a half days! Each round is 45 minutes, followed by a 15-minute break. Each time I would have this yearning in the past, my brain would kick in and say things like: *You can't do that; You've never done that before; You're not in shape; You hurt your knee two years ago while dancing;* and *You'll be away from home for a whole week*...and on and on. But in November, unsure of how I'd make room in my life for it, I simply decided to join a health club and begin the task of preparing my body to be a lead dancer. In December I found an opening in my schedule, enrolled in a club, hired a trainer and began a regimen of three to five workout sessions a week. Along with the training, I joined Weight Watchers to lose weight, and within just a few months I began to see a big change in me.

"Releasing all the reasons that said 'I can't,' allowed the yearning for what I wanted, to come through and flower. Otherwise my yearning never would have become reality. Being able to manage my emotions, mind, and thoughts, rather than having thoughts and emotions manage me is an important part of me being a *spiritual warrior.*

"The first heroes or mentors for me were Pele Rouge and FireHawk, a couple who I became acquainted with when I attended my first ceremony four years ago. Being in their mid to late 50s, they were a little older than me and took me under their wings. In a sense they *reparented* me for awhile. During that time, I was experiencing a great deal of emotional pain, and they provided me with a lot of nurturing.

"When I attended my first Sun Dance I knew little about the significance of the dance, but I knew I yearned to play the huge five-foot drum they used. Once I told them, Pele Rouge and FireHawk said, 'Come and sit, and follow us.' I proceeded to drum with them and learned the beat and they taught me the songs. When I look back on that I realize how healing those moments were. With the power of the drum, and them on either side of me, it was as if I was being lovingly held in a cocoon. When we were done with the drumming I was told that I was free to come back and play this drum anytime I wanted. For me, it was as if they, the teachers, had given me, the student, a little gold star! (Laughing)

"My teachers WindEagle and RainbowHawk, the founders of the Ehama Institute, and WhiteEagle, now founder of Dancehammers—her own teaching circle—are the elders, or the grandparents as we call them. They have been important mentors for me, and they are my role models for never *flinching.* Adversity is where you can really see yourself tumble, so I'm just amazed at the way they don't hold attachments and yet their intention remains very clear. In the course of their own life, they have walked through many tragedies, yet at the same time, they've established a center in California, sold it, and have now created a center in New Mexico, with plans for an adjoining village where people can come and live…and RainbowHawk is 84 years old! This is not what most people in their 80s in our society would be giving their time to!

"When I was a young adult my hero was my mom. She'd gone through a divorce, like me, and had to make her own way as a single parent in the 1970s. Married women couldn't have a credit card of their own because they were *Mrs. so and so,* but I remember mom, after her divorce, receiving her first credit card, in her name, and then buying her first car. She was also an artist and art teacher. Her heart and soul would go into her sculptures, some taking as long as a year to complete. I could see *her story* in her work; it was part of her. I think she did her healing work through her art and I'm so proud of her for that. She never faltered.

"Nancy Howes, who has since passed on and was my mentor at Antioch New England Graduate School where I was doing my graduate work in Education, believed in me and continually told me I could *do it* when I was struggling academically. She also lovingly and gently showed me that I could think *outside the box.*

"Leslie Haas, who has since passed away, was a midwife for me when I gave birth to my daughter. She taught me to be in touch with my body and to allow my body's natural rhythms and wisdom to guide me. I recall during those sessions, thinking that my entire self-image was shifting because Leslie was modeling for me, a sense of confidence and what it was to be a strong woman.

"During delivery I was in terrible pain from the contractions, and I was yelling '*I don't care, get these clothes off me, I just want to deliver this baby!*' Leslie and her partner Betsy, both midwives, loved and accepted me, while I was at my absolute worst. Being far less than perfect, yet still accepted and loved by others, is, I think, one of the peak experiences of being human."

As you share the story of your passion, it's apparent that acceptance and a growing love of yourself as a woman has been a vital part of this journey for you.

"I'd say that's very true for me. Growing up I was a tomboy. I learned to play baseball and football long before I could play softball, as most girls my age were doing at that time. Although I excelled in a lot of boy's activities, the development and ownership of my feminine qualities took much longer. In my early days of working with the medicine wheel, there were times when we women would be in the inner ring while the men were in the outer ring and I found there was something in the energy of the men circling the energy of the women that was beautiful and incredibly healing for me. There were also times in our gatherings when the woman and men would have separate lodgings. The women would share thoughts and feelings about being a woman, and the men would have the opportunity to talk among themselves about life as a man. Later, the men and women would come together, and share how the experience affected each group. I can't tell you how beautiful it is for me to say, 'I honor both the masculine and feminine within me, and I honor the fact that I'm a woman. I don't have to pretend to be a man or have the qualities of a man. I do not have to prove to anyone that I have to be a *man* to survive or to be OK in this world. My aim is to claim myself as a woman; claim the strengths that come with being feminine; and truly be myself in this world."

Have there been trade-offs or sacrifices for as you've pursued this spiritual journey?

"Probably the most prominent sacrifice is the time spent away from my children. I've been on a spiritual journey since 1999, but when I stepped into formal training in 2001, I was required to be away from my kids four times a year for a week, for the next two years. I also attend local trainings and sometimes I'm able to bring them along, but not always. Now that I'm in the advanced phase of training, I have to leave them twice a year for 11 days. Preparing me and the children for my departure can also take up to three weeks. In some ways I look at it and think, well, that's not such a huge sacrifice, they really are benefiting by being able to live with their dad for two weeks. On the other hand, I miss them a great deal. I think we're all aware, though, that each time we do this it gets a little easier for us. Although I seem to miss out on some important event in their lives—his baseball game or her birthday—each time I'm gone, I have to accept that and hope they know why I do this work. That's truly my biggest sacrifice in following this passion of mine."

In what ways have your spiritual beliefs been impacted by this passion of yours?

"Well, I was raised Catholic, but not so heavily indoctrinated that I couldn't still have an appreciation for Christ as a beautiful man who came into the world to bring a bounty of spiritual teachings to us. I have a sweet spot in my heart for the Christian tradition. In my spiritual journey, however, I've come to a much broader definition of spirituality and what it means to be a spiritual person. My spiritual focus isn't limited solely to seeing through the lens of the Christian tradition that says, *Christ came to save us, and by following Christ I will then go to heaven.* My viewpoint today is that spirituality, life, and energy is present in everything. Consequently, my approach today is much more an earth—based tradition that allows me to see all things in the universe as spiritual entities—Mother Earth which gives us life, being one of the most precious. If we live as *spiritual warriors* with a real discipline towards holding a perspective in our minds for beauty, love and compassion, I believe we have a chance to *live heaven* right here and now, every day.

"I hope this work I do can help to awaken peoples' consciousness to the truth that they are not separate, but connected to all things. If I can just touch them, so they can realize their potential, and what they can bring to the world with *their* particular gifts, I would fulfill my greatest hope. I want to *flower* people open, so they can experience their beauty, and the beauty of every human, as beings of light and love. One day those people can then become the teachers. I guess I see myself as just the "can opener." (Laughing)

Darci may be reached at darci.humanspirit@verizon.net

Epilogue

Below is a list of common elements identified in the preceding interviews that have guided and focused the storytellers in living life with meaning and a healthy passion. Sprinkled among these points are some thoughts of my own. I make no claim to this list as the be-all and end-all of how to live a passionate life, so I invite you, the reader, to be open to what you may discover through your own experiences in leading a life of high energy and fulfillment.

Be bold. Think big, break through that self-limiting belief that says you're not good enough, or that your idea is crazy, or that no one will support your dreams. You will do no favor for the world if you play small. Contributor Darci D'ercole says, "What is your truth, and how courageous and how *big* can you be to passionately stand up and choose to be your authentic self"?

Be present. Listen to and notice the needs of others that touch you. Listen to what others are excited about. Create quiet time each day, even if only for a few minutes, and listen to your own strong feelings, the exciting, the painful, the sad, as well as the deep desires and that still small voice that will not go away, but, if given a chance, will guide you to what is passionate for you.

If unable to find something to be passionate about, look back to the times of the greatest pain or trauma in your life or to the things that you can recall that have really excited you. Remember the events and activities that you just couldn't wait to participate in as a child, an adolescent, or as a young adult. Remember the dreams you had for your young life.

Identify an overriding purpose or intention for your life and for the work you do beyond simply satisfying your own desires. Then ask yourself if your life and the work you do are in sync with your intention. If not, and you wish to change that, explore ways in which you can begin to bring what you love into your life, even as a hobby or part-time job. Having some fear as you begin pursuit of your passion is a given, but your willingness to walk through that fear, coupled with your attention to your higher intention, can empower and strengthen you. Often, just prior to the beginning of a workshop or retreat that I am facilitating, my mind will begin to *attack*, leaving me frightened and anxious about what could go wrong. Over time I have discovered that when I can remember my purpose is to be an open channel for the Divine to work through instead of being in charge of the results, I am usually restored to peace. Remembering my higher purpose takes me out of the "driver's seat."

Make Time for what matters—No matter how busy your day, allot some time to what you love to do. In that way your passion will grow; if you don't make time, your passion will shrivel and die. On this subject, filmmaker Amy Hart said, "I'm acutely aware of how I allocate my time; even more so than how I spend my money. If you're spending your time out drinking, or talking on the phone, or sitting in front of the television, those are choices you're making about how you're using those valuable hours. For a person who desires to manifest a passionate life,…just two hours a day is a lot of time if you use it well."

Find friends or mentors who will support you in your passionate adventures. Resolutely following your dream can sometimes feel very lonely and intimidating. Friends can encourage and support you as you take those first, tentative steps. There may be few among your immediate circle of friends and family who can appreciate the depth of feeling and commitment you have for following your dream. In time they may understand, but you need support *now*.

Surrender the "All or Nothing" approach to finding your passion or to working on what fulfills and excites you. As writer Paul Ehmann states, "…when you can find ways to fulfill yourself, in even very small ways to begin with, you can find what you will ultimately feel passionate about. There is no feeling of fulfillment or joy in *all or nothing* for me."

Deal with your anger. Anger is often the initial impetus of the creation of a passionate pursuit, i.e., righting a wrong, or involvement in a meaningful cause. That's normal. What you do with that anger, however, and how you focus it is a key to fulfillment and your effectiveness. If anger runs wild and is allowed to motivate and accompany every action, it will inevitably lead to frustration for you and others and destroy the spiritual element of what you do. Unless you deal with anger, anger will deal with you and what you want to accomplish.

Stay focused. If you dilute your energy with too many pursuits you will become scattered, unable to finish, and dissipate your positive energy. Identify your priorities and decide how you will use your time to achieve them.

Commitment—Maintaining a conscious commitment to regularly work at the exercise of what you are passionate about will continue to open one door after another in pursuing your dream. Immerse yourself in the subject and learn as much as possible.

Use your spiritual warrior. Each of us has the innate elements of toughness, courage, and stick-to-it-iveness that embody the *spiritual warrior*. This great energy can push us forward in our commitment to perform the tasks that may frighten or challenge us, and, enable us to manage our runaway and illogical thoughts and emotions. Like any muscle in the body, the more we use this *spiritual* part of ourselves, the stronger it becomes and the more our confidence in our ability to succeed will grow.

Explore your limiting beliefs such as, "I'm not good enough," "I never finish anything," "This won't work," etc., which may be keeping you from taking action on your dream. When faced and seen for their faulty logic, limiting beliefs will lose most of their power. A professional therapist, cleric, or trusted friend could be of enormous help in this area as well.

Realize and accept your limits. Your willingness to accept a reasonable level of success or acknowledging the degree of change you can bring about through your passion will bring you peace, a healthy perspective, and significantly diminish your risk of burnout.

Laugh a lot. Actualizing and using our dreams, gifts, and talents in the service of something greater than ourselves, can be exhilarating, but very challenging at times. Frequently, it can be very serious business, so it is important to laugh at and see the humor in our obstacles, frustrations, and even our shortcomings. To remain serious and driven over a long period of time can create great stress and even debilitating illness if we allow it. A humorous perspective has the power to release stress and re-energize the spirit. As contributor Bob Moore states, "Sit loosely in the saddle of life."

Be Grateful each and every day. Persist in maintaining an attitude of gratitude. Gratitude will enable you to not only survive the challenges and frustrations your passion will inevitably face, but it will also allow you to look at "your glass as half-full rather than half-empty." Such an attitude can actually change body chemistry, elevate your outlook on life, and free your creative spirit.

"Life can beat you down, close your mind and imprison your spirit, but only if you let it. Choose not to let it."
Ralph Marston, *The Daily Motivator*

Note—I would also like to mention the book, *The Passion Test,* written by Janet Bray Attwood and Chris Attwood as a wonderful resource for understanding the process of discovering your passion.

In the course of writing this book, I've developed a deep appreciation for all the contributors. Having the privilege to be present to the telling of these stories has allowed me to know human beings at their core and consequently at their best. We are indeed the "stuff of stars." Take the time to really pay attention the next time someone begins to excitedly relate how they feel about a hobby, their work, a special interest; or even some deep hurt or injustice. Turn off your brain and lay aside your own agenda as they speak. Let them know you hear and understand what they have to tell you. If you do, you may well be rewarded, because what you are doing is an act of kindness and respect, and you are taking part in an intimate event between you and the storyteller. And, oh yes, be careful! If you listen closely with an open heart, you just might become "contaminated" by the most virulent of transmissions—human passion.

References
(By Chapter)

Chapter 1: Author's notes
- **Jiddu Krishnamurti** (May 12, 1895—February 17, 1986) was a renowned writer and speaker on philosophical and spiritual subjects. His subject matter included: psychological revolution, the nature of the mind, meditation, human relationships, and how to enact positive change in society. www.jkrishnamurti.org
- **Walter Ruether** (1907—1970)—Labor Leader and civil rights activist. Information and history at www.reuther.wayne.edu/
- **Janet Bray Attwood and Chris Attwood, authors—*The Passion Test: The Effortless Path to Discovering Your Destiny*— www.thepassiontest.com**
- *Storycatcher: Making Sense of Our Lives through the Power and Practice of Story*— author, Christina Baldwin—*website www.storycatcher.net*

Chapter 2: Pana Columbus
- **Circle of Stones Ritual Theatre Ensemble** is a professional, non-profit theatre company based in Emmaus, Pennsylvania and dedicated to using theatre to inspire positive community transformations.

Chapter 4: Jennifer Hanson

• **Appalachian Trail**, completed in 1937 is the nations longest marked footpath, at approximately 2,178 miles. It touches 14 states, beginning in the south at Springer Mountain in Georgia and terminating in the North on Mount Katahdin in Maine. www.appalachiantrail.org
• The term **Thru-Hiker** pertains to those hiking the entire 2,175 miles of the Appalachian Trail in one trip. The average thru hiker takes 6 months to complete the hike while only one of four who begin actually finishes the feat.
• **The Continental Divide** National Scenic Trail (in short Continental Divide Trail) is a United States National Scenic Trail running 3,100 miles (5,000 km) between Mexico and Canada www.cdtrail.org
• **Prayer of Protection** See entire prayer at www.unityonthebay.org/prayer_protection.html

Chapter 5: Anne Waldorf

• **Alcoholics Anonymous**. AA is a voluntary, worldwide fellowship of men and women from all walks of life who aim to recover from alcoholism by sharing their experience, strength, and hope with each other and by helping others recover from the disease of alcoholism. Information at www.aa.org
• **Sharon Wegscheider-Cruise** www.*sharonwcruse.com* Sharon is a family therapist, author, and has conducted workshops around the world. She has won awards in communication and has appeared on "The Oprah Winfrey Show", "Good Morning America", and countless other TV and radio shows.
• **Claudia Black** is an author, consultant, and workshop leader. Claudia Black, M.S.W., Ph.D. is a renowned addictions and codependency expert, author and trainer internationally recognized for her pioneering and contemporary work with family systems and addictive disorders. www.claudiablack.com
• **Dr. Janet Woititz**, author and family therapist, who has been

described as the "mother" of the Adult Child of Alcoholics movement www.drjan.com

Chapter 6: Howard Meyer

• **Axial Theatre** is located in Pleasantville, New York. Its mission is to create relevant, original plays in collaboration and to cultivate theatre artists through year-round educational programming. www.axialtheatre.org

• **Athol Fugard** (born 11 June 1932) is a South African playwright, novelist, actor, and director, best known for his political plays opposing the South African system of apartheid and for the 2005 Academy-Award winning film of his novel *Tsotsi*. www.answers.com/athol-fugard

• **Johann Wolfgang von Goethe** (1749-1832) was a German writer whose work spans the fields of poetry, drama, literature, theology, philosophy, humanism and science. Biography and links to poetry, speeches, and poems— www.wikipedia.org/wiki/Johann_Wolfgang_Von_Goethe

Chapter 7: Francis Endryck

• *Periodization*-**5th Edition: Theory and Methodology of Training**—Hardcover (Jun 22, 2009) by Tudor Bompa and G. Gregory Haff. This book teaches how to vary the intensity and volume of training to optimize the body's ability to recover and rebuild, resulting in better performance and less risk of injury.

• **Charles Poliquin** is a Canadian strength training coach who has trained and/or consulted numerous world class athletes and professional sports teams. www.charlespoliquin.com

• **Mel Cunningham Siff** is an international sports science and biomechanics consultant. www.melsiff.com

• **Dr. Nicholas Romanov** created and published *The POSE METHOD OF RUNNING* Book in 2002. www.posetech.com/posemethod

- **Total Immersion,** is an approach created by Terry Laughlin, to the coaching of swimming which concentrates on the hydrodynamics of the human body. www.totalimmersion.net

Chapter 10: Sandesh Naik

- **Mentalism** is a performing art in which its practitioners, known as mentalists, use mental acuity, cold reading, hot reading, principles of stage magic, and/or suggestion to present the illusion of mind reading, psychokinesis, extra-sensory perception, precognition, clairvoyance or mind control. Hypnosis may also be used as a stage tool. Information at wikipedia.org/wiki/**Mentalism**_(psychology)

Chapter 11: Norma Seaward

- **Carolyn Myss,**—is a five-time *New York Times* bestselling author and internationally renowned speaker in the fields of human consciousness, spirituality and mysticism, health, energy medicine, and the science of medical intuition. Her books include *ENTERING THE CASTLE* in 2007 and 2009's *DEFY GRAVITY*, a book exploring the mystical phenomenon of healing that transcends reason. www.*myss.com*

Chapter 12: Robert LoBue

- **Meher Baba**(1894—1969) Indian spiritual master. He created a system of spiritual beliefs according to which the goal of life was to realize the oneness of God, from whom the whole universe emanates. Source—www.concise.britannica.com
- **Carl Gustav Jung,** (1875-1961) Swiss psychologist and writer. www.cgjungpage.org
- **Narcotics Anonymous** is an international, community-based association of recovering drug addicts with more than 43,900 weekly meetings in over 127 countries worldwide. Website http://www.na.org

Chapter 13: Jackie Hawkins

• **Delta Sigma Theta** (ÄÓÈ) is a non-profit Greek-lettered sorority of college—educated women who perform public service and place emphasis on the African-American community. It was founded in 2001. www.thetadeltasigma.org

Chapter 14: Ruth Alsop

• **Arthur Leon Judson** (February 17, 1881—January 28, 1975) was a violinist, conductor, an artists' manager who also managed the New York Philharmonic and Philadelphia Orchestra—www.Wikipedia.org
• **The National Museum of Dance & Hall of Fame** in Saratoga Springs, New York was established in 1986 and is the only museum in the nation dedicated to professional dance. The museum houses a growing collection of photographs, videos, artifacts, costumes, biographies and archives comprising a contemporary and retrospective examination of seminal contributions to dance. www.dancemuseum.org
• **New York City Ballet** is one of the foremost and most unique dance companies in the world, solely responsible for training its own artists and creating its own works. It has two permanent homes, Lincoln Center in New York City, and the Saratoga Performing Arts Center in Saratoga Springs, New York. www.nycballet.org

Chapter 16: Robert Moore

• **Greater Capital Region Teacher's Center** website—www.teachercenter.org
• **Chautauqua Institute** is a National Historic Landmark and a thriving community located in Chautauqua, New York where visitors come to find intellectual and spiritual growth and renewal. Its dramatic lakeside setting and the beauty of its architecture make the Chautauqua Institution an ideal spot for learning www.*ciweb.org*

Chapter 17: Christopher Ringwald

• **Carroll Quigley**, 1910-1977), lecturer, writer, and professor of history at the foreign service School of Georgetown University, formerly taught at Princeton and at Harvard. Information and lectures at www.carrollquigley.net

• **Melvin Mencher**, and is the author of *News Reporting and Writing*, now in its 12th edition. He is professor emeritus, having taught at the Graduate School of Journalism at Columbia University. More information at: *journalism.columbia.edu/cs/.../JRNFacultyDetail.htm—13k*

• **Annie Dillard** (born April 30, 1945 is a Pulitzer Prize-winning American author, best known for her narrative nonfiction. www.anniedillard.com

Chapter 18: Jim Garrett

• The book, *Invitational Intervention*: A Step by Step Guide for Clinicians Helping Families Engage Resistant Substance Abusers in Treatment by Dr. Judith Landau and James Garrett may be viewed and purchased at Amazon and other major online booksellers.

Chapter 19: Connie Messit

• **The Priory Retreat House** is an interfaith retreat/renewal center staffed by sisters of St. Joseph and lay staff. The Center has been hosting groups and individuals since 1987. www.prioryretreathouse.org

• **Thich Nhat Hanh** (born October 11 1926 in Vietnam) is a Zen Buddhist monk, teacher, author, poet and peace activist. www.plumvillage.org

• **Julian of Norwich** (1342—1416) is thought of as one of the greatest English mystics, yet little is known of her life aside from her writings. More information at www.luminarium.org/medlit/julian.htm

Chapter 20: Cary Bayer

• **Hermann Hesse** (July 2, 1877—August 9, 1962) was a German Swiss poet, novelist, and painter. In 1946 he received the Nobel Prize in Literature. www.hermanhesse.de/eng

• **Joseph Campbell** (March 26, 1904—October 31, 1987) was an American mythologist, writer and lecturer, best known for his work in comparative mythology and comparative religion. www.jcf.org

• **Maharishi Mahesh Yogi**—founder of Transcendental Meditation www.maharishi.org

• **Alan Watts** (January 6, 1915—November 16, 1973) was a British philosopher, writer, speaker, and is best known as an interpreter of Zen Buddhism www.alanwatts.com

• **Walt Whitman**, (May 31, 1819—March 26, 1892) was a great American poet, essayist, journalist, and humanist. He is famous as the poet who wrote the collection, *Leaves of Grass.* www.whitmanarchive.org

Chapter 21: John Anthony Frederick

• **A Course in Miracles (Also referred to as the Course or ACIM)** is an experiential, self-study guide written by Dr. Helen Schucman and Dr. William Thetford that describes a new approach to spirituality, based on Christian teachings, that helps to bring about the Illumination of the Mind and Body through the process of the practical application of Love, Healing, and Forgiveness. www.acim.org

• **John Calvi**—has been working with people surviving traumatic experiences and those with AIDS since 1982. He is a certified massage therapist who has a spiritual gift for the release of emotional and physical pain. www.johncalvi.

Chapter 22: Steve Anderson

• **Dances of Universal Peace (DUP)** employs meditative and spiritual practices using the mantras of all world religions to promote peace. The

dances, of Sufi origin, combine chants from world faiths with dancing, whirling, and a variety of movement with singing. WWW.dup-co,com
• **Stephen R. Covey**, internationally respected teacher and consultant, and winner of the International Man of Peace Award, is the author of *The Seven Habits of Highly Effective People*, named by many as the most influential business book of the 20th century. Read more about him at www.stephencovey.com
• **The Peace Corps** was established by President John F. Kennedy in 1961 to promote world peace and friendship by creating a better understanding of Americans on the part of the peoples they served, and by advancing an increased understanding of other peoples on the part of Americans. www.peacecorps.gov

Chapter 23: Steve Holmes

• **The Self-Advocacy Association of New York State, Inc. (SANYS)** is a not-for profit, grassroots organization run by and for people with developmental disabilities. www.sanys.org
• **Rudolph Steiner** (Feb.25, 1861—March 30,1925) was an Austrian philosopher, social thinker, architect and esotericist. Information at www.steiner.edu
• **Daniel Berrigan** SJ, (born May 9, 1921) is a poet, American peace activist, and Roman Catholic priest. Daniel and his brother Philip were for a time on the FBI Ten Most Wanted Fugitives list for committing acts of vandalism including destroying government property. From 1966 to 1970 he was the assistant director of Cornell United Religious Work (CURW), during which time he played an instrumental role in the national peace movement.[1] He now resides in New York City and teaches at Fordham University in addition to serving as its poet in residence. (Wikipedia)
• **Neil Percival Young** (born November 12, 1945) is a Canadian singer-songwriter, musician and film director. He was inducted into the Rock and Roll Hall of Fame as a solo artist in 1995 and also as a member of Buffalo Springfield in 1997. www.*neilyoung.com*

Chapter 24: Steve Rock

- **North American Mycological Association,**www.namyco.org
- **COMA**—www.comafungi.org website

Chapter 25: Amy Hart

- *Water First* Is a documentary film dealing with the Global Water Crisis, produced by Amy Hart of Hart Productions. *www.hartproductions.org/ & WaterFirstFilm.Org*

Chapter 26: Carol Sue Hart

- **Clowns on Rounds, Inc.** provides professional entertainers, disguised as clown doctors to hospitals and nursing homes in New York State's Capital District. Transforming their regular acts and props into medically related routines, they tend to poke fun at conventional procedures and staff, thus diffusing some of the anxiety and fear experienced during treatment and long term care. www.clownsonrounds.com
- **Rick Warren** (born January 28, 1954 in San Jose, California) is an American Christian minister and best-selling author. He is the founder and senior pastor of Saddleback Church, an evangelical megachurch located in Lake Forest, California, currently the eighth-largest church in the United States. http://www.rickwarren.com/
- **Joyce Meyer** (born on June 4, 1943) is a Charismatic Christian best-selling author, bible teacher, and speaker. www.joycemeyer.org/ourministries/broadcast

Chapter 27: Steve Carty Cordry

- **Maria Nemeth PhD.** is a licensed clinical psychologist, Master Certified Coach, author, international lecturer, and President of the Academy for Coaching Excellence.

www.academyforcoachingexcellence.com Her newest book is *Mastering Life's Energies: Simple Steps to a Luminous Life at Work and Play*

Chapter 28: Bonnie Kriss

• **Community Hospice of Schenectady, NY**—info: www.hpcanys.org/county.asp—ID=47
• **Joan Nicole Prince Home**—www.Joannicoleprincehome.org
• **Marianne Williamson**, author and international lecturer on spiritual, personal and political issues. www.**marianne**.com

Chapter 29: Paul Ehmann

• **Marion Roach** —author, editor, blogger, and teacher; http://marionroach.com

Chapter 30: Debra Burger

• **Unity Church**—known as the Unity School of Christianity and informally as Unity Church, is a religious movement within the wider New Thought movement. Information at www.unity.org
• **Old Songs Inc.,** located in Voorheesville, New York, is a not-for-profit, educational organization dedicated to preserving traditional music and dance. More information at www.oldsongs.org

Chapter 31: Bob Blood

• **Pablo Picasso**—(25 October 1881—8 April 1973) a Spanish painter and sculptor, and one of the most world-renown artists of all time. www.*picasso.com*
• **Frèdèric Back**, (4/8/24—present) illustrator and film maker, created the classic short film, *The Man Who Planted Trees*, from the story by Jean Giono. www.fredericback.com

Chapter 32: Matt George
•   **Capital District Civil War Roundtable is an** educational organization whose purpose is to foster education, awareness and respect for America's historic heritage, with special focus on the Civil War period. Website at: www.timesunion.memlink.com/—_id=0700145601300001
•   **Joshua Chamberlain** (September 8, 1828—February 24, 1914) A college professor, Civil War hero, and later the Governor of Maine. Biography and links to speeches at: www.nps.gov/archive/gett/getttour/sidebar/chambln.htm
•   **Victor Frankel,** (1905-1997) —Holocaust survivor, psychoanalyst, and author of *"Man's Search for Meaning."* www.viktorfrankl.org

Chapter 33: Jim Fuller
•   **Edgar Cayce** (March 18, 1877—January 3, 1945), known as "The Sleeping Prophet" and "America's Greatest Mystic", is one of America's famous psychics. www.edgarcayce.org
•   **Leo Buscaglia**, 1924—1998), Ph.D.; also known as "Dr Love"... was an author and motivational speaker, and a professor in the Department of Special Education at the University of Southern California. He gained fame at USC through his non-credit course titled "Love 1A," which became the basis for his first book, titled simply LOVE. His dynamic speaking style was discovered by the Public Broadcasting System (PBS) and his televised lectures and best-selling books earned great popularity in the 1980s. www.buscaglia.com
•   ***A Journey without Distance.*** The complete inspirational story of how *The Course in Miracles* came to be. www.acim.org

Chapter 34: Darci Der'cole McGinn
•   **Ehama Institute** is dedicated to the mending of the sacred hoop of

the people and to the calling forth of unity and relationships among all peoples. www.ehama.org

• **Mandala**—*Oriental Art.* a schematized representation of the cosmos, chiefly characterized by a concentric configuration of geometric shapes, each of which contains an image of a deity or an attribute of a deity. In Jungian psychology) a symbol representing the effort to reunify the self.

• Source—Dictionary.com

Breinigsville, PA USA
21 October 2010
247833BV00003B/2/P